Nissan Sentra Automotive Repair Manual

**by Jay Storer
and John H Haynes**

Member of the Guild of Motoring Writers

Models covered:

All front-wheel drive Nissan Sentra models with gasoline engines
1982 through 1994

Does not cover diesel, 4WD, Pulsar or NX models

(6F9 - 72050)

(982)

ABCDE
FGHIJ
KLMNO
PQ
2

Haynes Publishing Group
Sparkford Nr Yeovil
Somerset BA22 7JJ England

Haynes North America, Inc
861 Lawrence Drive
Newbury Park
California 91320 USA

Acknowledgements
Technical writers who contributed to this project include Rob Maddox, Mike Stubblefield and Larry Warren.

© **Haynes North America, Inc. 1995, 1998**
With permission from J.H. Haynes & Co. Ltd.

A book in the Haynes Automotive Repair Manual Series

Printed in the U.S.A.

ISBN 1 56392 150 2

Library of Congress Catalog Card Number 95-79511

Contents

Haynes mechanic, author and photographer with 1994 Nissan Sentra

About this manual

Its purpose

The purpose of this manual is to help you get the best value from your vehicle. It can do so in several ways. It can help you decide what work must be done, even if you choose to have it done by a dealer service department or a repair shop; it provides information and procedures for routine maintenance and servicing; and it offers diagnostic and repair procedures to follow when trouble occurs.

We hope you use the manual to tackle the work yourself. For many simpler jobs, doing it yourself may be quicker than arranging an appointment to get the vehicle into a shop and making the trips to leave it and pick it up. More importantly, a lot of money can be saved by avoiding the expense the shop must pass on to you to cover its labor and overhead costs. An added benefit is the sense of satisfaction and accomplishment that you feel after doing the job yourself.

Using the manual

The manual is divided into Chapters. Each Chapter is divided into numbered Sections, which are headed in bold type between horizontal lines. Each Section consists of consecutively numbered paragraphs.

At the beginning of each numbered Section you will be referred to any illustrations which apply to the procedures in that Section. The reference numbers used in illustration captions pinpoint the pertinent Section and the Step within that Section. That is, illustration 3.2 means the illustration refers to Section 3 and Step (or paragraph) 2 within that Section.

Procedures, once described in the text, are not normally repeated. When it's necessary to refer to another Chapter, the reference will be given as Chapter and Section number. Cross references given without use of the word "Chapter" apply to Sections and/or paragraphs in the same Chapter. For example, "see Section 8" means in the same Chapter.

References to the left or right side of the vehicle assume you are sitting in the driver's seat, facing forward.

Even though we have prepared this manual with extreme care, neither the publisher nor the author can accept responsibility for any errors in, or omissions from, the information given.

NOTE

A **Note** provides information necessary to properly complete a procedure or information which will make the procedure easier to understand.

CAUTION

A **Caution** provides a special procedure or special steps which must be taken while completing the procedure where the Caution is found. Not heeding a Caution can result in damage to the assembly being worked on.

WARNING

A **Warning** provides a special procedure or special steps which must be taken while completing the procedure where the Warning is found. Not heeding a Warning can result in personal injury.

Introduction to the Nissan Sentra

Nissan Sentra models are available in hatchback, two- and four-door sedan and station wagon body styles.

The transversely mounted inline four-cylinder engines used in these models are equipped with either a carburetor or electronic fuel injection.

The engine drives the front wheels through either a four- or five-speed manual or a three- or four-speed automatic transaxle via independent driveaxles.

Independent suspension, featuring coil spring/strut damper units, is used on the front wheels, while independent suspension using shock absorbers and coil springs or coil spring/strut dampers is used at the rear.

The rack and pinion steering unit is mounted behind the engine with power-assist available as an option.

The brakes are disc at the front and drums or disc at the rear, with power assist standard. An Anti-lock Brake System (ABS) became available on later models.

Vehicle identification numbers

Vehicle identification number
(Chassis number)

Vehicle identification plate

F.M.V.S.S. certification label

Vehicle identification number plate

Emission control information label

The Vehicle Identification Number (VIN) is visible through the driver's side of the windshield

Modifications are a continuing and unpublicized process in vehicle manufacturing. Since spare parts manuals and lists are compiled on a numerical basis, the individual vehicle numbers are essential to correctly identify the component required.

Vehicle Identification Number (VIN)

This very important identification number is stamped on the firewall in the engine compartment and on a plate attached to the dashboard inside the windshield on the driver's side of the vehicle (see illustration). The VIN also appears on the Vehicle Certificate of Title and Registration. It contains information such as where and when the vehicle was manufactured, the model year and the body style.

VIN engine code

One particularly important piece of information found in the VIN is the engine code. Counting from the left, the engine code letter designation is the 4th digit.

On the models covered by this manual the engine codes are:

H E15 1.5L SOHC (1982)
P E16 1.6L SOHC (1982 through 1988)
G GA16i 1.6L SOHC (1989 and 1990)
E GA16DE 1.6L DOHC (1991 through 1994)
G SR20DE 2.0L DOHC (1991 through 1994)

Manufacturer's Certification Regulation label

The manufacturer's Certification Regulation label is attached to the driver's side door end or post. The plate contains the name of the manufacturer, the month and year of production, the Gross Vehicle Weight Rating (GVWR), the Gross Axle Weight Rating (GAWR) and the certification statement.

Engine number

The engine code number can be found on a pad on the front (radiator) side of the cylinder block, near the transaxle (see illustration).

FRONT

The engine number is stamped onto a machined pad on the front side of the engine block, near the transaxle

Buying parts

Replacement parts are available from many sources, which generally fall into one of two categories - authorized dealer parts departments and independent retail auto parts stores. Our advice concerning these parts is as follows:

Retail auto parts stores: Good auto parts stores will stock frequently needed components which wear out relatively fast, such as clutch components, exhaust systems, brake parts, tune-up parts, etc. These stores often supply new or reconditioned parts on an exchange basis, which can save a considerable amount of money. Discount auto parts stores are often very good places to buy materials and parts needed for general vehicle maintenance such as oil, grease, filters, spark plugs, belts, touch-up paint, bulbs, etc. They also usually sell tools and general accessories, have convenient hours, charge lower prices and can often be found not far from home.

Authorized dealer parts department: This is the best source for parts which are unique to the vehicle and not generally available elsewhere (such as major engine parts, transmission parts, trim pieces, etc.).

Warranty information: If the vehicle is still covered under warranty, be sure that any replacement parts purchased - regardless of the source - do not invalidate the warranty!

To be sure of obtaining the correct parts, have engine and chassis numbers available and, if possible, take the old parts along for positive identification.

Maintenance techniques, tools and working facilities

Maintenance techniques

There are a number of techniques involved in maintenance and repair that will be referred to throughout this manual. Application of these techniques will enable the home mechanic to be more efficient, better organized and capable of performing the various tasks properly, which will ensure that the repair job is thorough and complete.

Fasteners

Fasteners are nuts, bolts, studs and screws used to hold two or more parts together. There are a few things to keep in mind when working with fasteners. Almost all of them use a locking device of some type, either a lockwasher, locknut, locking tab or thread adhesive. All threaded fasteners should be clean and straight, with undamaged threads and undamaged corners on the hex head where the wrench fits. Develop the habit of replacing all damaged nuts and bolts with new ones. Special locknuts with nylon or fiber inserts can only be used once. If they are removed, they lose their locking ability and must be replaced with new ones.

Rusted nuts and bolts should be treated with a penetrating fluid to ease removal and prevent breakage. Some mechanics use turpentine in a spout-type oil can, which works quite well. After applying the rust penetrant, let it work for a few minutes before trying to loosen the nut or bolt. Badly rusted fasteners may have to be chiseled or sawed off or removed with a special nut breaker, available at tool stores.

If a bolt or stud breaks off in an assembly, it can be drilled and removed with a special tool commonly available for this purpose.

Most automotive machine shops can perform this task, as well as other repair procedures, such as the repair of threaded holes that have been stripped out.

Flat washers and lockwashers, when removed from an assembly, should always be replaced exactly as removed. Replace any damaged washers with new ones. Never use a lockwasher on any soft metal surface (such as aluminum), thin sheet metal or plastic.

Grade 1 or 2   Grade 5   Grade 8

Bolt strength marking (standard/SAE/USS; bottom - metric)

Grade	Identification
Hex Nut Grade 5	3 Dots
Hex Nut Grade 8	6 Dots

Standard hex nut strength markings

Grade	Identification
Hex Nut Property Class 9	Arabic 9
Hex Nut Property Class 10	Arabic 10

Metric hex nut strength markings

Class 10.9   Class 9.8   Class 8.8

Metric stud strength markings

00-1 HAYNES

Fastener sizes

For a number of reasons, automobile manufacturers are making wider and wider use of metric fasteners. Therefore, it is important to be able to tell the difference between standard (sometimes called U.S. or SAE) and metric hardware, since they cannot be interchanged.

All bolts, whether standard or metric, are sized according to diameter, thread pitch and length. For example, a standard 1/2 - 13 x 1 bolt is 1/2 inch in diameter, has 13 threads per inch and is 1 inch long. An M12 - 1.75 x 25 metric bolt is 12 mm in diameter, has a thread pitch of 1.75 mm (the distance between threads) and is 25 mm long. The two bolts are nearly identical, and easily confused, but they are not interchangeable.

In addition to the differences in diameter, thread pitch and length, metric and standard bolts can also be distinguished by examining the bolt heads. To begin with, the distance across the flats on a standard bolt head is measured in inches, while the same dimension on a metric bolt is sized in millimeters (the same is true for nuts). As a result, a standard wrench should not be used on a metric bolt and a metric wrench should not be used on a standard bolt. Also, most standard bolts have slashes radiating out from the center of the head to denote the grade or strength of the bolt, which is an indication of the amount of torque that can be applied to it. The greater the number of slashes, the greater the strength of the bolt. Grades 0 through 5 are commonly used on automobiles. Metric bolts have a property class (grade) number, rather than a slash, molded into their heads to indicate bolt strength. In this case, the higher the number, the stronger the bolt. Property class numbers 8.8, 9.8 and 10.9 are commonly used on automobiles.

Strength markings can also be used to distinguish standard hex nuts from metric hex nuts. Many standard nuts have dots stamped into one side, while metric nuts are marked with a number. The greater the number of dots, or the higher the number, the greater the strength of the nut.

Metric studs are also marked on their ends according to property class (grade). Larger studs are numbered (the same as metric bolts), while smaller studs carry a geometric code to denote grade.

It should be noted that many fasteners, especially Grades 0 through 2, have no distinguishing marks on them. When such is the case, the only way to determine whether it is standard or metric is to measure the thread pitch or compare it to a known fastener of the same size.

Standard fasteners are often referred to as SAE, as opposed to metric. However, it should be noted that SAE technically refers to a non-metric fine thread fastener only. Coarse thread non-metric fasteners are referred to as USS sizes.

Since fasteners of the same size (both standard and metric) may have different

Metric thread sizes	Ft-lbs	Nm
M-6	6 to 9	9 to 12
M-8	14 to 21	19 to 28
M-10	28 to 40	38 to 54
M-12	50 to 71	68 to 96
M-14	80 to 140	109 to 154
Pipe thread sizes		
1/8	5 to 8	7 to 10
1/4	12 to 18	17 to 24
3/8	22 to 33	30 to 44
1/2	25 to 35	34 to 47
U.S. thread sizes		
1/4 - 20	6 to 9	9 to 12
5/16 - 18	12 to 18	17 to 24
5/16 - 24	14 to 20	19 to 27
3/8 - 16	22 to 32	30 to 43
3/8 - 24	27 to 38	37 to 51
7/16 - 14	40 to 55	55 to 74
7/16 - 20	40 to 60	55 to 81
1/2 - 13	55 to 80	75 to 108

Standard (SAE and USS) bolt dimensions/grade marks

G   Grade marks (bolt strength)
L   Length (in inches)
T   Thread pitch (number of threads per inch)
D   Nominal diameter (in inches)

Metric bolt dimensions/grade marks

P   Property class (bolt strength)
L   Length (in millimeters)
T   Thread pitch (distance between threads in millimeters)
D   Diameter

strength ratings, be sure to reinstall any bolts, studs or nuts removed from your vehicle in their original locations. Also, when replacing a fastener with a new one, make sure that the new one has a strength rating equal to or greater than the original.

Tightening sequences and procedures

Most threaded fasteners should be tightened to a specific torque value (torque is the twisting force applied to a threaded component such as a nut or bolt). Overtightening the fastener can weaken it and cause it to break, while undertightening can cause it to eventually come loose. Bolts, screws and studs, depending on the material they are

made of and their thread diameters, have specific torque values, many of which are noted in the Specifications at the beginning of each Chapter. Be sure to follow the torque recommendations closely. For fasteners not assigned a specific torque, a general torque value chart is presented here as a guide. These torque values are for dry (unlubricated) fasteners threaded into steel or cast iron (not aluminum). As was previously mentioned, the size and grade of a fastener determine the amount of torque that can safely be applied to it. The figures listed here are approximate for Grade 2 and Grade 3 fasteners. Higher grades can tolerate higher torque values.

Fasteners laid out in a pattern, such as cylinder head bolts, oil pan bolts, differential cover bolts, etc., must be loosened or tight-

Micrometer set

Dial indicator set

ened in sequence to avoid warping the component. This sequence will normally be shown in the appropriate Chapter. If a specific pattern is not given, the following procedures can be used to prevent warping.

Initially, the bolts or nuts should be assembled finger-tight only. Next, they should be tightened one full turn each, in a criss-cross or diagonal pattern. After each one has been tightened one full turn, return to the first one and tighten them all one-half turn, following the same pattern. Finally, tighten each of them one-quarter turn at a time until each fastener has been tightened to the proper torque. To loosen and remove the fasteners, the procedure would be reversed.

Component disassembly

Component disassembly should be done with care and purpose to help ensure that the parts go back together properly. Always keep track of the sequence in which parts are removed. Make note of special characteristics or marks on parts that can be installed more than one way, such as a grooved thrust washer on a shaft. It is a good idea to lay the disassembled parts out on a clean surface in the order that they were removed. It may also be helpful to make sketches or take instant photos of components before removal.

When removing fasteners from a component, keep track of their locations. Sometimes threading a bolt back in a part, or putting the washers and nut back on a stud, can prevent mix-ups later. If nuts and bolts cannot be returned to their original locations, they should be kept in a compartmented box or a series of small boxes. A cupcake or muffin tin is ideal for this purpose, since each cavity can hold the bolts and nuts from a particular area (i.e. oil pan bolts, valve cover bolts, engine mount bolts, etc.). A pan of this type is especially helpful when working on assemblies with very small parts, such as the carburetor, alternator, valve train or interior dash and trim pieces. The cavities can be marked with paint or tape to identify the contents.

Whenever wiring looms, harnesses or connectors are separated, it is a good idea to identify the two halves with numbered pieces of masking tape so they can be easily reconnected.

Gasket sealing surfaces

Throughout any vehicle, gaskets are used to seal the mating surfaces between two parts and keep lubricants, fluids, vacuum or pressure contained in an assembly.

Many times these gaskets are coated with a liquid or paste-type gasket sealing compound before assembly. Age, heat and pressure can sometimes cause the two parts to stick together so tightly that they are very difficult to separate. Often, the assembly can be loosened by striking it with a soft-face hammer near the mating surfaces. A regular hammer can be used if a block of wood is placed between the hammer and the part. Do not hammer on cast parts or parts that could be easily damaged. With any particularly stubborn part, always recheck to make sure that every fastener has been removed.

Avoid using a screwdriver or bar to pry apart an assembly, as they can easily mar the gasket sealing surfaces of the parts, which must remain smooth. If prying is absolutely necessary, use an old broom handle, but keep in mind that extra clean up will be necessary if the wood splinters.

After the parts are separated, the old gasket must be carefully scraped off and the gasket surfaces cleaned. Stubborn gasket material can be soaked with rust penetrant or treated with a special chemical to soften it so it can be easily scraped off. A scraper can be fashioned from a piece of copper tubing by flattening and sharpening one end. Copper is recommended because it is usually softer than the surfaces to be scraped, which reduces the chance of gouging the part. Some gaskets can be removed with a wire brush, but regardless of the method used, the mating surfaces must be left clean and smooth. If for some reason the gasket surface is gouged, then a gasket sealer thick enough to fill scratches will have to be used during reassembly of the components. For most applications, a non-drying (or semi-drying) gasket sealer should be used.

Hose removal tips

Warning: *If the vehicle is equipped with air conditioning, do not disconnect any of the A/C hoses without first having the system depressurized by a dealer service department or a service station.*

Hose removal precautions closely parallel gasket removal precautions. Avoid scratching or gouging the surface that the hose mates against or the connection may leak. This is especially true for radiator hoses. Because of various chemical reactions, the rubber in hoses can bond itself to the metal spigot that the hose fits over. To remove a hose, first loosen the hose clamps that secure it to the spigot. Then, with slip-joint pliers, grab the hose at the clamp and rotate it around the spigot. Work it back and forth until it is completely free, then pull it off. Silicone or other lubricants will ease removal if they can be applied between the hose and the outside of the spigot. Apply the same lubricant to the inside of the hose and the outside of the spigot to simplify installation.

As a last resort (and if the hose is to be replaced with a new one anyway), the rubber can be slit with a knife and the hose peeled from the spigot. If this must be done, be careful that the metal connection is not damaged.

If a hose clamp is broken or damaged, do not reuse it. Wire-type clamps usually weaken with age, so it is a good idea to replace them with screw-type clamps whenever a hose is removed.

Tools

A selection of good tools is a basic requirement for anyone who plans to maintain and repair his or her own vehicle. For the owner who has few tools, the initial investment might seem high, but when compared to the spiraling costs of professional auto maintenance and repair, it is a wise one.

To help the owner decide which tools are needed to perform the tasks detailed in this manual, the following tool lists are offered: *Maintenance and minor repair, Repair/overhaul* and *Special*.

The newcomer to practical mechanics

Dial caliper

Hand-operated vacuum pump

Timing light

Compression gauge with spark plug
hole adapter

Damper/steering wheel puller

General purpose puller

Hydraulic lifter removal tool

Valve spring compressor

Valve spring compressor

Ridge reamer

Piston ring groove cleaning tool

Ring removal/installation tool

Ring compressor

Cylinder hone

Brake hold-down spring tool

Brake cylinder hone

Clutch plate alignment tool

Tap and die set

should start off with the *maintenance and minor repair* tool kit, which is adequate for the simpler jobs performed on a vehicle. Then, as confidence and experience grow, the owner can tackle more difficult tasks, buying additional tools as they are needed. Eventually the basic kit will be expanded into the *repair and overhaul* tool set. Over a period of time, the experienced do-it-yourselfer will assemble a tool set complete enough for most repair and overhaul procedures and will add tools from the special category when it is felt that the expense is justified by the frequency of use.

Maintenance and minor repair tool kit

The tools in this list should be considered the minimum required for performance of routine maintenance, servicing and minor repair work. We recommend the purchase of combination wrenches (box-end and open-end combined in one wrench). While more expensive than open end wrenches, they offer the advantages of both types of wrench.

Combination wrench set (1/4-inch to 1 inch or 6 mm to 19 mm)
Adjustable wrench, 8 inch
Spark plug wrench with rubber insert
Spark plug gap adjusting tool
Feeler gauge set
Brake bleeder wrench
Standard screwdriver (5/16-inch x 6 inch)

Phillips screwdriver (No. 2 x 6 inch)
Combination pliers - 6 inch
Hacksaw and assortment of blades
Tire pressure gauge
Grease gun
Oil can
Fine emery cloth
Wire brush
Battery post and cable cleaning tool
Oil filter wrench
Funnel (medium size)
Safety goggles
Jackstands (2)
Drain pan

Note: *If basic tune-ups are going to be part of routine maintenance, it will be necessary to purchase a good quality stroboscopic timing light and combination tachometer/dwell meter. Although they are included in the list of special tools, it is mentioned here because they are absolutely necessary for tuning most vehicles properly.*

Repair and overhaul tool set

These tools are essential for anyone who plans to perform major repairs and are in addition to those in the maintenance and minor repair tool kit. Included is a comprehensive set of sockets which, though expensive, are invaluable because of their versatility, especially when various extensions and drives are available. We recommend the 1/2-inch drive over the 3/8-inch drive. Although the larger drive is bulky and more expensive,

it has the capacity of accepting a very wide range of large sockets. Ideally, however, the mechanic should have a 3/8-inch drive set and a 1/2-inch drive set.

Socket set(s)
Reversible ratchet
Extension - 10 inch
Universal joint
Torque wrench (same size drive as sockets)
Ball peen hammer - 8 ounce
Soft-face hammer (plastic/rubber)
Standard screwdriver (1/4-inch x 6 inch)
Standard screwdriver (stubby - 5/16-inch)
Phillips screwdriver (No. 3 x 8 inch)
Phillips screwdriver (stubby - No. 2)
Pliers - vise grip
Pliers - lineman's
Pliers - needle nose
Pliers - snap-ring (internal and external)
Cold chisel - 1/2-inch
Scribe
Scraper (made from flattened copper tubing)
Centerpunch
Pin punches (1/16, 1/8, 3/16-inch)
Steel rule/straightedge - 12 inch
Allen wrench set (1/8 to 3/8-inch or 4 mm to 10 mm)
A selection of files
Wire brush (large)
Jackstands (second set)
Jack (scissor or hydraulic type)

Note: *Another tool which is often useful is an electric drill with a chuck capacity of 3/8-inch and a set of good quality drill bits.*

Special tools

The tools in this list include those which are not used regularly, are expensive to buy, or which need to be used in accordance with their manufacturer's instructions. Unless these tools will be used frequently, it is not very economical to purchase many of them. A consideration would be to split the cost and use between yourself and a friend or friends. In addition, most of these tools can be obtained from a tool rental shop on a temporary basis.

This list primarily contains only those tools and instruments widely available to the public, and not those special tools produced by the vehicle manufacturer for distribution to dealer service departments. Occasionally, references to the manufacturer's special tools are included in the text of this manual. Generally, an alternative method of doing the job without the special tool is offered. However, sometimes there is no alternative to their use. Where this is the case, and the tool cannot be purchased or borrowed, the work should be turned over to the dealer service department or an automotive repair shop.

> *Valve spring compressor*
> *Piston ring groove cleaning tool*
> *Piston ring compressor*
> *Piston ring installation tool*
> *Cylinder compression gauge*
> *Cylinder ridge reamer*
> *Cylinder surfacing hone*
> *Cylinder bore gauge*
> *Micrometers and/or dial calipers*
> *Hydraulic lifter removal tool*
> *Balljoint separator*
> *Universal-type puller*
> *Impact screwdriver*
> *Dial indicator set*
> *Stroboscopic timing light (inductive pick-up)*
> *Hand operated vacuum/pressure pump*
> *Tachometer/dwell meter*
> *Universal electrical multimeter*
> *Cable hoist*
> *Brake spring removal and installation tools*
> *Floor jack*

Buying tools

For the do-it-yourselfer who is just starting to get involved in vehicle maintenance and repair, there are a number of options available when purchasing tools. If maintenance and minor repair is the extent of the work to be done, the purchase of individual tools is satisfactory. If, on the other hand, extensive work is planned, it would be a good idea to purchase a modest tool set from one of the large retail chain stores. A set can usually be bought at a substantial savings over the individual tool prices, and they often come with a tool box. As additional tools are

needed, add-on sets, individual tools and a larger tool box can be purchased to expand the tool selection. Building a tool set gradually allows the cost of the tools to be spread over a longer period of time and gives the mechanic the freedom to choose only those tools that will actually be used.

Tool stores will often be the only source of some of the special tools that are needed, but regardless of where tools are bought, try to avoid cheap ones, especially when buying screwdrivers and sockets, because they won't last very long. The expense involved in replacing cheap tools will eventually be greater than the initial cost of quality tools.

Care and maintenance of tools

Good tools are expensive, so it makes sense to treat them with respect. Keep them clean and in usable condition and store them properly when not in use. Always wipe off any dirt, grease or metal chips before putting them away. Never leave tools lying around in the work area. Upon completion of a job, always check closely under the hood for tools that may have been left there so they won't get lost during a test drive.

Some tools, such as screwdrivers, pliers, wrenches and sockets, can be hung on a panel mounted on the garage or workshop wall, while others should be kept in a tool box or tray. Measuring instruments, gauges, meters, etc. must be carefully stored where they cannot be damaged by weather or impact from other tools.

When tools are used with care and stored properly, they will last a very long time. Even with the best of care, though, tools will wear out if used frequently. When a tool is damaged or worn out, replace it. Subsequent jobs will be safer and more enjoyable if you do.

How to repair damaged threads

Sometimes, the internal threads of a nut or bolt hole can become stripped, usually from overtightening. Stripping threads is an all-too-common occurrence, especially when working with aluminum parts, because aluminum is so soft that it easily strips out.

Usually, external or internal threads are only partially stripped. After they've been cleaned up with a tap or die, they'll still work. Sometimes, however, threads are badly damaged. When this happens, you've got three choices:

1) *Drill and tap the hole to the next suitable oversize and install a larger diameter bolt, screw or stud.*
2) *Drill and tap the hole to accept a threaded plug, then drill and tap the plug to the original screw size. You can also buy a plug already threaded to the original size. Then you simply drill a hole to the specified size, then run the threaded plug into the hole with a bolt and jam*

nut. Once the plug is fully seated, remove the jam nut and bolt.
3) *The third method uses a patented thread repair kit like Heli-Coil or Slimsert. These easy-to-use kits are designed to repair damaged threads in straight-through holes and blind holes. Both are available as kits which can handle a variety of sizes and thread patterns. Drill the hole, then tap it with the special included tap. Install the Heli-Coil and the hole is back to its original diameter and thread pitch.*

Regardless of which method you use, be sure to proceed calmly and carefully. A little impatience or carelessness during one of these relatively simple procedures can ruin your whole day's work and cost you a bundle if you wreck an expensive part.

Working facilities

Not to be overlooked when discussing tools is the workshop. If anything more than routine maintenance is to be carried out, some sort of suitable work area is essential.

It is understood, and appreciated, that many home mechanics do not have a good workshop or garage available, and end up removing an engine or doing major repairs outside. It is recommended, however, that the overhaul or repair be completed under the cover of a roof.

A clean, flat workbench or table of comfortable working height is an absolute necessity. The workbench should be equipped with a vise that has a jaw opening of at least four inches.

As mentioned previously, some clean, dry storage space is also required for tools, as well as the lubricants, fluids, cleaning solvents, etc. which soon become necessary.

Sometimes waste oil and fluids, drained from the engine or cooling system during normal maintenance or repairs, present a disposal problem. To avoid pouring them on the ground or into a sewage system, pour the used fluids into large containers, seal them with caps and take them to an authorized disposal site or recycling center. Plastic jugs, such as old antifreeze containers, are ideal for this purpose.

Always keep a supply of old newspapers and clean rags available. Old towels are excellent for mopping up spills. Many mechanics use rolls of paper towels for most work because they are readily available and disposable. To help keep the area under the vehicle clean, a large cardboard box can be cut open and flattened to protect the garage or shop floor.

Whenever working over a painted surface, such as when leaning over a fender to service something under the hood, always cover it with an old blanket or bedspread to protect the finish. Vinyl covered pads, made especially for this purpose, are available at auto parts stores.

Booster battery (jump) starting

Observe these precautions when using a booster battery to start a vehicle:

a) *Before connecting the booster battery, make sure the ignition switch is in the Off position.*
b) *Turn off the lights, heater and other electrical loads.*
c) *Your eyes should be shielded. Safety goggles are a good idea.*
d) *Make sure the booster battery is the same voltage as the dead one in the vehicle.*
e) *The two vehicles MUST NOT TOUCH each other!*
f) *Make sure the transaxle is in Neutral (manual) or Park (automatic).*
g) *If the booster battery is not a maintenance-free type, remove the vent caps and lay a cloth over the vent holes.*

Connect the red jumper cable to the positive (+) terminals of each battery **(see illustration)**.

Connect one end of the black jumper cable to the negative (-) terminal of the booster battery. The other end of this cable should be connected to a good ground on the vehicle to be started, such as a bolt or bracket on the body.

Start the engine using the booster battery, then, with the engine running at idle speed, disconnect the jumper cables in the reverse order of connection.

Make the booster battery cable connections in the numerical order shown (note that the negative cable of the booster battery is NOT attached to the negative terminal of the dead battery)

Jacking and towing

Jacking

Warning: *The jack supplied with the vehicle should only be used for changing a tire or placing jackstands under the frame. Never work under the vehicle or start the engine while this jack is being used as the only means of support.*

The vehicle should be on level ground. Place the shift lever in Park, if you have an automatic, or Reverse if you have a manual

The jack fits over the rocker panel flange (there are two jacking points on each side of the vehicle, indicated by a notch in the rocker panel flange)

transaxle. Block the wheel diagonally opposite the wheel being changed. Set the parking brake.

Remove the spare tire and jack from stowage. Remove the wheel cover and trim ring (if so equipped) with the tapered end of the lug nut wrench by inserting and twisting the handle and then prying against the back of the wheel cover. Loosen the wheel lug nuts about 1/4-to-1/2 turn each.

Place the scissors-type jack under the side of the vehicle and adjust the jack height until it fits in the notch in the vertical rocker panel flange nearest the wheel to be changed. There is a front and rear jacking point on each side of the vehicle **(see illustration).**

Turn the jack handle clockwise until the tire clears the ground. Remove the lug nuts and pull the wheel off. Replace it with the spare.

Install the lug nuts with the beveled edges facing in. Tighten them snugly. Don't attempt to tighten them completely until the vehicle is lowered or it could slip off the jack. Turn the jack handle counterclockwise to lower the vehicle. Remove the jack and tighten the lug nuts in a diagonal pattern.

Install the cover (and trim ring, if used) and be sure it's snapped into place all the way around.

Stow the tire, jack and wrench. Unblock the wheels.

Towing

As a general rule, the vehicle should be towed with the front (drive) wheels off the ground. If they can't be raised, place them on a dolly. The ignition key must be in the ACC position, since the steering lock mechanism isn't strong enough to hold the front wheels straight while towing.

Vehicles equipped with an automatic transaxle can be towed from the front only with all four wheels on the ground, provided that speeds don't exceed 30 mph and the distance is not over 50 miles. Before towing, check the transmission fluid level (see Chapter 1). If the level is below the HOT line on the dipstick, add fluid or use a towing dolly.

When towing a vehicle equipped with a manual transaxle with all four wheels on the ground, be sure to place the shift lever in neutral and release the parking brake.

Equipment specifically designed for towing should be used. It should be attached to the main structural members of the vehicle, not the bumpers or brackets.

Safety is a major consideration when towing and all applicable state and local laws must be obeyed. A safety chain system must be used at all times.

Automotive chemicals and lubricants

A number of automotive chemicals and lubricants are available for use during vehicle maintenance and repair. They include a wide variety of products ranging from cleaning solvents and degreasers to lubricants and protective sprays for rubber, plastic and vinyl.

Cleaners

Carburetor cleaner and choke cleaner is a strong solvent for gum, varnish and carbon. Most carburetor cleaners leave a dry-type lubricant film which will not harden or gum up. Because of this film it is not recommended for use on electrical components.

Brake system cleaner is used to remove grease and brake fluid from the brake system, where clean surfaces are absolutely necessary. It leaves no residue and often eliminates brake squeal caused by contaminants.

Electrical cleaner removes oxidation, corrosion and carbon deposits from electrical contacts, restoring full current flow. It can also be used to clean spark plugs, carburetor jets, voltage regulators and other parts where an oil-free surface is desired.

Demoisturants remove water and moisture from electrical components such as alternators, voltage regulators, electrical connectors and fuse blocks. They are non-conductive, non-corrosive and non-flammable.

Degreasers are heavy-duty solvents used to remove grease from the outside of the engine and from chassis components. They can be sprayed or brushed on and, depending on the type, are rinsed off either with water or solvent.

Lubricants

Motor oil is the lubricant formulated for use in engines. It normally contains a wide variety of additives to prevent corrosion and reduce foaming and wear. Motor oil comes in various weights (viscosity ratings) from 0 to 50. The recommended weight of the oil depends on the season, temperature and the demands on the engine. Light oil is used in cold climates and under light load conditions. Heavy oil is used in hot climates and where high loads are encountered. Multi-viscosity oils are designed to have characteristics of both light and heavy oils and are available in a number of weights from 5W-20 to 20W-50.

Gear oil is designed to be used in differentials, manual transmissions and other areas where high-temperature lubrication is required.

Chassis and wheel bearing grease is a heavy grease used where increased loads and friction are encountered, such as for wheel bearings, balljoints, tie-rod ends and universal joints.

High-temperature wheel bearing grease is designed to withstand the extreme temperatures encountered by wheel bearings in disc brake equipped vehicles. It usually contains molybdenum disulfide (moly), which is a dry-type lubricant.

White grease is a heavy grease for metal-to-metal applications where water is a problem. White grease stays soft under both low and high temperatures (usually from -100 to +190-degrees F), and will not wash off or dilute in the presence of water.

Assembly lube is a special extreme pressure lubricant, usually containing moly, used to lubricate high-load parts (such as main and rod bearings and cam lobes) for initial start-up of a new engine. The assembly lube lubricates the parts without being squeezed out or washed away until the engine oiling system begins to function.

Silicone lubricants are used to protect rubber, plastic, vinyl and nylon parts.

Graphite lubricants are used where oils cannot be used due to contamination problems, such as in locks. The dry graphite will lubricate metal parts while remaining uncontaminated by dirt, water, oil or acids. It is electrically conductive and will not foul electrical contacts in locks such as the ignition switch.

Moly penetrants loosen and lubricate frozen, rusted and corroded fasteners and prevent future rusting or freezing.

Heat-sink grease is a special electrically non-conductive grease that is used for mounting electronic ignition modules where it is essential that heat is transferred away from the module.

Sealants

RTV sealant is one of the most widely used gasket compounds. Made from silicone, RTV is air curing, it seals, bonds, waterproofs, fills surface irregularities, remains flexible, doesn't shrink, is relatively easy to remove, and is used as a supplementary sealer with almost all low and medium temperature gaskets.

Anaerobic sealant is much like RTV in that it can be used either to seal gaskets or to form gaskets by itself. It remains flexible, is solvent resistant and fills surface imperfections. The difference between an anaerobic sealant and an RTV-type sealant is in the curing. RTV cures when exposed to air, while an anaerobic sealant cures only in the absence of air. This means that an anaerobic sealant cures only after the assembly of parts, sealing them together.

Thread and pipe sealant is used for sealing hydraulic and pneumatic fittings and vacuum lines. It is usually made from a Teflon compound, and comes in a spray, a paint-on liquid and as a wrap-around tape.

Chemicals

Anti-seize compound prevents seizing, galling, cold welding, rust and corrosion in fasteners. High-temperature ant-seize, usually made with copper and graphite lubricants, is used for exhaust system and exhaust manifold bolts.

Anaerobic locking compounds are used to keep fasteners from vibrating or working loose and cure only after installation, in the absence of air. Medium strength locking compound is used for small nuts, bolts and screws that may be removed later. High-strength locking compound is for large nuts, bolts and studs which aren't removed on a regular basis.

Oil additives range from viscosity index improvers to chemical treatments that claim to reduce internal engine friction. It should be noted that most oil manufacturers caution against using additives with their oils.

Gas additives perform several functions, depending on their chemical makeup. They usually contain solvents that help dissolve gum and varnish that build up on carburetor, fuel injection and intake parts. They also serve to break down carbon deposits that form on the inside surfaces of the combustion chambers. Some additives contain upper cylinder lubricants for valves and piston rings, and others contain chemicals to remove condensation from the gas tank.

Miscellaneous

Brake fluid is specially formulated hydraulic fluid that can withstand the heat and pressure encountered in brake systems. Care must be taken so this fluid does not come in contact with painted surfaces or plastics. An opened container should always be resealed to prevent contamination by water or dirt.

Weatherstrip adhesive is used to bond weatherstripping around doors, windows and trunk lids. It is sometimes used to attach trim pieces.

Undercoating is a petroleum-based, tar-like substance that is designed to protect metal surfaces on the underside of the vehicle from corrosion. It also acts as a sound-deadening agent by insulating the bottom of the vehicle.

Waxes and polishes are used to help protect painted and plated surfaces from the weather. Different types of paint may require the use of different types of wax and polish. Some polishes utilize a chemical or abrasive cleaner to help remove the top layer of oxidized (dull) paint on older vehicles. In recent years many non-wax polishes that contain a wide variety of chemicals such as polymers and silicones have been introduced. These non-wax polishes are usually easier to apply and last longer than conventional waxes and polishes.

Conversion factors

Length (distance)
Inches (in)	X	25.4	= Millimetres (mm)	X 0.0394	= Inches (in)
Feet (ft)	X	0.305	= Metres (m)	X 3.281	= Feet (ft)
Miles	X	1.609	= Kilometres (km)	X 0.621	= Miles

Volume (capacity)
Cubic inches (cu in; in^3)	X	16.387	= Cubic centimetres (cc; cm^3)	X 0.061	= Cubic inches (cu in; in^3)
Imperial pints (Imp pt)	X	0.568	= Litres (l)	X 1.76	= Imperial pints (Imp pt)
Imperial quarts (Imp qt)	X	1.137	= Litres (l)	X 0.88	= Imperial quarts (Imp qt)
Imperial quarts (Imp qt)	X	1.201	= US quarts (US qt)	X 0.833	= Imperial quarts (Imp qt)
US quarts (US qt)	X	0.946	= Litres (l)	X 1.057	= US quarts (US qt)
Imperial gallons (Imp gal)	X	4.546	= Litres (l)	X 0.22	= Imperial gallons (Imp gal)
Imperial gallons (Imp gal)	X	1.201	= US gallons (US gal)	X 0.833	= Imperial gallons (Imp gal)
US gallons (US gal)	X	3.785	= Litres (l)	X 0.264	= US gallons (US gal)

Mass (weight)
Ounces (oz)	X	28.35	= Grams (g)	X 0.035	= Ounces (oz)
Pounds (lb)	X	0.454	= Kilograms (kg)	X 2.205	= Pounds (lb)

Force
Ounces-force (ozf; oz)	X	0.278	= Newtons (N)	X 3.6	= Ounces-force (ozf; oz)
Pounds-force (lbf; lb)	X	4.448	= Newtons (N)	X 0.225	= Pounds-force (lbf; lb)
Newtons (N)	X	0.1	= Kilograms-force (kgf; kg)	X 9.81	= Newtons (N)

Pressure
Pounds-force per square inch (psi; lbf/in^2; lb/in^2)	X	0.070	= Kilograms-force per square centimetre (kgf/cm^2; kg/cm^2)	X 14.223	= Pounds-force per square inch (psi; lbf/in^2; lb/in^2)
Pounds-force per square inch (psi; lbf/in^2; lb/in^2)	X	0.068	= Atmospheres (atm)	X 14.696	= Pounds-force per square inch (psi; lbf/in^2; lb/in^2)
Pounds-force per square inch (psi; lbf/in^2; lb/in^2)	X	0.069	= Bars	X 14.5	= Pounds-force per square inch (psi; lbf/in^2; lb/in^2)
Pounds-force per square inch (psi; lbf/in^2; lb/in^2)	X	6.895	= Kilopascals (kPa)	X 0.145	= Pounds-force per square inch (psi; lbf/in^2; lb/in^2)
Kilopascals (kPa)	X	0.01	= Kilograms-force per square centimetre (kgf/cm^2; kg/cm^2)	X 98.1	= Kilopascals (kPa)

Torque (moment of force)
Pounds-force inches (lbf in; lb in)	X	1.152	= Kilograms-force centimetre (kgf cm; kg cm)	X 0.868	= Pounds-force inches (lbf in; lb in)
Pounds-force inches (lbf in; lb in)	X	0.113	= Newton metres (Nm)	X 8.85	= Pounds-force inches (lbf in; lb in)
Pounds-force inches (lbf in; lb in)	X	0.083	= Pounds-force feet (lbf ft; lb ft)	X 12	= Pounds-force inches (lbf in; lb in)
Pounds-force feet (lbf ft; lb ft)	X	0.138	= Kilograms-force metres (kgf m; kg m)	X 7.233	= Pounds-force feet (lbf ft; lb ft)
Pounds-force feet (lbf ft; lb ft)	X	1.356	= Newton metres (Nm)	X 0.738	= Pounds-force feet (lbf ft; lb ft)
Newton metres (Nm)	X	0.102	= Kilograms-force metres (kgf m; kg m)	X 9.804	= Newton metres (Nm)

Vacuum
Inches mercury (in. Hg)	X	3.377	= Kilopascals (kPa)	X 0.2961	= Inches mercury
Inches mercury (in. Hg)	X	25.4	= Millimeters mercury (mm Hg)	X 0.0394	= Inches mercury

Power
Horsepower (hp)	X	745.7	= Watts (W)	X 0.0013	= Horsepower (hp)

Velocity (speed)
Miles per hour (miles/hr; mph)	X	1.609	= Kilometres per hour (km/hr; kph)	X 0.621	= Miles per hour (miles/hr; mph)

Fuel consumption*
Miles per gallon, Imperial (mpg)	X	0.354	= Kilometres per litre (km/l)	X 2.825	= Miles per gallon, Imperial (mpg)
Miles per gallon, US (mpg)	X	0.425	= Kilometres per litre (km/l)	X 2.352	= Miles per gallon, US (mpg)

Temperature
Degrees Fahrenheit = (°C x 1.8) + 32

Degrees Celsius (Degrees Centigrade; °C) = (°F - 32) x 0.56

*It is common practice to convert from miles per gallon (mpg) to litres/100 kilometres (l/100km), where mpg (Imperial) x l/100 km = 282 and mpg (US) x l/100 km = 235

Safety first!

Regardless of how enthusiastic you may be about getting on with the job at hand, take the time to ensure that your safety is not jeopardized. A moment's lack of attention can result in an accident, as can failure to observe certain simple safety precautions. The possibility of an accident will always exist, and the following points should not be considered a comprehensive list of all dangers. Rather, they are intended to make you aware of the risks and to encourage a safety conscious approach to all work you carry out on your vehicle.

Essential DOs and DON'Ts

DON'T rely on a jack when working under the vehicle. Always use approved jackstands to support the weight of the vehicle and place them under the recommended lift or support points.

DON'T attempt to loosen extremely tight fasteners (i.e. wheel lug nuts) while the vehicle is on a jack - it may fall.

DON'T start the engine without first making sure that the transmission is in Neutral (or Park where applicable) and the parking brake is set.

DON'T remove the radiator cap from a hot cooling system - let it cool or cover it with a cloth and release the pressure gradually.

DON'T attempt to drain the engine oil until you are sure it has cooled to the point that it will not burn you.

DON'T touch any part of the engine or exhaust system until it has cooled sufficiently to avoid burns.

DON'T siphon toxic liquids such as gasoline, antifreeze and brake fluid by mouth, or allow them to remain on your skin.

DON'T inhale brake lining dust - it is potentially hazardous (see Asbestos below).

DON'T allow spilled oil or grease to remain on the floor - wipe it up before someone slips on it.

DON'T use loose fitting wrenches or other tools which may slip and cause injury.

DON'T push on wrenches when loosening or tightening nuts or bolts. Always try to pull the wrench toward you. If the situation calls for pushing the wrench away, push with an open hand to avoid scraped knuckles if the wrench should slip.

DON'T attempt to lift a heavy component alone - get someone to help you.

DON'T rush or take unsafe shortcuts to finish a job.

DON'T allow children or animals in or around the vehicle while you are working on it.

DO wear eye protection when using power tools such as a drill, sander, bench grinder, etc. and when working under a vehicle.

DO keep loose clothing and long hair well out of the way of moving parts.

DO make sure that any hoist used has a safe working load rating adequate for the job.

DO get someone to check on you periodically when working alone on a vehicle.

DO carry out work in a logical sequence and make sure that everything is correctly assembled and tightened.

DO keep chemicals and fluids tightly capped and out of the reach of children and pets.

DO remember that your vehicle's safety affects that of yourself and others. If in doubt on any point, get professional advice.

Asbestos

Certain friction, insulating, sealing, and other products - such as brake linings, brake bands, clutch linings, torque converters, gaskets, etc. - may contain asbestos. Extreme care must be taken to avoid inhalation of dust from such products, since it is hazardous to health. If in doubt, assume that they do contain asbestos.

Fire

Remember at all times that gasoline is highly flammable. Never smoke or have any kind of open flame around when working on a vehicle. But the risk does not end there. A spark caused by an electrical short circuit, by two metal surfaces contacting each other, or even by static electricity built up in your body under certain conditions, can ignite gasoline vapors, which in a confined space are highly explosive. Do not, under any circumstances, use gasoline for cleaning parts. Use an approved safety solvent.

Always disconnect the battery ground (-) cable at the battery before working on any part of the fuel system or electrical system. Never risk spilling fuel on a hot engine or exhaust component. It is strongly recommended that a fire extinguisher suitable for use on fuel and electrical fires be kept handy in the garage or workshop at all times. Never try to extinguish a fuel or electrical fire with water.

Fumes

Certain fumes are highly toxic and can quickly cause unconsciousness and even death if inhaled to any extent. Gasoline vapor falls into this category, as do the vapors from some cleaning solvents. Any draining or pouring of such volatile fluids should be done in a well ventilated area.

When using cleaning fluids and solvents, read the instructions on the container carefully. Never use materials from unmarked containers.

Never run the engine in an enclosed space, such as a garage. Exhaust fumes contain carbon monoxide, which is extremely poisonous. If you need to run the engine, always do so in the open air, or at least have the rear of the vehicle outside the work area.

If you are fortunate enough to have the use of an inspection pit, never drain or pour gasoline and never run the engine while the vehicle is over the pit. The fumes, being heavier than air, will concentrate in the pit with possibly lethal results.

The battery

Never create a spark or allow a bare light bulb near a battery. They normally give off a certain amount of hydrogen gas, which is highly explosive.

Always disconnect the battery ground (-) cable at the battery before working on the fuel or electrical systems.

If possible, loosen the filler caps or cover when charging the battery from an external source (this does not apply to sealed or maintenance-free batteries). Do not charge at an excessive rate or the battery may burst.

Take care when adding water to a non maintenance-free battery and when carrying a battery. The electrolyte, even when diluted, is very corrosive and should not be allowed to contact clothing or skin.

Always wear eye protection when cleaning the battery to prevent the caustic deposits from entering your eyes.

Household current

When using an electric power tool, inspection light, etc., which operates on household current, always make sure that the tool is correctly connected to its plug and that, where necessary, it is properly grounded. Do not use such items in damp conditions and, again, do not create a spark or apply excessive heat in the vicinity of fuel or fuel vapor.

Secondary ignition system voltage

A severe electric shock can result from touching certain parts of the ignition system (such as the spark plug wires) when the engine is running or being cranked, particularly if components are damp or the insulation is defective. In the case of an electronic ignition system, the secondary system voltage is much higher and could prove fatal.

Troubleshooting

Contents

This section provides an easy reference guide to the more common problems which may occur during the operation of your vehicle. These problems and their possible causes are grouped under headings denoting various components or systems, such as Engine, Cooling system, etc. They also refer you to the chapter and/or section which deals with the problem.

Remember that successful troubleshooting is not a mysterious black art practiced only by professional mechanics. It is simply the result of the right knowledge combined with an intelligent, systematic approach to the problem. Always work by a process of elimination, starting with the simplest solution and working through to the most complex - and never overlook the obvious. Anyone can run the gas tank dry or leave the lights on overnight, so don't assume that you are exempt from such oversights.

Finally, always establish a clear idea of why a problem has occurred and take steps to ensure that it doesn't happen again. If the electrical system fails because of a poor connection, check the other connections in the system to make sure that they don't fail as well. If a particular fuse continues to blow, find out why - don't just replace one fuse after another. Remember, failure of a small component can often be indicative of potential failure or incorrect functioning of a more important component or system.

Engine

1 Engine will not rotate when attempting to start

1   Battery terminal connections loose or corroded (Chapter 1).
2   Battery discharged or faulty (Chapter 1).
3   Automatic transaxle not completely engaged in Park (Chapter 7) or clutch pedal not completely depressed (Chapter 8).
4   Broken, loose or disconnected wiring in the starting circuit (Chapters 5 and 12).
5   Starter motor pinion jammed in flywheel ring gear (Chapter 5).
6   Starter solenoid faulty (Chapter 5).
7   Starter motor faulty (Chapter 5).
8   Ignition switch faulty (Chapter 12).
9   Starter pinion or flywheel teeth worn or broken (Chapter 5).

2 Engine rotates but will not start

1   Fuel tank empty.
2   Battery discharged (engine rotates slowly) (Chapter 5).
3   Battery terminal connections loose or corroded (Chapter 1).
4   Leaking carburetor, fuel injector(s), faulty fuel pump, pressure regulator, etc. (Chapter 4).
5   Broken or stripped timing belt or chain (Chapter 2).

6   Ignition components damp or damaged (Chapter 5).
7   Worn, faulty or incorrectly gapped spark plugs (Chapter 1).
8   Broken, loose or disconnected wiring in the starting circuit (Chapter 5).
9   Loose distributor is changing ignition timing (Chapter 5).
10   Broken, loose or disconnected wires at the ignition coil or faulty coil (Chapter 5).

3 Engine hard to start when cold

1   Battery discharged or low (Chapter 1).
2   Malfunctioning fuel system (Chapter 4).
3   Faulty coolant temperature sensor or intake air temperature sensor (Chapter 6).
4   Injector(s) leaking (Chapter 4B).
5   Carburetor or choke problem (Chapter 4A).
6   Faulty ignition system (Chapter 5).

4 Engine hard to start when hot

1   Air filter clogged (Chapter 1).
2   Fuel not reaching the carburetor or fuel injection system (Chapter 4).
3   Corroded battery connections, especially ground (Chapter 1).
4   Faulty coolant temperature sensor or intake air temperature sensor (Chapter 6).
5   Carburetor or choke problem (Chapter 4A).

5 Starter motor noisy or excessively rough in engagement

1   Pinion or flywheel gear teeth worn or broken (Chapter 5).
2   Starter motor mounting bolts loose or missing (Chapter 5).

6 Engine starts but stops immediately

1   Loose or faulty electrical connections at distributor, coil or alternator (Chapter 5).
2   Insufficient fuel reaching the carburetor or fuel injector(s) (Chapters 1 and 4).
3   Vacuum leak at the gasket between the intake manifold/plenum and throttle body or carburetor (Chapters 1 and 4).
4   Idle speed incorrect (Chapter 1).

7 Oil puddle under engine

1   Oil pan gasket and/or oil pan drain bolt washer leaking (Chapter 2).
2   Oil pressure sending unit leaking (Chapter 2).
3   Cylinder head covers leaking (Chapter 2).

4   Engine oil seals leaking (Chapter 2).
5   Oil pump housing leaking (Chapter 2).

8 Engine lopes while idling or idles erratically

1   Vacuum leakage (Chapters 2 and 4).
2   Leaking EGR valve (Chapter 6).
3   Air filter clogged (Chapter 1).
4   Fuel pump not delivering sufficient fuel to the carburetor or fuel injection system (Chapter 4).
5   Leaking head gasket (Chapter 2).
6   Timing belt or chain and/or pulleys worn (Chapter 2).
7   Camshaft lobes worn (Chapter 2).

9 Engine misses at idle speed

1   Spark plugs worn or not gapped properly (Chapter 1).
2   Faulty spark plug wires (Chapter 1).
3   Vacuum leaks (Chapter 1).
4   Incorrect ignition timing (Chapter 1).
5   Uneven or low compression (Chapter 2).
6   Problem with the carburetor or fuel injection system (Chapter 4).

10 Engine misses throughout driving speed range

1   Fuel filter clogged and/or impurities in the fuel system (Chapter 1).
2   Low fuel output at the carburetor or injector(s) (Chapter 4).
3   Faulty or incorrectly gapped spark plugs (Chapter 1).
4   Incorrect ignition timing (Chapter 5).
5   Cracked distributor cap, disconnected distributor wires or damaged distributor components (Chapters 1 and 5).
6   Leaking spark plug wires (Chapters 1 or 5).
7   Faulty emission system components (Chapter 6).
8   Low or uneven cylinder compression pressures (Chapter 2).
9   Weak or faulty ignition system (Chapter 5).
10   Vacuum leak in fuel injection system, carburetor, intake manifold, air control valve or vacuum hoses (Chapter 4).

11 Engine stumbles on acceleration

1   Spark plugs fouled (Chapter 1).
2   Problem with fuel injection system or carburetor (Chapter 4).
3   Fuel filter clogged (Chapters 1 and 4).
4   Incorrect ignition timing (Chapter 5).
5   Intake manifold air leak (Chapters 2 and 4).
6   Problem with the emissions control system (Chapter 6).

12 Engine surges while holding accelerator steady

1   Intake air leak (Chapter 4).
2   Fuel pump or fuel pressure regulator faulty (Chapter 4).
3   Problem with carburetor or fuel injection system (Chapter 4).
4   Problem with the emissions control system (Chapter 6).

13 Engine stalls

1   Idle speed incorrect (Chapter 1).
2   Fuel filter clogged and/or water and impurities in the fuel system (Chapters 1 and 4).
3   Distributor components damp or damaged (Chapter 5).
4   Faulty emissions system components (Chapter 6).
5   Faulty or incorrectly gapped spark plugs (Chapter 1).
6   Faulty spark plug wires (Chapter 1).
7   Vacuum leak in the carburetor or fuel injection system, intake manifold or vacuum hoses (Chapters 2 and 4).
8   Valve clearances incorrectly set (Chapter 1).

14 Engine lacks power

1   Incorrect ignition timing (Chapter 5).
2   Excessive play in distributor shaft (Chapter 5).
3   Worn rotor, distributor cap, spark plug wires or faulty coil (Chapters 1 and 5).
4   Faulty or incorrectly gapped spark plugs (Chapter 1).
5   Problem with the carburetor or fuel injection system (Chapter 4).
6   Plugged air filter (Chapter 1).
7   Brakes binding (Chapter 9).
8   Automatic transaxle fluid level incorrect (Chapter 1).
9   Clutch slipping (Chapter 8).
10 Fuel filter clogged and/or impurities in the fuel system (Chapters 1 and 4).
11 Emission control system not functioning properly (Chapter 6).
12 Low or uneven cylinder compression pressures (Chapter 2).
13 Obstructed exhaust system (Chapter 4).

15 Engine backfires

1   Emission control system not functioning properly (Chapter 6).
2   Ignition timing incorrect (Chapter 5).
3   Faulty secondary ignition system (cracked spark plug insulator, faulty plug wires, distributor cap and/or rotor) (Chapters 1 and 5).
4   Problem with the carburetor or fuel injection system (Chapter 4).

5   Vacuum leak at fuel injector(s), intake manifold, air control valve or vacuum hoses (Chapters 2 and 4).
6   Valve clearances incorrectly set and/or valves sticking (Chapter 1).

16 Pinging or knocking engine sounds during acceleration or uphill

1   Incorrect grade of fuel.
2   Ignition timing incorrect (Chapter 5).
3   Carburetor or fuel injection system faulty (Chapter 4).
4   Improper or damaged spark plugs or wires (Chapter 1).
5   Worn or damaged distributor components (Chapter 5).
6   EGR valve not functioning (Chapter 6).
7   Vacuum leak (Chapters 2 and 4).

17 Engine runs with oil pressure light on

1   Low oil level (Chapter 1).
2   Idle rpm below specification (Chapter 1).
3   Short in wiring circuit (Chapter 12).
4   Faulty oil pressure sender (Chapter 2).
5   Worn engine bearings and/or oil pump (Chapter 2).

18 Engine diesels (continues to run) after switching off

1   Idle speed too high (Chapter 1).
2   Excessive engine operating temperature (Chapter 3).
3   Ignition timing in need of adjustment (Chapter 5).

Engine electrical system

19 Battery will not hold a charge

1   Alternator drivebelt defective or not adjusted properly (Chapter 1).
2   Battery electrolyte level low (Chapter 1).
3   Battery terminals loose or corroded (Chapter 1).
4   Alternator not charging properly (Chapter 5).
5   Loose, broken or faulty wiring in the charging circuit (Chapter 5).
6   Short in vehicle wiring (Chapter 12).
7   Internally defective battery (Chapters 1 and 5).

20 Alternator light fails to go out

1   Faulty alternator or charging circuit (Chapter 5).

2   Alternator drivebelt defective or out of adjustment (Chapter 1).
3   Alternator voltage regulator inoperative (Chapter 5).

21 Alternator light fails to come on when key is turned on

1   Warning light bulb defective (Chapter 12).
2   Fault in the printed circuit, dash wiring or bulb holder (Chapter 12).

Fuel system

22 Excessive fuel consumption

1   Dirty or clogged air filter element (Chapter 1).
2   Incorrectly set ignition timing (Chapter 5).
3   Emissions system not functioning properly (Chapter 6).
4   Carburetor or fuel injection system not functioning properly (Chapter 4).
5   Low tire pressure or incorrect tire size (Chapter 1).

23 Fuel leakage and/or fuel odor

1   Leaking fuel feed or return line (Chapters 1 and 4).
2   Tank overfilled.
3   Evaporative canister filter clogged (Chapters 1 and 6).
4   Problem with carburetor or fuel injection system (Chapter 4).

Cooling system

24 Overheating

1   Insufficient coolant in system (Chapter 1).
2   Water pump drivebelt defective or out of adjustment (Chapter 1).
3   Radiator core blocked or grille restricted (Chapter 3).
4   Thermostat faulty (Chapter 3).
5   Electric coolant fan inoperative or blades broken (Chapter 3).
6   Radiator cap not maintaining proper pressure (Chapter 3).
7   Ignition timing incorrect (Chapter 5).

25 Overcooling

1   Faulty thermostat (Chapter 3).
2   Inaccurate temperature gauge sending unit (Chapter 3).

26 External coolant leakage

1   Deteriorated/damaged hoses; loose clamps (Chapters 1 and 3).
2   Water pump defective (Chapter 3).
3   Leakage from radiator core or coolant reservoir bottle (Chapter 3).
4   Engine drain or water jacket core plugs leaking (Chapter 2).

27 Internal coolant leakage

1   Leaking cylinder head gasket (Chapter 2).
2   Cracked cylinder bore or cylinder head (Chapter 2).

28 Coolant loss

1   Too much coolant in system (Chapter 1).
2   Coolant boiling away because of overheating (Chapter 3).
3   Internal or external leakage (Chapter 3).
4   Faulty radiator cap (Chapter 3).

29 Poor coolant circulation

1   Inoperative water pump (Chapter 3).
2   Restriction in cooling system (Chapters 1 and 3).
3   Water pump drivebelt defective/out of adjustment (Chapter 1).
4   Thermostat sticking (Chapter 3).

Clutch

30 Pedal travels to floor - no pressure or very little resistance

1   Damaged cable (Chapter 8).
2   Broken release bearing or fork (Chapter 8).

31 Unable to select gears

1   Faulty transaxle (Chapter 7).
2   Faulty clutch disc or pressure plate (Chapter 8).
3   Faulty release lever or release bearing (Chapter 8).
4   Faulty shift lever assembly or rods (Chapter 8).

32 Clutch slips (engine speed increases with no increase in vehicle speed)

1   Clutch plate worn (Chapter 8).
2   Clutch plate is oil soaked by leaking rear main seal (Chapter 8).

3   Clutch plate not seated (Chapter 8).
4   Warped pressure plate or flywheel (Chapter 8).
5   Weak diaphragm springs (Chapter 8).
6   Clutch plate overheated. Allow to cool.

33 Grabbing (chattering) as clutch is engaged

1   Oil on clutch plate lining, burned or glazed facings (Chapter 8).
2   Worn or loose engine or transaxle mounts (Chapters 2 and 7).
3   Worn splines on clutch plate hub (Chapter 8).
4   Warped pressure plate or flywheel (Chapter 8).
5   Burned or smeared resin on flywheel or pressure plate (Chapter 8).

34 Transaxle rattling (clicking)

1   Release lever loose (Chapter 8).
2   Clutch plate damper spring failure (Chapter 8).
3   Low engine idle speed (Chapter 1).

35 Noise in clutch area

1   Fork shaft improperly installed (Chapter 8).
2   Faulty bearing (Chapter 8).

36 Clutch pedal stays on floor

Broken cable, release bearing or fork (Chapter 8).

37 High pedal effort

1   Piston binding in bore (Chapter 8).
2   Pressure plate faulty (Chapter 8).
3   Incorrect size master or release cylinder (Chapter 8).

Manual transaxle

38 Knocking noise at low speeds

1   Worn driveaxle constant velocity (CV) joints (Chapter 8).
2   Worn side gear shaft counterbore in differential case (Chapter 7A).*

39 Noise most pronounced when turning

Differential gear noise (Chapter 7A).*

40 Clunk on acceleration or deceleration

1   Loose engine or transaxle mounts (Chapters 2 and 7A).
2   Worn differential pinion shaft in case.*
3   Worn side gear shaft counterbore in differential case (Chapter 7A).*
4   Worn or damaged driveaxle inboard CV joints (Chapter 8).

41 Clicking noise in turns

Worn or damaged outboard CV joint (Chapter 8).

42 Vibration

1   Rough wheel bearing (Chapters 1 and 10).
2   Damaged driveaxle (Chapter 8).
3   Out of round tires (Chapter 1).
4   Tire out of balance (Chapters 1 and 10).
5   Worn CV joint (Chapter 8).

43 Noisy in neutral with engine running

1   Damaged input gear bearing (Chapter 7A).*
2   Damaged clutch release bearing (Chapter 8).

44 Noisy in one particular gear

1   Damaged or worn constant mesh gears (Chapter 7A).*
2   Damaged or worn synchronizers (Chapter 7A).*
3   Bent reverse fork (Chapter 7A).*
4   Damaged fourth speed gear or output gear (Chapter 7A).*
5   Worn or damaged reverse idler gear or idler bushing (Chapter 7A).*

45 Noisy in all gears

1   Insufficient lubricant (Chapter 7A).
2   Damaged or worn bearings (Chapter 7A).*
3   Worn or damaged input gear shaft and/or output gear shaft (Chapter 7A).*

46 Slips out of gear

1   Worn or improperly adjusted linkage (Chapter 7A).
2   Transaxle loose on engine (Chapter 7A).
3   Shift linkage does not work freely, binds (Chapter 7A).
4   Input gear bearing retainer broken or loose (Chapter 7A).*
5   Dirt between clutch cover and engine housing (Chapter 7A).
6   Worn shift fork (Chapter 7A).*

47 Leaks lubricant

1   Side gear shaft seals worn (Chapter 7).
2   Excessive amount of lubricant in transaxle (Chapters 1 and 7A).
3   Loose or broken input gear shaft bearing retainer (Chapter 7A).*
4   Input gear bearing retainer O-ring and/or lip seal damaged (Chapter 7A).*

48 Locked in gear

Lock pin or interlock pin missing (Chapter 7A).*

Although the corrective action necessary to remedy the symptoms described is beyond the scope of this manual, the above information should be helpful in isolating the cause of the condition so that the owner can communicate clearly with a professional mechanic.

Automatic transaxle

Note: *Due to the complexity of the automatic transaxle, it is difficult for the home mechanic to properly diagnose and service this component. For problems other than the following, the vehicle should be taken to a dealer or transaxle shop.*

49 Fluid leakage

1   Automatic transaxle fluid is a deep red color. Fluid leaks should not be confused with engine oil, which can easily be blown onto the transaxle by air flow.
2   To pinpoint a leak, first remove all built-up dirt and grime from the transaxle housing with degreasing agents and/or steam cleaning. Then drive the vehicle at low speeds so air flow will not blow the leak far from its source. Raise the vehicle and determine where the leak is coming from. Common areas of leakage are:
   a) *Pan (Chapters 1 and 7)*
   b) *Dipstick tube (Chapters 1 and 7)*
   c) *Transaxle oil lines (Chapter 7)*
   d) *Speed sensor (Chapter 7)*
   e *Driveaxle oil seals (Chapter 7).*

50 Transaxle fluid brown or has a burned smell

Transaxle fluid overheated (Chapter 1).

51 General shift mechanism problems

1   Chapter 7, Part B, deals with checking and adjusting the shift linkage on automatic transaxles. Common problems which may be attributed to poorly adjusted linkage are:
   a) *Engine starting in gears other than Park or Neutral.*
   b) *Indicator on shifter pointing to a gear other than the one actually being used.*
   c) *Vehicle moves when in Park.*
2   Refer to Chapter 7B for the shift linkage adjustment procedure.

52 Transaxle will not downshift with accelerator pedal pressed to the floor

Throttle valve cable out of adjustment (Chapter 7B).

53 Engine will start in gears other than Park or Neutral

Neutral start switch malfunctioning (Chapter 7B).

54 Transaxle slips, shifts roughly, is noisy or has no drive in forward or reverse gears

There are many probable causes for the above problems, but the home mechanic should be concerned with only one possibility - fluid level. Before taking the vehicle to a repair shop, check the level and condition of the fluid as described in Chapter 1. Correct the fluid level as necessary or change the fluid and filter if needed. If the problem persists, have a professional diagnose the cause.

Driveaxles

55 Clicking noise in turns

Worn or damaged outboard CV joint (Chapter 8).

56 Shudder or vibration during acceleration

1   Excessive toe-in (Chapter 10).
2   Incorrect spring heights (Chapter 10).
3   Worn or damaged inboard or outboard CV joints (Chapter 8).
4   Sticking inboard CV joint assembly (Chapter 8).

57 Vibration at highway speeds

1   Out of balance front wheels and/or tires (Chapters 1 and 10).
2   Out of round front tires (Chapters 1 and 10).
3   Worn CV joint(s) (Chapter 8).

Brakes

Note: *Before assuming that a brake problem exists, make sure that:*
   a) *The tires are in good condition and properly inflated (Chapter 1).*
   b) *The front end alignment is correct (Chapter 10).*
   c) *The vehicle is not loaded with weight in an unequal manner.*

58 Vehicle pulls to one side during braking

1   Incorrect tire pressures (Chapter 1).
2   Front end out of alignment (have the front end aligned).
3   Front, or rear, tire sizes not matched to one another.
4   Restricted brake lines or hoses (Chapter 9).
5   Malfunctioning drum brake or caliper assembly (Chapter 9).
6   Loose suspension parts (Chapter 10).
7   Loose calipers (Chapter 9).
8   Excessive wear of brake shoe or pad material or disc/drum on one side.

59 Noise (high-pitched squeal when the brakes are applied)

Front and/or rear disc brake pads worn out. The noise comes from the wear sensor rubbing against the disc (does not apply to all vehicles). Replace pads with new ones immediately (Chapter 9).

60 Brake roughness or chatter (pedal pulsates)

1   Excessive lateral runout (Chapter 9).
2   Uneven pad wear (Chapter 9).
3   Defective disc (Chapter 9).

61 Excessive brake pedal effort required to stop vehicle

1   Malfunctioning power brake booster (Chapter 9).
2   Partial system failure (Chapter 9).
3   Excessively worn pads or shoes (Chapter 9).
4   Piston in caliper or wheel cylinder stuck or sluggish (Chapter 9).
5   Brake pads or shoes contaminated with oil or grease (Chapter 9).
6   Brake disc grooved and/or glazed (Chapter 1).
7   New pads or shoes installed and not yet seated. It will take a while for the new material to seat against the disc or drum.

62 Excessive brake pedal travel

1   Partial brake system failure (Chapter 9).
2   Insufficient fluid in master cylinder (Chapters 1 and 9).
3   Air trapped in system (Chapters 1 and 9).

63 Dragging brakes

1   Incorrect adjustment of brake light switch (Chapter 9).
2   Master cylinder pistons not returning correctly (Chapter 9).
3   Restricted brakes lines or hoses (Chapters 1 and 9).
4   Incorrect parking brake adjustment (Chapter 9).

64 Grabbing or uneven braking action

1   Malfunction of proportioning valve (Chapter 9).
2   Malfunction of power brake booster unit (Chapter 9).
3   Binding brake pedal mechanism (Chapter 9).

65 Brake pedal feels spongy when depressed

1   Air in hydraulic lines (Chapter 9).
2   Master cylinder mounting bolts loose (Chapter 9).
3   Master cylinder defective (Chapter 9).

66 Brake pedal travels to the floor with little resistance

1   Little or no fluid in the master cylinder reservoir caused by leaking caliper piston(s) (Chapter 9).

2   Loose, damaged or disconnected brake lines (Chapter 9).

67 Parking brake does not hold

Parking brake linkage improperly adjusted (Chapters 1 and 9).

Suspension and steering systems

Note: *Before attempting to diagnose the suspension and steering systems, perform the following preliminary checks:*

a) *Tires for wrong pressure and uneven wear.*
b) *Steering universal joints from the column to the rack and pinion for loose connectors or wear.*
c) *Front and rear suspension and the rack and pinion assembly for loose or damaged parts.*
d) *Out-of-round or out-of-balance tires, bent rims and loose and/or rough wheel bearings.*

68 Vehicle pulls to one side

1   Mismatched or uneven tires (Chapter 10).
2   Broken or sagging springs (Chapter 10).
3   Wheel alignment out-of-specifications (Chapter 10).
4   Front brake dragging (Chapter 9).

69 Abnormal or excessive tire wear

1   Wheel alignment out-of-specifications (Chapter 10).
2   Sagging or broken springs (Chapter 10).
3   Tire out-of-balance (Chapter 10).
4   Worn strut damper (Chapter 10).
5   Overloaded vehicle.
6   Tires not rotated regularly.

70 Wheel makes a thumping noise

1   Blister or bump on tire (Chapter 10).
2   Improper strut damper action (Chapter 10).

71 Shimmy, shake or vibration

1   Tire or wheel out-of-balance or out-of-round (Chapter 10).
2   Loose or worn wheel bearings (Chapters 1, 8 and 10).
3   Worn tie-rod ends (Chapter 10).
4   Worn lower balljoints (Chapters 1 and 10).
5   Excessive wheel runout (Chapter 10).
6   Blister or bump on tire (Chapter 10).

72 Hard steering

1   Lack of lubrication at balljoints, tie-rod ends and rack and pinion assembly (Chapter 10).
2   Front wheel alignment out-of-specifications (Chapter 10).
3   Low tire pressure(s) (Chapters 1 and 10).

73 Poor returnability of steering to center

1   Lack of lubrication at balljoints and tie-rod ends (Chapter 10).
2   Binding in balljoints (Chapter 10).
3   Binding in steering column (Chapter 10).
4   Lack of lubricant in steering gear assembly (Chapter 10).
5   Front wheel alignment out-of-specifications (Chapter 10).

74 Abnormal noise at the front end

1   Lack of lubrication at balljoints and tie-rod ends (Chapters 1 and 10).
2   Damaged strut mounting (Chapter 10).
3   Worn control arm bushings or tie-rod ends (Chapter 10).
4   Loose stabilizer bar (Chapter 10).
5   Loose wheel nuts (Chapters 1 and 10).
6   Loose suspension bolts (Chapter 10)

75 Wander or poor steering stability

1   Mismatched or uneven tires (Chapter 10).
2   Lack of lubrication at balljoints and tie-rod ends (Chapters 1 and 10).
3   Worn strut assemblies (Chapter 10).
4   Loose stabilizer bar (Chapter 10).
5   Broken or sagging springs (Chapter 10).
6   Wheels out of alignment (Chapter 10).

76 Erratic steering when braking

1   Wheel bearings worn (Chapter 10).
2   Broken or sagging springs (Chapter 10).
3   Leaking wheel cylinder or caliper (Chapter 10).
4   Warped rotors or drums (Chapter 10).

77 Excessive pitching and/or rolling around corners or during braking

1   Loose stabilizer bar (Chapter 10).
2   Worn strut dampers or mountings (Chapter 10).
3   Broken or sagging springs (Chapter 10).
4   Overloaded vehicle.

78 Suspension bottoms

1   Overloaded vehicle.
2   Worn strut dampers (Chapter 10).
3   Incorrect, broken or sagging springs (Chapter 10).

79 Cupped tires

1   Front wheel or rear wheel alignment out-of-specifications (Chapter 10).
2   Worn strut dampers (Chapter 10).
3   Wheel bearings worn (Chapter 10).
4   Excessive tire or wheel runout (Chapter 10).
5   Worn balljoints (Chapter 10).

80 Excessive tire wear on outside edge

1   Inflation pressures incorrect (Chapter 1).

2   Excessive speed in turns.
3   Front end alignment incorrect (excessive toe-in). Have professionally aligned.
4   Suspension arm bent or twisted (Chapter 10).

81 Excessive tire wear on inside edge

1   Inflation pressures incorrect (Chapter 1).
2   Front end alignment incorrect (toe-out). Have professionally aligned.
3   Loose or damaged steering components (Chapter 10).

82 Tire tread worn in one place

1   Tires out-of-balance.
2   Damaged or buckled wheel. Inspect and replace if necessary.
3   Defective tire (Chapter 1).

83 Excessive play or looseness in steering system

1   Wheel bearing(s) worn (Chapter 10).
2   Tie-rod end loose (Chapter 10).
3   Steering gear loose (Chapter 10).
4   Worn or loose steering intermediate shaft (Chapter 10).

84 Rattling or clicking noise in steering gear

1   Steering gear loose (Chapter 10).
2   Steering gear defective.

Chapter 1
Tune-up and routine maintenance

Contents

Specifications

Recommended lubricants and fluids

Note: *Listed here are manufacturer recommendations at the time this manual was written. Manufacturers occasionally upgrade their fluid and lubricant specifications, so check with your local auto parts store for current recommendations.*

Engine oil .... PI grade SG or SG/CD multigrade and fuel efficient oil
  Viscosity .... See accompanying chart

Recommended engine oil viscosity

Recommended lubricants and fluids

Fuel .... Unleaded gasoline, 87 octane or higher
Automatic transaxle fluid .... DEXRON II automatic transmission fluid
Manual transaxle lubricant............................ API GL-4 75W-90 gear oil
Brake fluid... DOT 3 brake fluid
Power steering system .... DEXRON II automatic transmission fluid
Wheel bearings.. NLGI no. 2 lithium-base grease

Capacities*

Engine oil (including filter)............................. 3.5 qts
Coolant .... 6 qts
Transaxle
   Automatic (drain and refill) .... 2.6 qts
   Manual.. 2.5 qts
All capacities approximate. Add as necessary to bring up to appropriate level.

Ignition system

Spark plug type and gap
  1988 and earlier
    US
      Type.. NGK BPR5ES-11 or equivalent
      Gap.. 0.043 inch
    Canada
      Type.. NGK BPR5ES or equivalent
      Gap.. 0.035 inch

  1989 and 1990
    Type.. NGK BCPR5ES-11 or equivalent
    Gap... 0.043 inch
  1991 through 1993
    SR20DE engine
      Type.. NGK BKR6E or equivalent
      Gap.. 0.043 inch
    GA16DE engine
      Type.. NGK BKR5E or equivalent
      Gap.. 0.043 inch

The blackened terminal shown on the distributor cap indicates the Number One spark plug wire position

Cylinder location and distributor rotation

  1994
    SR20DE engine
      Type.. NGK BKR6E or equivalent
      Gap.. 0.043 inch
    GA16DE engine
      Type.. NGK BKR5E-11 or equivalent
      Gap.. 0.043 inch
Spark plug wire resistance .... 10,000 to 25,000 ohms
Engine firing order 1-3-4-2

Ignition timing

1982
  US
    All except MPG model
      Manual transaxle .... 2-degrees ATDC
      Automatic transaxle................................. 6-degrees ATDC
    MPG model... 2-degrees ATDC
  Canada
    All except MPG model
      Manual transaxle .... 4-degrees ATDC
      Automatic transaxle................................. 6-degrees ATDC
    MPG model
      Manual transaxle .... 2-degrees ATDC
1983
  US
    All except MPG model
      Manual transaxle .... 5-degrees ATDC
      Automatic transaxle................................. 5-degrees ATDC
    MPG model... 2-degrees ATDC
  Canada
    Manual transaxle....................................... 5-degrees ATDC
    Automatic transaxle .... 5-degrees ATDC

1984 and 1985
  California
    Manual transaxle .... 5-degrees ATDC
    Automatic transaxle .... 5-degrees ATDC
  49-state
    Manual transaxle .... 15-degrees BDTC
    Automatic transaxle .... 8-degrees BTDC
  Canada
    Manual transaxle .... 5-degrees ATDC
    Automatic transaxle .... 5-degrees ATDC
1986
  California
    Manual transaxle .... 5-degrees ATDC
    Automatic transaxle .... 5-degrees ATDC
  49-state
    Manual transaxle .... 10-degrees BDTC
    Automatic transaxle .... 10-degrees BTDC
  Canada
    Manual transaxle .... 5-degrees ATDC
    Automatic transaxle .... 5-degrees ATDC
1987 through 1990 (all) .... 7-degrees BTDC
1991 and later
  SR20DE engine .... 15-degrees BTDC
  GA16DE engine .... 10-degrees BTDC

Idle speed adjustment
1982
  All except MPG model
    Manual transaxle .... 700 rpm
    Automatic transaxle .... 600 rpm
  MPG model .... 700 rpm
1983 and 1984
  US
    All except MPG model
      Manual transaxle .... 750 rpm
      Automatic transaxle .... 650 rpm
    MPG model .... 700 rpm
  Canada
    All except MPG model
      Manual transaxle .... 750 rpm
      Automatic transaxle .... 650 rpm
    MPG model .... 700 rpm
1985 and 1986
  California
    Manual transaxle .... 800 rpm
    Automatic transaxle .... 650 rpm
  49-state
    Manual transaxle .... 800 rpm
    Automatic transaxle .... 650 rpm
  Canada
    Manual transaxle .... 800 rpm
    Automatic transaxle .... 650 rpm
1987
  E16i engine
    Manual transaxle .... 800 rpm
    Automatic transaxle .... 700 rpm
  49-state
    Manual transaxle .... 800 rpm
    Automatic transaxle .... 700 rpm
  Canada and California
    Manual transaxle .... 800 rpm
    Automatic transaxle .... 700 rpm
1988 and 1989
  Manual transaxle .... 800 rpm
  Automatic transaxle .... 700 rpm
1990
  Manual transaxle .... 800 rpm
  Automatic transaxle .... 900 rpm

Idle speed adjustment
1991 and later
  SR20DE engine
    Manual transaxle.. 800 rpm
    Automatic transaxle .... 900 rpm
  GA16DE engine
    Manual transaxle
      US .... 650 rpm
      Canada .... 750 rpm
    Automatic transaxle (all).. 800 rpm

Valve clearances (engine hot)
1988 and earlier E16 engine (Section 22)
  Intake valve .... 0.011 inch
  Exhaust valve .... 0.011 inch
1991 and later GA16DE engine (Section 41)
  Intake valve .... 0.008 to 0.019 inch
  Exhaust valve .... 0.012 to 0.023 inch

Cooling system
Thermostat rating
  Starts to open... 190-degrees F
  Fully open .... 212-degrees F

Clutch pedal
Freeplay .... 1/8 to 5/32 inch
Height
  1984 and earlier models.. 7 1/2 to 8 inches
  1985 .... 8 1/4 to 8 1/2 inches
  1986 .... 7 3/4 to 8 inches
  1987 .... 6 1/2 to 6 3/4 inches
  1988 through 1990 .... 5 1/2 to 5 7/8 inches
  1991 and later .... 6 to 6 1/4 inches
Release lever freeplay .... 1/8 to 9/64 inch
Clutch interlock switch freeplay... 1/64 to 3/64 inch

Brakes
Disc brake pad lining thickness (minimum)................................ 1/16 inch
Drum brake shoe lining thickness (minimum)............................ 1/16 inch
Parking brake adjustment
  1986 and earlier.. 6 to 7 clicks
  1987 through 1990 .... 7 to 11 clicks
  1990 and later
    Drum brake .... 5 to 7 clicks
    Disc brake .... 7 to 9 clicks
Brake pedal
  Freeplay
    1986 and earlier .... 1/32 inch
    1987 and later .... 1/8 inch
  Free height
    1986 and earlier
      Manual transaxle .... 7.64 to 8.03 inch
      Automatic transaxle... 7.76 to 8.15 inch
    1987 and 1988
      Manual transaxle .... 6.10 to 6.50 inch
      Automatic transaxle... 6.46 to 6.85 inch
    1989 and 1990
      Manual transaxle .... 6.30 to 6.61 inch
      Automatic transaxle... 6.46 to 6.85 inch
    1991 and later
      Manual transaxle .... 5.83 to 6.22 inch
      Automatic transaxle... 6.18 to 6.57 inch
  Depressed height
    1990 and earlier
      Manual transaxle .... 3.35 inch
      Automatic transaxle... 3.15 inch

Depressed height
   1991 and later
      GA16DE engine
         Manual transaxle... 2.95 inch
         Automatic transaxle .... 3.15 inch
      SRD20 engine
         Manual transaxle... 3.15 inch
         Automatic transaxle .... 3.35 inch

Suspension and steering
Steering wheel freeplay limit.. 1-3/16 inch
Balljoint allowable movement .... 0 inch

Torque specifications   Ft-lbs
Automatic transaxle drain plug... 30
Manual transaxle drain and filler plugs 29
Spark plugs.. 14 to 28
Wheel lug nuts 72

**Engine compartment components
(1994 model shown)**

 1 *PCV valve (Section 37)*
 2 *Fuel filter (Section 23)*
 3 *Brake fluid reservoir (Section 4)*
 4 *Air filter housing (Section 17)*
 5 *Battery (Section 11)*
 6 *Relay block (Chapter 12)*
 7 *Clutch release lever*
 8 *Distributor (Section 25)*
 9 *Upper radiator hose (Section 13)*
10 *Oxygen sensor (Section 40)*
11 *Engine oil dipstick (Section 4)*
12 *Spark plugs (Section 24)*
13 *Radiator cap (Section 14)*
14 *Oil filler cap (Section 4)*
15 *Coolant reservoir (Section 4)*
16 *Windshield washer fluid reservoir
   (Section 4)*

**Engine compartment underside
components (1994 model shown)**

1 *Manual transaxle check/fill plug
  (Section 19)*
2 *Clutch release lever (Section 10)*
3 *Disc brake caliper (Section 16)*
4 *Driveaxle boot (Section 22)*
5 *Manual transaxle drain plug (Section 19)*
6 *Exhaust system (Section 31)*
7 *Engine oil pan drain plug (Section 8)*
8 *Suspension strut (Section 20)*

1

**Typical rear underside components
(1994 model shown)**

1 *Gas tank filler hose (Section 18)*
2 *Muffler (Section 31)*
3 *Suspension strut and spring (Section 20)*
4 *Gas tank (Section 18)*

**Engine compartment components
(1988 model shown)**

1 *Fuel filter (Section 23)*
2 *Evaporative canister (Section 30)*
3 *Brake fluid reservoir (Section 4)*
4 *Fuse block (Chapter 12)*
5 *Battery (Section 11)*
6 *Upper radiator hose (Section 13)*
7 *Distributor (Section 25)*
8 *Spark plugs (Section 24)*
9 *Engine oil dipstick (Section 4)*
10 *Oil filler cap (Section 4)*
11 *Radiator cap (Section 14)*
12 *Windshield washer fluid reservoir
     (Section 4)*
13 *Coolant reservoir (Section 4)*

1   Introduction

This chapter is designed to help the home mechanic maintain the Nissan Sentra for peak performance, economy, safety and long life.

On the following pages is a master maintenance schedule, followed by sections dealing specifically with each item on the schedule. Visual checks, adjustments, component replacement and other helpful items are included. Refer to the accompanying illustrations of the engine compartment and the underside of the vehicle for the location of various components.

Servicing your Sentra in accordance with the mileage/time maintenance schedule and the following Sections will provide it with a planned maintenance program that should result in a long and reliable service life. This is a comprehensive plan, so maintaining some items but not others at the specified service intervals will not produce the same results.

As you service your Sentra, you will discover that many of the procedures can - and should - be grouped together because of the nature of the particular procedure you're performing or because of the close proximity of two otherwise unrelated components to one another.

For example, if the vehicle is raised for any reason, you should inspect the exhaust, suspension, steering and fuel systems while you're under the vehicle. When you're rotating the tires, it makes good sense to check the brakes and wheel bearings since the wheels are already removed.

Finally, let's suppose you have to borrow or rent a torque wrench. Even if you only need to tighten the spark plugs, you might as well check the torque of as many critical fasteners as time allows.

The first step of this maintenance program is to prepare yourself before the actual work begins. Read through all sections pertinent to the procedures you're planning to do, then make a list of and gather together all the parts and tools you will need to do the job. If it looks as if you might run into problems during a particular segment of some procedure, seek advice from your local parts man or dealer service department.

2 Nissan Sentra Maintenance schedule

The maintenance intervals in this manual are provided with the assumption that you, not the dealer, will be doing the work. These are the minimum maintenance intervals recommended by the factory for Sentras that are driven daily. If you wish to keep your vehicle in peak condition at all times, you may wish to perform some of these procedures even more often. Because frequent maintenance enhances the efficiency, performance and resale value of your car, we encourage you to do so. If you drive in dusty areas, tow a trailer, idle or drive at low speeds for extended periods or drive for short distances (less than four miles) in below freezing temperatures, shorter intervals are also recommended.

When your vehicle is new, it should be serviced by a factory authorized dealer service department to protect the factory warranty. In many cases, the initial maintenance check is done at no cost to the owner.

Every 250 miles or weekly, whichever comes first

Check the engine oil level (Section 4)
Check the engine coolant level (Section 4)
Check the windshield washer fluid level (Section 4)
Check the brake fluid level (Section 4)
Check the tires and tire pressures (Section 5)

Every 3000 miles or 3 months, whichever comes first

All items listed above plus:
Check the power steering fluid level (Section 6)
Check the automatic transaxle fluid level (Section 7)
Change the engine oil and oil filter (Section 8)

Every 7500 miles or 6 months, whichever comes first

Inspect and replace if necessary the windshield wiper blades (Section 9)
Check the clutch pedal and release lever for proper freeplay (Section 10)
Check and service the battery (Section 11)
Check and adjust if necessary the engine drivebelts (Section 12)
Inspect and replace if necessary all underhood hoses (Section 13)
Check the cooling system (Section 14)
Rotate the tires (Section 15)

Every 15,000 miles or 12 months, whichever comes first

All items listed above plus:
Inspect the brake system (Section 16)*
Replace the air filter (Section 17)
Inspect the fuel system (Section 18)
Check the manual transaxle lubricant level (Section 19)
Inspect the suspension and steering components (Section 20)
Check the driveaxle boots (Section 21)
Check and adjust if necessary the valve clearances (1988 and earlier models) (Section 22)

Every 30,000 miles or 24 months, whichever comes first

All items listed above plus:
Replace the fuel filter (Section 23)
Check and replace if necessary the spark plugs (Section 24)
Inspect and replace if necessary the spark plug wires, distributor cap and rotor (Section 25)
Service the cooling system (drain, flush and refill) (Section 26)
Check and adjust if necessary, the engine ignition timing (Section 27)
Check and adjust if necessary, the engine idle speed (Section 28)
Check the operation of the carburetor choke (Section 29)
Inspect the evaporative emissions control system (Section 30)
Check the exhaust system (Section 31)
Change the automatic transaxle fluid (Section 32) **
Change the manual transaxle lubricant (Section 33)**
Check, repack and adjust. the rear wheel bearings (Section 34)
Check the operation of the Exhaust Gas Recirculation (EGR) system (Section 35)
Check the operation of the thermostatic air cleaner (Section 36)
Check and replace if necessary the PCV valve (Section 37)
Replace the Air Induction valve filter (1982 and earlier models only) (Section 38)
Replace the vacuum control modulator filter (some 1985 and 1987 models) (Section 39)
Replace the Idle Speed Control actuator filter (some 1985 through 1987 models) (Section 39)
Check and replace if necessary, the oxygen sensor (Section 40)

Every 60,000 miles or 48 months, whichever comes first

Replace the timing belt (1988 and earlier models) (Chapter 2A)
Check and adjust if necessary, the valve clearances (1990 and later GA16DE engine only (Section 41)
* This item is affected by "severe" operating conditions as described below. If your vehicle is operated under "severe" conditions, perform all maintenance indicated with an asterisk (*) at 3000 mile/3 month intervals. Severe conditions are indicated if you mainly operate your vehicle under one or more of the following conditions:
Operating in dusty areas
Towing a trailer
Idling for extended periods and/or low speed operation
Operating when outside temperatures remain below freezing and when most trips are less than 4 miles
** If operated under one or more of the following conditions, change the, manual or automatic transaxle fluid and differential lubricant every 15,000 miles:
In heavy city traffic where the outside temperature regularly reaches 90-degrees F (32-degrees C) or higher
In hilly or mountainous terrain
Frequent trailer pulling

4.2 The engine oil dipstick (arrow) is located on the front side of the engine

4.4 The oil level should be at or near the H mark - if it isn't, add enough oil to bring the level to near the H mark (it takes one full quart to raise the level from the L to the H mark)

4.6 The threaded oil filler cap is located on the valve cover - always make sure the area around the opening is clean before unscrewing the cap to prevent dirt from contaminating the engine

3 Tune-up general information

The term tune-up is used in this manual to represent a combination of individual operations rather than one specific procedure.

If, from the time the vehicle is new, the routine maintenance schedule is followed closely and frequent checks are made of fluid levels and high wear items, as suggested throughout this manual, the engine will be kept in relatively good running condition and the need for additional work will be minimized.

More likely than not, however, there will be times when the engine is running poorly due to lack of regular maintenance. This is even more likely if a used vehicle, which has not received regular and frequent maintenance checks, is purchased. In such cases, an engine tune-up will be needed outside of the regular routine maintenance intervals.

The first step in any tune-up or engine diagnosis to help correct a poor running engine would be a cylinder compression check. A check of the engine compression (Chapter 2 Part B) will give valuable information regarding the overall performance of many internal components and should be used as a basis for tune-up and repair procedures. If, for instance, a compression check indicates serious internal engine wear, a conventional tune-up will not help the running condition of the engine and would be a waste of time and money.

The following series of operations are those most often needed to bring a generally poor running engine back into a proper state of tune.

Minor tune-up

Check all engine related fluids (Section 4)
Clean, inspect and test the battery (Section 11)
Check and adjust the drivebelts (Section 12)
Check all underhood hoses (Section 13)

Check the cooling system (Section 14)
Check the air filter (Section 17)
Replace the spark plugs (Section 24)
Inspect the distributor cap and rotor (Section 25)
Inspect the spark plug and coil wires (Section 25)
Check and adjust the idle speed (Section 28)

Major tune-up

All items listed under Minor tune-up, plus . . .
Replace the air filter (Section 17)
Check the fuel system (Section 18)
Check the charging system (Chapter 5)
Replace the spark plug wires (Section 25)
Replace the distributor cap and rotor (Section 25)
Check the ignition system (Section 27)

4 Fluid level checks (every 250 miles or weekly)

1   Fluids are an essential part of the lubrication, cooling, brake, clutch and other systems. Because these fluids gradually become depleted and/or contaminated during normal operation of the vehicle, they must be periodically replenished. See *Recommended lubricants* and *fluids* and *capacities* at the beginning of this Chapter before adding fluid to any of the following components. **Note:** *The vehicle must be on level ground before fluid levels can be checked.*

Engine oil

Refer to illustrations 4.2, 4.4 and 4.6
2   The engine oil level is checked with a dipstick located at the front side of the engine **(see illustration)**. The dipstick extends through a metal tube from which it protrudes down into the engine oil pan.
3   The oil level should be checked before the vehicle has been driven, or about 15 minutes after the engine has been shut off. If the oil is checked immediately after driving

the vehicle, some of the oil will remain in the upper engine components, producing an inaccurate reading on the dipstick.
4   Pull the dipstick from the tube and wipe all the oil from the end with a clean rag or paper towel. Insert the clean dipstick all the way back into its metal tube and pull it out again. Observe the oil at the end of the dipstick. At its highest point, the level should be between the L and H marks **(see illustration)**.
5   It takes one quart of oil to raise the level from the L mark to the H mark on the dipstick. Do not allow the level to drop below the L mark or oil starvation may cause engine damage. Conversely, overfilling the engine (adding oil above the H mark) may cause oil fouled spark plugs, oil leaks or oil seal failures.
6   Remove the threaded cap from the valve cover to add oil **(see illustration)**. Use a funnel to prevent spills. After adding the oil, install the filler cap hand tight. Start the engine and look carefully for any small leaks around the oil filter or drain plug. Stop the engine and check the oil level again after it has had sufficient time to drain from the upper block and cylinder head galleys.
7   Checking the oil level is an important preventive maintenance step. A continually dropping oil level indicates oil leakage through damaged seals, from loose connections, or past worn rings or valve guides. If the oil looks milky in color or has water droplets in it, a cylinder head gasket may be blown. The engine should be checked immediately. The condition of the oil should also be checked. Each time you check the oil level, slide your thumb and index finger up the dipstick before wiping off the oil. If you see small dirt or metal particles clinging to the dipstick, the oil should be changed (see Section 8).

Engine coolant

Refer to illustration 4.8
Warning: *Do not allow antifreeze to come in contact with your skin or painted surfaces of the vehicle. Flush contaminated areas immediately with plenty of water. Don't store*

4.8 The coolant reservoir is located in the right or left front corner of the engine compartment - make sure the level is near the MAX mark on the reservoir

4.14 The windshield washer fluid reservoir is located on the side of the engine compartment

4.17 The brake fluid level should be kept between the MIN and MAX marks on the translucent plastic reservoir

new coolant or leave old coolant lying around where it's accessible to children or pets – they're attracted by its sweet smell. Ingestion of even a small amount of coolant can be fatal! Wipe up garage floor and drip pan spills immediately. Keep antifreeze containers covered and repair cooling system leaks as soon as they're noticed.

8   All vehicles covered by this manual are equipped with a pressurized coolant recovery system. A white coolant reservoir located in the right or left (depending on model year) front corner of the engine compartment is connected by a hose to the base of the coolant filler cap **(see illustration)**. If the coolant gets too hot during engine operation, coolant can escape through a pressurized filler cap, then through a connecting hose into the reservoir. As the engine cools, the coolant is automatically drawn back into the cooling system to maintain the correct level.

9   The coolant level should be checked regularly. It must be between the Max and Min lines on the tank. The level will vary with the temperature of the engine. When the engine is cold, the coolant level should be at or slightly above the Min mark on the tank. Once the engine has warmed up, the level should be at or near the Max mark. If it isn't, allow the fluid in the tank to cool, then remove the cap from the reservoir and add coolant to bring the level up to the Max line. Use only ethylene/glycol type coolant and water in the mixture ratio recommended by your owner's manual. Do not use supplemental inhibitor additives. If only a small amount of coolant is required to bring the system up to the proper level, water can be used. However, repeated additions of water will dilute the recommended antifreeze and water solution. In order to maintain the proper ratio of antifreeze and water, it is advisable to top up the coolant level with the correct mixture. Refer to your owner's manual for the recommended ratio.

10   If the coolant level drops within a short time after replenishment, there may be a leak in the system. Inspect the radiator, hoses, engine coolant filler cap, drain plugs, air bleeder plugs and water pump. If no leak is evident, have the radiator cap pressure

tested by your dealer. **Warning:** Never remove the radiator cap or the coolant recovery reservoir cap when the engine is running or has just been shut down, because the cooling system is hot. Escaping steam and scalding liquid could cause serious injury.

11   If it is necessary to open the radiator cap, wait until the system has cooled completely, then wrap a thick cloth around the cap and turn it to the first stop. If any steam escapes, wait until the system has cooled further, then remove the cap.

12   When checking the coolant level, always note its condition. It should be relatively clear. If it is brown or rust colored, the system should be drained, flushed and refilled. Even if the coolant appears to be normal, the corrosion inhibitors wear out with use, so it must be replaced at the specified intervals.

13   Do not allow antifreeze to come in contact with your skin or painted surfaces of the vehicle. Flush contacted areas immediately with plenty of water.

Windshield washer fluid

Refer to illustration 4.14

14   Fluid for the windshield washer system is stored in a plastic reservoir which is located on the left (driver's) or right (passenger) side (depending on model year) of the engine compartment **(see illustration)**. In milder climates, plain water can be used to top up the reservoir, but the reservoir should be kept no more than two-thirds full to allow for expansion should the water freeze. In colder climates, the use of a specially designed windshield washer fluid, available at your dealer and any auto parts store, will help lower the freezing point of the fluid. Mix the solution with water in accordance with the manufacturer's directions on the container. Do not use regular antifreeze. It will damage the vehicle's paint.

Battery electrolyte

15   On models not equipped with a sealed battery, check the electrolyte level of all six battery cells. It must be between the upper and lower levels. If the level is low, remove

the filler/vent cap and add distilled water. Install and securely re-tighten the cap. **Caution:** *Overfilling the cells may cause electrolyte to spill over during periods of heavy charging, causing corrosion or damage.*

Brake fluid

Refer to illustration 4.17

16   The brake master cylinder is mounted on the front of the power booster unit in the engine compartment.

17   To check the fluid level of the brake master cylinder, simply look at the MAX and MIN marks on the reservoir **(see illustration)**. The level should be within the specified distance from the maximum fill line.

18   If the level is low, wipe the top of the reservoir cover with a clean rag to prevent contamination of the brake system before lifting the cover.

19   Add only the specified brake fluid to the brake reservoir (refer to Recommended lubricants and fluids at the front of this chapter or to your owner's manual). Mixing different types of brake fluid can damage the system. Fill the brake master cylinder reservoir only to the MAX line. **Warning:** Use caution when filling either reservoir - brake fluid can harm your eyes and damage painted surfaces. Do not use brake fluid that has been opened for more than one year or has been left open. Brake fluid absorbs moisture from the air. Excess moisture can cause a dangerous loss of braking.

20   While the reservoir cap is removed, inspect the master cylinder reservoir for contamination. If deposits, dirt particles or water droplets are present, the system should be drained and refilled.

21   After filling the reservoir to the proper level, make sure the lid is properly seated to prevent fluid leakage and/or system pressure loss.

22   The brake fluid in the master cylinder will drop slightly as the brake pads at each wheel wear down during normal operation. If the master cylinder requires repeated replenishing to keep it at the proper level, this is an indication of leakage in the brake system,

5.2 A tire tread depth indicator should be used to monitor tire wear - they are available at auto parts stores and service stations and cost very little

which should be corrected immediately. Check all brake lines and connections, along with the wheel cylinders and booster (see Section 16 for more information).

23 If, upon checking the master cylinder fluid level, you discover one or both reservoirs empty or nearly empty, the brake system should be bled (see Chapter 9).

UNDERINFLATION

CUPPING

Cupping may be caused by:
• Underinflation and/or mechanical irregularities such as out-of-balance condition of wheel and/or tire, and bent or damaged wheel.
• Loose or worn steering tie-rod or steering idler arm.
• Loose, damaged or worn front suspension parts.

INCORRECT TOE-IN OR EXTREME CAMBER

OVERINFLATION

FEATHERING DUE TO MISALIGNMENT

5.3 This chart will help you determine the condition of your tires, the probable cause(s) of abnormal wear and the corrective action necessary

5 Tire and tire pressure checks (every 250 miles or weekly)

Refer to illustrations 5.2, 5.3, 5.4a, 5.4b and 5.8

1 Periodic inspection of the tires may spare you from the inconvenience of being stranded with a flat tire. It can also provide you with vital information regarding possible problems in the steering and suspension systems before major damage occurs.

2 Normal tread wear can be monitored with a simple, inexpensive device known as a tread depth indicator **(see illustration)**. When the tread depth reaches the specified minimum, replace the tire(s).

3 Note any abnormal tread wear **(see illustration)**. Tread pattern irregularities such as cupping, flat spots and more wear on one side than the other are indications of front end alignment and/or balance problems. If

any of these conditions are noted, take the vehicle to a tire shop or service station to correct the problem.

4 Look closely for cuts, punctures and embedded nails or tacks. Sometimes a tire will hold its air pressure for a short time or leak down very slowly even after a nail has embedded itself into the tread. If a slow leak persists, check the valve stem core to make sure it is tight **(see illustration)**. Examine the tread for an object that may have embedded itself into the tire or for a "plug" that may have begun to leak (radial tire punctures are repaired with a plug that is installed in a puncture). If a puncture is suspected, it can be easily verified by spraying a solution of soapy water onto the puncture area **(see illustration)**. The soapy solution will bubble if there is a leak. Unless the puncture is inordinately large, a tire shop or gas station can usually repair the punctured tire.

5 Carefully inspect the inner sidewall of

each tire for evidence of brake fluid leakage. If you see any, inspect the brakes immediately.

6 Correct tire air pressure adds miles to the lifespan of the tires, improves mileage and enhances overall ride quality. Tire pressure cannot be accurately estimated by looking at a tire, particularly if it is a radial. A tire pressure gauge is therefore essential. Keep an accurate gauge in the glove box. The pressure gauges fitted to the nozzles of air hoses at gas stations are often inaccurate.

7 Always check tire pressure when the tires are cold. "Cold," in this case, means the vehicle has not been driven over a mile in the three hours preceding a tire pressure check. A pressure rise of four to eight pounds is not uncommon once the tires are warm.

8 Unscrew the valve cap protruding from the wheel or hubcap and push the gauge firmly onto the valve **(see illustration)**. Note the reading on the gauge and compare this

5.4a If a tire loses air on a steady basis, check the valve core first to make sure it's snug (special inexpensive wrenches are commonly available at auto parts stores)

5.4b If the valve core is tight, raise the corner of the vehicle with the low tire and spray a soapy water solution onto the tread as the tire is turned slowly - slow leaks will cause small bubbles to appear

5.8 To extend the life of your tires, check the air pressure at least once a week with an accurate gauge (don't forget the spare!)

6.6 The power steering fluid is checked with a dipstick which is part of the cap - the fluid level varies with temperature, so the fluid can be checked hot or cold

7.4a The automatic transaxle dipstick is located in a tube which extends forward from the transaxle

figure to the recommended tire pressure shown on the tire placard on the left door. Be sure to reinstall the valve cap to keep dirt and moisture out of the valve stem mechanism. Check all four tires and, if necessary, add enough air to bring them up to the recommended pressure levels.

9   Don't forget to keep the spare tire inflated to the specified pressure (consult your owner's manual). Note that the air pressure specified for the compact spare is significantly higher than the pressure of the regular tires.

6   Power steering fluid level check (every 3000 miles or 3 months)

Refer to illustration 6.6

1   Unlike manual steering, the power steering system relies on fluid which may, over a period of time, require replenishing.
2   The fluid reservoir for the power steering pump is located on the inner fender panel near the front of the engine.
3   For the check, the front wheels should be pointed straight ahead and the engine should be off.
4   Use a clean rag to wipe off the reservoir cap and the area around the cap. This will help prevent any foreign matter from entering the reservoir during the check.
5   Twist off the cap and check the temperature of the fluid at the end of the dipstick with your finger.
6   Wipe off the fluid with a clean rag, reinsert it, then withdraw it and read the fluid level **(see illustration)**. The level should be near the upper mark on the dipstick. On some models the dipstick is marked so the fluid can be checked either cold or hot. The level should be at the HOT mark if the fluid was hot to the touch. It should be at the COLD mark if the fluid was cool to the touch. At no time should the fluid level drop below the upper mark for each heat range.
7   If additional fluid is required, pour the

specified type directly into the reservoir, using a funnel to prevent spills.
8   If the reservoir requires frequent fluid additions, all power steering hoses, hose connections, the power steering pump and the rack and pinion assembly should be carefully checked for leaks.

7   Automatic transaxle fluid level check (every 3000 miles or 3 months)

Refer to Illustrations 7.4a and 7.4b

1   The level of the automatic transaxle fluid should be carefully maintained. Low fluid level can lead to slipping or loss of drive, while overfilling can cause foaming, loss of fluid and transaxle damage.
2   The transaxle fluid level should only be checked when the transaxle is hot (at its normal operating temperature). If the vehicle has just been driven over 10 miles (15 miles in a frigid climate), and the fluid temperature is 160 to 175-degrees F, the transaxle is hot. **Caution:** If the vehicle has just been driven for a long time at high speed or in city traffic in hot weather, or if it has been pulling a trailer, an accurate fluid level reading cannot

7.4b If the automatic transaxle fluid is cold, the level should be between the two lower notches; if it's at operating temperature, the level should be between the two upper marks

be obtained. Allow the fluid to cool down for about 30 minutes.
3   If the vehicle has not just been driven, park the vehicle on level ground, set the parking brake and start the engine. While the engine is idling, depress the brake pedal and move the selector lever through all the gear ranges, beginning and ending in Park.
4   With the engine still idling, remove the dipstick from its tube **(see illustration)**. Check the level of the fluid on the dipstick **(see illustration)** and note its condition.
5   Wipe the fluid from the dipstick with a clean rag and reinsert it back into the filler tube until the cap seats.
6   Pull the dipstick out again and note the fluid level. If the transaxle is cold, the level should be in the COLD or COOL range on the dipstick. If it is hot, the fluid level should be in the HOT range. If the level is at the low side of either range, add the specified automatic transmission fluid through the dipstick tube with a funnel.
7   Add just enough of the recommended fluid to fill the transaxle to the proper level. It takes about one pint to raise the level from the low mark to the high mark when the fluid is hot, so add the fluid a little at a time and keep checking the level until it is correct.
8   The condition of the fluid should also be checked along with the level. If the fluid at the end of the dipstick is black or a dark reddish brown color, or if it emits a burned smell, the fluid should be changed (see Section 32). If you are in doubt about the condition of the fluid, purchase some new fluid and compare the two for color and smell.

8   Engine oil and oil filter change (every 3000 miles or 3 months)

Refer to illustrations 8.2, 8.7, 8.13 and 8.15

1   Frequent oil changes are the best preventive maintenance the home mechanic can give the engine, because aging oil becomes diluted and contaminated, which leads to premature engine wear.

1 **Drain pan** - It should be fairly shallow in depth, but wide in order to prevent spills
2 **Rubber gloves** - When removing the drain plug and filter, it is inevitable that you will get oil on your hands (the gloves will prevent burns)
3 **Breaker bar** - Sometimes the oil drain plug is pretty tight and a long breaker bar is needed to loosen it
4 **Socket** – To be used with the breaker bar or a ratchet (must be the correct size to fit the drain plug)
5 **Filter wrench** - This is a metal band-type wrench, which requires clearance around the filter to be effective
6 **Filter wrench** - This type fits on the bottom of the filter and can be turned with a ratchet or breaker bar (different size wrenches are available for different types of filters)

8.2 These tools are required when changing the engine oil and filter

2   Make sure that you have all the necessary tools before you begin this procedure **(see illustration)**. You should also have plenty of rags or newspapers handy for mopping up any spills.
3   Access to the underside of the vehicle is greatly improved if the vehicle can be lifted on a hoist, driven onto ramps or supported by jackstands. **Warning:** *Do not work under a vehicle which is supported only by a bumper, hydraulic or scissors-type jack.*
4   If this is your first oil change, get under the vehicle and familiarize yourself with the location of the oil drain plug. The engine and exhaust components will be warm during the actual work, so try to anticipate any potential problems before the engine and accessories are hot.
5   Park the vehicle on a level spot. Start the engine and allow it to reach its normal operating temperature (the needle on the temperature gauge should be at least above the bottom mark). Warm oil and sludge will

flow out more easily. Turn off the engine when it's warmed up. Remove the filler cap in the rear cam cover.
6   Raise the vehicle and support it on jackstands. **Warning:** *To avoid personal injury, never get beneath the vehicle when it is supported by only by a jack. The jack provided with your vehicle is designed solely for raising the vehicle to remove and replace the wheels. Always use jackstands to support the vehicle when it becomes necessary to place your body underneath the vehicle.*
7   Being careful not to touch the hot exhaust components, place the drain pan under the drain plug in the bottom of the pan and remove the plug **(see illustration)**. You may want to wear gloves while unscrewing the plug the final few turns if the engine is really hot.
8   Allow the old oil to drain into the pan. It may be necessary to move the pan farther under the engine as the oil flow slows to a trickle. Inspect the old oil for the presence of metal shavings and chips.

9   After all the oil has drained, wipe off the drain plug with a clean rag. Even minute metal particles clinging to the plug would immediately contaminate the new oil.
10   Clean the area around the drain plug opening, reinstall the plug and tighten it securely, but do not strip the threads.
11   Move the drain pan into position under the oil filter.
12   Remove all tools, rags, etc. from under the vehicle, being careful not to spill the oil in the drain pan, then lower the vehicle.
13   Loosen the oil filter **(see illustration)** by turning it counterclockwise with the filter wrench. Any standard filter wrench should work. Once the filter is loose, use your hands to unscrew it from the block. Just as the filter is detached from the block, immediately tilt the open end up to prevent the oil inside the filter from spilling out. **Warning:** *The engine exhaust manifold may still be hot, so be careful.*
14   With a clean rag, wipe off the mounting surface on the block. If a residue of old oil is allowed to remain, it will smoke when the block is heated up. It will also prevent the new filter from seating properly. Also make sure that the none of the old gasket remains stuck to the mounting surface. It can be removed with a scraper if necessary.
15   Compare the old filter with the new one to make sure they are the same type. Smear some engine oil on the rubber gasket of the new filter and screw it into place **(see illustration)**. Because over-tightening the filter will damage the gasket, do not use a filter wrench to tighten the filter. Tighten it by hand until the gasket contacts the seating surface. Then seat the filter by giving it an additional 3/4-turn.
16   Add new oil to the engine through the oil filler cap in the valve cover. Use a spout or funnel to prevent oil from spilling onto the top of the engine. Pour three quarts of fresh oil into the engine. Wait a few minutes to allow the oil to drain into the pan, then check the level on the oil dipstick (see Section 4 if necessary). If the oil level is at or near the H mark, install the filler cap hand tight, start the engine and allow the new oil to circulate.
17   Allow the engine to run for about a minute. While the engine is running, look

8.7 Use a proper size box-end wrench or socket to remove the oil drain plug and avoid rounding it off

8.13 Since the oil filter is usually on very tight, you'll need a special wrench for removal - DO NOT use the wrench to tighten the new filter

8.15 Lubricate the oil filter gasket with clean engine oil before installing the filter on the engine

9.5 On earlier models, push up on the lever to remove the blade from the arm

9.7 On 1985 and 1986 models, push on the lock knob to detach the blade

9.9 On 1987 and later models, press on the release tab and push the blade assembly down out of the hook in the arm

9.10 On later models, use needle-nose pliers to pull out the two metal rods, then slide the old element out - slide the new element in and lock in place with the metal rods

under the vehicle and check for leaks at the oil pan drain plug and around the oil filter. If either is leaking, stop the engine and tighten the plug or filter slightly.

18 Wait a few minutes to allow the oil to trickle down into the pan, then recheck the level on the dipstick and, if necessary, add enough oil to bring the level to the H mark.

19 During the first few trips after an oil change, make it a point to check frequently for leaks and proper oil level.

20 The old oil drained from the engine cannot be reused in its present state and should be discarded. Oil reclamation centers, auto repair shops and gas stations will normally accept the oil, which can be refined and used again. After the oil has cooled, it can be drained into a suitable container (capped plastic jugs, topped bottles, milk cartons, etc.) for transport to one of these disposal sites.

9 Windshield wiper blade inspection and replacement (every 7500 miles or 6 months)

Refer to illustrations 9.5, 9.7, 9.9 and 9.10

1 The windshield wiper and blade assembly should be inspected periodically for damage, loose components and cracked or worn blade elements.

2 Road film can build up on the wiper blades and affect their efficiency, so they should be washed regularly with a mild detergent solution.

3 The action of the wiping mechanism can loosen bolts, nuts and fasteners, so they should be checked and tightened, as necessary, at the same time the wiper blades are checked.

4 If the wiper blade elements are cracked, worn or warped, or no longer clean adequately, they should be replaced with new ones.

1984 and earlier models

5 Lift the arm assembly away from the glass for clearance, reach up under the blade assembly and push up on the release lever,

then detach the wiper blade assembly from the arm **(see illustration)**.

6 Remove the rubber blade from the frame, discard it and install a new one.

1985 and 1986 models

7 Lift the arm assembly away from the glass for clearance, reach under the frame and push up on the lock knob to detach the wiper blade assembly **(see illustration)**.

8 Remove the rubber blade from the blade frame, discard it and install a new one.

1987 and later models

9 Lift the arm assembly away from the glass for clearance, press on the release lever, then slide the wiper blade assembly out of the hook in the end of the arm **(see illustration)**.

10 Use needle-nose pliers to pull out the two metal rods from the blade element, then slide the element out of the frame and discard it **(see illustration)**.

11 Installation is the reverse of removal.

10 Clutch pedal height, freeplay and release lever freeplay check and adjustment (every 7500 miles or 6 months)

Pedal height

Refer to illustration 10.1

1 With the clutch pedal fully released, measure the distance from the top of the pad to the floor **(see illustration)**.

2 If the height is not as listed in the Specifications at the beginning of this Chapter it must be adjusted.

3 Loosen the locknut on the pedal stopper or cruise control (ASCD) switch **(see illustration 10.1)**.

4 Turn the pedal stopper or cruise control switch until the pedal height is correct.

5 Tighten the locknut.

6 After adjusting the pedal height, check the release lever freeplay.

Release lever freeplay

Refer to illustration 10.7

7 In the engine compartment, move the

10.1 To check clutch pedal height, measure the distance between the pedal pad and the floor. To check clutch pedal freeplay, measure the distance between the natural resting place of the pedal and the point at which you encounter resistance

10.7 Move the release lever back-and-forth to check the freeplay (B) - adjustments are made by loosening the locknut and turning the threaded adjusting nut

end of the release lever back-and-forth and measure the freeplay **(see illustration)**. Compare the freeplay measurement to the one in the Specifications Section at the beginning of this Chapter.

8   If freeplay is incorrect, loosen the locknut and turn the adjusting nut until the height is correct. Tighten the locknut.

9   After checking the release lever freeplay, check the clutch pedal freeplay.

Pedal freeplay

10   Press down lightly on the clutch pedal and, with a small steel ruler, measure the distance that it moves freely before the clutch resistance is felt **(see illustration 10.1)**. The freeplay should be within the specified limits. If it isn't, it must be adjusted.

11   Loosen the locknut on the pedal stopper or cruise control (ASCD) switch **(see illustration 10.1)**.

10.15 Clutch interlock switch freeplay (C) adjustment details

12   Turn the pedal stopper or cruise control switch until the pedal freeplay is correct.

13   Tighten the locknut.

Clutch interlock switch freeplay

Refer to illustration 10.15

14   On later models with an interlock switch, the switch freeplay must be must be checked once all other adjustments are made.

15   Measure the clearance (freeplay) between the pedal stopper rubber and the tip of the interlock switch **(see illustration)**.

16   If the freeplay isn't as listed in the Specifications Section at the beginning of this Chapter, adjust it by loosening the locknut on the switch. Rotate the switch to achieve the specified freeplay and tighten the locknut.

11   Battery check, maintenance and charging (every 7500 miles or 6 months)

Refer to illustrations 11.1, 11.6a, 11.6b, 11.7a and 11.7b

Warning: Certain precautions must be followed *when checking and servicing the battery. Hydrogen gas, which is highly flammable, is always present in the battery cells, so keep lighted tobacco and all other open flames and sparks away from the battery. The electrolyte inside the battery is actually dilute sulfuric acid, which will cause injury if splashed on your skin or in your eyes. It will also ruin clothes and painted surfaces. When removing the battery cables, always detach the negative cable first and hook it up last!*

1   A routine preventive maintenance program for the battery in your vehicle is the only way to ensure quick and reliable starts. But before performing any battery maintenance, make sure that you have the proper equipment necessary to work safely around the battery **(see illustration)**.

2   There are also several precautions that should be taken whenever battery maintenance is performed. Before servicing the battery, always turn the engine and all acces-

11.1 Tools and materials required for battery maintenance

1   *Face shield/safety goggles - When removing corrosion with a brush, the acidic particles can easily fly up into your eyes*

2   *Baking soda - A solution of baking soda and water can be used to neutralize corrosion*

3   *Petroleum jelly - A layer of this on the battery posts will help prevent corrosion*

4   *Battery post/cable cleaner - This wire brush cleaning tool will remove all traces of corrosion from the battery posts and cable clamps*

5   *Treated felt washers - Placing one of these on each post, directly under the cable clamps, will help prevent corrosion*

6   *Puller - Sometimes the cable clamps are very difficult to pull off the posts, even after the nut/bolt has been completely loosened. This tool pulls the clamp straight up and off the post without damage*

7   *Battery post/cable cleaner - Here is another cleaning tool which is a slightly different version of number 4 above, but it does the same thing*

8   *Rubber gloves - Another safety item to consider when servicing the battery; remember that's acid inside the battery*

11.6a Battery terminal corrosion usually appears as light, fluffy powder

11.6b Removing a cable from the battery post with a wrench - sometimes special battery pliers are required for this procedure if corrosion has caused deterioration of the nut hex (always remove the ground cable first and hook it up last!)

11.7a When cleaning the cable clamps, all corrosion must be removed (the inside of the clamp is tapered to match the taper on the post, so don't remove too much material)

11.7b Regardless of the type of tool used to clean the battery posts, a clean, shiny surface should be the result

1

sories off and disconnect the cable from the negative terminal of the battery.

3   The battery produces hydrogen gas, which is both flammable and explosive. Never create a spark, smoke or light a match around the battery. Always charge the battery in a ventilated area.

4   Electrolyte contains poisonous and corrosive sulfuric acid. Do not allow it to get in your eyes, on your skin or on your clothes. Never ingest it. Wear protective safety glasses when working near the battery. Keep children away from the battery.

5   Note the external condition of the battery. If the positive terminal and cable clamp on your vehicle's battery is equipped with a rubber protector, make sure it isn't torn or damaged. It should completely cover the terminal. Look for any corroded or loose connections, cracks in the case or cover or loose hold-down clamps. Also check the entire length of each cable for cracks and frayed conductors.

6   If corrosion, which looks like white, fluffy deposits **(see illustration)** is evident, particularly around the terminals, the battery should be removed for cleaning. Loosen the cable clamp bolts with a wrench, being careful to remove the ground cable first, and slide them off the terminals **(see illustration)**. Then disconnect the hold-down clamp bolt and nut, remove the clamp and lift the battery from the engine compartment.

7   Clean the cable clamps thoroughly with a battery brush or a terminal cleaner and a solution of warm water and baking soda **(see illustration)**. Wash the terminals and the top of the battery case with the same solution but make sure that the solution doesn't get into the battery. When cleaning the cables, terminals and battery top, wear safety goggles and rubber gloves to prevent any solution from coming in contact with your eyes or hands. Wear old clothes too - even diluted, sulfuric acid splashed onto clothes will burn holes in them. If the terminals have been extensively corroded, clean them up with a terminal cleaner **(see illustration)**. Thoroughly wash all cleaned areas with plain water.

8   Make sure the battery tray is in good condition and the hold-down clamp bolt or nut is tight. If the battery is removed from the

tray, make sure no parts remain in the bottom of the tray when the battery is reinstalled. When reinstalling the hold-down clamp bolt or nut, do not over-tighten it.

9   Information on removing and installing the battery can be found in Chapter 5. Information on jump starting can be found at the front of this manual. For more detailed battery checking procedures, refer to the *Haynes Automotive Electrical Manual.*

Cleaning

10   Corrosion on the hold-down components, battery case and surrounding areas can be removed with a solution of water and baking soda. Thoroughly rinse all cleaned areas with plain water.

11   Any metal parts of the vehicle damaged by corrosion should be covered with a zinc-based primer, then painted.

Charging

Warning: *When batteries are being charged, hydrogen gas, which is very explosive and flammable, is produced. Do not smoke or allow open flames near a charging or a recently charged battery. Wear eye protection when near the battery during charging. Also, make sure the charger is unplugged before connecting or disconnecting the battery from the charger.*

12   Slow-rate charging is the best way to restore a battery that's discharged to the point where it will not start the engine. It's also a good way to maintain the battery charge in a vehicle that's only driven a few miles between starts. Maintaining the battery charge is particularly important in the winter when the battery must work harder to start the engine and electrical accessories that drain the battery are in greater use.

13   It's best to use a one or two-amp battery charger (sometimes called a "trickle" charger). They are the safest and put the least strain on the battery. They are also the least expensive. For a faster charge, you can use a higher amperage charger, but don't use one rated more than 1/10th the amp/hour

rating of the battery. Rapid boost charges that claim to restore the power of the battery in one to two hours are hardest on the battery and can damage batteries not in good condition. This type of charging should only be used in emergency situations.

14   The average time necessary to charge a battery should be listed in the instructions that come with the charger. As a general rule, a trickle charger will charge a battery in 12 to 16 hours.

12   Drivebelt check, adjustment and replacement (every 7500 miles or 6 months)

Refer to illustrations 12.3, 12.4, 12.5, 12.6 and 12.9

Check

1   The alternator, power steering pump and air conditioning compressor drivebelts, also referred to as simply "fan" belts, are located at the right end of the engine. The good condition and proper adjustment of the alternator belt is critical to the operation of the engine. Because of their composition and the high stresses to which they are subjected, drivebelts stretch and deteriorate as they get older. They must therefore be periodically inspected.

STREAKED SIDEWALL

FRAYING

CRACKS

SEPARATION

GLAZING

OIL SOAKED

TENSILE BREAK

12.3 Here are some of the more common problems associated with drivebelts (check the belts very carefully to prevent an untimely breakdown)

12.4 Measuring drivebelt deflection with a straightedge and ruler

2   The number of belts used on a particular vehicle depends on the accessories installed. One belt transmits power from the crankshaft to the alternator and air conditioning. If the vehicle is equipped with power steering, the pump is driven by it's own belt.

3   With the engine off, open the hood and locate the drivebelts at the left end of the engine. With a flashlight, check each belt for separation of the adhesive rubber on both sides of the core, core separation from the belt side, a severed core, separation of the ribs from the adhesive rubber, cracking or separation of the ribs, and torn or worn ribs or cracks in the inner ridges of the ribs **(see illustration)**. Also check for fraying and glazing, which gives the belt a shiny appearance. Both sides of the belt should be inspected, which means you will have to twist the belt to check the underside. Use your fingers to feel the belt where you can't see it. If any of the above conditions are evident, replace the belt (go to Step 7).

12.5 On some components, such as the alternator, the drivebelt is adjusted using a slotted bracket

4   Check the belt tension by pushing firmly on the belt with your thumb at a distance halfway between the pulleys and note how far the belt can be pushed (deflected). Measure this deflection with a ruler **(see illustration)**. The belt should deflect 1/4-inch if the distance from pulley center to pulley center is between 7 and 11 inches; the belt should deflect 1/2-inch if the distance from pulley center to pulley center is between 12 and 16 inches.

Adjustment

5   Some belts are adjusted by loosening the adjustment bolt that secures it to the slotted bracket and pivoting it (away from the engine to tighten the belt, toward it to loosen it) **(see illustration)**. Repeat the procedure until the drivebelt tension is correct and tighten the bolt.

6   Some components have a built-in adjusting bolt or idler **(see illustration)**.

12.6 Some components use idlers or threaded brackets for drivebelt adjustment

12.9 When installing a ribbed V-belt, make sure it is centered - it must not overlap either edge of the pulley

Loosen the locknut and turn the adjusting bolt. Measure the belt tension in accordance with one of the above methods. Repeat this step until the drivebelt is adjusted.

Replacement

7   To replace a belt, follow the above procedures for drivebelt adjustment but slip the belt off the crankshaft pulley and remove it. If you are replacing the power steering pump belt, you may have to remove the air conditioning compressor belt first because of the way they are arranged on the crankshaft pulley. Because of this and because belts tend to wear out more or less together, it is a good idea to replace both belts at the same time. Mark each belt and its appropriate pulley groove so the replacement belts can be installed in their proper positions.
8   Take the old belts to the parts store in order to make a direct comparison for length, width and design.
9   After replacing ribbed drivebelts, make sure that it fits properly in the ribbed grooves in the pulleys **(see illustration)**. It is essential that the belt be properly centered.
10   Adjust the belt(s) in accordance with the procedure outlined above.

13 Underhood hose check and replacement (every 7500 miles or 6 months)

Caution: *Replacement of air conditioning hoses must be left to a dealer service department or air conditioning shop that has the equipment to depressurize the system safely. Never remove air conditioning components or hoses until the system has been depressurized.*

General

1   High temperatures in the engine compartment can cause the deterioration of the rubber and plastic hoses used for engine, accessory and emission systems operation. Periodic inspection should be made for cracks, loose clamps, material hardening and leaks.
2   Information specific to the cooling system hoses can be found in Section 14.
3   Some, but not all, hoses are secured to the fittings with clamps. Where clamps are used, check to be sure they haven't lost their tension, allowing the hose to leak. If clamps aren't used, make sure the hose has not expanded and/or hardened where it slips over the fitting, allowing it to leak.

Vacuum hoses

4   It's quite common for vacuum hoses, especially those in the emissions system, to be color coded or identified by colored stripes molded into them. Various systems require hoses with different wall thickness, collapse resistance and temperature resistance. When replacing hoses, be sure the new ones are made of the same material.
5   Often the only effective way to check a hose is to remove it completely from the vehicle. If more than one hose is removed, be sure to label the hoses and fittings to ensure correct installation.
6   When checking vacuum hoses, be sure to include any plastic T-fittings in the check. Inspect the fittings for cracks and the hose where it fits over the fitting for distortion, which could cause leakage.
7   A small piece of vacuum hose (1/4-inch inside diameter) can be used as a stethoscope to detect vacuum leaks. Hold one end of the hose to your ear and probe around vacuum hoses and fittings, listening for the "hissing" sound characteristic of a vacuum leak. **Warning:** *When probing with the vacuum hose stethoscope, be very careful not to come into contact with moving engine components such as the drivebelts, cooling fan, etc.*

Fuel hose

Warning: *There are certain precautions which must be taken when inspecting or servicing fuel system components. Work in a well ventilated area and do not allow open flames (cigarettes, appliance pilot lights, etc.) or bare light bulbs near the work area. Mop up any spills immediately and do not store fuel soaked rags where they could ignite.*
8   Check all rubber fuel lines for deterioration and chafing. Check especially for cracks in areas where the hose bends and just before fittings, such as where a hose attaches to the fuel filter.
9   High quality fuel line, usually identified by the word Fluoroelastomer printed on the hose, should be used for fuel line replacement. Never, under any circumstances, use unreinforced vacuum line, clear plastic tubing or water hose for fuel lines.
10   Spring-type clamps are commonly used on fuel lines. These clamps often lose their tension over a period of time, and can be "sprung" during removal. Replace all spring-type clamps with screw clamps whenever a hose is replaced.

Metal lines

11   Sections of metal line are often used for fuel line between the fuel pump and carburetor or fuel injection unit. Check carefully to be sure the line has not been bent or crimped and that cracks have not started in the line.
12   If a section of metal fuel line must be replaced, only seamless steel tubing should be used, since copper and aluminum tubing don't have the strength necessary to withstand normal engine vibration.
13   Check the metal brake lines where they enter the master cylinder and brake proportioning unit (if used) for cracks in the lines or loose fittings. Any sign of brake fluid leakage calls for an immediate thorough inspection of the brake system.

14 Cooling system check (every 7500 miles or 6 months)

Refer to illustration 14.4
1   Many major engine failures can be attributed to a faulty cooling system. If the vehicle is equipped with an automatic transaxle, the cooling system also cools the transaxle fluid and thus plays an important role in prolonging transaxle life.
2   The cooling system should be checked with the engine cold. Do this before the vehicle is driven for the day or after the engine has been shut off for at least three hours.
3   Remove the radiator cap by turning it to the left until it reaches a stop. If you hear a hissing sound (indicating there is still pressure in the system), wait until it stops. Now press down on the cap with the palm of your hand and continue turning to the left until the cap can be removed. Thoroughly clean the cap, inside and out, with clean water. Also clean the filler neck on the radiator. All traces of corrosion should be removed. The coolant inside the radiator should be relatively transparent. If it's rust colored, the system should be drained and refilled (see Section 26). If the coolant level isn't up to the top, add additional antifreeze/coolant mixture (see Section 4).
4   Carefully check the large upper and lower radiator hoses along with the smaller diameter heater hoses which run from the engine to the firewall. Inspect each hose along its entire length, replacing any hose which is cracked, swollen or shows signs of deterioration. Cracks may become more apparent if the hose is squeezed **(see illustration on following page)**. Regardless of condition, it's a good idea to replace hoses with new ones every two years.
5   Make sure that all hose connections are tight. A leak in the cooling system will usually show up as white or rust colored deposits on the areas adjoining the leak. If wire-type clamps are used at the ends of the hoses, it

Check for a chafed area that could fail prematurely.

Check for a soft area indicating the hose has deteriorated inside.

Overtightening the clamp on a hardened hose will damage the hose and cause a leak.

Check each hose for swelling and oil-soaked ends. Cracks and breaks can be located by squeezing the hose.

14.4 Hoses, like drivebelts, have a habit of failing at the worst possible time - to prevent the inconvenience of a blown radiator or heater hose, inspect them carefully as shown here

may be a good idea to replace them with more secure screw-type clamps.

6   Use compressed air or a soft brush to remove bugs, leaves, etc. from the front of the radiator or air conditioning condenser. Be careful not to damage the delicate cooling fins or cut yourself on them.

7   Every other inspection, or at the first indication of cooling system problems, have the cap and system pressure tested. If you don't have a pressure tester, most gas stations and repair shops will do this for a minimal charge.

15   Tire rotation (every 7500 miles or 6 months))

Refer to illustration 15.2

1   The tires should be rotated at the specified intervals and whenever uneven wear is noticed. Since the vehicle will be

RADIAL TIRE ROTATION

[1-AJ HAYNES]

15.2 The recommended tire rotation pattern for these vehicles

raised and the tires removed anyway, check the brakes (see Section 16) at this time.

2   Radial tires must be rotated in a specific pattern **(see illus-tration)**.

3   Refer to the information in Jacking and towing at the front of this manual for the proper procedures to follow when raising the vehicle and changing a tire. If the brakes are to be checked, do not apply the parking brake as stated. Make sure the tires are blocked to prevent the vehicle from rolling.

4   Preferably, the entire vehicle should be raised at the same time. This can be done on a hoist or by jacking up each corner and then lowering the vehicle onto jackstands placed under the frame rails. Always use four jackstands and make sure the vehicle is firmly supported.

5   After rotation, check and adjust the tire pressures as necessary and be sure to check the lug nut tightness.

6   For further information on the wheels and tires, refer to Chapter 10.

16   Brake check (every 15,000 miles or 12 months)

Warning: *The dust created by the brake system may contain asbestos, which is harmful to your health. Never blow it out with compressed air and don't inhale any of it. An approved filtering mask should be worn when working on the brakes. Do not, under any circumstances, use petroleum-based solvents to clean brake parts. Use brake system cleaner only! Try to use non-asbestos replacement parts whenever possible.*
Note: *For detailed photographs of the brake system, refer to Chapter 9.*

1   In addition to the specified intervals, the brakes should be inspected every time the wheels are removed or whenever a defect is suspected. Any of the following symptoms could indicate a potential brake system defect: The vehicle pulls to one side when the

brake pedal is depressed; the brakes make squealing or dragging noises when applied; brake pedal travel is excessive; the pedal pulsates; brake fluid leaks, usually onto the inside of the tire or wheel.

2   The disc brake pads have built-in wear indicators which should make a high pitched squealing or scraping noise when they are worn to the replacement point. When you hear this noise, replace the pads immediately or expensive damage to the discs can result.

3   Loosen the wheel lug nuts.

4   Raise the vehicle and place it securely on jackstands.

5   Remove the wheels (see Jacking and towing at the front of this book, or your owner's manual, if necessary).

Disc brakes

Refer to illustration 16.6

6   There are two pads - an outer and an inner - in each caliper. The pads are visible through inspection holes in each caliper **(see illustration)**.

7   Check the pad thickness by looking at each end of the caliper and through the inspection hole in the caliper body. If the lining material is less than the thickness listed in this Chapter's Specifications, replace the pads. **Note:** Keep in mind that the lining material is riveted or bonded to a metal backing plate and the metal portion is not included in this measurement.

8   If it is difficult to determine the exact thickness of the remaining pad material by the above method, or if you are at all concerned about the condition of the pads, remove the caliper(s), then remove the pads from the calipers for further inspection (refer to Chapter 9).

9   Once the pads are removed from the calipers, clean them with brake cleaner and re-measure them with a ruler or a vernier caliper.

10   Measure the disc thickness with a micrometer to make sure that it still has service life remaining. If any disc is thinner than the specified minimum thickness, replace it (refer to Chapter 9). Even if the disc has service life remaining, check its

16.6 You will find an inspection hole like this in each caliper - placing a steel ruler across the hole should enable you to determine the thickness of remaining pad material for both inner and outer pads

16.12 A quick check of the remaining drum brake shoe lining material can be made by removing the rubber plug in the backing plate and looking through the inspection hole

16.14 If the lining is bonded to the brake shoe, measure the lining thickness from the outer surface to the metal shoe, as shown here; if the lining is riveted to the shoe, measure from the lining outer surface to the rivet head

16.16 Carefully peel back the wheel cylinder boots and check for leaking fluid indicating that the cylinder must be replaced or rebuilt

condition. Look for scoring, gouging and burned spots. If these conditions exist, remove the disc and have it resurfaced (see Chapter 9).

11   Before installing the wheels, check all brake lines and hoses for damage, wear, deformation, cracks, corrosion, leakage, bends and twists, particularly in the vicinity of the rubber hoses at the calipers. Check the clamps for tightness and the connections for leakage. Make sure that all hoses and lines are clear of sharp edges, moving parts and the exhaust system. If any of the above conditions are noted, repair, reroute or replace the lines and/or fittings as necessary (see Chapter 9).

Rear drum brakes

Refer to illustrations 16.12, 16.14 and 16.16

12   On most models, it is possible to check the brake shoe lining thickness without removing the brake drums by removing the rubber plug from the backing plate and use a flashlight to inspect the linings **(see illustration)**. For a more thorough brake inspection, follow the procedure below.

13   Refer to Section 34 and remove the rear brake drums.

14   Note the thickness of the lining material on the rear brake shoes **(see illustration)** and look for signs of contamination by brake fluid and grease. If the lining material is within 1/16-inch of the recessed rivets or metal shoes, replace the brake shoes with new ones. The shoes should also be replaced if they are cracked, glazed (shiny lining surfaces) or contaminated with brake fluid or grease. See Chapter 9 for the replacement procedure.

15   Check the shoe return and hold-down springs and the adjusting mechanism to make sure they're installed correctly and in good condition. Deteriorated or distorted springs, if not replaced, could allow the linings to drag and wear prematurely.

16   Check the wheel cylinders for leakage by carefully peeling back the rubber boots **(see illustration)**. If brake fluid is noted

behind the boots, the wheel cylinders must be replaced (see Chapter 9).

17   Check the drums for cracks, score marks, deep scratches and hard spots, which will appear as small discolored areas. If imperfections cannot be removed with emery cloth, the drums must be resurfaced by an automotive machine shop (see Chapter 9 for more detailed information).

18   Refer to Section 34 and install the brake drums.

19   Install the wheels and snug the wheel lug nuts finger tight.

20   Remove the jackstands and lower the vehicle.

21   Tighten the wheel lug nuts to the torque listed in this Chapter's Specifications.

Brake booster check

22   Sit in the driver's seat and perform the following sequence of tests.

23   With the engine stopped, depress the brake pedal several times - the travel distance should not change.

24   With the brake fully depressed, start the engine - the pedal should move down a little when the engine starts.

25   Depress the brake, stop the engine and hold the pedal in for about 30 seconds - the pedal should neither sink nor rise.

26   Restart the engine, run it for about a minute and turn it off. Then firmly depress the brake several times - the pedal travel should decrease with each application.

27   If your brakes do not operate as described above when the preceding tests are performed, the brake booster is either in need of repair or has failed. Refer to Chapter 9 for the removal procedure.

Parking brake

28   Slowly pull up on the parking brake and count the number of clicks you hear until the handle is up as far as it will go. The adjustment is correct if you hear the specified number of clicks. If you hear more or fewer clicks, it's time to adjust the parking brake (refer to Chapter 9).

29   An alternative method of checking the parking brake is to park the vehicle on a steep hill with the parking brake set and the transaxle in Neutral (be sure to stay in the vehicle during this check!). If the parking brake cannot prevent the vehicle from rolling, it is in need of adjustment (see Chapter 9).

Brake pedal height and freeplay check and adjustment

Brake pedal released height

Refer to illustrations 16.30a and 16.30b

30   With the brake pedal fully released, measure the distance from the top of the pad to the floor **(see illustrations)**.

16.30a 1986 and earlier brake pedal adjustment details

C   Brake switch freeplay
H   Pedal released height

16.30b 1987 and later model brake pedal adjustment details

A   Pedal released freeplay
D   Pedal depressed height
H   Pedal released height

31   If the height is not as listed in the Specifications Section at the beginning of this Chapter it must be adjusted.
32   Loosen the locknut on the brake booster input rod **(see illustrations 16.30a and 16.30b).**
33   Turn the input rod until the pedal height is correct.
34   Tighten the locknut.
35   After adjusting the pedal height, check the freeplay.

Brake pedal freeplay

1986 and earlier models

36   Measure the clearance (freeplay) between the pedal stopper rubber and the tip of the brake lamp switch **(see illustration 16.30a).**
37   If the freeplay isn't as listed in the Specifications Section at the beginning of this Chapter, adjust it by loosening the locknut on the switch. Rotate the switch to achieve the specified freeplay and tighten the locknut.

17.3a Detach the clips and separate the cover from the air cleaner housing

17.2 The PCV filter is located in a housing next to the air cleaner element

1987 and later models

38   Press down lightly on the brake pedal and, with a ruler, measure the distance that it moves freely before resistance is felt **(see illustration 16.30b).** The freeplay should be within the specified limits. If it isn't, it must be adjusted.
39   Loosen the locknut on the brake input rod **(see illustration 16.30b).**
40   Turn the input rod until the pedal freeplay is correct.
41   Tighten the locknut.

Brake pedal depressed height (all models)

42   After checking and, if necessary, adjusting the pedal released height and freeplay, the pedal depressed height must be checked.
43   With the engine running, press the brake pedal fully and measure the pedal pad-to-floor distance **(see illustration 16.30b).**
44   If the minimum depressed height is below that listed in the Specifications Section listed at the beginning of this Chapter, check the brake system for leaks or other damage.

17   Air filter replacement (every 15,000 miles or 12 months)

Refer to illustrations 17.2, 17.3a and 17.3b

1   On carburetor-and throttle body fuel injection-equipped models, the filter is

17.3b Lift the cover up and slide the element out of the housing

located inside a housing on top of the engine.
2   Release the spring clips (if equipped), remove the wingnut(s) and detach the cover, then lift the element out. If equipped, remove the PCV filter and replace it with a new one **(see illustration).**
3   On port fuel-injected models, the air filter is located inside a housing at the left (driver's) side of the engine compartment. To remove the air filter, release the four spring clips that keep the two halves of the air cleaner housing together, then lift the cover up and remove the air filter element **(see illustrations).**
4   Inspect the outer surface of the filter element. If it is dirty, replace it. If it is only moderately dusty, it can be reused by blowing it clean from the back to the front surface with compressed air. Because it is a pleated paper type filter, it cannot be washed or oiled. If it cannot be cleaned satisfactorily with compressed air, discard and replace it. While the cover is off, be careful not to drop anything down into the housing or carburetor. **Caution:** *Never drive the vehicle with the air cleaner removed. Excessive engine wear could result and backfiring could even cause a fire under the hood.*
5   Wipe out the inside of the air cleaner housing.
6   Place the new filter into the air cleaner housing, making sure it seats properly.
7   Installation of the cover is the reverse of removal.

18   Fuel system check (every 15,000 miles or 12 months)

Refer to illustration 18.5
Warning: *Gasoline is extremely flammable, so take extra precautions when you work on any part of the fuel system. Don't smoke or allow open flames or bare light bulbs near the work area, and don't work in a garage where a natural gas-type appliance (such as a water heater or clothes dryer) with a pilot light is present. Since gasoline is carcinogenic, wear latex gloves when there's a possibility of being exposed to fuel, and, if you spill any fuel on your skin, rinse it off immediately with soap and water. Mop up any spills immediately and do not store fuel-soaked rags where they could ignite. The fuel system is under constant pressure, so, if any fuel lines are to be disconnected, the fuel pressure in the system must be relieved first (see Chapter 4 for more information). When you perform any kind of work on the fuel system, wear safety glasses and have a Class B type fire extinguisher on hand.*
1   If you smell gasoline while driving or after the vehicle has been sitting in the sun, inspect the fuel system immediately.
2   Remove the gas filler cap and inspect if for damage and corrosion. The gasket should have an unbroken sealing imprint. If the

18.5 Inspect fuel filler hoses for cracks and make sure the clamps are tight (arrows)

19.1 The manual transaxle filler plug (arrow) is located on the front side of the transaxle housing

20.1 Steering wheel freeplay is the amount of travel between an initial steering input and the point at which the front wheels begin to turn (indicated by a slight resistance)

gasket is damaged or corroded, remove it and install a new one.

3   Inspect the fuel feed and return lines for cracks. Make sure the threaded flare nut type connectors which secure the metal fuel lines to the carburetor or fuel injection system and the clamps which secure the hoses to the in-line fuel filter are tight.

4   Since some components of the fuel system - the fuel tank and part of the fuel feed and return lines, for example - are underneath the vehicle, they can be inspected more easily with the vehicle raised on a hoist. If that's not possible, raise the vehicle and support it securely on jackstands.

5   With the vehicle raised and safely supported, inspect the gas tank and filler neck for punctures, cracks and other damage. The connection between the filler neck and the tank is particularly critical. Sometimes a rubber filler neck will leak because of loose clamps or deteriorated rubber (see illustration). These are problems a home mechanic can usually rectify. **Warning:** *Do not, under any circumstances, try to repair a fuel tank (except rubber components). A welding torch or any open flame can easily cause fuel vapors inside the tank to explode.*

6   Carefully check all rubber hoses and metal lines leading away from the fuel tank. Check for loose connections, deteriorated hoses, crimped lines and other damage. Carefully inspect the lines from the tank to the fuel injection system. Repair or replace damaged sections as necessary (see Chapter 4).

19 Manual transaxle lubricant level check
(every 15,000 miles or 12 months)

Refer to illustration 19.1

1   The manual transaxle does not have a dipstick. To check the fluid level, raise the vehicle and support it securely on jackstands. On the lower front side of the transaxle housing, you will see a plug **(see illustration)**. Remove it. If the lubricant level

is correct, it should be up to the lower edge of the hole.

2   If the transaxle needs more lubricant (if the level is not up to the hole), use a funnel or a gear oil pump to add more. Stop filling the transaxle when the lubricant begins to run out the hole.

3   Install the plug and tighten it securely. Drive the vehicle a short distance, then check for leaks.

20 Steering and suspension check
(every 15,000 miles or 12 months)

Refer to illustration 20.1
Note: *For detailed illustrations of the steering and suspension components, refer to Chapter 10.*

With the wheels on the ground

1   With the vehicle stopped and the front wheels pointed straight ahead, rock the steering wheel gently back and forth. If freeplay **(see illustration)** is excessive, a front wheel bearing, main shaft yoke, intermediate shaft yoke, lower arm balljoint or steering system joint is worn or the steering gear is out of adjustment or broken. Refer to Chapter 10 for the appropriate repair procedure.

2   Other symptoms, such as excessive vehicle body movement over rough roads, swaying (leaning) around corners and binding as the steering wheel is turned, may indicate faulty steering and/or suspension components.

3   Check the shock absorbers by pushing down and releasing the vehicle several times at each corner. If the vehicle does not come back to a level position within one or two bounces, the shocks/struts are worn and must be replaced. When bouncing the vehicle up and down, listen for squeaks and noises from the suspension components. Additional information on suspension components can be found in Chapter 10.

Under the vehicle

4   Raise the vehicle with a floor jack and

support it securely on jackstands. See Jacking and towing at the front of this book for the proper jacking points.

5   Check the tires for irregular wear patterns and proper inflation. See Section 5 in this Chapter for information regarding tire wear, Section 34 for wheel bearing adjustment (1986 and earlier models) and Chapter 10 for the wheel bearing replacement procedures (later models).

6   Inspect the universal joint between the steering shaft and the steering gear housing. Check the steering gear housing for grease leakage or oozing. Make sure that the dust seals and boots are not damaged and that the boot clamps are not loose. Check the steering linkage for looseness or damage. Check the tie-rod ends for excessive play. Look for loose bolts, broken or disconnected parts and deteriorated rubber bushings on all suspension and steering components. While an assistant turns the steering wheel from side to side, check the steering components for free movement, chafing and binding. If the steering components do not seem to be reacting with the movement of the steering wheel, try to determine where the slack is located.

7   Check the balljoints moving each lower arm up and down with a pry bar to ensure that its balljoint has no play. If any balljoint does have play, replace it. See Chapter 10 for the front balljoint replacement procedure.

8   Inspect the balljoint boots for damage and leaking grease. Replace the balljoints with new ones if they are damaged (see Chapter 10).

21 Driveaxle boot check
(every 15,000 miles or 12 months)

Refer to illustration 21.2

1   The driveaxle boots are very important because they prevent dirt, water and foreign material from entering and damaging the constant velocity (CV) joints. Oil and grease can cause the boot material to deteriorate prematurely, so it's a good idea to wash the boots with soap and water.

1

21.2 Flex the driveaxle boots by hand to check for cracks and/or leaking grease

22.5 When the no. 1 piston is at TDC on the compression stroke, the valve clearances for valves 1, 2, 3 and 6 can be measured and with no. 4 piston at TDC on the compression stroke, valves 4, 5, 7 and 8 can be measured

22.6 Measure the clearance for each valve with a feeler gauge of the specified thickness - if the clearance is correct, you should feel a slight drag on the gauge as you pull it out

2   Inspect the boots for tears and cracks as well as loose clamps **(see illustration)**. If there is any evidence of cracks or leaking lubricant, they must be replaced as described in Chapter 8.

22 Valve clearance check and adjustment (1988 and earlier models only) (every 15,000 miles or 12 months)

Refer to illustrations 22.5 and 22.6

1   Disconnect the negative cable from the battery.
2   Disconnect the cruise control cable, air cleaner assembly or other components which will interfere with valve cover removal.
3   Remove the valve cover (refer to Chapter 2).
4   Refer to Chapter 2 and position the number 1 piston at TDC on the compression stroke. The number one cylinder rocker arms (closest to the timing belt end of the engine) should be loose and the camshaft lobes facing away from the rocker arms.
5   With the crankshaft in this position, valve numbers 1, 2, 3 and 6 can be checked and adjusted **(see illustration)**.
6   Measure the clearances of the indicated valves with a feeler gauge of the specified thickness as shown **(see illustration)**. To adjust the clearance, loosen the locknut, turn the adjusting screw counterclockwise and insert the appropriate size feeler gauge between the rocker arm and the camshaft. Carefully tighten the adjusting screw until you can feel a slight drag on the feeler gauge as you withdraw it from between the rocker arm and camshaft.
7   Hold the adjusting screw with a screwdriver (to keep it from turning) and tighten the locknut. Recheck the clearance to make sure it hasn't changed.
8   Turn the crankshaft one complete revolution and realign the timing marks. Measure the valve numbers 4, 5, 7 and 8 **(see illustration 22.5)**.
9   Repeat this procedure until all the valves

which are out of clearance have been corrected.
10   Installation of the valve cover, air cleaner duct, etc. is the reverse of removal.

23 Fuel filter replacement (every 30,000 miles or 24 months)

Refer to illustrations 23.2 and 23.11

Carbureted models

1   Disconnect the cable from the negative terminal of the battery.
2   The translucent plastic fuel filter is located in a spring clip on the firewall **(see illustration)**.
3   For easier access, pull the filter out of the clip so both fittings can be reached.
4   Release the hose clamps at the filter fittings and slide them back up the hoses.
5   Disconnect the hose and remove the filter.
6   Push the hoses onto the new filter and position the clamps approximately 1/4-inch back from the ends.
7   Press the filter into the spring clip. Check to make sure its held securely and the hoses aren't kinked.
8   Start the engine and check for leaks.
Fuel-injected models
9   The canister filter is mounted in a clip on

the firewall near the brake master cylinder.
10   Depressurize the fuel system (see Chapter 4), then disconnect the cable from the negative terminal of the battery.
11   Detach the filter from the bracket, loosen the screw clamps, then detach the hoses from the top and bottom of the fuel filter and remove it **(see illustration)**.
12   Note that the inlet and outlet pipes are clearly labeled on their respective ends of the filter. Make sure the new filter is installed so that it's facing the proper direction as noted above. When correctly installed, the filter should be installed so the outlet pipe faces up and the inlet pipe faces down.
13   Install the inlet and outlet fittings and tighten the screw clamps securely. Reconnect the battery cable, start the engine and check for leaks.

24 Spark plug check and replacement (every 30,000 miles or 24 months)

Refer to illustrations 24.1, 24.4a, 24.4b, 24.6, 24.8, 24.10a and 24.10b

1   Spark plug replacement requires a spark plug socket which fits onto a ratchet wrench. This socket is lined with a rubber grommet to protect the porcelain insulator of the spark plug and to hold the plug while you

23.2 On carbureted models, the fuel filter is clipped to a bracket on the firewall

23.11 On fuel-injected models, the fuel filter is mounted in a clip below the brake master cylinder

24.1 Tools required for changing spark plugs

1   *Spark plug socket - This will have special padding inside to protect the spark plug porcelain insulator*

2   *Torque wrench - Although not mandatory, use of this tool is the best way to ensure that the plugs are tightened properly*

3   *Ratchet - Standard hand tool to fit the plug socket*

4   *Extension - Depending on model and accessories, you may need special extensions and universal joints to reach one or more of the plugs*

5   *Spark plug gap gauge - This gauge for checking the gap comes in a variety of styles. Make sure the gap for your engine is included*

insert it into the spark plug hole. You will also need a wire-type feeler gauge to check and adjust the spark plug gap and a torque wrench to tighten the new plugs to the specified torque **(see illustration)**.

2   If you are replacing the plugs, purchase the new plugs, adjust them to the proper gap and then replace each plug one at a time. **Note:** *When buying new spark plugs, it's essential that you obtain the correct plugs for your specific vehicle. This information can be found in the Specifications Section at the beginning of this Chapter, on the Vehicle Emissions Control Information (VECI) label located on the underside of the hood or in the owner's manual. If these sources specify different plugs, purchase the spark plug type specified on the VECI label because that information is provided specifically for your engine.*

24.4a Spark plug manufacturers recommend using a wire-type gauge when checking the gap - if the wire does not slide between the electrodes with a slight drag, adjustment is required

3   Inspect each of the new plugs for defects. If there are any signs of cracks in the porcelain insulator of a plug, don't use it.

4   Check the electrode gaps of the new plugs. Check the gap by inserting the wire gauge of the proper thickness between the electrodes at the tip of the plug **(see illustration)**. The gap between the electrodes should be identical to that listed in this Chapter's Specifications or on the VECI label. If the gap is incorrect, use the notched adjuster on the feeler gauge body to bend the curved side electrode slightly **(see illustration)**.

5   If the side electrode is not exactly over the center electrode, use the notched adjuster to align them. **Caution:** *If the gap of a new plug must be adjusted, bend only the base of the ground electrode - do not touch the tip.*

Removal

6   To prevent the possibility of mixing up spark plug wires, work on one spark plug at a time. Remove the wire and boot from one spark plug. Grasp the boot - not the cable - as shown, give it a half twisting motion and pull straight up **(see illustration)**.

7   If compressed air is available, blow any dirt or foreign material away from the spark plug area before proceeding (a common bicycle pump will also work).

8   Remove the spark plug **(see illustration)**.

24.4b To change the gap, bend the side electrode only, as indicated by the arrows, and be very careful not to crack or chip the porcelain insulator surrounding the center electrode

24.6 When removing the spark plug wires, pull only on the boot and use a twisting/pulling motion

9   Whether you are replacing the plugs at this time or intend to reuse the old plugs, compare each old spark plug with those shown in the accompanying photos to determine the overall running condition of the engine.

Installation

10   Prior to installation, apply a coat of anti-seize compound to the plug threads. It's often difficult to insert spark plugs into their holes without cross-threading them. To avoid this possibility, fit a short piece of 3/8-inch ID rubber hose over the end of the spark plug **(see illustrations)**. The flexible hose acts as a universal joint to help align the plug with the

24.8 Use a socket wrench with a long extension to unscrew the spark plugs on twin cam engines

24.10a Apply a coat of anti-seize compound to the spark plug threads

24.10b A length of 3/8-inch ID rubber hose will save time and prevent damaged threads when installing the spark plugs

1

plug hole. Should the plug begin to cross-thread, the hose will slip on the spark plug, preventing thread damage. Tighten the plug to the torque listed in this Chapter's Specifications.

11   Attach the plug wire to the new spark plug, again using a twisting motion on the boot until it is firmly seated on the end of the spark plug.

12   Follow the above procedure for the remaining spark plugs, replacing them one at a time to prevent mixing up the spark plug wires.

25   Spark plug wire, distributor cap and rotor check and replacement (every 30,000 miles or 24 months)

Refer to illustrations 25.8, 25.11 and 25.12

1   The spark plug wires should be checked whenever new spark plugs are installed.

2   Begin this procedure by making a visual check of the spark plug wires while the engine is running. In a darkened garage (make sure there is ventilation) start the engine and observe each plug wire. Be careful not to come into contact with any moving engine parts. If there is a break in the wire, you will see arcing or a small spark at the damaged area. If arcing is noticed, make a note to obtain new wires, then allow the engine to cool and check the distributor cap and rotor.

3   The spark plug wires should be inspected one at a time to prevent mixing up the order, which is essential for proper engine operation. Each original plug wire should be numbered to help identify its location. If the number is illegible, a piece of tape can be marked with the correct number and wrapped around the plug wire.

4   Disconnect the plug wire from the spark plug. A removal tool can be used for this purpose or you can grasp the rubber boot, twist the boot half a turn and pull the boot free. Do not pull on the wire itself.

5   Check inside the boot for corrosion, which will look like a white crusty powder.

6   Push the wire and boot back onto the end of the spark plug. It should fit tightly onto the end of the plug. If it doesn't, remove the wire and use pliers to carefully crimp the metal connector inside the wire boot until the fit is snug.

7   Using a clean rag, wipe the entire length of the wire to remove built-up dirt and grease. Once the wire is clean, check for burns, cracks and other damage. Do not bend the wire sharply, because the conductor might break.

8   Remove the rubber boot (if equipped) and disconnect the wire from the distributor **(see illustration)**. Again, pull only on the rubber boot. Check for corrosion and a tight fit. Replace the wire in the distributor.

9   Inspect the remaining spark plug wires, making sure that each one is securely fastened at the distributor and spark plug when the check is complete.

10   If new spark plug wires are required, purchase a set for your specific engine model. Pre-cut wire sets with the boots already installed are available. Remove and replace the wires one at a time to avoid mix-ups in the firing order.

11   Detach the distributor cap by loosening the two cap retaining screws. Look inside it for cracks, carbon tracks and worn, burned or loose contacts **(see illustration)**.

12   Loosen the retaining screw and pull the rotor off the distributor shaft and examine it for cracks and carbon tracks **(see illustration)**. Replace the cap and rotor if any damage or defects are noted.

13   It is common practice to install a new cap and rotor whenever new spark plug wires are installed, but if you wish to continue using the old cap, check the resistance between the spark plug wires and the cap first. If the indicated resistance is more than the maximum value listed in this Chapter's Specifications, replace the cap and/or wires.

14   When installing a new cap, remove the wires from the old cap one at a time and attach them to the new cap in the exact same location - do not simultaneously remove all the wires from the old cap or firing order mix-ups may occur.

26   Cooling system servicing (draining, flushing and refilling) (every 30,000 miles or 24 months)

Warning: *Do not allow engine coolant (antifreeze) to come in contact with your skin or painted surfaces of the vehicle. Rinse off spills immediately with plenty of water. Antifreeze is highly toxic if ingested. Never leave antifreeze laying around in an open container or in puddles on the floor; children and pets are attracted by it's sweet smell and may drink it. Check with local authorities about disposing of used antifreeze. Many communities have collection centers which will see that antifreeze is disposed of safely.*

1   Periodically, the cooling system should be drained, flushed and refilled to replenish the antifreeze mixture and prevent formation of rust and corrosion, which can impair the performance of the cooling system and cause engine damage. When the cooling system is serviced, all hoses and the radiator cap should be checked and replaced if necessary.

Draining

Refer to illustrations 26.3a, 26.3b, 26.3c, 26.3d, 26.3e, 26.4 and 26.5

2   Apply the parking brake and block the wheels. If the vehicle has just been driven, wait several hours to allow the engine to cool down before beginning this procedure.

3   Move the temperature lever on the heater control panel to HOT. Remove the radiator cap and, on 1989 and later models,

25.8 Unsnap the rubber cover and pull it out of the way for access to the distributor cap screws

25.11 Shown here are some of the common defects to look for when inspecting the distributor cap (if in doubt about its condition, install a new one)

25.12 The ignition rotor should be checked for wear and corrosion as indicated here (if in doubt about its condition, buy a new one)

26.3a On 1989 and 1990 models the air bleed plug is located at the end of the cylinder head, near the distributor

26.3b 1991 and 1992 GA16 models and 1993 and 1994 SR20 models have a bleeder plug on the thermostat housing . . .

26.3c . . . and an air bleeder cap on an elbow in one of the heater pipes

26.3d 1993 and later GA16 models have an air bleed plug in a fitting on the intake manifold . . .

26.3e . . . and another bleed plug below the distributor

26.4 On most models you will have to remove a cover for access to the radiator drain fitting (arrow) located at the bottom of the radiator

remove the air bleed plug(s) **(see illustrations)**.

4   Move a large container under the radiator drain to catch the coolant. Attach a 3/8-inch inner diameter hose to the drain fitting to direct the coolant into the container (some models are already equipped with a hose), then open the drain fitting (a pair of pliers may be required to turn it, while on later models a large screwdriver is needed) **(see illustration)**.

5   After the coolant stops flowing out of the radiator, move the container under the engine block drain plug **(see illustration)**. Loosen the plug and allow the coolant in the block to drain.

6   While the coolant is draining, check the condition of the radiator hoses, heater hoses and clamps (refer to Section 14 if necessary).

7   Replace any damaged clamps or hoses (see Chapter 3).

Flushing

8   Once the system is completely drained, flush the radiator with fresh water from a garden hose until water runs clear at the drain. The flushing action of the water will remove sediments from the radiator but will not remove rust and scale from the engine and cooling tube surfaces.

9   These deposits can be removed by the chemical action of a cleaner. Follow the procedure outlined in the manufacturer's instructions. If the radiator is severely

corroded, damaged or leaking, it should be removed (see Chapter 3) and taken to a radiator repair shop.

10   Remove the overflow hose from the coolant recovery reservoir. Drain the reservoir and flush it with clean water, then reconnect the hose.

Refilling

11   Close and tighten the radiator drain. Install and tighten the block drain plug.

12   Make sure the heater temperature control is in the maximum heat position.

13   Slowly add new coolant (a 50/50 mixture of water and antifreeze) to the radiator until it's full. On models equipped with air bleed plugs, fill the system until coolant runs out the air bleed hole(s), then install the air bleed bolt and/or cap. Add coolant to the reservoir up to the lower mark.

14   Leave the radiator cap off and run the engine in a well-ventilated area until the thermostat opens (coolant will begin flowing through the radiator and the upper radiator hose will become hot). Race the engine two or three times under no load.

15   Turn the engine off and let it cool. Add more coolant mixture to bring the level back up to the lip on the radiator filler neck.

16   Squeeze the upper radiator hose to expel air, then add more coolant mixture if necessary. Replace the radiator cap.

17   Start the engine, allow it to reach normal operating temperature and check for leaks.

26.5 After draining the radiator, be sure to fully drain the cooling system by removing the block drain plug located on the side of the engine block (arrow)

27   Ignition timing check and adjustment (every 30,000 miles or 24 months)

Refer to illustrations 27.2 and 27.5

1   All vehicles are equipped with an Emissions Control Information label inside the engine compartment. The label contains important ignition timing specifications and the proper timing procedure for your specific vehicle. If the information on the emissions label is different from the information included in this Section, follow the procedure on the label.

27.2 Tools needed to check and adjust the ignition timing

1   *Vacuum plugs - Vacuum hoses will, in most cases, have to be disconnected and plugged. Molded plugs in various shapes and sizes are available for this*

2   *Inductive pick-up timing light - Flashes a bright concentrated beam of light whenever the number one spark plug fires. Connect the leads according to the instructions supplied with the light*

3   *Distributor wrench - On some models, the hold-down bolt for the distributor is difficult to reach and turn with a conventional wrench or socket. A special wrench like this must be used*

2   At the specified intervals, or when the distributor has been removed, the ignition timing must be checked and adjusted if necessary. Tools required for this procedure include an inductive pick-up timing light, a tachometer, a distributor wrench and, in some cases, a means of plugging vacuum hoses **(see illustration)**.

3   Before you check the timing, make sure the idle speed is correct (see Section 28) and the engine is at normal operating temperature.

4   With the engine off, connect a timing light in accordance with the manufacturer's instructions. Usually, the light must be connected to the battery and the number one spark plug in some fashion. The number one spark plug wire or terminal should be marked at the distributor; trace it back to the spark plug and attach the timing light lead near the plug.

5   Locate the numbered timing scale on the front cover of the engine **(see illustration)**.

6   Locate the notched groove across the crankshaft pulley or the flywheel. It may be necessary to have an assistant temporarily turn the ignition on and off in short bursts without starting the engine in order to bring the groove into a position where it can easily be cleaned and marked. **Warning:** Stay clear of all moving engine components when the engine is turned over in this manner.

7   Use white soapstone, chalk or paint to mark the groove in the pulley or flywheel. Also, put a mark on the timing scale corresponding to the number of degrees specified on the Emission Control Information label in the engine compartment.

8   Aim the timing light at the marks, again being careful not to come into contact with moving parts. The marks made should appear stationary. If the marks are in alignment, the timing is correct. If the marks are not aligned, turn off the engine.

9   Loosen the hold-down bolt or nut at the base of the distributor. Loosen the bolt/nut only slightly, just enough to turn the distributor (see Chapter 5).

10   Now restart the engine and turn the distributor very slowly until the timing marks are aligned.

11   Shut off the engine and tighten the distributor bolt/nut, being careful not to move the distributor.

12   Start the engine and recheck the timing to make sure the marks are still in alignment.

13   Disconnect the timing light and tachometer and reconnect any components which were disconnected for this procedure.

28   Engine idle speed check and adjustment (every 30,000 miles or 24 months)

Refer to illustrations 28.8, 28.9, 28.11a and 28.11b

1   Engine idle speed is the speed at which the engine operates when no accelerator pedal pressure is applied, as when stopped at a traffic light. This speed is critical to the performance of the engine itself, as well as many engine subsystems.

2   Set the parking brake firmly and block the wheels to prevent the vehicle from rolling. Put the transaxle in Neutral. Unplug the engine fan electrical connector(s). If the fan(s) should come on during the idle adjustment procedure, idle speed is affected.

3   Connect a hand-held tachometer. **Caution:** *Don't allow the tachometer to touch ground or damage to the igniter and/or the ignition coil may occur.* **Note:** *Some tachometers may not be compatible with this ignition system. It is recommended that you consult the manufacturer of the tool.*

4   Start the engine and allow it to reach normal operating temperature.

5   Check, and adjust if necessary, the ignition timing (see Section 27).

6   Start the engine and allow it run at idle for two minutes.

7   On ECCS equipped models, clear any codes before checking the idle speed (see Chapter 6).

8   On 1985 and 1986 49-state models, turn off the engine and disconnect and plug the vacuum control modulator hose **(see illustration)**. Restart the engine.

9   On 1987 through 1990 models, shut off the engine and disconnect the electrical connector for the throttle sensor **(see illustration)**. Restart the engine.

10   Check the engine idle speed on the tachometer and compare it to those listed in the Specifications Section at the beginning of this Chapter or the Vehicle Emission Control Information label in the engine compartment. If there is a difference between the Specifica-

27.5 The timing marks are attached to the front of the engine and the crankshaft pulley has groove in it for reference on most models

28.8 Disconnect the hose from the vacuum control modulator (arrow) and plug it

28.9 Disconnect the TBI fuel injection throttle sensor

28.11a Adjust the idle by turning the adjusting screw with a screwdriver

28.11b Use a screwdriver to turn the adjusting screw on the fuel-injected models - note that the idle speed is quite sensitive to even the slightest turn of this screw

30.2 Check the evaporative canister for damage and the hose connections (arrows) for cracks and damage

tions Section and the VECI label, always assume that the information on the label is correct.

11   If the idle speed is too low or too high, use a screwdriver to turn the idle speed adjusting screw until the specified curb idle speed is obtained **(see illustrations)**.

12   Turn off the engine, disconnect the tachometer and reconnect any components which were disconnected.

29   Carburetor choke check (every 30,000 miles or 24 months)

1   The choke operates when the engine is cold, so this check can only be performed before the vehicle has been started for the day.

2   Open the hood and remove the top plate of the air cleaner assembly (see Section 17). If any vacuum hoses must be disconnected, make sure you tag the hoses for reinstallation in their original positions. Place the top plate and wing nut aside, out of the way of moving engine components.

3   Look at the center of the air cleaner housing. You will notice a flat plate at the carburetor opening.

4   Press the accelerator pedal to the floor. The plate should close completely. Start the engine while you watch the plate at the carburetor. **Warning:** *Do not position your face directly over the carburetor, as the engine could backfire, causing serious burns.* When the engine starts, the choke plate should open slightly.

5   Allow the engine to continue running at an idle speed. As the engine warms up to operating temperature, the plate should slowly open, allowing more air to enter through the top of the carburetor.

6   After a few minutes, the choke plate should be fully open to the vertical position. Lightly tap the accelerator to make sure the fast idle cam disengages.

7   You will notice that the engine speed corresponds with the plate opening. With the plate fully closed, the engine should run at a fast idle speed. As the plate opens and the throttle is moved to disengage the fast idle cam, the engine speed will decrease.

8   Refer to Chapter 4 for specific information on adjusting and servicing the choke components.

30   Evaporative emissions control system check (every 30,000 miles or 24 months)

Refer to illustration 30.2

1   The function of the evaporative emissions control system is to draw fuel vapors from the gas tank and fuel system, store them in a charcoal canister and then burn them during normal engine operation.

2   The most common symptom of a fault in the evaporative emissions system is a strong fuel odor in the engine compartment. If a fuel odor is detected, inspect the charcoal canister, located at the front of the engine compartment. Check the canister and all hoses for damage and deterioration **(see illustration)**.

3   The evaporative emissions control system is explained in more detail in Chapter 6.

31   Exhaust system check (every 30,000 miles or 24 months)

Refer to illustration 31.4

1   With the engine cold (at least three hours after the vehicle has been driven), check the complete exhaust system from its starting point at the engine to the end of the tailpipe. This should be done on a hoist where unrestricted access is available.

2   Check the pipes and connections for evidence of leaks, severe corrosion or damage. Make sure that all brackets and hangers are in good condition and tight.

3   At the same time, inspect the underside of the body for holes, corrosion, open seams, etc. which may allow exhaust gases to enter the passenger compartment. Seal all body openings with silicone or body putty.

4   Rattles and other noises can often be

traced to the exhaust system, especially the mounts and hangers **(see illustration)**. Try to move the pipes, muffler and catalytic converter. If the components can come in contact with the body or suspension parts, secure the exhaust system with new mounts.

5   Check the running condition of the engine by inspecting inside the end of the tailpipe. The exhaust deposits here are an indication of engine state-of-tune. If the pipe is black and sooty or coated with white deposits, the engine is in need of a tune-up, including a thorough fuel system inspection.

32   Automatic transaxle fluid change (every 30,000 miles or 24 months)

Refer to illustrations 32.7a and 32.7b

1   At the specified time intervals, the automatic transaxle fluid should be drained and replaced.

2   Before beginning work, purchase the specified transmission fluid (see Recommended fluids and lubricants at the front of this chapter).

3   Other tools necessary for this job include jackstands to support the vehicle in a raised position, a wrench, a drain pan capable of holding at least four quarts, newspapers and clean rags.

4   The fluid should be drained immediately after the vehicle has been driven. Hot fluid is more effective than cold fluid at removing built up sediment. **Warning:** *Fluid temper-*

31.4 Check the exhaust system hangers (arrow) for damage and cracks

32.7a On some automatic transaxles, the drain plug is located on the edge of the housing

32.7b On other automatic transaxles, the drain plug is located on the bottom of the fluid pan

33.1 Use a 3/8-inch ratchet or breaker bar to remove the manual transaxle drain plug

ature can exceed 350-degrees F in a hot transaxle. Wear protective gloves.

5   After the vehicle has been driven to warm up the fluid, raise it and place it on jackstands for access to the transaxle drain plugs.

6   Move the necessary equipment under the vehicle, being careful not to touch any of the hot exhaust components.

7   Place the drain pan under the drain plug in the transaxle housing or fluid pan and remove the drain plug **(see illustrations)**. Be sure the drain pan is in position, as fluid will come out with some force. Once the fluid is drained, reinstall the drain plug securely.

8   Lower the vehicle.

9   With the engine off, add new fluid to the transaxle through the dipstick tube (see *Recommended fluids and lubricants* for the recommended fluid type and capacity). Use a funnel to prevent spills. It is best to add a little fluid at a time, continually checking the level with the dipstick (see Section 7). Allow the fluid time to drain into the pan.

10   Start the engine and shift the selector into all positions from P through L, then shift into P and apply the parking brake.

11   With the engine idling, check the fluid

level. Add fluid up to the Cool level on the dipstick.

33 Manual transaxle lubricant change
(every 30,000 miles or 24 months)

Refer to illustration 33.1

1   Remove the drain plug and drain the fluid **(see illustration)**.

2   Reinstall the drain plug(s) securely.

3   Add new fluid until it begins to run out of the filler hole (see Section 19). Install the check/fill plug and tighten it securely. See *Recommended lubricants and fluids* for the specified lubricant type.

34 Rear wheel bearing check, repack and adjustment (1986 and earlier models only)
(ever 30,000 miles or 24 months)

Check
Refer to illustration 34.1

1   In most cases the rear wheel bearings will not need servicing until the brake shoes are changed. However, the bearings should be checked whenever the rear of the vehicle is raised for any reason. Several items, including a torque wrench and special grease, are required for this procedure **(see illustration)**.

2   With the vehicle securely supported on jackstands, spin each wheel and check for noise, rolling resistance and freeplay.

3   Grasp the top of each tire with one hand and the bottom with the other. Move the wheel in-and-out on the spindle. If there's any noticeable movement, the bearings should be checked and then repacked with grease or replaced if necessary.

Repack
Refer to illustrations 34.7, 34.8 and 34.14

4   Remove the wheel.

5   Pry the dust cap out of the hub using a screwdriver or hammer and chisel.

6   Straighten the bent ends of the cotter pin, then pull the cotter pin out of the nut lock. Discard the cotter pin and use a new one during reassembly.

34.1 Tools and materials needed for wheel bearing maintenance

1   *Hammer - A common hammer will do just fine*

2   *Grease - High-temperature grease that is formulated for wheel bearings should be used*

3   *Wood block - If you have a scrap piece of 2x4, it can be used to drive the new seal into the hub*

4   *Needle-nose pliers - Used to straighten and remove the cotter pin in the spindle*

5   *Torque wrench - This is very important in this procedure; if the bearing is too tight, the wheel won't turn freely - if it's too loose, the wheel will "wobble" on the spindle. Either way, it could mean extensive damage*

6   *Screwdriver - Used to remove the seal from the hub (a long screwdriver is preferred)*

7   *Socket/breaker bar - Needed to loosen the nut on the spindle if it's extremely tight*

8   *Brush - Together with some clean solvent, this will be used to remove old grease from the hub and spindle*

34.7 Typical rear hub and bearing components

7 Remove the nut lock cap, nut and washer from the end of the spindle **(see illustration)**.

8 Pull the hub/disc assembly out slightly, then push it back into its original position **(see illustration)**. This should force the outer bearing off the spindle enough so it can be removed.

9 Pull the hub/disc assembly off the spindle. If it does not come off easily, back off the adjuster as described in the drum brake shoe replacement procedure in Chapter 9.

10 Use a screwdriver to pry the seal out of the rear of the hub. As this is done, note how the seal is installed.

11 Remove the inner wheel bearing from the hub.

12 Use solvent to remove all traces of the old grease from the bearings, hub and spindle. A small brush may prove helpful; however make sure no bristles from the brush embed themselves inside the bearing rollers. Allow the parts to air dry.

13 Carefully inspect the bearings for cracks, heat discoloration, worn rollers, etc. Check the bearing races inside the hub for wear and damage. If the bearing races are

defective, the hubs should be taken to a machine shop with the facilities to remove the old races and press new ones in. Note that the bearings and races come as matched sets and old bearings should never be installed on new races.

14 Use high-temperature front wheel bearing grease to pack the bearings. Work the grease completely into the bearings, forcing it between the rollers, cone and cage from the back side **(see illustration)**.

15 Apply a thin coat of grease to the spindle at the outer bearing seat, inner bearing seat, shoulder and seal seat.

16 Put a small quantity of grease inboard of each bearing race inside the hub. Using your finger, form a dam at these points to provide extra grease availability and to keep thinned grease from flowing out of the bearing.

17 Place the grease-packed inner bearing into the rear of the hub and put a little more grease outboard of the bearing.

18 Place a new seal over the inner bearing and tap the seal evenly into place with a hammer and blunt punch until it's flush with the hub.

19 Carefully place the hub assembly onto

the spindle and push the grease-packed outer bearing into position.

20 Install the washer and spindle nut. Tighten the nut only slightly (no more than 12 ft-lbs of torque).

Adjustment

21 Spin the hub in a forward direction to seat the bearings and remove any grease or burrs which could cause excessive bearing play later.

22 Check to see that the tightness of the nut is still approximately 12 ft-lbs.

23 Loosen the nut until it's just loose, no more.

24 Using your hand (not a wrench of any kind), tighten the nut until it's snug. Install the nut lock and a new cotter pin through the hole in the spindle and lock. If the nut lock slots don't line up, take it off and rotate it to another position.

25 Bend the ends of the cotter pin until they're flat against the nut. Cut off any extra length which could interfere with the dust cap.

26 Install the dust cap, tapping it into place with a hammer.

27 Install the wheel on the hub and tighten the lug nuts.

28 Grasp the top and bottom of the tire and check the bearings in the manner described earlier in this Section.

29 Lower the vehicle.

35 Exhaust Gas Recirculation (EGR) valve check (every 30,000 miles or 24 months)

Refer to illustration 35.2

1 The EGR valve is located on the exhaust manifold, next to the carburetor or fuel injection unit. Most of the time when a problem develops in this emissions system, it's due to a stuck or corroded EGR valve.

34.8 Pull the drum/hub out slightly and push it back in to unseat the outer bearing

34.14 Pack each wheel bearing by working the grease into the rollers from the back side

35.2 Press up on the EGR valve diaphragm to make sure it moves easily

36.3 Use a mirror to check the position of the damper door

37.2 The PVC valve (arrow) threads into the valve cover on later models - remove the valve and verify that vacuum is felt at the valve with the engine running

2   With the engine cold to prevent burns, reach under the EGR valve and push up on the diaphragm. Using moderate pressure you should be able to press the diaphragm up-and-down within the housing **(see illustration)**.

3   If the diaphragm doesn't move, or moves only with much effort, replace the EGR valve with a new one. If in doubt about the condition of the valve, compare the free movement of your EGR valve with a new valve.

4   Refer to Chapter 6 for more information on the EGR system.

36   Thermostatic air cleaner check (every 30,000 miles or 24 months)

Refer to illustration 36.3

1   Some models are equipped with a thermostatically controlled air cleaner which draws air to the carburetor/throttle body from different locations, depending upon engine temperature.

2   This is a visual check. If access is limited, a small mirror may have to be used.

3   Open the hood and locate the damper door inside the air cleaner assembly **(see illustration)**.

4   If there is a flexible air duct attached to the end of the air cleaner, disconnect it at the air cleaner. This will enable you to see the damper inside.

5   The check should be done when the engine is cold. Start the engine and look at the damper, which should move to a closed position. With the damper closed, air cannot enter through the air cleaner opening, but instead enters the air cleaner through a flexible duct attached to a heat stove on the exhaust manifold.

6   As the engine warms up to operating temperature, the damper should open to allow air through the air cleaner opening. Depending on outside temperature, this may take 10 to 15 minutes. To speed up this check you can reconnect the air duct, drive the vehicle, then check to see if the damper is completely open.

7   If the thermo-controlled air cleaner is not operating properly, see Chapter 6 for more information.

37   Positive Crankcase Ventilation (PCV) valve and hose check and replacement (every 30,000 miles or 24 months)

Refer to illustration 37.2

1   The PCV valve is located in the intake manifold below the carburetor or throttle body (1989 and earlier models) or in the valve cover (1990 and later models).

2   Remove the PCV valve **(see illustration)**. **Note:** *It may be necessary to first remove the hose from the PCV valve, then unscrew the PCV valve and reattach the hose.*

3   With the engine idling at normal operating temperature, place your finger over the end of the valve. If there is no vacuum at the valve, check for a plugged hose. Replace the hose if it's plugged or deteriorated. If the hose is good, replace the valve.

4   When purchasing a replacement PCV valve, make sure it's for your particular vehicle and engine size. Compare the old valve with the new one to make sure they're the same.

38   Air Induction valve filter replacement (1982 and 1983 models only) (every 30,000 miles or 24 months)

Refer to illustration 38.1

1   Remove the screws, detach the air induction valve filter housing and remove the filter **(see illustration)**.

2   Place the new filter in position, reinstall the housing and tighten the screws securely.

39   Vacuum control modulator valve and Idle Speed Control (ISC) modulator filter replacement (1985 through 1987 49-state models only) (every 30,000 miles or 24 months)

Refer to illustration 39.1

1   Remove the air cleaner housing for access and remove the filters from the vacuum control and idle speed control actuators **(see illustration)**.

2   Replace the filters with new ones.

Air induction valve filter

38.1 Detach the air induction valve filter

Vacuum control modulator valve filter

Idle speed control actuator filter

39.1 Locations of the vacuum control modulator and idle speed control actuator filters

40.2 The exhaust gas sensor harness must be plugged and the ECC harness disconnected

40.7 The oxygen sensor (arrow) is mounted in the exhaust manifold

40.12 Push the reset button on the relay located under the right side of the dash

40 Oxygen sensor check and replacement (every 30,000 miles or 24 months)

Refer to illustrations 40.2, 40.7, 40.12, 40.13a and 40.13b

Check

1   On 1982 through 1987 models, the light in the instrument cluster marked ECC (California and MPG models) or Sensor (49-state models) will come on at the specified intervals, indicating that the oxygen sensor system requires service. Check the sensor using the procedure below and replace it with a new one if it fails. After checking and/or replacing the oxygen sensor, reset the light to turn it off (see reset procedure below). On later models without a sensor checking system, refer to Chapter 6 for oxygen sensor testing information.
2   With the engine off, connect the oxygen sensor inspection harness and unplug the ECC harness test connector **(see illustration)**.
3   With the engine at normal operating temperature, run the engine for about five minutes at approximately 2000 rpm with no load.
4   The instrument cluster light should not come on.
5   Plug in the ECC connector and make

sure the cluster light flashes five or more times over a ten second interval.
6   If the oxygen sensor fails either test, refer to Chapter 6 for information on checking the oxygen sensor.

Replacement

7   The oxygen sensor is threaded into the exhaust pipe or manifold **(see illustration)**.
8   Unplug the connector and unscrew the sensor with a suitable deep socket or box-end wrench.
9   Use a tap to clean the threads in the exhaust pipe or manifold.
10   If the old sensor is to be reinstalled, apply anti-seize compound to the threads. New sensors will already have the anti-seize compound on the threads.
11   Install the sensor and tighten it securely.
Reset
12   After checking the oxygen sensor, the light can be reset by pressing the button on the side of the relay **(see illustration)**.
13   The manufacturer doesn't require this check after 90,000 miles, so the harness connector located above the fuse block can be unplugged at this time **(see illustrations)**.

41 Valve clearance check and adjustment (1991 and later GA16DE engine only) (every 60,000 miles or 48 months)

Refer to illustrations 41.6a, 41.6b, 41.7, 41.9a, 41.9b and 41.10
Note: *The manufacturer recommends this procedure at the specified interval if the valve gear makes excessive noise. The following procedure requires the use of a special valve lifter tool.*
1   Disconnect the cable from the negative terminal of the battery.
2   Disconnect the air cleaner duct or other components which will interfere with valve cover removal.
3   Blow out the recessed area between the camshafts with compressed air, if available, to remove any debris that might fall into the cylinders, then remove the spark plugs (see Section 24).

40.13a 1986 and earlier model warning light connector

40.13b 1987 warning light connector location

41.6a When the no. 1 piston is at TDC on the compression stroke, the valve clearances for the no. 1 and no. 3 cylinder exhaust valves and the no. 1 and no. 2 cylinder intake valves can be measured

41.6b Measure the clearance for each valve with a feeler gauge of the specified thickness - if the clearance is correct, you should feel a slight drag on the gauge as you pull it out

41.7 When the no. 4 piston is at TDC on the compression stroke, the valve clearances for the no. 2 and no. 4 exhaust valves and the no. 3 and no. 4 intake valves can be measured

4   Remove the valve cover (see Chapter 2A).

5   Refer to Chapter 2A and position the number 1 piston at TDC on the compression stroke.

6   Measure the clearances of the indicated valves with a feeler gauge of the specified thickness **(see illustrations)**. Record the measurements which are out of specification. They will be used later to determine the required replacement shims.

7   Turn the crankshaft one complete revolution and realign the timing marks. Measure the remaining valves **(see illustration)**.

8   After all the valve clearances have been measured, turn the crankshaft pulley until the camshaft lobe above the first valve which you intend to adjust is pointing up, away from the shim.

9   Position the notch in the valve lifter toward the spark plug. Then press down the valve lifter with a special valve lifter tool, or equivalent, available at most parts stores

(see illustration). Place the special valve lifter tool in position as shown, with the longer jaw of the tool gripping the lower edge of the cast lifter boss and the upper, shorter jaw gripping the upper edge of the lifter itself. Press down the valve lifter by squeezing the handles of the valve lifter tool together and remove the adjusting shim with a small screwdriver or a pair of tweezers **(see illustration)**. Note that the wire hook on the end of one valve lifter tool handle can be used to clamp both handles together to keep the lifter depressed while the shim is removed.

10   Measure the thickness of the shim with a micrometer **(see illustration)**. To calculate the correct thickness of a replacement shim that will place the valve clearance within the specified value, use the following formula:

Intake side: $N = R + (M - 0.015\text{-inch})$
Exhaust side: $N = R + (M - 0.018\text{-inch})$
$R = $ *thickness of the old shim*
$M = $ *valve clearance measured*
$N = $ *thickness of the new shim*

11   Select a shim with a thickness as close

as possible to the valve clearance calculated. Shims, which are available in 50 sizes in increments of 0.0020-inch (0.050 mm), range in size from 0.1005-inch (2.00 mm) to 0.125-inch (2.98 mm). **Note:** *Through careful analysis of the shim sizes needed to bring all the out-of-specification valve clearances within specification, it is often possible to simply move a shim that has to come out anyway to another valve lifter requiring a shim of that particular size, thereby reducing the number of new shims that must be purchased.*

12   Place the special valve lifter tool in position as shown in **illustration 41.9a,** with the longer jaw of the tool gripping the lower edge of the cast lifter boss and the upper, shorter jaw gripping the upper edge of the lifter itself, press down the valve lifter by squeezing the handles of the valve lifter tool together and install the new adjusting shim (note that some valve lifter tools have a wire hook on the end that can be used to clamp the handles together to keep the lifter depressed while the shim is inserted). Measure the clearance with a feeler gauge to make sure that your calculations are correct.

13   Repeat this procedure until all the valves which are out of clearance have been corrected.

14   Installation of the spark plugs, valve cover, spark plug wires and boots, accelerator cable bracket, etc. is the reverse of removal.

41.9a Install the valve lifter tool as shown and squeeze the handles together to lower the valve lifter so the shim can be removed

41.9b Remove the shim with a small screwdriver, a pair of tweezers or a magnet

41.10 Measure the shim thickness with a micrometer

Chapter 2 Part A Engines

Contents

2A

Specifications

General

Displacement	
E15	1488cc (90.80 cubic inches)
E16/GA16	1597cc (97.45 cubic inches)
SR20	1998cc (121.92 cubic inches)
Cylinder numbers (drivebelt end-to-transaxle end)	1-2-3-4
Firing order	1-3-4-2

FRONT   1990 and earlier

Warpage limits

Cylinder head-to-block surface	0.004 inch

Camshaft

FRONT   1991 and later

The blackened terminal shown on the distributor cap indicates the Number One spark plug wire position

Cylinder location and distributor rotation

Thrust clearance (endplay)	
1982 through 1988	0.0059 to 0.0114 inch
1989 and 1990	0.0012 to 0.0051 inch
1991 through 1994	0.0022 to 0.0055 inch
Camshaft journal diameter	
1982 through 1988	
No. 1, 3 and 5	1.6515 to 1.6522 inches
No. 2 and 4	1.6498 to 1.6505 inches
1989 and 1990	1.6510 to 1.6518 inches
1991 through 1994	
SR20	1.0998 to 1.1006 inches
GA16	
No. 1	1.0998 to 1.1006 inches
No. 2 through 5	0.9423 to 0.9431 inches
Camshaft bearing inside diameter	
1982 through 1990	1.6535 to 1.6545 inches
Bearing oil clearance	
1982 through 1988	
Standard	
No. 1, 3 and 5	0.0014 to 0.0030 inch
No. 2 and 4	0.0031 to 0.0047 inch
Service limit	
No. 1, 3 and 5	0.0059 inch
No. 2 and 4	0.0079 inch
1989 through 1994	
Standard	0.0018 to 0.0034 inch
Service limit	0.0059 inch

Camshaft (continued)

Runout limit (all)	0.004 inch maximum
Intake lobe height	
1982 through 1988	1.4128 to 1.4226 inches
1989 and 1990	1.4147 to 1.4222 inches
1991 through 1994	
SR20	1.5121 to 1.5196 inches
GA16	1.5984 to 1.6059 inches
Exhaust lobe height	
1982 through 1988	1.4031 to 1.4130 inches
1989 and 1990	1.4073 to 1.4148 inches
1991 through 1994	
SR20	1.4929 to 1.5004 inches
GA16	1.5701 to 1.5776 inches

Oil pump

1982 through 1988	
Outer rotor-to-pump body clearance	0.0059 to 0.0083 inch
Side clearance (with gasket)	0.0020 to 0.0047 inch
Rotor tip clearance	less than 0.0047 inch
1989 through 1994 (except SR20)	
Body-to-outer gear clearance	0.0045 to 0.0079 inch
Inner gear-to-crescent clearance	0.0085 to 0.0129 inch
Outer gear-to-crescent clearance	0.0083 to 0.0126 inch
Body-to-inner gear clearance	0.0020 to 0.0035 inch
Body-to-outer gear clearance	0.0020 to 0.0043 inch
1991 through 1994 (SR20)	
Body-to-outer gear clearance	0.0045 to 0.0079 inch
Inner gear-to-outer gear tip clearance	less than 0.0071 inch
Body-to-inner gear clearance	0.0020 to 0.0035 inch
Body-to-outer gear clearance	0.0020 to 0.0043 inch
Rocker arm shaft diameter	
1981 to 1988	0.7866 to 0.7874 inch
1989 to 1990	0.8653 to 0.8661 inch

Torque specifications

	Ft-lbs (unless otherwise indicated)
Intake manifold bolts/nuts	12 to 15
Exhaust manifold-to-block bolts/nuts	12 to 15
Crankshaft pulley-to-crankshaft bolt	
1982 through 1985	83 to 108
1986 through 1988	80 to 94
1989 through 1994 (except SR20)	98 to 112
1991 through 1994 (SR20)	105 to 112
Flywheel bolts	
1982 through 1988	58 to 65
1989 through 1994	61 to 69
Driveplate bolts	69 to 76
Cylinder head bolts	
1982 and 1983	
Step 1	29 to 33
Step 2	51 to 54
1984 through 1988	
Step 1	22
Step 2	51
Step 3	Loosen all bolts completely
Step 4	22
Step 5	51 to 54
1989 through 1994 (GA16)	
Step 1 (bolts 1 through 10)	22
Step 2 (bolts 1 through 10)	43
Step 3 (bolts 1 through 10)	Loosen all bolts completely
Step 4 (bolts 1 through 10)	22
Step 5 (bolts 1 through 10)	43 to 47
Step 6 (bolts 11 through 15)	55 to 73 in-lbs
1991 through 1994 (SR20)	
Step 1	29
Step 2	58
Step 3	Loosen all bolts completely
Step 4	25 to 33
Step 5	Tighten an additional 90 degrees
Step 6	Tighten an additional 90 degrees

Torque specifications (continued)

	Ft-lbs (unless otherwise indicated)
Camshaft bearing cap bolts (1991 through 1994)	
GA16	80 to 104 in-lbs
SR20	
All except distributor bracket bolts	80 to 104 in-lbs
Distributor bracket bolts	13 to 19
Camshaft sprocket bolt	
1982 and 1983 (E15)	51 to 69 in-lbs.
1983 through 1988 (E16)	78 to 104 in-lbs.
1989 through 1994 (except SR20)	72 to 94 ft.-lbs.
1991 through 1994 (SR20)	101 to 116 ft-lbs.
Idler sprocket bolt (GA16DE only)	32 to 43
Engine mount through-bolts	
1982 through 1985	29 to 36
1986 through 1988	29 to 40
1989 through 1994	33 to 40
Oil pump-to-block bolts	
1982 and 1983 (E15)	80 to 104 in-lbs
1983 through 1986 (E16)	69 to 86 in-lbs
1987 and 1988	144 to 180 in-lbs
Oil pump-to-front cover bolts	
1989 and 1990	43 to 61 in-lbs
1991 through 1994	
GA16	55 to 73 in-lbs
SR20	56 to 66 in-lbs
Oil pump-to-front cover screws	
1989 and 1990	26 to 43 in-lbs
1991 through 1994	32 to 44 in-lbs
Oil pick-up (strainer) nuts/bolts	55 to 73 in-lbs
Oil pan-to-block bolts	
1982 through 1986	32 to 44 in-lbs
1987 through 1994 (except SR20)	55 to 73 in-lbs
1991 through 1994 (SR20)	
Aluminum section-to-block	
Large bolts	12 to 14
Small nuts	56 to 66 in-lbs
Steel pan-to aluminum section	56 to 66 in-lbs
Rocker arm shaft bolts	
1982 through 1988	12 to 15
1989 through 1990	27 to 31
Valve cover bolts/nuts	
1982 through 1986	34 to 69 in-lbs
1987 and 1988	
Step 1	16-34-in-lbs
Step 2	34 to 51 in-lbs
1989 through 1994 (except SR20DE)	16 to 34 in-lbs
1991 through 1994 (SR20DE)	69 to 86 in-lbs

2A

1 General information

This Part of Chapter 2 is devoted to in-vehicle repair procedures for all engines. All information concerning engine removal and installation and engine block and cylinder head overhaul can be found in Part B of this Chapter.

The following repair procedures are based on the assumption that the engine is installed in the vehicle. If the engine has been removed from the vehicle and mounted on a stand, many of the steps outlined in this Part of Chapter 2 will not apply.

The Specifications included in this Part of Chapter 2 apply only to the procedures contained in this Part. Part B of Chapter 2 contains the Specifications necessary for cylinder head and engine block rebuilding.

The 1982 and 1983 Sentras were equipped with a 1488cc, SOHC, carbureted 4-cylinder engine(E15). In 1983, an additional, slightly larger version (E16, 1597cc) was offered and became the standard engine until 1989. The E15 and E16 engines feature an external oil pump driven by an internal jackshaft, adjustable rocker arms, two valve per cylinder, and a timing belt. In 1989 and 1990, the standard engine type in the Sentra was the GA16i, also 1597cc, but equipped with a timing chain, hydraulic lifters, a three-valve head, and an oil pump inside the front cover. In 1991 two new engines replaced the earlier models. The GA16DE (1597cc) and SR20DE (1998cc) both utilize DOHC and four-valves-per-cylinder. The main difference between them being that the GA16DE has two timing chains, and the SR20DE has only one.

2 Repair operations possible with the engine in the vehicle

Warning: *Some later models are equipped with airbags. The airbag Is armed and can deploy (inflate) any time the battery is connected. To prevent accidental deployment (and possible injury), disconnect the negative battery cable whenever working near airbag components. After the battery is disconnected, wait at least ten minutes before beginning work (the system has a back-up capacitor that must fully discharge). See Chapter 12 for more information.*

Many major repair operations can be accomplished without removing the engine from the vehicle.

Clean the engine compartment and the exterior of the engine with some type of

3.4 The crankshaft can be turned with a ratchet and socket on the crankshaft pulley bolt. It is necessary on some models to remove the plastic splash shield for access

3.8a Timing mark location on early models

3.8b Timing mark location on later models

degreaser before any work is done. It will make the job easier and help keep dirt out of the internal areas of the engine.

Depending on the components involved, it may be helpful to remove the hood to improve access to the engine as repairs are performed (refer to Chapter 11 if necessary). Cover the fenders to prevent damage to the paint. Special pads are available, but an old bedspread or blanket will also work.

If vacuum, exhaust, oil or coolant leaks develop, indicating a need for gasket or seal replacement, the repairs can generally be made with the engine in the vehicle. The intake and exhaust manifold gaskets, oil pan gasket, crankshaft oil seals and cylinder head gasket are all accessible with the engine in place.

Exterior engine components, such as the intake and exhaust manifolds, the oil pan, the oil pump, the water pump, the starter motor, the alternator, the distributor and the fuel system components can be removed for repair with the engine in place.

Since the cylinder head can be removed without pulling the engine, camshaft and valve component servicing can also be accomplished with the engine in the vehicle. Replacement of the timing belt and pulleys is also possible with the engine in the vehicle.

In extreme cases caused by a lack of necessary equipment, repair or replacement of piston rings, pistons, connecting rods and rod bearings is possible with the engine in the vehicle. However, this practice is not recommended because of the cleaning and preparation work that must be done to the components involved.

3   Top Dead Center (TDC) for number one piston - locating

Refer to illustrations 3.4, 3.8a and 3.8b
Note: *The following procedure is based on the assumption that the distributor is correctly installed. If you are trying to locate TDC to install the distributor correctly, piston position must be determined by feeling for compression at the number one spark plug*

hole, then aligning the ignition timing marks as described in step 8.

1   Top Dead Center (TDC) is the highest point in the cylinder that each piston reaches as it travels up-and-down when the crankshaft turns. Each piston reaches TDC on the compression stroke and again on the exhaust stroke, but TDC generally refers to piston position on the compression stroke.

2   Positioning the number one piston at TDC is an essential part of many procedures, such as camshaft and timing belt/chain removal and distributor removal.

3   Before beginning this procedure, be sure to place the transmission in Neutral and apply the parking brake or block the rear wheels. Also, disable the ignition system by disconnecting the primary (low voltage) electrical connectors at the distributor) (see Chapter 5). Remove the spark plugs (see Chapter 1).

4   In order to bring any piston to TDC, the crankshaft must be turned using one of the methods outlined below. When looking at the front of the engine (timing belt end), normal crankshaft rotation is clockwise.

   a) *The preferred method is to turn the crankshaft with a socket and ratchet attached to the bolt threaded into the front of the crankshaft* **(see illustration)**.

   b) *A remote starter switch, which may save some time, can also be used. Follow the instructions included with the switch. Once the piston is close to TDC, use a socket and ratchet as described in the previous paragraph.*

   c) *If an assistant is available to turn the ignition switch to the Start*

      position in short bursts, you can get the piston close to TDC without a remote starter switch. Make sure your assistant is out of the vehicle, away from the ignition switch, then use a socket and ratchet as described in Paragraph a) to complete the procedure.

5   Note the position of the terminal for the number one spark plug wire on the distributor cap. If the terminal isn't marked, follow the plug wire from the number one cylinder spark plug to the cap.

6   Use a felt-tip pen or chalk to make a mark on the distributor body directly under the number one terminal.

7   Detach the cap from the distributor and set it aside (see Chapter 1 if necessary).

8   Turn the crankshaft (see Step 4) until the notch in the crankshaft pulley is aligned with the 0 on the timing plate (located at the front of the engine) **(see illustrations)**.

9   Look at the distributor rotor - it should be pointing directly at the mark you made on the distributor body.

10   If the rotor is 180-degrees off, the number one piston is at TDC on the exhaust stroke.

11   To get the piston to TDC on the compression stroke, turn the crankshaft one complete revolution (360-degrees) clockwise. The rotor should now be pointing at the mark on the distributor. When the rotor is pointing at the number one spark plug wire terminal in the distributor cap and the ignition timing marks are aligned, the number one piston is at TDC on the compression stroke. **Note:** *It it's impossible to align the ignition timing marks when the rotor is pointing at the mark on the distributor body, the timing belt may have jumped the teeth on the pulleys or may have been installed incorrectly.*

12   After the number one piston has been positioned at TDC on the compression stroke, TDC for any of the remaining pistons can be located by turning the crankshaft and following the firing order. Mark the remaining spark plug wire terminals on the distributor body just like you did for the number one terminal, then number the marks to correspond with the cylinder numbers. As you turn the crankshaft, the rotor will also turn. When it's pointing directly at one of the marks on the distributor, the piston for that particular cylinder is at TDC on the compression stroke.

4   Valve cover - removal and installation

Removal

Refer to illustrations 4.2 and 4.4

1   Disconnect the battery cable from the negative battery terminal. **Caution:** *If the stereo in your vehicle is equipped with an anti-theft system, make sure you have the correct activation code before disconnecting the battery.*

4.2 Carbureted models require disconnecting the following items for valve cover removal

1 *PCV (positive crankcase ventilation) hoses*
2 *Acorn nuts*
3 *Accelerator cable*

2   On carbureted models, detach the air intake breather duct, PCV hose, and throttle cable from the valve cover **(see illustration)**. On later models, remove the spark plug wires from the spark plugs, remove the PCV hoses, and remove the throttle cable from its brackets and position it out of the way.
3   Detach the spark plug wires from the clips on the valve cover.
4   Remove the acorn-type cap nuts and sealing washers, then detach the cover and gasket from the head. Later models are retained by screws around the cover's perimeter **(see illustration)**. If the cover is stuck to the head, bump the end with a wood block and a hammer to jar it loose. If that doesn't work, try to slip a flexible putty knife between the head and cover to break the seal. **Caution:** *Don't pry at the cover or housing-to-head joint or damage to the sealing surfaces may occur, leading to oil leaks after the cover is reinstalled.*
5   Remove the gasket from the valve cover.

Installation

6   The mating surfaces of the valve cover and cylinder head must be clean when the cover is installed. Use a gasket scraper to remove all traces of sealant and old gasket material, then clean the mating surfaces with

5.3 The various hoses should be marked to ensure correct reinstallation

4.4 On later models, remove the PCV hoses, remove the throttle cable from its brackets and remove the retaining screws (arrows)

lacquer thinner or acetone. If there's residue or oil on the mating surfaces when the cover is installed, oil leaks may develop.
7   Install the valve cover with a new gasket.
8   Tighten the nuts or screws to the torque listed in this Chapter's Specifications, starting with the center fasteners and working out toward each end.

---

5   Intake manifold - removal and installation

Removal

Refer to illustrations 5.3 and 5.6

1   If you're working on a fuel-injected model, relieve the fuel system pressure (see Chapter 4b). Disconnect the cable from the negative battery terminal. **Caution:** *If the stereo in your vehicle is equipped with an anti-theft system, make sure you have the correct activation code before disconnecting the battery.*
2   Drain the cooling system (see Chapter 1).
3   Label and detach all wire harnesses, control cables, coolant and vacuum hoses connected to the intake manifold **(see illustration)**. For carbureted engines, proceed to step 6.
4   Remove the fuel rail and injectors (see Chapter 4b).
5   Unbolt the intake manifold from the brace underneath (at the timing belt end of

5.6 Remove the air intake plenum first, giving better access to wires and hoses underneath

the manifold).There are three supports on the SR20DE engine.
6   Remove the mounting nuts/bolts, then detach the manifold from the engine. **Note:** *The intake manifold on later fuel-injected engines is a two-piece design. It is easier to remove the manifold in sections, rather than as one piece. Remove the plenum first, giving greater access to hose and pipes connected to the lower section* **(see illustration)**.

Installation

7   Use a scraper to remove all traces of old gasket material and sealant from the manifold and cylinder head, then clean the mating surfaces with lacquer thinner or acetone.
8   Install a new gasket, then position the manifold on the head and install the nuts/bolts.
9   Tighten the nuts/bolts in three or four equal steps to the torque listed in this Chapter's Specifications. Work from the center out towards the ends to avoid warping the manifold.
10   Install the remaining parts in the reverse order of removal. Refill the cooling system (see Chapter 1).
11   Before starting the engine, check the throttle linkage for smooth operation.
12   Run the engine and check for coolant and vacuum leaks.
13   Road test the vehicle and check for proper operation of all accessories.

---

6   Exhaust manifold - removal and Installation

Warning: *The engine must be completely cool before beginning this procedure.*

Removal

Refer to illustrations 6.3; 6.8, and 6.10

1   Disconnect the cable from the negative battery terminal. **Caution:** *If the stereo in your vehicle is equipped with an anti-theft system, make sure you have the correct activation code before disconnecting the battery.*
2   Remove the oxygen sensor (see Chapter 6).
3   Remove the heat shield from the manifold **(see illustration)**.

6.3 Remove the exhaust manifold heat shield

2A

6.8 Remove the nuts (arrows) retaining the exhaust pipe to the exhaust manifold

6.10 Remove the nuts and/or bolts attaching the exhaust manifold to the cylinder head and remove the manifold

7.16 Before removing the timing cover, remove the bolt retaining the ground wire terminals

4   Block the rear wheels and set the parking brake.

5   Support the front of the vehicle securely on jackstands (see Chapter 1).

6   Remove the engine splash shields.

7   Apply penetrating oil to the exhaust manifold-to-head and manifold-to-exhaust pipe mounting nuts/bolts.

8   From beneath the vehicle, disconnect the exhaust pipe from the exhaust manifold **(see illustration)**. Early models have only two nuts, later models have three.

9   Unbolt the exhaust pipe brace at the engine mount, if equipped.

10   Remove the manifold-to-head nuts/bolts and detach the manifold and gaskets **(see illustration)**.

Installation

11   Use a scraper to remove all traces of old gasket material and carbon deposits from the manifold and cylinder head mating surfaces.

12   Position the new exhaust manifold gaskets over the cylinder head studs.

13   Install the manifold and thread the mounting nuts/bolts into place.

14   Working from the center out, tighten the nuts/bolts to the torque listed in this Chapter's Specifications in three or four equal steps.

15   Reinstall the remaining parts in the reverse order of removal.

16   Run the engine and check for exhaust leaks.

7   Timing belt and sprockets (1982 through 1988 models) - removal, inspection and installation

Removal

Refer to illustrations 7.16, 7.17, 7.19a, 7.19b, 7.20 and 7.21

1   Disconnect the cable from the negative battery terminal. **Caution:** *If the stereo in your vehicle is equipped with an anti-theft system, make sure you have the correct activation code before disconnecting the battery.*

2   Block the rear wheels and set the parking brake.

3   Loosen the lug nuts on the right front wheel and raise the vehicle. Support the front of the vehicle securely on jackstands. Remove the right-front wheel.

4   Remove the right (passenger's) side engine splash shield and under-cover.

5   Remove the valve cover (see Section 4).

6   Remove the drivebelts, including alternator, air conditioning and/or power steering if equipped (see Chapter 1).

7   Remove the air cleaner (see Chapter 4).

8   Support the engine with a floor jack and a wood block. **Warning:** *DO NOT support the engine to the point where the vehicle comes off the jackstands. Just raise the engine up enough to unload the weight from the mounts.*

9   Unbolt the passenger-side engine

mount from the engine(see Section 19).

10   Remove the upper alternator bracket (see Chapter 5).

11   Remove the spark plugs.

12   Bring the engine to TDC on the number one cylinder (see Section 3). Check to be sure the rocker arms on the number one cylinder are loose. If they aren't, rotate the crankshaft 360-degrees (one complete revolution), clockwise.

13   Remove water pump pulley and crankshaft pulley.

14   Hold the damper/pulley from turning with a screwdriver or prybar wedged between the damper and engine block. **Caution:** *DON'T allow the prybar to bottom against the oil pan.* Remove the bolt.

15   Remove the damper/pulley. If necessary, pry it off with two large screwdrivers or use a bolt-type puller that bears on the hub of the damper. **Caution:** *DON'T use a jaw-type gear puller on the outer edge of the damper or damage the damper will result.*

16   Disconnect the ground wires attached to the bolt protruding through the cover **(see illustration)**.

17   With the engine mount pulled up for clearance, remove the timing belt covers and gaskets **(see illustration)**.

18   If you plan to reuse the timing belt, paint an arrow on the belt indicating direction of rotation.

19   Mark, or make note of, the positions of the timing alignment marks **(see illustrations)**.

7.17 With the engine supported by a jack from underneath, and the fasteners removed from the cover, lift up the front engine mount for clearance as the cover is removed

7.19a Note and highlight the position of the upper timing sprocket alignment marks (arrows)

7.19b Note and highlight the position of the lower timing sprocket alignment marks (arrows)

7.20 Timing belt and related component details

7.21 Loosen the tensioner locknut and rotate the tensioner with a screwdriver

7.23 Carefully inspect the timing belt for the conditions shown here

2A

20   Slide the timing belt guide (see illustration) off the end of the crankshaft.
21   Loosen the timing belt tensioner locknut and rotate the tensioner clockwise, then retighten the locknut (see illustration). Check that tensioner rotates freely.
22   Slip the timing belt off the sprockets.

Inspection

Refer to illustration 7.23
Caution: *Do not bend, twist or turn the timing belt inside out. Do not allow it to come in contact with oil, coolant or fuel. Do not turn the crankshaft or camshaft more than a few degrees (if necessary for tooth alignment) while the timing belt is removed, or valves may hit the pistons.*
23   If the belt teeth are cracked or missing (see illustration), the distributor, water pump, oil pump or camshaft may have

seized. **Caution:** *If the timing belt broke during engine operation, the valves may have come in contact with the pistons, causing damage. Check the valve clearance at the rocker arms (see Chapter 1), bent valves usually will have excessive clearance, indicating damage that will require head removal to repair.*
24   If there is noticeable wear or cracks in the belt, check to see if there are nicks or burrs on the sprockets.
25   Replace the timing belt with a new one if obvious wear or damage is noted or if it is the least bit questionable. Correct any problems which contributed to belt failure prior to belt installation. **Note:** *Professionals recommend replacing the belt whenever it is removed, since belt failure can lead to expensive engine damage. The factory recommends changing the belt at 60,000-mile intervals.*

Installation

Refer to illustrations 7.27, 7.30 and 7.31
26   Remove all dirt and oil from the timing belt area at the front of the engine.
27   Recheck the camshaft and crankshaft timing marks to be sure they are properly aligned (see illustration).
28   Install the timing belt on the crankshaft, jackshaft and camshaft pulleys. If the original belt is being reinstalled make sure the arrow is pointed in the correct direction (clockwise).
29   Slip the belt guide onto the crankshaft with the cupped side facing out.
30   Loosen the timing belt tensioner locknut and rotate the tensioner against belt (see illustration).
31   Turn the camshaft sprocket clockwise approximately 20 degrees (two cogs) clockwise, this will load the proper tension on the timing belt (see illustration).

7.27 Camshaft and crankshaft sprocket alignment mark details

7.30 Loosen the tensioner locknut and apply pressure against the belt (belt not shown for clarity)

7.31 Rotate the camshaft sprocket approximately twenty degrees clockwise to properly tension the timing belt

8.10 Unbolt the engine mount and front support bracket

8.15 Remove the chain tensioner from the front cover

8.17 Remove the cam sprocket cover from the cylinder head

32   Tighten the tensioner locknut without allowing the tensioner to rotate.

33   Slowly turn the crankshaft clockwise two complete revolutions (720-degrees) from the alignment marks, by hand. **Caution:** *If you feel resistance while rotating the engine by hand, do not use force. The valves may be contacting the pistons due to incorrect valve timing.*

34   Recheck the timing marks. If the marks are not aligned exactly as shown, repeat the belt installation procedure. **Caution:** *DO NOT start the engine until you're absolutely certain that the timing belt is installed correctly. Serious and costly engine damage could occur if the belt is installed wrong.*

35   Reinstall the remaining parts in the reverse order of removal.

36   Start the engine and check for proper operation.

8   Timing chain (1989 and 1990 models) - removal, inspection and installation

Removal

Refer to illustrations 8.10, 8.15, 8.17, 8.19 and 8.20

1   Refer to Section 7, and perform steps 1 through 7.

2   Support the engine with a chain from overhead. **Warning:** *DO NOT support the engine to the point where the vehicle comes off the jackstands. Just raise the engine up*

enough to unload the weight from the mounts.

3   Remove the passenger-side engine mount (see Section 19).

4   Remove the passenger side engine mount insulator (see Section 19).

5   Remove the front exhaust pipe.

6   Remove the center crossmember.

7   Drain the engine oil and remove the oil pan (see Section 15).

8   Remove the drivebelts for the alternator, power steering and air-conditioner, if equipped.

9   Remove the power steering pump bracket.

10   Remove the engine mounting bracket **(see illustration)**.

11   Remove the spark plugs.

8.20 Timing chain component details, with the front cover removed

12   Drain the cooling system (see Chapter 1).

13   Remove the water pump.

14   Position the engine at TDC for the number one cylinder on its compression stroke (see Section 3).

15   Remove the chain tensioner from the front cover **(see illustration)**.

16   Remove crankshaft pulley.

17   Remove the cam-sprocket cover from the front of the cylinder head **(see illustration)**.

18   Unbolt and remove the front cover.

19   Using a suitable tool which will fit into the sprocket's holes, hold the cam sprocket from turning and unbolt the camshaft sprocket. **(see illustration)**.

20   After removing the two chain guides, the chain, camshaft sprocket and crankshaft sprocket can be removed **(see illustration)**.

Inspection

21   Inspect both camshaft and crankshaft sprockets for wear of the teeth and keyways. Inspect the chain for cracks or excessive wear of the rollers. Inspect the facing of the chain guides for excessive wear.

Installation

Refer to illustration 8.22

22   Install the timing chain together with the camshaft and crankshaft sprockets, aligning the mating marks of the chain with the mating marks on the sprockets. The top of the chain has a colored link to line up with the camshaft sprocket, while the opposite end of the chain has a colored link to line up with the crankshaft sprocket **(see illustration)**. When installed, the timing chain should have 23 links equally on either side, between the top and bottom mating marks.

23   Install the camshaft sprocket bolt and washer (the washer should have its chamfered edge toward the sprocket) and using a suitable tool to hold the camshaft, tighten the bolt to the torque listed in this Chapter's Specifications.

24   Install the timing chain guides. Apply RTV sealant to the front cover sealing surface and install the cover. **Caution:** *When*

8.19 Use a suitable tool to hold the camshaft sprocket while removing the camshaft sprocket bolt

8.22 Timing chain alignment marks (1989 and 1990 models)

installing the front cover, align the flats on the oil pump with the flats on the crankshaft, and be careful to not disturb the gasket under the front end of the cylinder head. It may help to lubricate the top of the front cover with grease to allow it to slide in easier under the head. Install the timing chain tensioner using a new gasket.

25 Reinstall the remaining parts in the reverse order of removal.

9 Timing chain (1991 through 1994 models) - removal, inspection and installation

GA16DE engines

Removal

Refer to illustrations 9.6a, 9.6b, 9.10, 9.12, 9.13, 9.15, 9.16, 9.17, 9.19 and 9.21

9.13 With the sprocket cover removed, remove the following upper timing chain components:

1 Valve Timing Control (VTC) cam sprocket
2 Upper chain guide
3 Idler chain guide
4 Upper chain tensioner
5 Cover gusset stud

9.6a Remove the bolts (arrows) from the front engine-to-transaxle brace and remove the brace

9.10 With the engine supported by a jack from underneath, remove the front engine mount (A) and front brace (B)

1 Refer to Section 7, and perform steps 1 through 7. Valve cover screws should be removed in sequence, staring with the front, then the rear, then the center fasteners.
2 Relieve the fuel line pressure (see Chapter 4).
3 Drain the cooling system (see Chapter 1).
4 Remove the air duct connected to the intake manifold.
5 Remove the thermostat housing from the water pump, and the water pump pulley (see Chapter 3).
6 Remove the two engine-to-transaxle braces **(see illustrations)**.
7 Drain the engine oil and remove the oil pan and oil pump pick-up (see Section 15).
8 Position the engine at TDC for number one cylinder (see Section 3).
9 Lower the vehicle and support the

9.15 Remove the lower chain tensioner (arrow)

9.6b Remove the bolts (arrows) from the rear engine-to-transaxle brace and remove the brace

9.12 Remove the cam sprocket cover

engine with a jack and wood block placed under the front main bearing saddle.
10 Remove the engine mount at the front (passenger side) of the engine and the brace around the front of the cylinder head **(see illustration)**.
11 Remove the distributor (see Chapter 5).
12 Remove the cam sprocket cover **(see illustration)**.
13 Remove the two upper chain guides, cover gusset (stud) and upper chain tensioner **(see illustration)**.
14 Remove the crankshaft pulley.
15 Remove the lower chain tensioner from the front cover **(see illustration)**.
16 Hold the exhaust camshaft with a wrench in the hex-shaped area, while using another wrench to remove the bolt from the cam sprocket. **(see illustration)**.

9.16 To remove either camshaft sprocket, hold the flats on the cam with a wrench as shown, while removing the sprocket bolt

2A

9.17 Remove the VTC sprocket from the intake camshaft

9.19 Note the numbers and positions of the camshaft bearing caps, unbolt the bearing caps and remove the camshafts

9.21 The cylinder head may be removed with the exhaust and intake manifolds still in place

17   Hold the intake cam and remove the VTC cam sprocket, leaving the upper chain collapsed **(see illustration)**.
18   Remove the idler sprocket bolt.
19   Loosen the camshaft bearing caps in two or three steps, in numerical sequence (see Section 12). The camshaft bearing caps have arrows indicating the front of the engine, are numbered from 1 to 5, and are stamped with an "I" or an "E", to indicate intake or exhaust. **Caution:** *Keep the caps in order. They must go back in the same*

location they were removed from. Number these caps, if there are no identification marks. Remove the bearing caps and the camshafts **(see illustration)**.
20   Following the reverse order of the tightening sequence (see Section 14), loosen the head bolts in several steps and remove them (see Section 14).
21   With all hoses and wires disconnected and marked, the cylinder head can be removed with the exhaust manifold and intake manifold still attached **(see illustration)**.
22   Remove the timing cover.
23   Remove the upper and lower chains and the idler sprocket.

Inspection

24   Inspect camshaft, idler and crankshaft sprockets for wear of the teeth and keyways. Inspect the chains for cracks or excessive wear of the rollers. Inspect the facing of the chain guides for excessive wear.

Installation

Refer to illustrations 9.26, 9.27 and 9.30
25   Install the lower chain with either of its two mating (silver-colored) links aligned with the mark on the crank pulley.
26   Position the idler sprocket in place with its mating mark aligned with the silver-colored link on the lower chain **(see illustration)**.
27   Apply a bead of RTV sealant to the timing cover sealing surface and install the cover. **Note:** *Be sure to apply sealant to the water passage sealing area, and make sure new O-rings are in place* **(see illustration)**.
28   Position the upper chain in place on the idler sprocket with its gold-colored link aligned with the mating mark on the idler's smaller front sprocket **(see illustration 9.26)**.
29   Install the cylinder head with a new gasket (see Section 14). Install the camshafts (see Section 12).
30   The remainder of the installation is the reverse of the disassembly sequence. Install the cam sprockets and upper chain with the cams at TDC and the upper chain aligned with its silver links aligned with the sprocket mating marks **(see illustration)**. Do not install the lower chain tensioner until after the cam

9.26 Timing chain alignment details - GA16DE engine

9.27 Install new O-rings (A) and apply sealant to both mating edges of the timing cover and to the water-passage sealing area (B)

9.30 Alignment details of the upper timing chain and sprockets (arrows) (GA16DE engine)

9.32 Upper timing chain alignment marks (SR20DE engine)

9.34 Location of chain tensioner

9.39 The knock sensor harness connector is located under the intake manifold

2A

and idler sprockets and chains are properly aligned. Tighten all the sprocket bolts to the torque listed in this Chapter's Specifications.

SR20DE engines
Removal
Refer to illustrations 9.32, 9.34, 9.39 and 9.42

31 Refer to GA16DE engine disassembly sequence and perform steps 1 through 10. **Note:** *This engine has only one timing chain.*

32 Rotate the engine until the left and right camshaft sprocket marks are aligned **(see illustration)**.

33 Remove the crankshaft pulley.

34 Remove the chain tensioner **(see illustration)**.

35 Remove the distributor.

36 Remove the upper chain guide and, using a suitable tool to hold the camshafts, remove the camshaft sprockets.

37 Remove the starter (see Chapter 5).

38 Loosen the camshaft bearing caps in two or three steps, in numerical sequence (see Section 12). Carefully lift out the camshafts, oil tubes and baffle plate.

39 Remove the knock sensor harness connector **(see illustration)**.

40 Loosen the cylinder head bolts in sequence and remove them (see Section 14).

41 Lift off the cylinder head with intake manifold lower section and exhaust manifold connected.

42 Remove the front cover **(see illustration)**.

43 Remove the timing chain and the two chain guides.

9.42 Location of the front cover bolts

Inspection
44 Inspect camshaft, and crankshaft sprockets for wear of the teeth and keyways. Inspect the chain for cracks or excessive wear of the rollers. Inspect the facing of the chain guides for excessive wear.

Installation
Refer to illustrations 9.45, 9.46, 9.48 and 9.49

45 Install the timing chain with the bottom mating mark aligned with the mark on the crankshaft sprocket **(see illustration)**.

46 Install the chain guides and the front cover, keeping the excess upper chain laying over the right-hand guide (as you face the front of the engine). Apply a bead of RTV sealant to the outer perimeter of the cover, but not to the groove indicated **(see illustration)**.

47 Install the cylinder head (see

9.45 Timing chain-to-crankshaft sprocket alignment marks (SR20DE engine)

Section 14). Install the camshafts (see Section 12).

48 Install the camshaft sprockets, aligning the silver-colored chain links with the mating marks on the cam sprockets **(see illustration)**. Tighten the camshaft sprocket bolts to the torque listed in this Chapter's Specifications.

49 Retract the chain tensioner by holding the cam stopper back while depressing the sleeve until the hook can be latched over the pin **(see illustration)**. Install the chain tensioner with the (cast-in) arrow pointing to the front of the engine. The hook will be released automatically as the tensioner is bolted in.

50 The remainder of the installation is the reverse of the removal procedure.

9.46 Apply sealant to the front cover in the areas indicated

9.48 Timing chain alignment mark details (SR20DE engine)

9.49 The chain tensioner must be retracted before installation, and installed with the (cast-in) arrow pointing to the front of the engine

10 Crankshaft front oil seal, camshaft oil seal, jackshaft oil seal - replacement

Models with a timing belt (1982 to 1988)

Refer to illustrations 10.3 and 10.7

1   Remove the timing belt (see Section 7).
2   Remove the camshaft and crankshaft timing belt sprockets.
3   Remove the upper front cover from the cylinder head **(see illustration)**, and the lower front cover from the block.
4   Because of the work necessary to access the seals, all three seals should be replaced at the same time.
5   Wrap the tip of a small screwdriver with tape, and use it to pry out the seals, being careful not to damage the seal bores.
6   Clean the bores in the housings and coat the outer edge of the new seals with engine oil or multi-purpose grease. Also lubricate the seal lips.
7   Using a socket with an outside diameter slightly smaller than the outside diameter of the seal, carefully drive the new seal into place with a hammer **(see illustration)**. Make sure it's installed squarely and driven in to the same depth as the original. If a socket isn't available, a short section of large diameter pipe will also work. Check the seal after installation to make sure the garter spring didn't pop out of place.
8   Reinstall the crankshaft sprocket and timing belt (see Section 7).
9   Run the engine and check for oil leaks.

10.3 The camshaft oil seal is located in the upper front cover on engines equipped with a timing belt

Models with a timing chain (1989-1994)

These models do not have a camshaft oil seal or jackshaft oil seal. Crankshaft oil seal replacement procedure is the same as for the timing-belt engines, and can be done with the timing cover on the engine.

11 Camshaft and rocker arms (1982 to 1990 models) - removal, inspection and installation

Note: *1982 to 1988 models utilize rocker arms with lash adjustment at the valve stem end, and require periodic adjustment. 1989 and 1990 models have rocker arms with hydraulic adjusters built-in, and do not require periodic adjustment.*

Removal

Refer to illustrations 11.5 and 11.8

1   Detach the cable from the negative terminal of the battery. **Caution:** *If the stereo in your vehicle is equipped with an anti-theft system, make sure you have the correct activation code before disconnecting the battery.*
2   Remove the valve cover (see Section 4).
3   Position the engine on TDC for number one cylinder(see Section 3).
4   Remove the timing belt/chain and the camshaft sprocket (see Section 7).
5   Use a dial indicator to check camshaft endplay **(see illustration)**. Mount the dial indicator so the gauge tip can be placed at

10.7 The seals can be pried or driven out, and new seals installed with a hammer and large socket

the end of the camshaft. Move the camshaft all the way to the rear and zero the dial indicator. Next, use a screwdriver to pry it all the way forward. If the endplay, the total amount of movement, exceeds the limit listed in this Chapter's Specifications, replace the camshaft and/or cylinder head.
6   Remove the cylinder head front cover (1982 to 1988 models only).
7   Loosen the bolts retaining the rocker shaft in two or three stages and lift the rocker arm assembly off the head.
8   On 1989 and 1990 models, remove the camshaft locator plate **(see illustration)**. Slide the camshaft out from the front of the head. **Note:** *On some models, it may be necessary to support the engine with a jack and, with the front engine mount removed, raise the belt/chain end up to allow enough clearance for the camshaft to be removed.*

Inspection

Refer to illustrations 11.9a, 11.9b, 11.14a and 11.14b

9   Examine the front of the rocker shaft for an identifying mark or stamp. If none is found, make a mark with paint or a punch. Remove the rocker arms from the shaft and clean all components with solvent or thinner. Keep the parts in order **(see illustrations)**.

11.5 With a dial indicator in place, pry the camshaft forward and back to check the camshaft endplay

11.8 Remove the camshaft locator plate and slide the camshaft out from the front of the cylinder head

11.9a Remove the rocker arm assembly, keeping the rocker arms, springs, and retainers in order

11.9b Rocker arm assembly details on 1989 and 1990 models, note the two intake rockers for each cylinder

11.14a Measure each journal diameter with a micrometer (if any journal measures less than the specified limit, replace the camshaft)

11.14b Measure the lobe heights - if any lobe height is less than the minimum listed in this Chapter's Specifications, replace that camshaft

Camshaft front view

11.18 Rotate the camshaft until the knock pin is at the twelve o'clock position

Caution: *The hydraulic lifters on 1989 and 1990 models are part of the rocker arms. These must be kept in a vertical plane (as installed) or oil may bleed out and air may enter. They may be stored on their side, submerged in a pan of engine oil.*

10   Inspect the rocker arms for excessive wear on the tips that contact the valve stem and camshaft.

11   Inspect the rocker arm shaft for scoring, excessive wear or other damage.

12   Slide each rocker arm, one at a time, onto the shaft to its normal position. Wiggle the rocker arm to check for freeplay, and compare this with the same action when the rocker arm is placed on an unworn section of the shaft. If there is a substantial difference, the rocker arm and/or shaft will need replacing.

13   The shaft can be measured with a micrometer in the area that the rocker arms ride, and the measurement compared to this Chapter's Specifications. If the shaft diameter is smaller than specified, it should be replaced.

14   The camshaft should be examined for signs of wear or scoring. Measure the camshaft journal diameter and lobe height with a micrometer **(see illustrations)**. Compare your measurements with this Chapter's Specifications. If the camshaft has worn beyond the specified limits, replace it with a new one. Measure the inside diameter of the camshaft bearing with an inside micrometer. Subtract the inside measurement from the camshaft journal diameter to determine the bearing oil clearance. If the bearing oil clearance is greater than the specified limit, replace the camshaft and/or the cylinder head.

Installation

Refer to illustration 11.18

15   Lubricate the camshaft journals and lobes with moly-base grease and install the camshaft into the cylinder head, being careful not to nick the lobes or bearing surfaces.

16   On 1988 and earlier models, install a new camshaft oil seal in the front cover (see Section 10), and bolt the cover to the cylinder head. On 1989 and 1990 models, install the locator plate.

17   Lubricate the rocker arms and shaft with clean engine oil, and assemble the arms on the shaft in proper sequence. Make sure the

marked end of the shaft is to the front. **Note:** *The center rocker shaft retainer has a small cutout which must be installed facing the exhaust side of the engine on 1982 through 1988 models, and toward the intake side on 1989 and 1990 models.*

18   Rotate the camshaft until the knock pin is in the twelve o'clock position **(see illustration)**. Install the camshaft sprocket, hold the sprocket with a suitable tool and tighten the bolt to the torque listed in this Chapter's Specifications.

19   Install the rocker arm shaft assembly and tighten the bolts to the torque listed in this Chapter's Specifications, working from the center out in two or three steps.

20   Install the timing belt or chain (see Sections 7 or 8). Rotate the crankshaft 360-degrees (number 4 cylinder TDC) and tighten the rocker arm bolts, again, to the torque listed in this Chapter's Specifications.

21   Install the remaining components in reverse order of disassembly and adjust valve clearances (see Chapter 1).

12   Camshaft (1991 through 1994 models) - removal, inspection and installation

Removal

Refer to illustrations 12.4, 12.7a, 12.7b and 12.9

1   Detach the cable from the negative terminal of the battery. **Caution:** *If the stereo*

in your vehicle is equipped with an anti-theft system, make sure you have the correct activation code before disconnecting the battery.

2   Remove the valve cover (see Section 4).

3   Remove the cam sprocket cover and cover gusset (stud).

4   Use a dial indicator to check camshaft endplay **(see illustration)**. Mount the dial indicator so the gauge tip can be placed at the end of the camshaft. Move the camshaft all the way to the rear and zero the dial indicator. Next, use a screwdriver to pry it all the way forward. If the endplay, the total amount of movement, exceeds the limit listed in this Chapter's Specifications, replace the camshaft and/or cylinder head.

5   Position the engine at TDC for number one cylinder (see Section 3) and remove the distributor (see Chapter 5).

6   Remove the camshaft sprockets and position the upper timing chain out of the way (see Section 9).

7   Loosen the camshaft bearing caps in two or three steps, in numerical sequence **(see illustrations)**. The camshaft bearing caps have arrows indicating the front of the engine. They are numbered from 1 to 5, and are stamped with an "I" or an "E" to indicate intake or exhaust. **Caution:** *Keep the caps in order. They must go back in the same location they were removed from. Number these caps, if there are no identification marks.*

8   Remove the bearing caps and camshafts.

12.4 A dial indicator is used as shown to check camshaft endplay

Loosen in numerical order.

12.7a Using the sequence shown, loosen the camshaft retainers in two or three steps (GA16DE engine)

12.7b Using the sequence shown, loosen the camshaft retainers in two or three steps (SR20DE engine)

12.9 Location of VTC solenoid on front/intake side of cylinder head - GA16DE engine

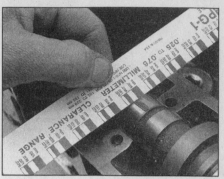

12.12 Compare the width of the crushed Plastigage to the scale on the envelope to determine the oil clearance

9   On 1991 through 1994 GA series engines, remove the Valve Timing Control (VTC) solenoid, located on the right-rear of the cylinder head, for inspection **(see illustration)**.

Inspection

Refer to illustrations 12.12 and 12.14

10   Visually examine the camshaft lobes, journals, bearing caps, pivot points and metal-to-metal contact areas. Check for score marks, pitting and evidence of overheating (blue, discolored areas). If wear is excessive or damage is evident, the component will have to be replaced.

11   Using a micrometer, measure camshaft journal diameter and lobe height **(see illustrations 11.14a and 11.14b)**, and compare your measurements to this Chapter's Specifications. If the lobe height is less than the minimum allowable, the camshaft is worn and must be replaced.

12   Check the oil clearance for each camshaft journal as follows:

a)   *Clean the bearing caps and the camshaft journals with lacquer thinner or acetone.*

b)   *Carefully lay the camshafts in place in the head. DON'T use any lubrication.*

c)   *Lay a strip of Plastigage on each journal.*

d)   *Install the bearing caps with the arrows pointing toward the front (timing chain end) of the engine.*

12.14 On GA16DE engines, the VTC solenoid can be tested by applying battery voltage to the terminals, the plunger should protrude

e)   *Tighten the bolts in sequence (use the sequence opposite the one shown in* **illustration 12.7b**) *to the torque listed in this Chapter's Specifications in 1/4-turn increments.* **Caution:** *Don't turn the camshaft while the Plastigage is in place.*

f)   *Remove the bolts, in the proper sequence, and detach the bearing caps*

g)   *Compare the width of the crushed Plastigage (at it's widest point) to the scale on the Plastigage envelope (see illustration).*

h)   *If the clearance is greater than specified, replace the camshaft and/or cylinder head.*

13   Scrape off the Plastigage with your fingernail or the edge of a credit card - don't scratch or nick the journals or bearing caps.

14   The VTC solenoid controls oil flow to the VTC unit incorporated into the intake cam sprocket. With the VTC solenoid removed from the head, it can be tested by applying battery voltage to the terminals of the solenoid. With battery voltage applied, the plunger shaft should protrude from the solenoid body **(see illustration)**.

Installation

Refer to illustration 12.17

15   On GA16DE engines, install the VTC solenoid.

16   Apply moly-based engine assembly lubricant to the camshaft lobes and journals. Also apply the same lubricant to the rocker arm contact surfaces on SR20DE engines.

12.17 Before installing the camshaft sprockets, position the camshafts as shown (GA16DE engine)

17   Install the camshafts in their original positions. **Note:** *The slotted end of the exhaust camshaft is the rear (transaxle end). The distributor is driven by the camshaft when inserted in this slot.* On SR20DE engines, position the knock pin of the intake camshaft at approximately ten o'clock and the knock pin on the exhaust camshaft at approximately twelve o'clock. On GA16DE engines, position the knock pins as shown **(see illustration)**.

18   Install the bearing cap bolts and tighten them, in sequence; use the sequence opposite the one shown in illustration 12.7a (GA16DE engine) or 12.7b (SR20DE engine), to the torque listed in this Chapter's Specifications. **Note:** *Apply RTV sealant to the end cap (distributor bracket) of the exhaust cam.*

19   Install the camshaft sprockets and timing chain (see Section 9).

20   The remainder of installation is the reverse of removal. If any part of the valve train was replaced, check and adjust, if necessary, the valve clearance (see Chapter 1).

13   Valve springs, retainers and seals - replacement

Refer to illustrations 13.4, 13.9, 13.10, 13.15, and 13.17

Note: *Broken valve springs and leaking/worn out valve stem seals can be replaced without removing the cylinder head. Two special tools and a compressed air source are normally required to perform this operation, so read through this Section carefully and rent or buy the tools before beginning the job. If compressed air isn't available, a length of nylon rope can be used to keep the valves from falling into the cylinder during this procedure.*

1   Refer to Sections 11 or 12, depending on the model, and remove the rocker arm shaft assembly and/or camshaft(s).

2   Remove the spark plug from the cylinder which has the defective component. If all of the valve stem seals are being replaced, all of the spark plugs should be removed.

3   Rotate the crankshaft until the piston in the affected cylinder is at Top Dead Center (TDC) on the compression stroke (see Section 3). If you're replacing all of the valve

13.4 This is what the air hose adapter that threads into the spark plug hole looks like - they're commonly available from auto parts stores

13.9 Compress the valve spring(s) and remove the two keepers (arrow) with needle-nose pliers or a magnet

stem seals, begin with cylinder number one and work on the valves for one cylinder at a time. Move from cylinder-to-cylinder following the firing order sequence (see the Specifications).

4   Thread an adapter into the spark plug hole **(see illustration)** and connect an air hose from a compressed air source to it. Most auto parts stores can supply the air hose adapter. **Note:** *Many cylinder compression gauges utilize a screw-in fitting that may work with your air hose quick-disconnect fitting.*

5   Apply compressed air to the cylinder. **Warning:** *The piston may be forced down by compressed air, causing the crankshaft to turn suddenly. If the wrench used when positioning the number one piston at TDC is still attached to the bolt in the crankshaft nose, it could cause damage or injury when the crankshaft moves.*

6   The valves should be held in place by the air pressure. If the valve faces or seats are in poor condition, leaks may prevent air pressure from retaining the valves - refer to the alternative procedure below.

7   If you don't have access to compressed air, an alternative method can be used. Position the piston at a point approximately 45-degrees before TDC on the compression stroke, then feed a long piece of nylon rope through the spark plug hole until it fills the combustion chamber. Be sure to leave the end of the rope hanging out of the engine so it can be removed easily.

8   Use a large ratchet and socket to rotate the crankshaft in the normal direction of rotation (clockwise, viewed from the front) until slight resistance is felt.

9   Stuff shop rags into the cylinder head areas, above and below the valves, to prevent parts and tools from falling into the engine, then use a valve spring compressor to compress the spring **(see illustration)**. Remove the keepers with small needle-nose pliers or a magnet.

10   Remove the spring retainer, valve spring and shim(s) then remove the stem oil seal with pliers **(see illustration)**. **Note:** *If air pressure fails to hold the valve in the closed position during this operation, the valve face and/or seat is probably damaged. If so, the cylinder head will have to be removed for additional repair operations.*

11   Wrap a rubber band or tape around the top of the valve stem so the valve won't fall into the combustion chamber, then release the air pressure. **Note:** *If a rope was used instead of air pressure, turn the crankshaft slightly in the direction opposite normal rotation.*

12   Inspect the valve stem for damage. Rotate the valve in the guide and check the end for eccentric movement, which would indicate that the valve is bent.

13   Move the valve up-and-down in the guide and make sure it doesn't bind. If the valve stem binds, either the valve is bent or the guide is damaged. In either

case, the head will have to be removed for repair.

14   Reapply air pressure to the cylinder to retain the valve in the closed position, then remove the tape or rubber band from the valve stem. If a rope was used instead of air pressure, rotate the crankshaft in the normal direction of rotation until slight resistance is felt.

15   Lubricate the valve stem with engine oil and install the new oil seal, using an installation tool or deep socket **(see illustration)**.

16   Install the spring in position over the valve. The tapered (progressively-wound) springs should be installed with the smaller (tighter-wound) ends down, or with the paint marks toward the head. **Caution:** *Make sure the valve spring seat is in place before the spring is installed.*

17   Install the valve spring retainer. Compress the valve spring and carefully position the keepers in the groove. Apply a small dab of grease to the inside of each keeper to hold it in place if necessary **(see illustration)**.

18   Remove the pressure from the spring tool and make sure the keepers are seated.

19   Disconnect the air hose and remove the adapter from the spark plug hole. If a rope was used in place of air pressure, pull it out of the cylinder.

20   The procedure is the same for all valve stems seals, both intake and exhaust.

21   Refer to Section 10, 11, or 12, depending on model, and install the camshaft(s).

22   The rest of the installation is the reverse of the removal procedure.

23   Start and run the engine, then check for oil leaks and unusual sounds coming from the valve cover area.

14   Cylinder head - removal and installation

Note: *The engine must be completely cool before beginning this procedure.*

Removal

1   Relieve the fuel system pressure on fuel-injected models (see Chapter 4b), then disconnect the cable from the negative

13.10 Remove the retainer and valve spring, then use pliers or a puller to remove the valve-stem seal (arrow)

13.15 Place the new seals on the valve guides squarely, then tap them in place with hammer and socket, do not continue to hammer once the seals are seated

13.17 Apply a small dab of grease to each keeper before installation to hold them in place on the valve stem until the spring is released

2A

14.15 Remove all traces of old gasket material - the cylinder head and block mating surfaces must be perfectly clean to ensure a good gasket seal

14.18 A die should be used to remove sealant and corrosion from the head bolt threads prior to installation

14.21 When placing the head gasket on the block, place the appropriate holes over the alignment dowels on the block deck surface

battery terminal. **Caution:** *If the stereo in your vehicle is equipped with an anti-theft system, make sure you have the correct activation code before disconnecting the battery.*

2   Drain the coolant from the engine block and radiator (see Chapter 1).

3   Drain the engine oil and remove the oil filter (see Chapter 1).

4   Remove the carburetor or fuel rail and injectors, depending on which fuel system is on the vehicle (see Chapter 4).

5   Remove the intake manifold (see Section 5).

6   Remove the exhaust manifold (see Section 6).

7   Remove the timing belt or chain (see Sections 7, 8, and 9).

8   Remove the alternator and distributor (see Chapter 5).

9   Remove the power steering pump (see Chapter 10) and set it aside without disconnecting the hoses.

10   Label and remove any remaining items attached to the cylinder head, such as coolant fittings, tubes, cables, hoses or wires.

11   Using a breaker bar and the appropriate sized socket, loosen the cylinder head bolts in 1/4-turn increments until they can be removed by hand. Loosen the bolts in a pattern *opposite* that of the tightening sequence **(see illustrations 14.24a through 14.24d)** to avoid warping or cracking the head. **Note:** *On 1991 through 1994 GA series engines, you will need a 10mm Allen wrench at least one and a half inches long to remove the head bolts under the cams.*

12   Lift the cylinder head off the engine block. If it's stuck, very carefully pry up at the transaxle end, beyond the gasket surface, at a casting protrusion.

13   Remove all external components from the head to allow for thorough cleaning and inspection. **Note:** *See Chapter 2, Part B, for cylinder head servicing procedures.*

Installation

Refer to illustrations 14.15, 14.18, 14.21, 14.24a, 14.24b, 14.24c and 14.24d

14   The mating surfaces of the cylinder head and block must be perfectly clean when the head is installed.

15   Use a gasket scraper to remove all traces

of carbon and old gasket material **(see illustration)**, then clean the mating surfaces with lacquer thinner or acetone. If there's oil on the mating surfaces when the head is installed, the gasket may not seal correctly and leaks could develop. When working on the block, stuff the cylinders with clean shop rags to keep out debris. Use a vacuum cleaner to remove material that falls into the cylinders.

16   Check the block and head mating surfaces for nicks, deep scratches and other damage. If damage is slight, it can be removed with a file; if it's excessive, machining may be the only alternative.

17   Use a tap of the correct size to chase the threads in the head bolt holes, then clean the holes with compressed air - make sure that nothing remains in the holes. **Warning:** *Wear eye protection when using compressed air!*

18   Mount each bolt in a vise and run a die down the threads to remove corrosion and

restore the threads **(see illustration)**. Dirt, corrosion, sealant and damaged threads will affect torque readings.

19   Check the cylinder head for warpage (see Chapter 2B). Check the head gasket, intake and exhaust manifold surfaces.

20   Install the components that were removed from the head.

21   Position the new cylinder head gasket over the dowel pins in the block **(see illustration)**.

22   Carefully set the head on the block without disturbing the gasket.

23   Before installing the head bolts, apply a small amount of clean engine oil to the threads and hardened washers (if equipped). The chamfered side of the washers must face the bolt heads.

24   Install the bolts in their original locations and tighten them finger tight. Then tighten all the bolts, following the proper sequence **(see illustrations),** to the torque listed in this

Tighten in numerical order.

14.24a Cylinder head bolt TIGHTENING sequence - 1982 through 1988 models

Tighten in numerical order

14.24b Cylinder head TIGHTENING sequence - 1989 and 1990 models

Tighten in numerical order.

14.24c Cylinder head TIGHTENING sequence -1991 through 1994 GA16DE engine

Tighten in numerical order.

14.24d Cylinder head TIGHTENING sequence -1991 through 1994 SR20DE engine

15.8 Remove the oil pan bolts starting from the ends and working towards the center

Chapter's Specifications. **Caution:** *On GA16 engines, the small hex-head bolts (no. 11 through 15) should only be tightened to 55 to 73 inch pounds.*

25 The remaining installation steps are the reverse of removal.

26 Check and adjust the valves as necessary (see Chapter 1).

27 Refill the cooling system, install a new oil filter and add oil to the engine (see Chapter 1).

28 Run the engine and check for leaks. Set the ignition timing (see Chapter 5) and road test the vehicle.

15 Oil pan - removal and installation

Removal

All - except SR20DE engine

Refer to illustration 15.8

1 Disconnect the cable from the negative battery terminal. **Caution:** *If the stereo in your vehicle is equipped with an anti-theft system, make sure you have the correct activation code before disconnecting the battery.*

2 Set the parking brake and block the rear wheels.

3 Raise the front of the vehicle and support it securely on jackstands (see Chapter 1).

1 Side gallery baffle plate
2 Aluminum section
3 Rear cover plate
4 Drain plug
5 Steel oil pan
6 Baffle plate

15.9 Details of the SR20DE engine oil pans

4 Remove the splash shields under the engine.

5 Drain the engine oil and remove the oil filter (see Chapter 1). Remove the oil dipstick.

6 Disconnect the front exhaust pipe from the engine (see Section 6).

7 On models equipped with GA16 series engines, remove the center crossmember.

8 Remove the nuts and bolts and separate the oil pan from the engine block **(see illustration)**. Use a soft-faced hammer to break the oil pan-to-block seal. Do not pry with a screwdriver between the pan and the block or the pan flange could be distorted and cause an oil leak.

SR20DE engine

Refer to illustrations 15.9, 15.10 and 15.12

9 The oil pan is a two piece design. A steel pan is attached to an aluminum section which is bolted to the engine block **(see illustration)**. Perform steps 1 through 5 and remove the steel pan and the baffle plate from the aluminum section. **Caution:** *Do not*

pry between the steel pan and the aluminum flange or damage to the sealing surface may result.

10 Disconnect the exhaust pipe from the exhaust manifold. Support the engine from above with an engine hoist and support the transaxle from below with a floor jack. Remove the center crossmember **(see illustration)**.

11 Remove the air conditioning compressor bracket-to-oil pan braces and the rear cover plate. Remove the bolts attaching the aluminum section to the block, working from the ends toward the center to prevent warpage.

12 To loosen the aluminum section, remove two transaxle bolts and insert them into two empty, threaded holes in the oil pan **(see illustration)**. Tightening these bolts into the indicated holes will separate the pan from the block. Remove the two transaxle bolts and reinstall them in their original location.

Installation

Refer to illustration 15.16

13 Use a scraper to remove all traces of old gasket material and sealant from the block and oil pan. Clean the mating surfaces with lacquer thinner or acetone. **Caution:** *Be careful not to scratch or gouge the gasket surface of the block or oil pan. A leak could develop after the repairs have been completed.*

14 Make sure the threaded bolt holes in the block are clean.

15 Check the oil pan flange for distortion, particularly around the bolt holes. If necessary, place the pan on a wood block and use a hammer to flatten and restore the gasket surface.

16 Apply a 3/16-inch wide bead of RTV

15.10 Support the transmission with a jack and remove the center crossmember

15.12 To remove the SR20DE aluminum pan, remove two bolts from the transaxle and tightened them into the pan bolt holes as shown

2A

15.16 Apply an even bead of RTV sealant to the oil pan before installation

16.2 To remove the oil pump, located beneath the intake manifold on 1982 to 1988 models, disconnect the oil pressure sender (arrow) and remove the bolts/nuts

16.5 The oil pump pressure relief assembly should be removed for cleaning and inspection

sealant around the oil pan flange (see illustration). Note: The oil pan must be installed within 15 minutes once the sealant has been applied.

17   Carefully position the oil pan on the engine block and install the nuts and bolts. Working from the center out, tighten the fasteners in three or four steps to the torque listed in this Chapter's Specifications.

18   The remainder of installation is the reverse of removal. Be sure to install a new oil filter and wait at least thirty minutes before adding oil.

16   Oil pump - removal, inspection and installation,

1982 through 1988 models
Removal
Refer to illustration 16.2

1   The oil pump is located on the intake manifold side of the engine, between the oil filter and the block/oil pan mating surface.

2   Remove the bolt and the two nuts and detach the oil pump assembly from the engine (see illustration). Caution: *If the pump doesn't come off by hand, tap it gently with a soft-faced hammer.*

3   Remove the bolts retaining the pump cover to the pump body, but do not disassemble the inner rotor and drive gear.

Caution: *Be very careful with these components, close tolerances are critical in creating the correct oil pressure. Any nicks or other damage will require replacement of the complete pump assembly.*

Inspection
Refer to illustrations 16.5, 16.6a and 16.6b

4   Clean all components, including the pump and block gasket surfaces, with solvent, then inspect all surfaces for excessive wear and/or damage.

5   Disassemble the relief valve by removing the cap, washer, spring and regulator valve (see illustration). Check the oil pressure regulator valve sliding surface and valve spring. The regulator, when clean and oiled, should slide easily in the valve bore. If either the spring or the valve is damaged, they must be replaced as a set. If no damage is found reassemble the relief valve components, coating the parts with oil, and install them in the pump body.

6   Check the oil pump component clearance with a feeler gauge (see illustrations) and compare the results to the Specifications at the beginning of this Chapter.

Installation

7   Attach the cover to the pump body with a new gasket.

8   Install the pump onto the engine with a new gasket and tighten the bolts to the torque listed in this Chapter's Specifications.

9   Install a new oil filter and add engine oil to the crankcase as necessary (see Chapter 1).

10   Start the engine and check for oil pressure and leaks.

11   Recheck the engine oil level.

1989-1994 models
Removal
Refer to illustration 16.14

12   The oil pump is located inside the lower part of the engine front cover, and is driven from the crankshaft.

13   The front cover must be removed for access to the oil pump, Refer to Section 8 or 9 and remove the front cover.

14   Remove the bolts retaining the pump cover to the pump body (see illustration), but do not disassemble the inner rotor and drive gear. Caution: *Be very careful with these components, close tolerances are critical in creating the correct oil pressure. Any nicks or other damage will require replacement of the complete pump assembly.*

Inspection
Refer to illustrations 16.16 and 16.17

15   Clean all components, including the pump and block gasket surfaces, with solvent, then inspect all surfaces for excessive wear and/or damage.

16   Disassemble the relief valve by removing the cap, washer, spring and

16.6a Measure the outer rotor-to-body clearance . . .

16.6b . . . and the rotor tip clearance

16.14 The oil pump is located inside the front cover - remove the screws and the pump cover

16.16 Remove the oil pump pressure regulator valve assembly for cleaning and inspection

16.17 Check the outer gear-to-body clearance with a feeler gauge as shown - also check the inner and outer gear-to-crescent clearance (arrow)

17.4 Mark the flywheel for realignment (arrow), and use a pry bar against two clutch cover bolts as shown, to keep the flywheel from turning when removing the bolts

2A

regulator valve **(see illustration)**.The regulator valve is in the pump cover on SR20DE engines, and in the engine front cover on all GA series engines. Check the oil pressure regulator valve sliding surface and valve spring. The regulator, when clean and oiled, should slide easily in the valve hole. If either the spring or the valve is damaged, they must be replaced as a set. If no damage is found reassemble the relief valve parts, coating the parts with oil, and reinstall it in the front cover.
17 Check the oil pump component clearance with a feeler gauge **(see illustration)** and compare the results to the specifications at the beginning of this Chapter.

Installation
18 Assemble the cover to the pump body.
19 Refer to Sections 8 or 9, install the front cover and any other components removed for disassembly, to the engine. **Note:** *The flats inside the oil pump must be turned to align with the flats on the crankshaft when installing the front cover.*
20 Install a new oil filter and add engine oil to the crankcase, if necessary (see Chapter 1).
21 Start the engine and check for oil pressure and leaks.
22 Recheck the engine oil level.

17 Flywheel/driveplate - removal and installation

Removal
Refer to illustration 17.4
1 Raise the vehicle and support it securely on jackstands (see Chapter 1), then remove the transaxle (see Chapter 7). If it's leaking, now would be a very good time to replace the front pump seal/O-ring (automatic transaxle only).
2 Remove the pressure plate and clutch disc (see Chapter 8) (manual transaxle models). Now is a good time to check/replace the clutch components bearing.

3 Use a center-punch, or paint, to make alignment marks on the flywheel/driveplate and crankshaft to ensure correct alignment during reinstallation.
4 Remove the bolts that secure the flywheel/driveplate to the crankshaft. If the crankshaft turns, reinstall two clutch cover bolts and use a large prybar across them to hold the flywheel. **(see illustration)**.
5 Remove the flywheel/driveplate from the crankshaft. **Warning:** *Since the flywheel is fairly heavy, be sure to support it while removing the last bolt. Flywheel teeth can be sharp, wear gloves or use rags to hold the flywheel.*

Installation
6 Clean the flywheel to remove grease and oil. Inspect the surface for cracks, rivet grooves, burned areas and score marks. Light scoring can be removed with emery cloth. Check for cracked and broken ring gear teeth. Lay the flywheel on a flat surface and use a straightedge to check for warpage.
7 Clean and inspect the mating surfaces of the flywheel/driveplate and the crankshaft. If the crankshaft rear seal is leaking, replace it before reinstalling the flywheel/driveplate.
8 Position the flywheel/driveplate against the crankshaft. Be sure to align the marks made during removal. Note that some engines have an alignment dowel or staggered bolt holes to ensure correct installation. Before installing the bolts, apply thread locking compound to the threads.

9 Wedge a screwdriver in the ring gear teeth to keep the flywheel/driveplate from turning as you tighten the bolts to the torque listed in this Chapter's Specifications. Follow a criss-cross pattern and work up to the final torque in three or four steps.
10 The remainder of installation is the reverse of the removal procedure.

18 Rear main oil seal - replacement

Refer to illustrations 18.3, 18.5 and 18.6
1 Remove the transaxle (see Chapter 7).
2 Remove the flywheel/driveplate (see Section 17).
3 Remove the rear oil seal retainer from the block **(see illustration)**. **Note:** if the seal retainer is removed, several oil pan bolts will have to be removed if the pan is still in place, and it may disturb the pan gasket.
4 Scrape any sealant or gasket material from the retainer, oil pan and the block.
5 Position the seal and retainer assembly between two wood blocks, to evenly support the aluminum housing, and drive the old seal out with a hammer and punch **(see illustration)**. A screwdriver can also be used to pry the seal out, being careful not to gouge or nick the housing during seal removal.
6 Place the new seal squarely on the retainer and drive it into the retainer with a

18.3 Remove the rear oil seal retainer

18.5 After removing the retainer from the block, support it between two wood blocks and drive out the old seal with a punch and hammer

18.6 Drive the new seal into the retainer with a wood block or a section of pipe, if you have one large enough - make sure that you don't cock the seal in the retainer bore

wood block **(see illustration)** or a section of pipe slightly smaller in diameter than the outside diameter of the seal.

7   Lubricate the crankshaft seal journal and the lip of the new seal with multi-purpose grease.

8   Apply a thin, uniform layer of RTV sealant to the seal retainer. Also apply sealant to the bottom of the retainer (oil pan mating surface).

9   Slowly and carefully push the seal onto the crankshaft. The seal lip is stiff, so work it onto the crankshaft with a smooth object such as the end of a socket extension as you push the retainer against the block.

10   Install and tighten the retainer bolts securely. The bottom sealing flange of the retainer must not extend below the bottom sealing flange (oil pan rail) of the block.

11   The remaining steps are the reverse of removal.

19   Engine mounts - check and replacement

Refer to illustration 19.1
Note: *See Chapter 7 for transaxle mount replacement.*

1   Engine mounts seldom require attention, but broken or deteriorated mounts should be replaced immediately or the added strain placed on the driveline components may cause damage or wear **(see illustration).**

Check

2   During the check, the engine must be raised slightly to remove the weight from the mounts.

3   Raise the vehicle and support it securely on jackstands and remove the splash shields.

4   Position a jack under the engine oil pan. Place a large wood block between the jack head and the oil pan, then carefully raise the engine *just enough* to take the weight off the mounts. Do not place the wood block under the oil pan drain plug. **Warning:** *DO NOT*

place any part of your body under the engine when it's supported only by a jack!

5   Check the mounts to see if the rubber is cracked, hardened or separated from the metal plates. Sometimes the rubber will split right down the center.

6   Check for relative movement between the mount plates and the engine or frame (use a large screwdriver or prybar to attempt to move the mounts). If movement is noted, lower the engine and tighten the mount fasteners.

7   Rubber preservative should be applied to the mounts to slow deterioration.

Replacement

8   Disconnect the negative battery cable from the battery, then raise the vehicle and support it securely on jackstands (if not already done). Support the engine as described in Step 3.

9   To remove the right engine mount, at the timing belt/chain end of the engine, remove the nut and withdraw the through-bolt from the frame bracket.

10   Remove the mount-to-bracket nuts and detach the mount.

11   To remove the front engine mount, remove the engine mount through bolt.

12   Remove the engine block-to-mount bolts and remove the mount.

13   Installation is the reverse of removal. Use thread locking compound on the mount bolts/nuts and be sure to tighten them securely.

19.1 Typical crossmember, motor and transaxle mount details

Chapter 2 Part B
General engine overhaul procedures

Contents

2B

Specifications

General

Cylinder compression pressure
  1982 through 1990 .... 181 psi (142 psi minimum)
  1991 through 1994
    GA16DE .... 192 psi (164 psi minimum)
    SR20DE .... 178 psi (149 psi minimum)

Oil pump pressure (at normal operating temperature)

1982 through 1988
  1050 rpm .... 28 psi
  1700 rpm .... 43 lbs
  5150 rpm .... 57 lbs
1989 through 1990
  Idle .... 7 to 27 psi
  3000 rpm .... 57 to 71 psi
1991 through 1994
  GA16DE
    Idle .... 7 to 27 psi
    3000 rpm .... 50 to 64 psi
  SR20DE
    Idle .... 11 psi
    3200 rpm .... 46 to 57 psi

Engine block

Deck surface warpage	0.004 inch
Bore diameter	
1982 through 1990	
E15	2.9908 to 2.9928 inches
E16 and GA16i	2.9921 to 2.9933 inches
1991 through 1994	
GA16DE	
Grade 1	2.9921 to 2.9925 inches
Grade 2	2.9925 to 2.9929 inches
Grade 3	2.9929 to 2.9933 inches
SR20DE	
Grade 1	3.3858 to 3.3862 inches
Grade 2	3.3862 to 3.3866 inches
Grade 3	3.3866 to 3.3870 inches
Out-of-round	
Service limit	
1982 and 1983	0.0008 inch
1983 through 1994	0.0006 inch
Taper	
Service limit	
1982 through 1988	0.0008 inch
1989 through 1994	0.0004 inch

Crankshaft and connecting rods

Crankshaft runout	
1982 and 1983	0.0039 inch maximum
1984 through 1988	0.0031 inch maximum
1989 through 1990	0.0016 inch maximum
1991 through 1994	0.0020 inch maximum
Endplay	
1982 through 1988	0.0118 inch maximum
1989 through 1994 (except SR20DE)	0.0120 inch maximum
1991 through 1994 (SR20DE)	0.0118 inch maximum
Main bearing journal	
Diameter	
1982 and 1983	1.9661 to 1.9671 inches
1984 through 1986	1.9663 to 1.9671 inches
1987 and 1988	1.9661 to 1.9671 inches
1989 and 1990	1.9668 to 1.967 inches
1991 through 1994	
GA16DE	
Grade 0	1.9668 to 1.9671 inches
Grade 1	1.9665 to 1.9668 inches
Grade 2	1.9661 to 1.9665 inches
SR20DE	
Grade 0	2.1643 to 2.1646 inches
Grade 1	2.1641 to 2.1643 inches
Grade 2	2.1639 to 2.1641 inches
Grade 3	2.1636 to 2.1639 inches
Taper	
1982 through 1988	0.0012 inch maximum
1989 through 1994 (except SR20DE)	0.0001 inch maximum
1991 through 1994 (SR20DE)	0.0002 inch maximum
Out-of-round	
1982 through 1988	0.0012 inch maximum
1989 through 1994	0.0002 inch maximum
Main bearing oil clearance	
1982 and 1983	
Standard	
No. 1 and 5	0.0012 to 0.0030 inch
No. 2, 3 and 4	0.0012 to 0.0036 inch
Limit	0.004 inch
1984 through 1988	
Standard	
No. 1, 3 and 5	0.0012 to 0.0022 inch
No. 2 and 4	0.0012 to 0.0036 inch
Limit	0.004 inch

1989 and 1990
  Standard .... 0.0008 to 0.0017 inch
  Limit .... 0.004 inch
1991 through 1994
  GA16DE
    Standard .... 0.0007 to 0.0017 inch
    Limit 0.004
  SR20DE
    Standard .... 0.0002 to 0.0009 inch
    Limit .... 0.002 inch
Connecting rod journal
  Diameter
    1982 through 1990 .... 1.5730 to 1.5738 inches
    1991 through 1994
      GA16DE
        Grade 0 .... 1.5735 to 1.5738 inches
        Grade 1 .... 1.5733 to 1.5735 inches
        Grade 2 .... 1.5731 to 1.5733 inches
      SR20DE
        Grade 0 .... 1.8885 to 1.8887 inches
        Grade 1 .... 1.8883 to 1.8885 inches
        Grade 2 .... 1.8880 to 1.8883 inches
Connecting rod oil clearance
  1982 and 1983
    Standard .... 0.0012 to 0.0024 inch
    Limit .... 0.004 inch
  1983 through 1988
    Standard .... 0.0004 to 0.0017 inch
    Limit .... 0.004 inch
  1989 through 1994
    GA series
      Standard .... 0.0004 to 0.0014 inch
      Limit .... 0.004 inch
    SR20DE
      Standard .... 0.0004 to 0.0014 inch
      Limit .... 0.0035 inch
Connecting rod side clearance (endplay)
  1982 through 1988
    Standard .... 0.0040 to 0.0146 inch
    Limit .... 0.020 inch
  1989 through 1994
    GA series
      Standard .... 0.0079 to 0.0185 inch
      Limit .... 0.0205 inch
    SR20DE
      Standard .... 0.0079 to 0.0138 inch
      Limit .... 0.020 inch

Piston and rings

Piston diameter
  1982 through 1988 .... 2.9908 to 2.9928 inches
  1989 through 1994
    GA series
      Grade 1 .... 2.9911 to 2.9915 inches
      Grade 2 .... 2.9915 to 2.9919 inches
      Grade 3 .... 2.9919 to 2.9923 inches
    SR20DE
      Grade 1 .... 3.3850 to 3.3854 inches
      Grade 2 .... 3.3854 to 3.3858 inches
      Grade 3 .... 3.3858 to 3.3862 inches
Piston-to-bore clearance
  1982 through 1988 .... 0.0009 to 0.0017 inch
  1989 through 1994
    GA series .... 0.0006 to 0.0014 inch
    SR20DE .... 0.0004 to 0.0012 inch
Piston ring end gap
  1982 through 1986
    No. 1 (top ring) .... 0.0079 to 0.0138 inch
    No. 2 (middle ring) .... 0.0059 to 0.0118 inch
    Oil ring .... 0.0118 to 0.0354 inch

Piston and rings

Piston ring end gap (continued)
  1987 and 1988
    No. 1 (top ring) .... 0.0079 to 0.0118 inch
    No. 2 (middle ring) .... 0.0059 to 0.0098 inch
    Oil ring .... 0.0079 to 0.0236 inch
  1989 through 1994
    GA series
      No. 1 (top ring) .... 0.0079 to 0.0138 inch
      No. 2 (middle ring) .... 0.0146 to 0.0205 inch
      Oil ring .... 0.0079 to 0.0236 inch
    SR20DE
      No. 1 (top ring) .... 0.0079 to 0.0118 inch
      No. 2 (middle ring) .... 0.0138 to 0.0197 inch
      Oil ring .... 0.0079 to 0.0236 inch
  Service limit (all models) .... 0.040 inch
Piston ring side clearance
  1982 through 1988
    No. 1 (top ring) .... 0.0016 to 0.0029 inch
    No. 2 (middle ring) .... 0.0012 to 0.0025 inch
  1989 through 1994
    GA series
      No. 1 (top ring) .... 0.0016 to 0.0031 inch
      No. 2 (middle ring) .... 0.0012 to 0.0028 inch
    SR20DE
      No. 1 (top ring) .... 0.0018 to 0.0031 inch
      No. 2 (middle ring) .... 0.0012 to 0.0026 inch
  Service limit (all models) .... 0.0080 inch

Valves and related components

Valve face angle .... 45 degrees
Valve spring free length
  1982 through 1988 .... 1.8386 inches
  1989 and 1990
    Intake .... 2.0709 inches
    Exhaust .... 2.1543 inches
  1991 through 1994
    GA16DE .... 1.6217 inches
    SR20DE .... 1.9433 inches
Valve spring out of square limit
  1982 through 1988 .... 0.0790 inch
  1989 and 1990
    Intake .... 0.0910 inch
    Exhaust .... 0.0940 inch
  1991 through 1994
    GA16DE .... 0.0709 inch
    SR20DE .... 0.0870 inch
Valve margin width
  1982 through 1990 .... 0.020 inch
  1991 through 1994
    GA16DE .... 0.035 to 0.043 inch
    SR20DE .... 0.020 inch
Valve stem diameter
  1982 through 1988
    Intake .... 0.2744 to 0.2750 inch
    Exhaust .... 0.2734 to 0.2740 inch
  1989 and 1990
    Intake .... 0.2348 to 0.2354 inch
    Exhaust .... 0.2582 to 0.2587 inch
  1991 through 1994
    GA16DE
      Intake .... 0.2152 to 0.2157 inch
      Exhaust .... 0.2144 to 0.2150 inch
    SR20DE
      Intake .... 0.2348 to 0.2354 inch
      Exhaust .... 0.2341 to 0.2346 inch
Valve stem-to-guide clearance
  1982 through 1988
    Intake .... 0.0008 to 0.0020 inch
    Exhaust .... 0.0018 to 0.0030 inch

1989 and 1990
  Intake .... 0.0008 to 0.0020 inch
  Exhaust.. 0.0012 to 0.0022 inch
1991 through 1994
  GA16DE
    Intake .... 0.0008 to 0.0020 inch
    Exhaust.. 0.0016 to 0.0028 inch
  SR20DE
    Intake .... 0.0008 to 0.0021 inch
    Exhaust.. 0.0016 to 0.0029 inch

Torque specifications*   Ft-lbs (unless otherwise indicated)

Main bearing cap bolts
  1982 through 1988 .... 36 to 43
  1989 through 1994
    GA series.. 36 to 38
    SR20DE
      Step 1 .... 24 to 28
      Step 2 .... Tighten an additional 45 degrees
Connecting rod cap nuts
  1982 through 1988 .... 23 to 27
  1989 through 1994
    GA series
      Step 1 .... 120 to 144 in-lbs
      Step 2 .... Tighten an additional 35 to 40 degrees
    SR20DE
      Step 1 .... 120 to 144 in-lbs
      Step 2 .... Tighten an additional 60 to 65 degrees

* Note: Refer to Part A for additional torque specifications

2B

1 General information

Included in this portion of Chapter 2 are the general overhaul procedures for the cylinder head and internal engine components.

The information ranges from advice concerning preparation for an overhaul and the purchase of replacement parts to detailed, step-by-step procedures covering removal and installation of internal engine components and the inspection of parts.

The following Sections have been written based on the assumption that the engine has been removed from the vehicle. For information concerning in-vehicle engine repair, as well as removal and installation of the external components necessary for the overhaul, see Section 7 and Chapter 2A.

The Specifications included in this Part are only those necessary for the inspection and overhaul procedures which follow. Refer to Part A for additional Specifications.

2 Engine overhaul - general information

It's not always easy to determine when, or if, an engine should be completely overhauled, as a number of factors must be considered.

High mileage is not necessarily an indication that an overhaul is needed, while low mileage doesn't preclude the need for an overhaul. Frequency of servicing is probably the most important consideration. An engine that's had regular and frequent oil and filter changes, as well as other required maintenance, will most likely give many thousands of miles of reliable service. Conversely, a neglected engine may require an overhaul very early in its life.

Excessive oil consumption is an indication that piston rings, valve seals and/or valve guides are in need of attention. Make sure that oil leaks aren't responsible before deciding that the rings and/or guides are bad. Perform a cylinder compression check to determine the extent of the work required (see Section 4).

Check the oil pressure with a gauge installed in place of the oil pressure sending unit and compare it to the Specifications. If it's extremely low, the bearings and/or oil pump are probably worn out.

Loss of power, rough running, knocking or metallic engine noises, excessive valve train noise and high fuel consumption rates may also point to the need for an overhaul, especially if they're all present at the same time. If a complete tune-up doesn't remedy the situation, major mechanical work is the only solution.

An engine overhaul involves restoring the internal parts to the specifications of a new engine. During an overhaul, the piston rings are replaced and the cylinder walls are reconditioned (rebored and/or honed). If a rebore is done by an automotive machine shop, new oversize pistons will also be installed. The main bearings, connecting rod bearings and camshaft bearings are generally replaced with new ones and, if necessary, the crankshaft may be reground to restore the journals. Generally, the valves are serviced as well, since they're usually in less-than-perfect condition at this point. The end result should be a like-new engine that will give many trouble free miles. **Note:** *Critical cooling system components such as the hoses, drivebelts, thermostat and water pump MUST be replaced with new parts when an engine is overhauled. The radiator should be checked carefully to ensure that it isn't clogged or leaking (see Chapter 3). If you purchase a rebuilt engine or shortblock, some rebuilders will not warranty their engines unless the radiator has been professionally flushed.*

Before beginning the engine overhaul, read through the entire procedure to familiarize yourself with the scope and requirements of the job. Overhauling an engine isn't difficult, but it is time consuming. Plan on the vehicle being tied up for a minimum of two weeks, especially if parts must be taken to an automotive machine shop for repair or reconditioning. Check on availability of parts and make sure that any necessary special tools and equipment are obtained in advance. Most work can be done with typical hand tools, although a number of precision measuring tools are required for inspecting parts to determine if they must be replaced. Often an automotive machine shop will handle the inspection of parts and offer advice concerning reconditioning and replacement. **Note:** *Always wait until the engine has been completely disassembled and all components, especially the engine block, have been inspected before deciding what service and repair operations must be performed by an automotive machine shop. Since the block's condition will be the major factor to consider when determining whether* to overhaul the original engine or buy a rebuilt one, never purchase parts or have machine work done on other components until the block has been thoroughly inspected. As a general rule, time is the primary cost of an overhaul, so it doesn't pay to install worn or substandard parts.

As a final note, to ensure maximum life and minimum trouble from a rebuilt engine, everything must be assembled with care in a spotlessly-clean environment.

3   Vacuum gauge diagnostic checks

A vacuum gauge provides valuable information about what is going on in the engine at a low-cost. You can check for worn rings or cylinder walls, leaking head or intake manifold gaskets, incorrect carburetor adjustments, restricted exhaust, stuck or burned valves, weak valve springs, improper ignition or valve timing and ignition problems.

Unfortunately, vacuum gauge readings are easy to misinterpret, so they should be used in conjunction with other tests to confirm the diagnosis.

Both the absolute readings and the rate of needle movement are important for accurate interpretation. Most gauges measure vacuum in inches of mercury (in-Hg). As a point of reference, normal atmospheric pressure at sea level is about 30 in-Hg. As vacuum increases (or atmospheric pressure decreases), the reading will decrease. Also, for every 1,000 foot increase in elevation above sea level, the gauge readings will decrease about one inch of mercury.

Connect the vacuum gauge directly to intake manifold vacuum, not to ported (carburetor) vacuum. Be sure no hoses are left disconnected during the test or false readings will result.

Before you begin the test, allow the engine to warm up completely. Block the wheels and set the parking brake. With the transmission in neutral (or Park, on automatics), start the engine and allow it to run at normal idle speed. **Warning:** *Carefully inspect the fan blades for cracks or damage before starting the engine. Keep your hands and the vacuum tester clear of the fan and do not stand in front of the vehicle or in line with the fan when the engine is running.*

Read the vacuum gauge; an average, healthy engine should normally produce between 17 and 22 inches of vacuum with a fairly steady needle.

Refer to the following vacuum gauge readings and what they indicate about the engines condition:

1   A low steady reading usually indicates a leaking gasket between the intake manifold and carburetor or throttle body, a leaky vacuum hose, late ignition timing or incorrect camshaft timing. Check ignition timing with a timing light and eliminate all other possible causes, utilizing the tests provided in this Chapter before you remove the timing chain cover to check the timing marks.

2   If the reading is three to eight inches below normal and it fluctuates at that low reading, suspect an intake manifold gasket leak at an intake port or a faulty injector (on port-injected models only).

3   If the needle has regular drops of about two to four inches at a steady rate the valves are probably leaking. Perform a compression or leak-down test to confirm this.

4   An irregular drop or down-flick of the needle can be caused by a sticking valve or an ignition misfire. Perform a compression or leak-down test and read the spark plugs.

5   A rapid vibration of about four in.-Hg vibration at idle combined with exhaust smoke indicates worn valve guides. Perform a leak-down test to confirm this. If the rapid vibration occurs with an increase in engine speed, check for a leaking intake manifold gasket or head gasket, weak valve springs, burned valves or ignition misfire.

6   A slight fluctuation, say one inch up and down, may mean ignition problems. Check all the usual tune-up items and, if necessary, run the engine on an ignition analyzer.

7   If there is a large fluctuation, perform a compression or leak-down test to look for a weak or dead cylinder or a blown head gasket.

8   If the needle moves slowly through a wide range, check for a clogged PCV system, incorrect idle fuel mixture, carburetor/throttle body or intake manifold gasket leaks.

9   Check for a slow return after revving the engine by quickly snapping the throttle open until the engine reaches about 2,500 rpm and let it shut. Normally the reading should drop to near zero, rise above normal idle reading (about 5 in.-Hg over) and then return to the previous idle reading. If the vacuum returns slowly and doesn't peak when the throttle is snapped shut, the rings may be worn. If there is a long delay, look for a restricted exhaust system (often the muffler or catalytic converter). An easy way to check this is to temporarily disconnect the exhaust ahead of the suspected part and redo the test.

4   Compression check

Refer to illustration 4.6

1   A compression check will tell you what mechanical condition the upper end (pistons, rings, valves, head gasket) of your engine is in. Specifically, it can tell you if the compression is down due to leakage caused by worn piston rings, defective valves and seats or a blown head gasket. **Note:** *The engine must be at normal operating temperature and the battery must be fully charged for this check.*

2   Begin by cleaning the area around the spark plugs before you remove them (compressed air should be used, if available, otherwise a small brush or even a bicycle tire

4.6 A compression gauge with a threaded fitting for the spark plug hole is preferred over the type that requires hand pressure to maintain the seal - be sure to open the throttle valve as far as possible during the compression check

pump will work). The idea is to prevent dirt from getting into the cylinders as the compression check is being done.

3   Remove all of the spark plugs from the engine (see Chapter 1).

4   Block the throttle wide open.

5   Detach the primary (low voltage) wiring from the coil (see Chapter 5), and on 1984 and later models, disconnect the crank-angle sensor plug at the distributor. The fuel pump circuit should also be disabled (see Chapters 4A and 4B).

6   Install the compression gauge in the spark plug hole **(see illustration)**.

7   Crank the engine over at least five compression strokes and watch the gauge. The compression should build up quickly in a healthy engine. Low compression on the first stroke, followed by gradually increasing pressure on successive strokes, indicates worn piston rings. A low compression reading on the first stroke, which doesn't build up during successive strokes, indicates leaking valves or a blown head gasket (a cracked head could also be the cause). Deposits on the undersides of the valve heads can also cause low compression. Record the highest gauge reading obtained.

8   Repeat the procedure for the remaining cylinders and compare the results to the Specifications.

9   Add some engine oil (about three squirts from a plunger-type oil can) to each cylinder, through the spark plug holes, and repeat the test.

10   If the compression increases after the oil is added, the piston rings are definitely worn. If the compression doesn't increase significantly, the leakage is occurring at the valves or head gasket. Leakage past the valves may be caused by burned valve seats and/or faces or warped, cracked or bent valves.

11   If two adjacent cylinders have equally low compression, there's a strong possibility that the head gasket between them is blown. The appearance of coolant in the combustion chambers or the crankcase would verify this condition.

12   If one cylinder is 20-percent lower than

the others, and the engine has a slightly rough idle, a worn exhaust lobe on the camshaft could be the cause.

13   If the compression is unusually high, the combustion chambers are probably coated with carbon deposits. If that's the case, the cylinder head(s) should be removed and decarbonized.

14   If compression is way down or varies greatly between cylinders, it would be a good idea to have a leak-down test performed by an automotive repair shop. This test will pinpoint exactly where the leakage is occurring and how severe it is.

5   Engine removal - methods and precautions

Warning: *If equipped with airbags, refer to Chapter 12 to disarm system.*

If you've decided that an engine must be removed for overhaul or major repair work, several preliminary steps should be taken.

Locating a suitable place to work is extremely important. Adequate work space, along with storage space for the vehicle, will be needed. If a shop or garage isn't available, at the very least a flat, level, clean work surface made of concrete or asphalt is required.

Cleaning the engine compartment and engine before beginning the removal procedure will help keep tools clean and organized.

An engine hoist or A-frame will also be necessary. Make sure the equipment is rated in excess of the combined weight of the engine and transaxle. Safety is of primary importance, considering the potential hazards involved in lifting the engine out of the vehicle.

If the engine is being removed by a novice, a helper should be available. Advice and aid from someone more experienced would also be helpful. There are many instances when one person cannot simultaneously perform all of the operations required when lifting the engine out of the vehicle.

Plan the operation ahead of time. Arrange for or obtain all of the tools and equipment you'll need prior to beginning the job. Some of the equipment necessary to perform engine removal and installation safely and with relative ease are (in addition to an engine hoist) a heavy duty floor jack, complete sets of wrenches and sockets as described in the front of this manual, wooden blocks and plenty of rags and cleaning solvent for mopping up spilled oil, coolant and gasoline. If the hoist must be rented, make sure that you arrange for it in advance and perform all of the operations possible without it beforehand. This will save you money and time.

Plan for the vehicle to be out of use for quite a while. A machine shop will be required to perform some of the work which the do-it-yourselfer can't accomplish without

special equipment. These shops often have a busy schedule, so it would be a good idea to consult them before removing the engine in order to accurately estimate the amount of time required to rebuild or repair components that may need work.

Always be extremely careful when removing and installing the engine. Serious injury can result from careless actions. Plan ahead, take your time and a job of this nature, although major, can be accomplished successfully.

6   Engine - removal and installation

Refer to illustrations 6.18, 6.23a and 6.23b
Warning: *Gasoline is extremely flammable, so take extra precautions when disconnecting any part of the fuel system. Don't smoke or allow open flames or bare light bulbs in or near the work area and don't work in a garage where a natural gas appliance (such as a clothes dryer or water heater) is installed. If you spill gasoline on your skin, rinse it off immediately. Have a fire extinguisher rated for gasoline fires handy and know how to use it.*
Note: *Read through the entire Section before beginning this procedure. The engine and transaxle may be removed as a unit, to be separated afterward on the garage floor, or either may be supported with jacks and/or chain hoists while the other is removed separately. Engines should be removed from the top when taken out separately, while transaxles should be lowered out the bottom when removed separately. To remove both engine and transaxle as a unit, lift out the unit from the top. For more on transaxle removal, see Chapter 7.*

Removal

1   On fuel-injected models, relieve the fuel system pressure (see Chapter 4). Disconnect the cable from the negative battery terminal.
Caution: *If the stereo in your vehicle is equipped with an anti-theft system, make sure you have the correct activation code before disconnecting the battery.*
2   Place protective covers on the fenders and cowl and remove the hood (see Chapter 11).
3   Remove the battery and battery tray (see Chapter 5).
4   Remove the air cleaner assembly (see Chapter 4).
5   Remove the cruise control actuator cable, if equipped.
6   Raise the vehicle and support it securely on jackstands. Drain the cooling system and engine oil and remove the drivebelts (see Chapter 1). **Note:** *Don't raise the vehicle any higher than necessary.*
7   Clearly label and disconnect all vacuum lines, coolant and emissions hoses, electrical connectors, ground straps and fuel lines (for fuel line removal see Chapter 4). Masking tape and/or a touch up paint applicator work well for marking items. Take instant photos or sketch the locations of components and

brackets, if necessary.
8   Remove the cooling fan(s), shroud and radiator (see Chapter 3).
9   Release the residual fuel pressure in the tank by removing the gas cap, then disconnect the fuel lines between the engine and chassis (see Chapter 4). Plug or cap all open fittings.
10   Disconnect the throttle linkage and transaxle shift control cable (if equipped) from the throttle body (see Chapter 4).
11   Remove the alternator and starter (see Chapter 5).
12   On power steering equipped vehicles, unbolt the power steering pump (see Chapter 10). Tie the pump aside without disconnecting the hoses.
13   On air conditioned models, unbolt the compressor and set it aside (see Chapter 3). **Warning:** *Do not disconnect the refrigerant hoses.*
14   Unbolt the exhaust pipe from the exhaust manifold **(see Chapter 2A).**
15   Unbolt and remove the engine-to-transmission reinforcement brackets **(see Chapter 2A, illustrations 9.6a and 9.6b).**
16   Remove the right front wheel and the right drive axle (see Chapter 8).
17   On automatic transaxle equipped models, detach the torque converter cover from the lower bellhousing. On some automatic transaxle models, the rear engine plate is one-piece and access to the converter bolts is through the starter hole in the plate.
18   Remove the torque converter-to-drive-plate fasteners **(see illustration)** and push the converter back slightly into the bellhousing.
19   Attach a lifting sling or chain to the brackets on the engine. Position a hoist and connect the sling or chain to it. Take up the slack until there is slight tension on the hoist. **Warning:** *Do not place any part of your body under the engine/transaxle when it's supported only by a hoist or other lifting device.*
20   Recheck to be sure nothing except the mounts are still connecting the engine/transaxle to the vehicle. Disconnect anything still remaining.

6.18 On automatic transaxle models, the converter nuts must be removed before the engine can be disconnected from the transaxle. Access to the bolts is through a dust cover (arrow) or the starter hole

2B

6.23a   In most cases, the engine can be removed from above as a unit with the transaxle as shown on this E16 model . . .

6.23b . . . or the transaxle can be left attached to the vehicle (and supported by a jack) and the engine pulled out separately, as on this 1994 model. Guide the engine/transaxle assembly as it comes up and out to clear any components in the engine compartment

21   Place a floor jack under the transmission bellhousing area, to support the transaxle when the engine is unbolted and removed. Be sure to place a wood block on the jack head to serve as a cushion.
22   Remove the remaining engine mounts **(see Chapter 2A, illustration 19.8)**, but leave the transaxle mounts connected.
23   Slowly raise the engine out of the vehicle **(see illustrations)**. It may be necessary to tilt the engine up at the front, using the jack under the transaxle to tilt it up as well. Have an assistant twist the engine sling to angle the engine as needed as it is raised with the hoist.
24   Move the engine away from the vehicle and carefully lower the hoist until the engine is on the floor, supported by wood blocks, or remove the flywheel or driveplate and mount the engine on an engine stand.

Installation

25   Check the engine/transaxle mounts. If they're worn or damaged, replace them.
26   On manual transaxle equipped models, inspect the clutch components (see Chapter 8) and, on automatic transaxle models, inspect the converter seal and bushing.
27   On automatic transaxle equipped models, apply a dab of grease to the nose of the torque converter and to the seal lips.
28   Attach the hoist to the engine and carefully guide the engine into place, following the procedure outlined in Chapter 7A or 7B. **Caution:** *Do not use the bolts to force the engine and transaxle into alignment. It may crack or damage major components.* Install the engine-to-transaxle bolts and tighten them to the torque listed in Chapter 7A or 7B Specifications.
29   If you're working on a model equipped with an automatic transaxle, install the torque converter-to-driveplate fasteners and tighten them to the torque listed in the Chapter 7B Specifications.
30   Install the mount bolts and tighten them securely.
31   Reinstall the remaining components and fasteners in the reverse order of removal.
32   Add coolant, oil, power steering and transmission fluids as needed (see Chapter 1).

33   Run the engine and check for proper operation and leaks. Shut off the engine and recheck the fluid levels.

7   Engine rebuilding alternatives

The do-it-yourselfer is faced with a number of options when performing an engine overhaul. The decision to replace the engine block, piston/connecting rod assemblies and crankshaft depends on a number of factors, with the number one consideration being the condition of the block. Other considerations are cost, access to machine shop facilities, parts availability, time required to complete the project and the extent of prior mechanical experience on the part of the do-it-yourselfer.

Some of the rebuilding alternatives include:

Individual parts - If the inspection procedures reveal that the engine block and most engine components are in reusable condition, purchasing individual parts may be the most economical alternative. The block, crankshaft and piston/connecting rod assemblies should all be inspected carefully. Even if the block shows little wear, the cylinder bores should be surface honed.

Short block - A short block consists of an engine block with a crankshaft and piston/connecting rod assemblies already installed. All new bearings are incorporated and all clearances will be correct. The existing camshaft, valve train components, cylinder head(s) and external parts can be bolted to the short block with little or no machine shop work necessary.

Long block - A long block consists of a short block plus an oil pump, oil pan, cylinder head, camshaft and valve train components, timing pulleys and belt. All components are installed with new bearings, seals and gaskets incorporated throughout. The installation of manifolds and external parts is all that's necessary.

Give careful thought to which alternative

is best for you and discuss the situation with local automotive machine shops, auto parts dealers and experienced rebuilders before ordering or purchasing replacement parts.

8   Engine overhaul - disassembly sequence

Refer to illustration 8.5

1   It's much easier to disassemble and work on the engine if it's mounted on a portable engine stand. A stand can often be rented quite cheaply from an equipment rental yard. Before the engine is mounted on a stand, the flywheel/driveplate and rear oil seal retainer should be removed from the engine.
2   If a stand isn't available, it's possible to disassemble the engine with it blocked up on the floor. Be extra careful not to tip or drop the engine when working without a stand.
3   If you're going to obtain a rebuilt engine, all external components must come off first, to be transferred to the replacement engine, just as they will if you're doing a complete engine overhaul yourself. These include:

Emissions control components
Distributor, spark plug wires and spark plugs
Thermostat and housing
Water pump
Caburetion/EFI components
Intake/exhaust manifolds
Oil filter (always use a new filter)
Engine mounts
Clutch and flywheel/driveplate
Engine rear plate

Note: *When removing the external components from the engine, pay close attention to details that may be helpful or important during installation. Note the installed position of gaskets, seals, spacers, pins, brackets, washers, bolts and other small items.*

4   If you're obtaining a short block, which consists of the engine block, crankshaft, pistons and connecting rods all assembled, then the cylinder head, oil pan, front timing cover and oil pump will have to be removed as well, to be reused on the rebuilt short block. See Section 7 for additional information regarding the different possibilities to be considered.
5   If you're planning a complete overhaul, the engine must be disassembled and the components removed in the following order **(see illustration)**.

Valve cover
Oil pan and pick-up tube
Timing belt/chain cover
Oil pump
Timing belt/chain and sprockets
Rocker arm and shaft assemblies (if equipped)
Camshaft(s) and lifters
Cylinder head
Piston/connecting rod assemblies
Crankshaft rear oil seal retainer
Crankshaft and main bearings

8.5 Typical internal engine components

Rocker cover

Rocker shaft

Gasket

Camshaft

Rocker arm

Valve cotter

Spring retainer

Spring

Spring seat

Oil seal

Locate plate

Cylinder head

Gasket

Cam sprocket cover

Cylinder head gasket

Liquid gasket

Intake valve

Water outlet

9.1 Typical cylinder head components

6   Before beginning the disassembly and overhaul procedures, make sure the following items are available. Also, refer to Section 21 for a list of tools and materials needed for engine reassembly.

Common hand tools
Small cardboard boxes or plastic bags for storing parts
Gasket scraper
Ridge reamer
Vibration damper puller
Micrometers
Telescoping gauges
Dial indicator set
Valve spring compressor
Cylinder surfacing hone
Piston ring groove cleaning tool
Electric drill motor
Tap and die set
Wire brushes
Oil gallery brushes
Cleaning solvent

9   Cylinder head - disassembly

Refer to illustrations 9.1, 9.2, 9.3 and 9.4
Note: *New and rebuilt cylinder heads are commonly available for most engines at dealerships and auto parts stores. Due to the fact that some specialized tools are necessary for the disassembly and inspection procedures, and replacement parts may not be readily available, it may be more practical and economical for the home mechanic to purchase a replacement head rather than taking the time to disassemble, inspect and recondition the original.*

1   Cylinder head disassembly involves removal of the intake and exhaust valves and related components **(see illustration)**. It's assumed that the lifters or rocker arms and camshaft(s) have already been removed (see Part A as needed).

2   Before the valves are removed, arrange to label and store them, along with their related components, so they can be kept separate and reinstalled in the same valve guides they are removed from **(see illustration)**.

9.2 A small plastic bag, with an appropriate label, can be used to store the valve train components so they can be kept together and reinstalled in the original position

9.3 Use a valve spring compressor to compress the spring, then remove the keepers (arrow) from the valve stem

9.4 If the valve won't pull through the guide, deburr the edge of the stem end and the area around the top of the keeper groove with a file or whetstone

3 Compress the springs on the first valve with a spring compressor and remove the keepers **(see illustration)**. Carefully release the valve spring compressor and remove the retainer, the spring and the spring seat (if used).

4 Pull the valve out of the head and remove the oil seal from the guide (in either order). If the valve binds in the guide (won't pull through), push it back into the head and deburr the area around the keeper groove with a fine file or whetstone **(see illustration)**.

5 Repeat the procedure for the remaining valves. Remember to keep all the parts for each valve together so they can be reinstalled in the same locations.

6 Once the valves and related components have been removed and stored in an organized manner, the head should be thoroughly cleaned and inspected. If a complete engine overhaul is being done, finish the engine disassembly procedures before beginning the cylinder head cleaning and inspection process.

10 Cylinder head - cleaning and inspection

1 Thorough cleaning of the cylinder head and related valve train components, followed by a detailed inspection, will enable you to decide how much valve service work must be done during the engine overhaul. **Note:** *If the engine was severely overheated, the cylinder head is probably warped* (see Step 12).

Cleaning

2 Scrape all traces of old gasket material and sealing compound off the head gasket, intake manifold and exhaust manifold sealing surfaces. Be very careful not to gouge the cylinder head. Special gasket removal solvents that soften gaskets and make removal much easier are available at auto parts stores.

3 Remove all built-up scale from the coolant passages.

4 Run a stiff wire brush through the various holes to remove deposits that may have formed in them.

5 Run an appropriate size tap into each of the threaded holes to remove corrosion and thread sealant that may be present. If compressed air is available, use it to clear the holes of debris produced by this operation. **Warning:** *Wear eye protection when using compressed air!*

6 Clean the exhaust and intake manifold stud threads with a wire brush.

7 Clean the cylinder head with solvent and dry it thoroughly. Compressed air will speed the drying process and ensure that all holes and recessed areas are clean. **Note:** *Decarbonizing chemicals are available and may prove very useful when cleaning cylinder heads and valve train components. They are very caustic and should be used with caution. Be sure to follow the instructions on the container.*

8 Clean the lifters and rocker arms (if used) with solvent and dry them thoroughly (don't mix them up during the cleaning process). Compressed air will speed the drying process and can be used to clean out the oil passages. **Caution:** *The hydraulic lifters on 1989 and 1990 models are part of the rocker arms. These must be kept in a vertical (as installed) plane or oil may bleed out and air may enter. They may be stored on their side submerged in a pan of engine oil. The hydraulic lash adjusters on 1991 through*

10.12 Check the cylinder head gasket surface for warpage by trying to slip a feeler gauge under the straightedge (see this Chapter's Specifications for the maximum warpage allowed and use a feeler gauge of that thickness)

1994 SR20DE engines must also be stored in engine oil. Both of these hydraulic adjuster types are very difficult to bleed down in engine operation if air is allowed in during disassembly procedures.

9 Clean all the valve springs, spring seats, keepers and retainers with solvent and dry them thoroughly. Do the components from one valve at a time to avoid mixing up the parts. Number the valve lifters and their shims and keep them together.

10 Scrape off any heavy deposits that may have formed on the valves, then use a motorized wire brush to remove deposits from the valve heads and stems. Again, make sure the valves don't get mixed up.

Inspection

Note: *Be sure to perform all of the following inspection procedures before concluding that machine shop work is required. Make a list of the items that need attention. The inspection procedures for the lifters and rocker arms, as well as the camshaft(s), can be found in Part A.*

Cylinder head

Refer to illustrations 10.12, 10.14, 10.15, and 10.16

11 Inspect the head very carefully for cracks, evidence of coolant leakage and other damage. If cracks are found, check with an automotive machine shop concerning repair. If repair isn't possible, a new cylinder head should be obtained.

12 Using a straightedge and feeler gauge, check the head gasket mating surface for warpage **(see illustration)**. If the warpage exceeds the specified limit, it can be resurfaced at an automotive machine shop.

13 Examine the valve seats in each of the combustion chambers. If they're pitted, cracked or burned, the head will require valve service that's beyond the scope of the home mechanic.

14 Measure the valve guide inside diameter with a small hole gauge and micrometer **(see illustration)**, then measure the valve stem diameter with a micrometer and subtract it from the valve guide inside diameter to obtain the stem-to-guide clearance. Also, check the valve stem deflection crosswise (parallel to the rocker arm) with a dial indicator attached securely to the head. The valve must be in

10.14 Use a small hole gauge to determine the inside diameter of the valve guides (the gauge is then measured with a micrometer)

10.15 Check for valve wear at the points shown here

10.16 The margin width on each valve must be as specified (if no margin exists, the valve cannot be reused)

10.17 Measure the free length of each valve spring with a dial or vernier caliper

the guide and approximately 1/16-inch off the seat. The total valve stem movement indicated by the gauge needle must be noted. If it exceeds the specified stem-to-guide clearance limit, the valve guides should be replaced. After this is done, if there's still some doubt regarding the condition of the valve guides they should be checked by an automotive machine shop (the cost should be minimal).

Valves

15   Carefully inspect each valve face for uneven wear, deformation, cracks, pits and burned areas. Check the valve stem for scuffing and galling and the neck for cracks. Rotate the valve and check for any obvious indication that it's bent. Look for pits and excessive wear on the end of the stem (see illustration). The presence of any of these conditions indicates the need for valve service by an automotive machine shop.
16   Measure the margin width on each valve (see illustration). Any valve with a margin narrower than specified will have to be replaced with a new one.

Valve components

Refer to illustrations 10.17 and 10.18
17   Check each valve spring for wear (on the ends) and pits. Measure the free height and compare it to the Specifications (see

10.18 Check each valve spring for squareness, if it is bent it should be replaced

illustration). Any springs that are shorter than specified have sagged and should not be reused. The tension of all springs should be checked with a special fixture before deciding that they're suitable for use in a rebuilt engine (take the springs to an automotive machine shop for this check).
18   Stand each spring on a flat surface and check it for squareness (see illustration). If any of the springs are distorted or sagged, replace all of them with new parts.
19   Check the spring retainers and keepers for obvious wear and cracks. Any questionable parts should be replaced with new ones, as extensive damage will occur if they fail during engine operation.
20   Any damaged or excessively worn parts must be replaced with new ones.
21   If the inspection process indicates that the valve components are in generally poor condition and worn beyond the limits specified, which is usually the case in an engine that's being overhauled, reassemble the valves in the cylinder head and refer to valve servicing recommendations (see Section 11).

11   Valves - servicing

1   Because of the complex nature of the job and the special tools and equipment needed, servicing of the valves, the valve seats and the valve guides, commonly known as a valve job, should be done by a professional.
2   The home mechanic can remove and disassemble the head, do the initial cleaning and inspection, then reassemble and deliver it to a dealer service department or an automotive machine shop for the actual service work. Doing the inspection will enable you to see what condition the head and valvetrain components are in and will ensure that you know what work and new parts are required when dealing with an automotive machine shop.
3   The dealer service department, or automotive machine shop, will remove the valves and springs, recondition or replace the valves and valve seats, check and replace the valve guides (as necessary), check and replace the valve springs, spring retainers

and keepers (as necessary), replace the valve seals with new ones, reassemble the valve components and make sure the installed spring height is correct. The cylinder head gasket surface will also be resurfaced (within specification limits) if it's warped.
4   After the valve job has been performed by a professional, the head will be in like-new condition. When the head is returned, be sure to clean it again before installation on the engine to remove any metal particles and abrasive grit that may still be present from the valve service or head resurfacing operations. Use compressed air, if available, to blow out all the oil holes and passages.

12   Cylinder head - reassembly

1   Regardless of whether or not the head was sent to an automotive repair shop for valve servicing, make sure it's clean before beginning reassembly.
2   If the head was sent out for valve servicing, the valves and related components will already be in place.
3   If the machine shop did not install them, install new seals on each of the valve guides. Gently tap each intake valve seal into place until it's seated on the guide (see Chapter 2A). **Caution:** *Don't hammer on the valve seals once they're seated or you may damage them. Don't twist or cock the seals during installation or they won't seat properly on the valve stems.*
4   Beginning at one end of the head, lubricate and install the first valve. Apply moly-base grease or clean engine oil to the valve stem.
5   Drop the spring seat or shim(s) (if equipped) over the valve guide and set the valve spring and retainer in place.
6   Compress the springs with a valve spring compressor and carefully install the keepers in the upper groove, then slowly release the compressor and make sure the keepers seat properly. Apply a small dab of grease to each keeper to hold it in place if necessary.
7   Repeat the procedure for the remaining valves. Be sure to return the components to their original locations - don't mix them up!

2B

13.1 A ridge reamer is required to remove the ridge from the top of each cylinder - do this before removing the pistons!

13.3 Check the connecting rod side clearance (endplay) with a feeler gauge as shown here

13.4 If not already marked, mark the rod bearing caps in order from the front of the engine to the rear (one mark for the front cap, two for the second one and so on) the marks should always be on the same side of the rod and cap

13   Pistons/connecting rods - removal

Refer to illustrations 13.1, 13.3, 13.4 and 13.6
Note: *Prior to removing the piston/connecting rod assemblies, remove the cylinder head, the oil pan and the oil pump pick-up tube by referring to the appropriate Sections in Part A.*

1   Use your fingernail to feel if a ridge has formed at the upper limit of ring travel (about 1/4-inch down from the top of each cylinder). If carbon deposits or cylinder wear have produced ridges, they must be completely removed with a special tool **(see illustration)**. Follow the manufacturer's instructions provided with the tool. Failure to remove the ridges before attempting to remove the piston/connecting rod assemblies may result in piston breakage. **Caution:** *When removing a ridge in the cylinder bore, DO NOT damage the top of the cylinder bore or the block deck surface with the ridge removal tool.*

2   After the cylinder ridges have been removed, turn the engine upside-down so the crankshaft is facing up.

3   Before the connecting rods are removed, check the endplay (side clearance) with feeler gauges. Slide them between each connecting rod and the crankshaft throw until the play is removed **(see illustration)**. The endplay is equal to the thickness of the feeler

gauge(s). If the endplay exceeds the service limit, new connecting rods will be required. If new rods (or a new crankshaft) are installed, the endplay may fall under the specified minimum (if it does, the rods will have to be machined to restore it - consult an automotive machine shop for advice if necessary). Repeat the procedure for the remaining connecting rods.

4   Check the connecting rods and caps for identification marks. If they aren't plainly marked, use a small center-punch to make the appropriate number of indentations on each rod and cap (1, 2, 3, etc., depending on the engine type and cylinder they're associated with) **(see illustration)**.

5   Loosen each of the connecting rod cap nuts 1/2-turn at a time until they can be removed by hand. Remove the number one connecting rod cap and bearing insert. Don't drop the bearing insert out of the cap.

6   Slip a short length of plastic or rubber hose over each connecting rod cap bolt to protect the crankshaft journal and cylinder wall as the piston is removed **(see illustration)**.

7   Remove the bearing insert and push the connecting rod/piston assembly out through the top of the engine. Use a wooden hammer handle to push on the upper bearing surface in the connecting rod. If resistance is felt, double-check to make sure that all of the ridge was removed from the cylinder.

8   Repeat the procedure for the remaining cylinders.

9   After removal, reassemble the connecting rod caps and bearing inserts in their respective connecting rods and install the cap nuts finger tight. Leaving the old bearing inserts in place until reassembly will help prevent the connecting rod bearing surfaces from being accidentally nicked or gouged.

10   Don't separate the pistons from the connecting rods (see Section 18).

14   Crankshaft - removal

Refer to illustrations 14.1 and 14.3
Note: *The crankshaft can be removed only after the engine has been removed from the vehicle. It's assumed that the flywheel or driveplate, crankshaft pulley, timing chain, oil pan, oil pick-up tube, oil pump and piston/connecting rod assemblies have already been removed. The rear main oil seal retainer must be unbolted and separated from the block before proceeding with crankshaft removal.*

1   Before the crankshaft is removed, check the endplay. Mount a dial indicator with the stem in line with the crankshaft and touching the crankshaft end **(see illustration)**.

2   Pry the crankshaft all the way to the rear and zero the dial indicator. Next, pry the crankshaft to the front as far as possible and check the reading on the dial indicator. The distance that it moves is the endplay. If it's greater than specified, check the crankshaft thrust surfaces for wear. If no wear is evident, new thrust bearings should correct the endplay.

3   If a dial indicator isn't available, feeler gauges can be used. Gently pry or push the crankshaft all the way to the front of the engine. Slip feeler gauges between the crankshaft and the front face of the thrust main bearing to determine the clearance **(see illustration)**. The thrust bearing is the number three (center) bearing.

4   Check the main bearing caps to see if they're marked to indicate their locations.

13.6 To prevent damage to the crankshaft journals and cylinder walls, slip sections of hose over the rod bolts before removing the piston/rod assembly

14.1 Checking crankshaft endplay with a dial indicator

14.3 Checking crankshaft endplay with a feeler gauge

15.1a A hammer and a large punch can be used to knock the core plugs sideways in their bores

15.1b Pull the core plugs from the block with pliers

They should be numbered consecutively from the front of the engine to the rear. If they aren't, mark them with number stamping dies or a center-punch. Main bearing caps generally have a cast-in arrow, which points to the front of the engine. Loosen the main bearing cap bolts 1/4-turn at a time each, starting with the front and rear caps and working toward the center, until they can be removed by hand. If any stud bolts are used and make sure they're returned to their original locations when the crankshaft is reinstalled. **Note:** *1982 through 1988 models have separate main caps for each main bearing, as does the later SR20DE engine, but all the 1597 cc GA series engines from 1989 through 1994 have two bearing saddles, which incorporate two bearing caps in each, plus a separate center bearing cap.*

5   Gently tap the caps with a soft-face hammer, then separate them from the engine block. If necessary, use the bolts as levers to remove the caps. Try not to drop the bearing inserts if they come out with the caps.
6   Carefully lift the crankshaft out of the engine. It may be a good idea to have an assistant available, since the crankshaft is quite heavy. With the bearing inserts in place in the engine block and main bearing caps or cap assembly, return the caps to their respective locations on the engine block and tighten the bolts finger tight.
Note: *1982 through 1988 engines have a jackshaft that drives the oil pump. During this part of the engine disassembly, the jackshaft should be removed and inspected for wear or nicks on its bearing surfaces and the oil pump drive gear. Remove the jackshaft sprocket to gain access to the screw and retainer plate that holds the jackshaft in the block.*

15   Engine block- cleaning

Refer to illustrations 15.1a, 15.1b, 15.8 and 15.10
Caution: *The core plugs (also known as freeze or soft plugs) may be difficult or impossible to retrieve if they're driven into the block coolant passages.*
1   Using the wide end of a punch **(see illustration)** tap in on one side of the outer

edge of the core plug to turn the plug sideways in the bore. Then, using a pair of pliers, pull the core plug from the engine block **(see illustration)**. Don't worry about the condition of the old core plugs as they are being removed because they will be replaced on reassembly with new plugs.
2   Using a gasket scraper, remove all traces of gasket material from the engine block. **Caution:** *Be EXTREMELY CAREFUL not to nick or gouge the gasket sealing surfaces.*
3   Remove the main bearing caps or cap assembly and separate the bearing inserts from the caps and the engine block. Tag the bearings, indicating which cylinder they were removed from and whether they were in the cap or the block, then set them aside.
4   Remove all of the threaded oil gallery plugs from the block. The plugs are usually very tight   they may have to be drilled out and the holes retapped. Use new plugs when the engine is reassembled.
5   If the engine is extremely dirty it should be taken to an automotive machine shop for cleaning.
6   After the block is returned, clean all oil holes and oil galleries one more time. Brushes specifically designed for this purpose are available at most auto parts stores. Flush the passages with warm water until the water runs clear, dry the block thoroughly and wipe all machined surfaces with a light, rust preventive oil. If you have

access to compressed air, use it to speed the drying process and to blow out all the oil holes and galleries. **Warning:** *Wear eye protection when using compressed air!*
7   If the block isn't extremely dirty or sludged up, you can do an adequate cleaning job with hot soapy water and a stiff brush. Take plenty of time and do a thorough job. Regardless of the cleaning method used, be sure to clean all oil holes and galleries very thoroughly, dry the block completely and coat all machined surfaces with light oil.
8   The threaded holes in the block must be clean to ensure accurate torque readings during reassembly. Run the proper size tap into each of the holes to remove rust, corrosion, thread sealant or sludge and restore damaged threads **(see illustration)**. If possible, use compressed air to clear the holes of debris produced by this operation. Now is a good time to clean the threads on the head bolts and the main bearing cap bolts as well.
9   Reinstall the main bearing caps and tighten the bolts finger tight.
10   After coating the sealing surfaces of the new core plugs with a non-hardening sealant, such as Permatex no. 2 sealant or equivalent, install them in the engine block **(see illustration)**. Make sure they're driven in straight or leakage could result. Special tools are available for this purpose, but a large socket, with an outside diameter that will just slip into the core plug, a 1/2-inch drive extension and a hammer will work just as well.

2B

15.8 All bolt holes in the block - particularly the main bearing cap and head bolt holes - should be cleaned and restored with a tap (be sure to remove debris from the holes after this is done)

15.10 A large socket on an extension can be used to drive the new core plugs into the bores

16.2 On 1989 to 1994 models, the rear of the oil pan surface on the block is stamped with two rows of numbers (arrows) - indicating the "grade" or size of the cylinder bores and main journals

1 Cylinder bore grade number (front to rear, cylinders 1 to 4)
2 Main journal grade number (front to rear, journals 1 to 5)

11 Apply non-hardening sealant (such as Permatex no. 2 or Teflon pipe sealant) to the new oil gallery plugs and thread them into the holes in the block. Make sure they're tightened securely.
12 If the engine isn't going to be reassembled right away, cover it with a large plastic trash bag to keep it clean.

16 Engine block - inspection

Refer to illustrations 16.2, 16.4a, 16.4b and 16.12

1 Before the block is inspected, it should be cleaned (see Section 15).
2 Visually check the block for cracks, rust and corrosion. Look for stripped threads in the threaded holes. It's also a good idea to have the block checked for hidden cracks by an automotive machine shop that has the special equipment to do this type of work. If defects are found, have the block repaired, if possible, or replaced. On 1991 through 1994 models, the blocks are marked with a "grade"

16.12 Check the block deck for distortion with a precision straightedge and a feeler gauge - lay the straightedge across the block, diagonally and from end-to-end when making the check

16.4a Measure the diameter of each cylinder - the ability to feel when the telescoping gauge is at the correct point will be developed over time, so work slowly and repeat the check until you're satisfied the bore measurement is accurate

indication, which refers to the sizes of the bores and other specifications (**see illustration**). This information can be important when ordering bearings and other parts.
3 Check the cylinder bores for scuffing and scoring.
4 Measure the diameter of each cylinder at the top (just under the ridge area), center and bottom of the cylinder bore, parallel to the crankshaft axis (**see illustrations**).
5 Next, measure each cylinder's diameter at the same three locations across the crankshaft axis. Compare the results to the Specifications.
6 If the required precision measuring tools aren't available, the piston-to-cylinder clearances can be obtained, though not quite as accurately, using feeler gauge stock. Feeler gauge stock comes in 12-inch lengths and various thickness and is generally available at auto parts stores.
7 To check the clearance, select a feeler gauge the same thickness as the recommended piston-to-bore clearance (see this chapter's specifications) and slip it into the cylinder along with the matching piston (with piston rings removed). The piston must be positioned exactly as it normally would be. The feeler gauge must be between the piston and cylinder on one of the thrust faces (90-degrees to the piston pin bore).
8 The piston should slip through the cylinder (with the feeler gauge in place) with moderate pressure.
9 If it falls through or slides through easily, the clearance is excessive and a new piston will be required. If the piston binds at the lower end of the cylinder and is loose toward the top, the cylinder is tapered. If tight spots are encountered as the piston/feeler gauge is rotated in the cylinder, the cylinder is out-of-round.
10 Repeat the procedure for the remaining pistons and cylinders.
11 If the cylinder walls are badly scuffed or scored, or if they're out-of-round or tapered beyond the limits given in this Chapter's Specifications, have the engine block rebored and honed at an automotive machine

16.4b The gauge is then measured with a micrometer to determine the bore size

shop. If a rebore is done, oversize pistons and rings will be required.
12 Using a precision straightedge and a feeler gauge, check the block deck (the surface that mates with the cylinder head) for distortion (**see illustration**). If it's distorted beyond the specified limit, it can be resurfaced by an automotive machine shop.
13 If the cylinders are in reasonably good condition and not worn to the outside of the limits, and if the piston-to-cylinder clearances can be maintained properly, then they don't have to be rebored. Honing is all that's necessary (see Section 17).

17 Cylinder honing

Refer to illustrations 17.3a and 17.3b

1 Prior to engine reassembly, the cylinder bores must be honed so the new piston rings will seat correctly and provide the best possible combustion chamber seal. **Note:** *If you don't have the tools or don't want to tackle the honing operation, most automotive machine shops will do it for a reasonable fee.*
2 Before honing the cylinders, install the main bearing caps (without bearing inserts) and tighten the bolts to the torque listed in this Chapter's Specifications.
3 Two types of cylinder hones are commonly available - the flex hone or "bottle brush" type and the more traditional surfacing hone with spring-loaded stones. Both will do the job, but for the less experienced mechanic the "bottle brush" hone will probably be easier to use. You'll also need some kerosene or honing oil, rags and an electric drill motor. Proceed as follows:

a) *Mount the hone in the drill motor, compress the stones and slip it into the first cylinder (see illustration). Be sure to wear safety goggles or a face shield!*
b) *Lubricate the cylinder with plenty of honing oil, turn on the drill and move the hone up-and-down in the cylinder at a pace that will produce a fine crosshatch pattern on the cylinder walls. Ideally, the*

17.3a A "bottle brush" hone will produce better results if you've never honed cylinders before

crosshatch lines should intersect at approximately a 60-degrees angle **(see illustration)**. *Be sure to use plenty of lubricant and don't take off any more material than is absolutely necessary to produce the desired finish.* **Note:** *Piston ring manufacturers may specify a smaller crosshatch angle than the traditional 60-degrees - read and follow any instructions included with the new rings.*

c) *Don't withdraw the hone from the cylinder while it's running. Instead, shut off the drill and continue moving the hone up-and-down in the cylinder until it comes to a complete stop, then compress the stones and withdraw the hone. If you're using a "bottle brush" type hone, stop the drill motor, then turn the chuck in the normal direction of rotation while withdrawing the hone from the cylinder.*

d) *Wipe the oil out of the cylinder and repeat the procedure for the remaining cylinders.*

4   After the honing job is complete, chamfer the top edges of the cylinder bores with a small file so the rings won't catch when the pistons are installed. Be very careful not to nick the cylinder walls with the end of the file.

5   The entire engine block must be washed again very thoroughly with warm, soapy water to remove all traces of the abrasive grit produced during the honing operation. **Note:** *The bores can be considered clean when a*

18.4 The piston ring grooves can be cleaned with a special tool, or a section of a broken ring as shown here

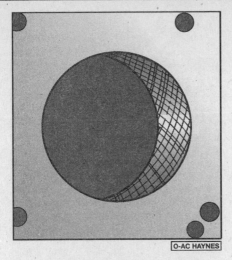

17.3b The cylinder hone should leave a smooth, crosshatch pattern with the lines intersecting at approximately a 60-degree angle

lint-free white cloth - dampened with clean engine oil - used to wipe them out doesn't pick up any more honing residue, which will show up as gray areas on the cloth. Be sure to run a brush through all oil holes and galleries and flush them with running water.

6   After rinsing, dry the block and apply a coat of light rust preventive oil to all machined surfaces. Wrap the block in a plastic trash bag to keep it clean and set it aside until reassembly.

18   Pistons/connecting rods - inspection

Refer to illustrations 18.4, 18.10 and 18.11

1   Before the inspection process can be carried out, the piston/connecting rod assemblies must be cleaned and the original piston rings removed from the pistons. **Note:** *Always use new piston rings when the engine is reassembled.*

2   Using a piston ring installation tool, carefully remove the rings from the pistons. Be careful not to nick or gouge the pistons in the process.

18.10 Check the ring side clearance with a feeler gauge at several points around the groove

3   Scrape all traces of carbon from the top of the piston. A hand-held wire brush or a piece of fine emery cloth can be used once the majority of the deposits have been scraped away. Do not, under any circumstances, use a wire brush mounted in a drill motor to remove deposits from the pistons. The piston material is soft and may be eroded away by the wire brush.

4   Use a piston ring groove cleaning tool to remove carbon deposits from the ring grooves. If a tool isn't available, a piece broken off the old ring will do the job. Be very careful to remove only the carbon deposits - don't remove any metal and do not nick or scratch the sides of the ring grooves **(see illustration)**.

5   Once the deposits have been removed, clean the piston/rod assemblies with solvent and dry them with compressed air (if available). **Warning:** *Wear eye protection when using compressed air!* Make sure the oil return holes in the back sides of the ring grooves and the oil hole in the lower end of each rod are clear.

6   If the pistons and cylinder walls aren't damaged or worn excessively, and if the engine block is not rebored, new pistons won't be necessary. Normal piston wear appears as even vertical wear on the piston thrust surfaces and slight looseness of the top ring in its groove. New piston rings, however, should always be used when an engine is rebuilt.

7   Carefully inspect each piston for cracks around the skirt, at the pin bosses and at the ring lands.

8   Look for scoring and scuffing on the thrust faces of the skirt, holes in the piston crown and burned areas at the edge of the crown. If the skirt is scored or scuffed, the engine may have been suffering from overheating and/or abnormal combustion, which caused excessively high operating temperatures. The cooling and lubrication systems should be checked thoroughly. A hole in the piston crown is an indication that abnormal combustion (preignition) was occurring. Burned areas at the edge of the piston crown are usually evidence of spark knock (detonation). If any of the above problems exist, the causes must be corrected or the damage will occur again. The causes may include intake air leaks, incorrect fuel/air mixture, incorrect ignition timing and EGR system malfunctions.

9   Corrosion of the piston, in the form of small pits, indicates that coolant is leaking into the combustion chamber and/or the crankcase. Again, the cause must be corrected or the problem may persist in the rebuilt engine.

10   Measure the piston ring side clearance by laying a new piston ring in each ring groove and slipping a feeler gauge in beside it **(see illustration)**. Check the clearance at three or four locations around each groove. Be sure to use the correct ring for each groove - they are different. If the side clearance is greater than specified, new pistons will have to be used.

2B

18.11 Measure the piston diameter at a 90-degree angle to the piston pin below the bottom of the piston pin bore

19.1 The oil holes should be chamfered so sharp edges don't gouge or scratch the new bearings

19.2 Use a wire or stiff plastic bristle brush to clean the oil passages In the crankshaft

11   Check the piston-to-bore clearance by measuring the bore (see Section 16) and the piston diameter. Make sure the pistons and bores are correctly matched. Measure the piston across the skirt, at a 90-degree angle to the piston pin and at approximately the bottom of the pin bore **(see illustration)**. Subtract the piston diameter from the bore diameter to obtain the clearance. If it's greater than specified, the block will have to be rebored and new pistons and rings installed.

12   Check the piston-to-rod clearance by twisting the piston and rod in opposite directions. Any noticeable play indicates excessive wear, which must be corrected. The piston/connecting rod assemblies should be taken to an automotive machine shop to have the pistons and rods re-sized and new pins installed.

13   If the pistons must be removed from the connecting rods for any reason, they should be taken to an automotive machine shop. While they are there, have the connecting rods checked for bend and twist, since automotive machine shops have special equipment for this purpose. **Note:** *Unless new pistons and/or connecting rods must be installed, do not disassemble the pistons and connecting rods.*

14   Check the connecting rods for cracks and other damage. Temporarily remove the

rod caps, lift out the old bearing inserts, wipe the rod and cap bearing surfaces clean and inspect them for nicks, gouges and scratches. After checking the rods, replace the old bearings, slip the caps into place and tighten the nuts finger tight. **Note:** *If the engine is being rebuilt because of a connecting rod knock, be sure to install new rods.*

19 Crankshaft - inspection

Refer to illustrations 19.1, 19.2, 19.4 and 19.6

1   Remove all burrs from the crankshaft oil holes with a stone, file or scraper **(see illustration)**.

2   Clean the crankshaft with solvent and dry it with compressed air (if available). Be sure to clean the oil holes with a stiff brush and flush them with solvent **(see illustration)**.

3   Check the main and connecting rod bearing journals for uneven wear, scoring, pits and cracks.

4   Rub a penny across each journal several times **(see illustration)**. If a journal picks up copper from the penny, it's too rough and must be reground.

5   Check the rest of the crankshaft for cracks and other damage. It should be magnafluxed to reveal hidden cracks - an automotive machine shop will handle the procedure.

6   Using a micrometer, measure the

diameter of the main and connecting rod journals and compare the results to this chapters specifications **(see illustration)**. By measuring the diameter at a number of points around each journal's circumference, you'll be able to determine whether or not the journal is out-of-round. Take the measurement at each end of the journal, near the crank throws, to determine if the journal is tapered. Crankshaft runout should be checked also, but large V-blocks and a dial indicator are needed to do it correctly. If you don't have the equipment, have a machine shop check the runout.

7   If the crankshaft journals are damaged, tapered, out-of-round or worn beyond the limits given in the Specifications, have the crankshaft reground by an automotive machine shop. Be sure to use the correct size bearing inserts if the crankshaft is reconditioned.

8   Check the oil seal journals at each end of the crankshaft for wear. If the seal has worn a groove in the journal, or if it's nicked or scratched, the new seal may leak when the engine is reassembled. In some cases, an automotive machine shop may be able to repair the journal by pressing on a thin sleeve. If repair isn't feasible, a new or different crankshaft should be installed.

9   Examine the main and rod bearing inserts (see Section 20).

10   If the crankshaft requires replacement make certain that you match the original crankshaft with any replacement purchased.

19.4 Rubbing a penny lengthwise on each journal will reveal its condition - if copper rubs off and is embedded in the crankshaft, the journals should be reground

19.6 Measure the diameter of each crankshaft journal at several points to detect taper and out-of-round conditions

20 Main and connecting rod bearings - inspection and selection

Inspection

Refer to illustrations 20.1 and 20.10

1   Even though the main and connecting rod bearings should be replaced with new ones during the engine overhaul, the old bearings should be retained for close examination, as they may reveal valuable infor-

20.1 Typical bearing failures

CRATERS OR POCKETS
FATIGUE FAILURE

BRIGHT (POLISHED) SECTIONS
IMPROPER SEATING

SCRATCHES
DIRT IMBEDDED INTO BEARING MATERIAL
SCRATCHED BY DIRT

OVERLAY WIPED OUT
LACK OF OIL

OVERLAY GONE FROM ENTIRE SURFACE
EXCESSIVE WEAR

RADIUS RIDE
TAPERED JOURNAL

mation about the condition of the engine (**see illustration**).

2   Bearing failure occurs because of lack of lubrication, the presence of dirt or other foreign particles, overloading the engine and corrosion. Regardless of the cause of bearing failure, it must be corrected before the engine is reassembled to prevent it from happening again.

3   When examining the bearings, remove them from the engine block, the main bearing caps, the connecting rods and the rod caps and lay them out on a clean surface in the same general position as their location in the engine. This will enable you to match any bearing problems with the corresponding crankshaft journal.

4   Dirt and other foreign particles get into the engine in a variety of ways. It may be left in the engine during assembly, or it may pass through filters or the PCV system. It may get into the oil, and from there into the bearings. Metal chips from machining operations and normal engine wear are often present. Abrasives are sometimes left in engine components after reconditioning, especially when parts are not thoroughly cleaned using the proper cleaning methods. Whatever the source, these foreign objects often end up embedded in the soft bearing material and are easily recognized. Large particles will not embed in the bearing and will score or gouge the bearing and journal. The best prevention for this cause of bearing failure is to clean all parts thoroughly and keep everything spotlessly clean during engine assembly. Frequent and regular engine oil and filter changes are also recommended.

5   Lack of lubrication (or lubrication breakdown) has a number of interrelated causes. Excessive heat (which thins the oil), overloading (which squeezes the oil from the bearing face) and oil leakage or throw off (from excessive bearing clearances, worn oil pump or high engine speeds) all contribute to lubrication breakdown. Blocked oil passages, which usually are the result of misaligned oil

holes in a bearing shell, will also oil starve a bearing and destroy it. When lack of lubrication is the cause of bearing failure, the bearing material is wiped or extruded from the steel backing of the bearing. Temperatures may increase to the point where the steel backing turns blue from overheating.

6   Driving habits can have a definite effect on bearing life. Low speed operation in too high a gear (lugging the engine) puts very high loads on bearings, which tends to squeeze out the oil film. These loads cause the bearings to flex, which produces fine cracks in the bearing face (fatigue failure). Eventually the bearing material will loosen in pieces and tear away from the steel backing. Short trip driving leads to corrosion of bearings because insufficient engine heat is produced to drive off the condensed water and corrosive gases. These products collect in the engine oil, forming acid and sludge. As the oil is carried to the engine bearings, the acid attacks and corrodes the bearing material.

7   Incorrect bearing installation during engine assembly will lead to bearing failure as well. Tight fitting bearings leave insufficient bearing oil clearance and will result in oil starvation. Dirt or foreign particles trapped behind a bearing insert result in high spots on the bearing which lead to failure.

Selection

8   If the original bearings are worn or damaged, or if the oil clearances are incorrect (see Section 23 or 25) and the crankshaft is undamaged or worn excessively, new bearings should be purchased for engine reassembly. However, if the crankshaft has been reground, new undersize bearings must be installed. The automotive machine shop that reconditions the crankshaft will provide or help you select the correct size bearings. Regardless of how the bearing sizes are determined, measure the oil clearance with Plastigage to ensure the bearings are the right size. **Note**: *1991 through 1994 engines are marked with "grade" numbers* (**see illustration 16.2**). *The lower row of numbers refers to the main bearing journal size. If the original crankshaft is being reused without regrinding, comparable size main bearings should be ordered.*

20.10 Just as the 1991 to 1994 blocks are "grade" marked, so are the crankshafts marked on the first counterweight

No. 4   No.1
Crank pin grade number
Crank journal grade number
No.5   No.1

9   If you need to use STANDARD size bearings, install bearings that have the same grade number as the original bearings.

10   Crankshafts on 1991 through 1994 models may be marked, like the blocks, with two rows of numbers on the front counterweight (**see illustration**). The top row as shown indicates the grade of the four rod journals, and the lower numbers the grade of the five main journals.

11   Remember, the oil clearance is the final judge when selecting new bearing sizes. If you have any questions or are unsure which bearings to use, get help from a dealer parts or service department or other parts supplier.

21   Engine overhaul - reassembly sequence

1   Before beginning engine reassembly, make sure you have all the necessary new parts, gaskets and seals as well as the following items on hand:

Common hand tools
A torque wrench
Piston ring installation tool
Piston ring compressor
Short lengths of rubber or plastic hose to fit over
connecting rod bolts
Plastigage
Feeler gauges
A fine-tooth file
New engine oil
Engine assembly lube or moly-base grease
Gasket sealant
Thread locking compound

2   In order to save time and avoid problems, engine reassembly must be done in the following general order:

Piston rings
Crankshaft and main bearings
Piston/connecting rod assemblies
Rear main oil seal
Jackshaft (if equipped)
Timing belt/chain, sprockets and cover (Part A)
Cylinder head and camshaft(s) (Part A)
Rocker arms or lifters (Part A)
Oil pump (Part A)
Oil pick-up tube
Oil pan (Part A)
Valve cover (Part A)
Intake and exhaust manifolds (Part A)
Flywheel/driveplate (Part A)

22   Piston rings - installation

Refer to illustrations 22.3, 22.4, 22.7a, 22.7b and 22.10

1   Before installing the new piston rings, the ring end gaps must be checked. It's assumed that the piston ring side clearance has been checked and verified correct (see Section 18).

2B

22.3 When checking piston ring end gap, the ring must be square in the cylinder bore (this is done by pushing the ring down with the top of a piston as shown)

22.4 With the ring square in the cylinder, measure the end gap with a feeler gauge

22.7a Installing the spacer/expander in the oil control ring groove

2   Lay out the piston/connecting rod assemblies and the new ring sets so the ring sets will be matched with the same piston and cylinder during the end gap measurement and engine assembly.

3   Insert the top (number one) ring into the first cylinder and square it up with the cylinder walls by pushing it in with the top of the piston **(see illustration)**. The ring should be near the bottom of the cylinder, at the lower limit of ring travel.

4   To measure the end gap, slip feeler gauges between the ends of the ring until a gauge equal to the gap width is found **(see illustration)**. The feeler gauge should slide between the ring ends with a slight amount of drag. Compare the measurement to the Specifications. If the gap is larger or smaller than specified, double-check to make sure you have the correct rings before proceeding.

5   Repeat the procedure for each ring that will be installed in the first cylinder and for each ring in the remaining cylinders. Remember to keep rings, pistons and cylinders matched up.

6   Once the ring end gaps have been checked the rings can be installed on the pistons.

7   The oil control ring (lowest one on the piston) is usually installed first. It's composed of three separate components. Slip the spacer/expander into the groove **(see illustration)**. If an anti-rotation tang is used, make sure it's inserted into the drilled hole in the ring groove. Next, install the lower side rail. Don't use a piston ring installation tool on the oil ring side rails, as they may be damaged. Instead, place one end of the side rail into the groove between the spacer/expander and the ring land, hold it firmly in place and slide a finger around the piston while pushing the rail into the groove **(see illustration)**. Next, install the upper side rail in the same manner.

8   After the three oil ring components have been installed, check to make sure that both the upper and lower side rails can be turned smoothly in the ring groove.

9   The number two (middle) ring is installed next. It's usually stamped with a mark which must face up, toward the top of the piston. **Note:** *Always follow the instructions printed on the ring package or box - different manufacturers may require different approaches. Do not mix up the top and middle rings, as they have different cross sections.*

10   Use a piston ring installation tool and make sure the identification mark is facing the top of the piston, then slip the ring into the middle groove on the piston. Don't expand the ring any more than necessary to slide it over the piston **(see illustration)**.

11   Install the number one (top) ring in the same manner. Make sure the mark is facing up. Be careful not to confuse the number one and number two rings.

12   Repeat the procedure for the remaining pistons and rings.

22.7b DO NOT use a piston ring installation tool when installing the oil ring side rails

22.10 Installing the compression rings with a ring expander - the mark (arrow) must face up

23 Crankshaft - installation and main bearing oil clearance check

Refer to illustrations 23.10, 23.12a, 23.12b, 23.12c and 23.14

1   Crankshaft installation is the first major step in engine reassembly. It's assumed at this point that the engine block and crankshaft have been cleaned, inspected and repaired or reconditioned.

2   Position the engine with the bottom facing up.

3   Remove the main bearing cap bolts and lift out the caps. Lay the caps out in the proper order to ensure correct installation.

4   If they're still in place, remove the old bearing inserts from the block and the main bearing caps. Wipe the main bearing surfaces of the block and caps with a clean, lint-free cloth. They must be kept spotlessly clean!

Main bearing oil clearance check

5   Clean the back sides of the new main bearing inserts and lay the bearing half with the oil groove and hole in each main bearing saddle in the block (on all engines covered by this manual, the bearings with oil holes go in the block and those without oil holes go in the caps). Lay the other bearing half from each bearing set in the corresponding main bearing cap. Make sure the tab on each bearing insert fits into the recess in the block or cap. Also, the oil holes in the block must line up with the oil holes in the bearing insert. **Caution:** *Do not hammer the bearings into place and don't nick or gouge the bearing faces. No lubrication should be used at this time.*

6   The thrust bearings (washers) must be installed in the number three main bearing saddle (on the cylinder block side). Be sure to install them with the oil grooves facing out (away from the main bearing saddle). 1982 through 1988 models have a one-piece (flanged) thrust bearing, while 1989 and later engines have a three-piece arrangement (bearing plus two thrust washers). Apply a thin film of moly-based grease or engine assembly lube to the back sides of the thrust bearings to hold them in place.

23.10 Lay the Plastigage strips (arrow) on the main bearing journals, parallel to the crankshaft centerline

23.12 Main bearing cap tightening sequence

23.14 Compare the width of the crushed Plastigage to the scale on the envelope to determine the main bearing oil clearance (always take the measurement at the widest point of the Plastigage); be sure to use the correct scale - standard and metric ones are included

7 Clean the faces of the bearings in the block and the crankshaft main bearing journals with a clean, lint-free cloth. Check or clean the oil holes in the crankshaft, as any dirt here can go only one way - straight through the new bearings.

8 Once you're certain the crankshaft is clean, carefully lay it in position in the main bearings. No lubricant should be used at this time.

9 Before the crankshaft can be permanently installed, the main bearing oil clearance must be checked.

10 Trim several pieces of the appropriate size Plastigage (they must be slightly shorter than the width of the main bearings) and place one piece on each crankshaft main bearing journal, parallel with the journal axis **(see illustration)**.

11 Clean the faces of the bearings in the caps and install the caps in their respective positions (don't mix them up) with the arrows pointing toward the front of the engine. The main bearing caps are numbered, starting with number one at the timing belt/chain end of the block. Don't disturb the Plastigage. Apply a light coat of oil to the bolt threads and the under sides of the bolt heads, then install them.

12 Following the recommended sequence **(see illustration)**, tighten the main bearing cap bolts, in three steps, to the torque listed in this Chapter's Specifications. Don't rotate the crankshaft at any time during this operation!

13 Remove the bolts and carefully lift off the main bearing caps. Keep them in order. Don't disturb the Plastigage or rotate the crankshaft. If any of the main bearing caps are difficult to remove, tap them gently from side-to-side with a soft-face hammer to loosen them.

14 Compare the width of the crushed Plastigage on each journal to the scale printed on the Plastigage envelope to obtain the main bearing oil clearance **(see illustration)**. Check the Specifications to make sure it's correct.

15 If the clearance is not as specified, the bearing inserts may be the wrong size which means different ones will be required (see Section 20). Before deciding that different

inserts are needed, make sure that no dirt or oil was between the bearing inserts and the caps or block when the clearance was measured. If the Plastigage is noticeably wider at one end than the other, the journal may be tapered (see Section 19).

16 Carefully scrape all traces of the Plastigage material off the main bearing journals and/or the bearing faces. Don't nick or scratch the bearing faces.

Final crankshaft installation

17 Carefully lift the crankshaft out of the engine. Clean the bearing faces in the block, then apply a thin, uniform layer of clean moly-base grease or engine assembly lube to each of the bearing surfaces. Coat the thrust washers as well (thrust flanges on one-piece thrust bearings).

18 Lubricate the crankshaft surfaces that contact the oil seals with moly-base grease, engine assembly lube or clean engine oil.

19 Make sure the crankshaft journals are clean, then lay the crankshaft back in place in the block. Clean the faces of the bearings in the caps or cap assembly, then apply the same lubricant to them. Install the caps in their respective positions with the arrows pointing toward the front of the engine.

20 Apply a light coat of oil to the bolt threads and the under sides of the bolt heads, then install them. Tighten the bolts to 10-to-12 ft-lbs following the recommended sequence **(see illustration 23.12)**. Tap the ends of the crankshaft forward and backward with a lead or brass hammer to line up the thrust washer and crankshaft surfaces. Re-tighten all main bearing cap bolts to the specified torque, following the recommended sequence (work from the center out and approach the final torque in three steps).

21 Rotate the crankshaft a number of times by hand to check for any obvious binding.

22 Check the crankshaft endplay with a feeler gauge or a dial indicator (see Section 14). The endplay should be correct if the crankshaft thrust faces aren't worn or damaged and new thrust bearings/washers have been installed.

23 Install a new rear main oil seal, then bolt the retainer to the block (see Section 24).

24 Rear main oil seal - installation

Refer to Chapter 2A for procedure and illustrations

1 The crankshaft must be installed first and the main bearing caps bolted in place, then the new seal should be installed in the retainer and the retainer bolted to the block. **Note:** *Depending on the design of the engine stand being used, you may not be able to install the rear main seal retainer with the engine on the stand. In this case, install the rear main seal retainer as the last step before engine installation, when the engine is off the stand and on the hoist.*

25 Pistons/connecting rods - installation and rod bearing oil clearance check

Refer to illustrations 25.5, 25.9a, 25.9b, 25.17 and 25.26

1 Before installing the piston/connecting rod assemblies, the cylinder walls must be perfectly clean, the top edge of each cylinder must be chamfered, and the crankshaft must be in place.

2 Remove the cap from the end of the number one connecting rod (refer to the marks made during removal). Remove the original bearing inserts and wipe the bearing surfaces of the connecting rod and cap with a clean, lint-free cloth. They must be kept spotlessly clean.

Connecting rod bearing oil clearance check

3 Clean the back side of the new upper bearing insert, then lay it in place in the connecting rod. Make sure the tab on the bearing fits into the recess in the rod so the oil holes line up. Don't hammer the bearing insert in place and be very careful not to nick or gouge the bearing face. Don't lubricate the bearing at this time.

2B

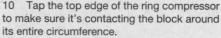

25.5 Ring end gap positions

A *Oil ring side rail gaps*
B *Middle compression ring gap*
C *Dimple in the piston (indicating front of engine)*
D *Oil spacer/expander gap*
E *Top compression ring gap*

25.9a Position the piston, when installing it, with the mark/notch (arrow) in the piston facing the front of the engine

4   Clean the back side of the other bearing insert and install it in the rod cap. Again, make sure the tab on the bearing fits into the recess in the cap, and don't apply any lubricant. It's critically important that the mating surfaces of the bearing and connecting rod are perfectly clean and oil free when they're assembled.

5   Position the piston ring gaps at staggered intervals around the piston **(see illustration)**.

6   Slip a section of plastic or rubber hose over each connecting rod cap bolt. **(see illustration** 13.6**)**.

7   Lubricate the piston and rings with clean engine oil and attach a piston ring compressor to the piston. Leave the skirt protruding about 1/4-inch to guide the piston into the cylinder. The rings must be compressed until they're flush with the piston.

8   Rotate the crankshaft until the number one connecting rod journal is at BDC (bottom dead center) and apply a coat of engine oil to the cylinder walls.

9   With the mark on top of the piston facing the front (timing chain end) of the engine **(see illustration)**, gently insert the piston/connecting rod assembly into the number one cylinder bore and rest the bottom edge of the ring compressor on the engine block **(see illustration)**.

10   Tap the top edge of the ring compressor to make sure it's contacting the block around its entire circumference.

11   Gently tap on the top of the piston with the end of a wooden or plastic hammer handle while guiding the end of the connecting rod into place on the crankshaft journal. The piston rings may try to pop out of the ring compressor just before entering the cylinder bore, so keep some pressure on the ring compressor. Work slowly, and if any resistance is felt as the piston enters the cylinder, stop immediately. Find out what's hanging up and fix it before proceeding. Do not, for any reason, force the piston into the cylinder - you might break a ring and/or the piston.

12   Once the piston/connecting rod assembly is installed, the connecting rod bearing oil clearance must be checked before the rod cap is permanently bolted in place.

13   Cut a piece of the appropriate size Plastigage slightly shorter than the width of

the connecting rod bearing and lay it in place on the number one connecting rod journal, parallel with the journal axis **(see illustration)**.

14   Clean the connecting rod cap bearing face, remove the protective hoses from the connecting rod bolts and install the rod cap. Make sure the mating mark on the cap is on the same side as the mark on the connecting rod. Check the cap to make sure the front mark is facing the timing belt/chain end of the engine.

15   Apply a light coat of oil to the under sides of the nuts, then install and tighten them to the torque listed in this Chapter's Specifications. Use a thin-wall socket to avoid erroneous torque readings that can result if the socket is wedged between the rod cap and nut. If the socket tends to wedge itself between the nut and the cap, lift up on it slightly until it no longer contacts the cap. Do not rotate the crankshaft at any time during this operation.

16   Remove the nuts and detach the rod cap, being very careful not to disturb the Plastigage.

17   Compare the width of the crushed Plastigage to the scale printed on the Plastigage envelope to obtain the oil clearance **(see illustration)**. Compare it to the Specifications to make sure the clearance is correct.

18   If the clearance is not as specified, the

25.9b With the ring compressor firmly seated against the block, the piston can be driven gently into the cylinder bore with the end of a wooden or plastic hammer handle

25.13 Lay a strip of Plastigage on each rod bearing journal, parallel to the crankshaft centerline

25.17 Measure the width of the crushed Plastigage to determine the rod bearing oil clearance (be sure to use the correct scale - standard and metric ones are included)

bearing inserts may be the wrong size (which means different ones will be required). Before deciding that different inserts are needed, make sure that no dirt or oil was between the bearing inserts and the connecting rod or cap when the clearance was measured. Also, recheck the journal diameter. If the Plastigage was wider at one end than the other, the journal may be tapered (see Section 19).

Final connecting rod installation

19   Carefully scrape all traces of the Plastigage material off the rod journal and/or bearing face. Be very careful not to scratch the bearing - use your fingernail or the edge of a credit card.

20   Make sure the bearing faces are perfectly clean, then apply a uniform layer of clean moly-base grease or engine assembly lube to both of them. You'll have to push the piston into the cylinder to expose the face of the bearing insert in the connecting rod - be sure to slip the protective hoses over the rod bolts first.

21   Slide the connecting rod back into place on the journal, remove the protective hoses from the rod cap bolts, install the rod cap and tighten the nuts to the torque listed in this Chapter's Specifications.

22   Repeat the entire procedure for the remaining pistons/connecting rods.

23   The important points to remember are:

a) *Keep the back sides of the bearing inserts and the insides of the connecting rods and caps perfectly clean when assembling them.*

b) *Make sure you have the correct piston/rod assembly for each cylinder.*

c) *The mark on the piston top must face the front (timing belt/chain end) of the engine.*

d) *Lubricate the cylinder walls with clean oil.*

e) *Lubricate the bearing faces when installing the rod caps after the oil clearance has been checked.*

24   After all the piston/connecting rod assemblies have been properly installed, rotate the crankshaft a number of times by hand to check for any obvious binding.

25   As a final step, the connecting rod side clearance (endplay) must be checked (see Section 13).

26   Compare the measured side clearance to the Specifications to make sure it's correct. If it was correct before disassembly and the original crankshaft and rods were reinstalled, it should still be right. If new rods or a new crankshaft were installed, the side clearance may be inadequate. If so, the rods will have to be removed and taken to an automotive machine shop for re-sizing.

27   On 1982 through 1988 models, lubricate the jackshaft bearing journals with engine assembly lube or moly-based grease and install it into the block **(see illustration)**.

---

26   Initial start-up and break-in after overhaul

Warning: *Have a fire extinguisher handy when starting the engine for the first time.*

1   Once the engine has been installed in the vehicle, double-check the engine oil and coolant levels.

2   With the spark plugs out of the engine and the ignition system disabled (see Section 4), crank the engine until oil pressure registers on the gauge or the light goes out.

3   Install the spark plugs, hook up the plug wires and reconnect the ignition coil wire, if it was removed earlier for the compression test in Section 4.

4   Start the engine. It may take a few moments for the fuel system to build up pressure, but the engine should start without a great deal of effort.

25.26 On 1982 through 1988 models, secure the jackshaft in the engine block with the retainer plate and screw (arrow)

5   After the engine starts, it should be allowed to warm up to normal operating temperature. While the engine is warming up, make a thorough check for fuel, oil and coolant leaks.

6   Shut the engine off and recheck the engine oil and coolant levels.

7   Drive the vehicle to an area with minimum traffic, accelerate from 30 to 50 mph, then allow the vehicle to slow to 30 mph with the throttle closed. Repeat the procedure 10 or 12 times. This will load the piston rings and cause them to seat properly against the cylinder walls. Check again for oil and coolant leaks.

8   Drive the vehicle gently for the first 500 miles (no sustained high speeds) and keep a constant check on the oil level. It is not unusual for an engine to use oil during the break-in period.

9   At approximately 500 to 600 miles, change the oil and filter.

10   For the next few hundred miles, drive the vehicle normally. Do not pamper it or abuse it.

11   After 2000 miles, change the oil and filter again and consider the engine broken in.

2B

Notes

Chapter 3
Cooling, heating and air conditioning systems

Contents

Specifications

General

Radiator cap pressure rating
| 1982 to 1986 | 13 psi |
| 1987 to 1994 | 11 to 14 psi |

Cooling system test pressure
1982 to 1988	23 psi
1989 and 1990	14 psi
1991 to 1994	23 psi

Thermostat rating (opening temperature)
| 1982 to 1988 | 180-degrees F |
| 1989 to 1994 | 170-degrees F |

| Cooling system capacity | 5.5 quarts |

Refrigerant capacity
1982 to 1986	1.8 to 2.2 lbs
1987	2.0 to 2.4 lbs
1988 to 1990	1.87 to 2.09 lbs
1991 to 1993	1.43 to 1.65 lbs
1994	1.32 to 1.54 lbs

Torque specifications

Thermostat housing bolts
1982 to 1987	69 to 96 in-lbs
1988	78 to 121 in-lbs
1989 and 1990	43 to 61 in-lbs
1991 to 1994	
GA16DE	75 to 99 in-lbs
SR20DE	55 to 73 in-lbs

Water pump-to-engine bolts
1982 to 1988	78 to 121 in-lbs
1989 and 1990	55 to 73 in-lbs
1991 to 1994	
GA16DE	55 to 73 in-lbs
SR20DE	144 to 180 in-lbs

1   General information

Engine cooling system

All vehicles covered by this manual employ a pressurized engine cooling system with thermostatically-controlled coolant circulation. An impeller type water pump mounted on the drivebelt end of the block pumps coolant through the engine. The coolant flows around each cylinder and toward the transaxle end of the engine. Cast-in coolant passages direct coolant around the intake and exhaust ports, near the spark plug areas and in close proximity to the exhaust valve guides.

A wax pellet type thermostat is located in a housing near the transaxle end of the engine on 1982-1988 models, and on the water pump on later engines (at the rear of the engine on the water pipes on the SR20DE engines). During warm up, the closed thermostat prevents coolant from circulating through the radiator. As the engine nears normal operating temperature, the thermostat opens and allows hot coolant to travel through the radiator, where it's cooled before returning to the engine.

The cooling system is sealed by a pressure type radiator cap, which raises the boiling point of the coolant and increases the cooling efficiency of the radiator. If the system pressure exceeds the cap pressure relief value, the excess pressure in the system forces the spring-loaded valve inside the cap off its seat and allows the coolant to escape through the overflow tube into a coolant reservoir. When the system cools, the excess coolant is automatically drawn from the reservoir back into the radiator.

The coolant reservoir does double duty as both the point at which fresh coolant is added to the cooling system to maintain the proper fluid level and as a holding tank for overheated coolant.

This type of cooling system is known as a closed design because coolant that escapes past the pressure cap is saved and re-used.

Heating system

The heating system consists of a blower fan and heater core located in the heater box, the hoses connecting the heater core to the engine cooling system and the heater/air conditioning control head on the dashboard. Hot engine coolant is circulated through the heater core. When the heater mode is activated, a flap opens to expose the heater box to the passenger compartment. A fan switch on the control head activates the blower motor, which forces air through the core, heating the air.

Air conditioning system

The air conditioning system consists of a condenser mounted in front of the radiator, an evaporator mounted adjacent to the heater core, a compressor mounted on the engine, a filter-drier which contains a high pressure relief valve and the plumbing connecting all of the above components.

A blower fan forces the warmer air of the passenger compartment through the evaporator core (sort of a radiator-in-reverse), transferring the heat from the air to the refrigerant. The liquid refrigerant boils off into low pressure vapor, taking the heat with it when it leaves the evaporator.

2   Antifreeze/coolant - general information

Refer to illustration 2.5

Warning: *Do not allow antifreeze to come in contact with your skin or painted surfaces of the vehicle. Rinse off spills immediately with plenty of water. Antifreeze is highly toxic if ingested. Never leave antifreeze lying around in an open container or in puddles on the floor; children and pets are attracted by it's sweet smell and may drink it. Check with local authorities about disposing of used antifreeze. Many communities have collection centers which will see that antifreeze is disposed of safely. Never dump used antifreeze on the ground or into drains.* **Note:** *Non-toxic coolant is available at most auto parts stores. Although the coolant is non-toxic, proper disposal is still required.*

1   The cooling system should be filled with a water/ethylene glycol-based antifreeze solution, which will prevent freezing down to at least -20-degrees F, or lower if local climate requires it. It also provides protection against corrosion and increases the coolant boiling point.
2   The cooling system should be drained, flushed and refilled at the specified intervals (see Chapter 1). Old or contaminated antifreeze solutions are likely to cause damage and encourage the formation of corrosion and scale in the system. Use distilled water with the antifreeze.
3   Before adding antifreeze, check all hose connections, because antifreeze tends to leak through very minute openings. Engines don't normally consume coolant, so if the level goes down, find the cause and correct it.
4   The exact mixture of antifreeze to water which you should use depends on the relative weather conditions. The mixture should contain at least 50-percent antifreeze, but should never contain more than 70-percent antifreeze. Consult the mixture ratio chart on the antifreeze container before adding coolant.

Antifreeze/coolant testing

Warning: *Do not remove the radiator cap to take a sample until the engine has cooled completely. The system is under pressure and extremely hot during and after running the engine, and will severely scald skin it comes in contact with.*

2.5 Inexpensive coolant hydrometers can be purchased at most auto parts stores

5   Hydrometers used to test the condition of the coolant are available at most auto parts stores **(see illustration)**. They are inexpensive and are very easy to use. To test coolant draw a small amount from the radiator, or coolant reservoir, with the hydrometer until all the balls are submerged (most of them will probably float). **Note:** *It is preferable to take the coolant sample from the radiator. The mixture in the coolant reservoir may be slightly diluted if any water has recently been added.* The strength of the mixture is shown by the number of balls that are floating. Exact temperature protection indicated by the hydrometer is clearly described on the package instructions. Always use antifreeze which meets the vehicle manufacturer's specifications.

3   Thermostat - check and replacement

Warning: *Do not remove the radiator cap, drain the coolant or replace the thermostat until the engine has cooled completely. Do not allow antifreeze to come in contact with your skin or painted surfaces of the vehicle. Rinse off spills immediately with plenty of water. Antifreeze is highly toxic if ingested. Never leave antifreeze lying around in an open container or in puddles on the floor; children and pets are attracted by it's sweet smell and may drink it. Check with local authorities about disposing of used antifreeze. Many communities have collection centers which will see that antifreeze is disposed of safely. Never dump used anti-freeze on the ground or into drains.* **Note:** *Non-toxic coolant is available at most auto parts stores. Although the coolant is non-toxic, proper disposal is still required.*

Check

1   Before assuming the thermostat is to blame for a cooling system problem, check the coolant level, drivebelt tension (see Chapter 1) and temperature gauge operation.
2   If the engine seems to be taking a long time to warm up (based on heater output or temperature gauge operation), the thermostat is probably stuck open. Replace the thermostat with a new one.

3.8 Loosen the clamp and detach the hose from the thermostat cover

3.11 Remove the bolts from the housing cover and separate the cover and thermostat

3.12 Note the position of the thermostat's air bleed valve (arrow) aligned with the casting and how the thermostat is installed (the spring end goes into the engine)

3   If the engine runs hot, use your hand to check the temperature of the radiator hose (check the upper hose on 1982 to 1988 models, the lower hose on later models). If the hose isn't hot, but the engine is, the thermostat is probably stuck closed, preventing the coolant from circulating through the radiator. Replace the thermostat. **Caution:** *Don't drive the vehicle without a thermostat. On computer-managed models, the engine may never reach the required temperature to allow the computer to go to closed loop operation. Performance, emissions and fuel economy will probably be poor.*

4   If the radiator-to-thermostat hose is hot, it means that the coolant is flowing and the thermostat is open. Consult the *Troubleshooting* section at the front of this manual for cooling system diagnosis.

Replacement

Refer to illustrations 3.8, 3.11 and 3.12

5   Disconnect the battery cable from the negative battery terminal. **Caution:** *If the stereo in your vehicle is equipped with an anti-theft system, make sure you have the correct activation code before disconnecting the battery.*

6   Drain the cooling system (see Chapter 1). If the coolant is relatively new, or tests in good condition (see Section 2), save it and re-use it.

4.1 On early models the cooling fan temperature switch is on the radiator

1 Thermostatic switch electrical connector
2 Thermostatic switch
3 Radiator draincock

7   Follow the upper radiator hose (lower hose on 1989 and later models) to the engine to locate the thermostat housing.

8   Loosen the hose clamp and detach the hose from the fitting **(see illustration)**. If the hose is stuck, grasp it near the end with a pair of large adjustable pliers and twist it to break the seal, then pull it off. If the hose is old or deteriorated, cut it off and install a new one.

9   If the outer surface of the large fitting that mates with the hose is deteriorated (corroded, pitted, etc.) it may be damaged further by hose removal. If it is, the thermostat housing cover will have to be replaced.

10   Unplug each of the electrical connections at the thermostat housing. **Note:** *Each of the connections should have matching colors on the male and female connector ends, to help in reassembly.*

11   Remove the bolts/nuts and detach the housing cover **(see illustration)**. If the cover is stuck, tap it with a soft-face hammer to jar it loose. Be prepared for some coolant to spill as the gasket seal is broken.

12   Note the position of the air bleed valve or air bleed hole **(see illustration)**.

13   Install the new thermostat in the housing. Make sure the air bleed faces up and the spring end is directed toward the engine.

14   Position a new gasket or apply liquid sealant to the thermostat cover.

15   Install the cover and bolts. Tighten the

4.4 Disconnect the fan electrical connector and use fused jumper wires to apply battery voltage

bolts to the torque listed in this Chapter's Specifications.

16   Reattach the hose to the fitting and tighten the hose clamp securely. Reconnect the electrical connector for the cooling fan switch.

17   Refill the cooling system (see Chapter 1).

18   Start the engine and allow it to reach normal operating temperature, then check for leaks and proper thermostat operation (as described in Steps 2 through 4).

4   Engine cooling fan(s) and circuit(s) - check and component replacement

Refer to illustrations 4.1, 4.4, 4.5a, 4.5b and 4.6

1   The engine cooling fan is controlled by a temperature switch which is mounted on the radiator (at bottom, driver's side) on 1982 through 1988 models **(see illustration)**, or on the thermostat housing on 1989 and 1990 models. When the coolant reaches a predetermined temperature, the switch closes, completing the circuit to ground.

2   On 1991 and later models, the engine cooling fan is controlled by the ECCS control module, using the coolant temperature sensor (part of the engine management system), the vehicle speed sensor and the air conditioner On signal as factors affecting fan operation. If equipped with airbags, see Chapter 12.

Check

3   First, check the fuses (see Chapter 12). Also check the fusible link (see Chapter 12).

4   To test a fan motor, unplug the electrical connector and use fused jumper wires to connect the fan directly to the battery **(see illustration)**. If the fan still does not work, replace the motor.

1990 and earlier models

5   If the motor tested OK, the fault lies in the coolant temperature switch, the relay

3

4.5a The location of the engine compartment relay box on early models is on the passenger side of the engine compartment, in front of the timing belt cover - the arrow points to the radiator fan relay

4.5b The radiator fan relay (arrow) on later models is located in the main relay box next to the battery

4.6 Test the fan circuit by using a jumper wire across the terminals of the electrical connector

(see illustrations) or the wiring harness (see Chapter 12).

6   Test the fan circuit by unplugging the connector from the coolant temperature switch, and with the ignition switch on, bridge the terminals of the connector with a jumper wire **(see illustration)**. If the fan now comes on, the circuit is OK but the switch is faulty. If the fan still does not operate, check the relay (see test below).

7   If the relay tested OK, check the wiring (see Chapter 12).

1991 and later models

8   If the motor tested OK in Step 4, check for trouble codes stored in the computer (see Chapter 6). If the coolant sensor and vehicle speed sensor check out OK, check the wiring.

Replacement

Engine cooling fan

Refer to illustrations 4.10, 4.11, and 4.12

9   Disconnect the cable from the negative battery terminal. **Caution:** *If the stereo in your vehicle is equipped with an anti-theft system, make sure you have the correct activation code before disconnecting the battery.*

10   Unbolt the cooling fan assembly from the radiator and remove it **(see illustration)**.

11   Remove the nut and detach the fan blade assembly from the motor shaft **(see illustration)**.

12   Take out the screws holding the fan motor to the mounting bracket, then detach the motor **(see illustration)**.

13   Installation is the reverse of removal.

Condenser fan (air-conditioned models only)

14   Air-conditioned models have an additional fan located next to the main engine cooling fan. The condenser fan is usually smaller than the cooling fan.

15   Disconnect the battery cable from the negative battery terminal. **Caution:** *If the stereo in your vehicle is equipped with an anti-theft system, make sure you have the correct activation code before disconnecting the battery.*

16   Unplug the electrical connector.

17   Remove the mounting bolts holding the fan assembly to the radiator support and remove the fan assembly.

18   Installation is the reverse of the removal procedure.

Engine cooling fan relay (1990 and earlier models)

Refer to illustration 4.19

19   Locate the cooling fan relay **(see illustrations 4.5a and 4.5b)** and check the relay for continuity using an ohmmeter **(see illustration)**. With the relay at rest (not energized by applying voltage to terminals 1 and 2), there should be no continuity between terminals 3 and 5.

20   With the relay energized, there should be continuity between terminals 3 and 5. If continuity isn't as specified, replace the relay.

Condenser fan relay

Refer to illustration 4.21

21   Locate the condenser fan (or "cooling fan 2") relay **(see illustrations 4.5a and 4.5b)** and inspect the relay for continuity using an ohmmeter **(see illustration)**. With no current supplied to terminals 1 or 2, there should be no continuity between terminals 3 and 5, or between 6 and 7. If continuity isn't as specified, replace the relay.

4.10 Unbolt and remove the four screws holding the fan frame to the radiator and lift the fan and housing out of the engine compartment

4.11 To replace the fan motor unbolt the fan blade nut and remove the fan blades

4.12 Remove the mounting screws that hold the motor to the fan housing and remove the motor

4.19 Cooling fan relay - continuity check

4.21 Condenser fan relay terminal designations

5.7 Remove the bracket hold-down bolt from the support on each side of the radiator

5.8 On automatic transmission models disconnect the cooler lines - have a drain pan ready to catch spilled fluid

22 Using jumper wires, apply battery voltage and ground by connecting the positive jumper wire to terminal number 1 and the negative jumper wire to terminal number 2.

23 With current applied, there now should be continuity between terminals 3 and 5, and between 6 and 7.

5 Radiator - removal and installation

Refer to illustrations 5.7, 5.8 and 5.9

Warning: *Do not start this procedure until the engine is completely cool. Do not allow antifreeze to come in contact with your skin or painted surfaces of the vehicle. Rinse off spills immediately with plenty of water. Antifreeze is highly toxic if ingested. Never leave antifreeze lying around in an open container or in puddles on the floor; children and pets are attracted by it's sweet smell and may drink it. Check with local authorities about disposing of used antifreeze. Many communities have collection centers which will see that antifreeze is disposed of safely. Never dump used anti-freeze on the ground or into drains.*

Note: *Non-toxic coolant is available at most auto parts stores. Although the coolant is non-toxic, proper disposal is still required.*

Removal

1 Disconnect the cable from the negative battery terminal. **Warning:** *On models equipped with airbags, wait at least ten minutes after the ignition has been turned off and the battery disconnected before starting work on the vehicle. The supplemental inflatable restraint (airbag) system has electrical capacitors that must bleed down to avoid the possibility of airbag deployment.* **Caution:** *If the stereo in your vehicle is equipped with an anti-theft system, make sure you have the correct activation code before disconnecting the battery.*

2 Raise the front of the vehicle and support it securely on jackstands. Remove the lower splash shields, if necessary to gain access to the radiator drain plug.

3 Drain the cooling system (see Chapter 1). If the coolant is relatively new, or tests in good condition, save it and reuse it (see Section 2).

4 Loosen the upper and lower hose clamps, then detach the radiator hoses from the fittings. If they're stuck, grasp each hose near the end with a pair of adjustable pliers and twist it to break the seal, then pull it off - be careful not to damage the radiator fittings! If the hoses are old or deteriorated, cut them off and install new ones.

5 Disconnect the coolant reservoir hose from the radiator.

6 Disconnect the cooling fan electrical connector.

7 Remove the bolts and mounting brackets **(see illustration)**.

8 If the vehicle is equipped with an automatic transaxle, disconnect the transmission oil cooler lines **(see illustration)** and plug the lines and fittings.

9 Carefully lift out the radiator **(see illustration)**. Don't spill coolant on the vehicle or scratch the paint. Remove the bolts securing the cooling fan to the radiator and pull it free.

10 Inspect the lower radiator rubber mounting pads. Replace them if they are deteriorated, split or broken.

11 With the radiator removed, it can be inspected for leaks and damage. If it needs repair, have a radiator shop or dealer service department perform the work as special techniques are required.

12 Bugs and dirt can be removed from the radiator with a soft brush, followed by forcing water from a garden hose through the core from the engine side. Don't bend the cooling fins as this is done.

Installation

13 Installation is the reverse of the removal procedure. Be sure the radiator mounting pads are seated properly at the base of the radiator **(see illustration 5.9)**.

14 After installation, fill the cooling system with the proper mixture of antifreeze and water (see Section 2 and Chapter 1).

15 Start the engine and check for leaks. Allow the engine to reach normal operating temperature, indicated by the upper radiator

hose becoming hot. Recheck the coolant level and add more if required.

16 If you're working on an automatic transaxle equipped vehicle, check and add transmission fluid as needed (see Chapter 1).

6 Coolant reservoir - removal and installation

Refer to illustration 6.2

Warning: *Do not start this procedure until the engine is completely cool. Do not allow antifreeze to come in contact with your skin or painted surfaces of the vehicle. Rinse off spills immediately with plenty of water. Antifreeze is highly toxic if ingested. Never leave antifreeze lying around in an open container or in puddles on the floor; children and pets are attracted by it's sweet smell and may drink it. Check with local authorities about disposing of used antifreeze. Many communities have collection centers which will see that antifreeze is disposed of safely. Never dump used anti-freeze on the ground or into drains.*

Note: *Non-toxic coolant is available at most auto parts stores. Although the coolant is non-toxic, proper disposal is still required.*

1 Disconnect the overflow hose from the reservoir, and plug to prevent coolant from spilling if the reservoir is full.

5.9 Carefully lift the radiator free, avoid scratching or spilling coolant on the vehicle - arrows indicate lower mounting pads

3

6.2 Detach the overflow hose from the radiator and lift the reservoir bottle out of its bracket

8.5 Loosen the water pump pulley bolts while the belt is still tight, then remove the belt and unbolt the pulley

8.7a On later models, unbolt and remove the thermostat housing before taking off the water pump

8.7b Early model water pump (pulley removed)

8.7c Later model water pump (pulley removed)

2   Unbolt the coolant reservoir and remove it from the vehicle **(see illustration)**. **Note:** *On some models, the neck of the windshield-washer tank must be pulled out to remove the coolant reservoir.*

3   Pour the coolant into a container. Wash out and inspect the reservoir for cracks and chafing. Replace it if any damage is found.

4   Installation is the reverse of removal.

7   Water pump - check

1   A failure in the water pump can cause serious engine damage due to overheating.

2   There are three ways to check the operation of the water pump while it's installed on the engine. If the pump is defective, it should be replaced with a new, or rebuilt unit.

3   With the engine running at normal operating temperature, squeeze the upper radiator hose. If the water pump is working properly, a pressure surge should be felt as the hose is released. **Warning:** *Keep your hands away from the fan blades! The fan can come on at any time.*

4   Water pumps are equipped with weep or vent holes. If a failure occurs in the pump seal, coolant will leak from the hole. In most cases you'll need a flashlight to find the hole on the water pump from underneath to check for leaks.

5   If the water pump shaft bearings fail there may be a howling sound at the drivebelt end of the engine while it's running. Shaft wear can be felt if the water pump pulley is rocked up and down. Don't mistake drivebelt slippage, which causes a squealing sound, for water pump bearing failure.

6   Turn the pump shaft by hand and feel for roughness in the bearing. Replace the pump if roughness is felt.

8   Water pump - replacement

Refer to illustrations 8.5, 8.7a, 8.7b and 8.7c

Warning: *Wait until the engine is completely cool before beginning this procedure. Do not allow antifreeze to come in contact with your skin or painted surfaces of the vehicle. Rinse off*

spills immediately with plenty of water. Antifreeze is highly toxic if ingested. Never leave antifreeze lying around in an open container or in puddles on the floor; children and pets are attracted by it's sweet smell and may drink it. Check with local authorities about disposing of used antifreeze. Many communities have collection centers which will see that antifreeze is disposed of safely. Never dump used antifreeze on the ground or into drains.

Note: *Non-toxic coolant is available at most auto parts stores. Although the coolant is non-toxic, proper disposal is still required.*

1   Disconnect the battery cable from the negative battery terminal. **Caution:** *If the stereo in your vehicle is equipped with an anti-theft system, make sure you have the correct activation code before disconnecting the battery.*

2   Drain the cooling system (see Chapter 1). If the coolant is relatively new, or tests in good condition (see Section 2), save it and re-use it.

3   Remove the right hand splash shield (see Chapter 1).

4   On 1991 and later models with the SR20DE engine, remove the right front wheel, engine side cover, and front engine mount for water pump access.

5   Remove the water pump pulley **(see illustration)**.

6   Remove any other accessory drivebelts that would interfere with removal (see Chapter 1).

7   On 1989 and later models, disconnect the coolant temperature switch and unbolt

the thermostat housing from the water pump **(see illustration)**. Remove the water pump **(see illustrations)**. If it is stuck, gently tap it with a soft faced hammer to break the seal.

8   Remove all traces of old gasket material from the sealing surface on the engine block.

9   Install the water pump, using a new gasket or sealant.

10   Tighten the bolts to the torque listed in this Chapter's Specifications in 1/4-turn increments. Don't over-tighten them or the pump may be damaged or leak.

11   Reinstall all parts removed for access to the pump.

12   Refill the cooling system (see Chapter 1). Run the engine and check for leaks.

9   Coolant temperature sending unit - check and replacement

Refer to illustrations 9.3a and 9.3b

Check

1   If the coolant temperature gauge is inoperative, check the fuses first (see Chapter 12).

2   If the temperature indicator shows excessive temperature after running awhile, see the *Troubleshooting* section in the front of the manual.

3   If the temperature gauge indicates Hot shortly after the engine is started cold, and the engine is not up to normal operating temperature, disconnect the wire at the

9.3a Location of the coolant temperature sending unit (arrow) on the GA16 engine

9.3b Location of the coolant temperature sending unit (arrow) on the SR20 engine

coolant temperature sending unit **(see illustrations). Note:** *The sending unit has a single wire terminal and is located at the end of the cylinder head under the distributor or screwed into the intake manifold on the right (passenger's) side of the engine.* If the gauge reading drops, replace the sending unit. If the reading remains high, the wire to the gauge may be shorted to ground or the gauge is faulty.

4   If the coolant temperature gauge fails to indicate after the engine has been warmed up (approximately 10 minutes) and the fuses checked out okay, shut off the engine. Disconnect the wire at the sending unit and using a jumper wire, connect it to a clean ground on the engine. Turn on the ignition without starting the engine. If the gauge now indicates Hot, replace the sending unit.

5   If the gauge still does not work, the circuit may be open or the gauge may be faulty.

Replacement

Warning: *The engine must be completely cool before removing the sending unit.*

6   With the engine completely cool, remove the cap from the radiator to release any pressure, then reinstall the cap. This reduces coolant loss during sending unit replacement.

7   Disconnect the electrical connector from the sending unit.

8   Prepare the new sending unit for installation by applying a light coat of sealant to

the threads, or by wrapping the threads with Teflon sealing tape.

9   Unscrew the sending unit from the radiator (or engine, depending on model) and quickly install the new one to prevent coolant loss.

10   Tighten the sending unit securely and attach the electrical connector.

11   Refill the cooling system (see Chapter 1) and run the engine. Check for leaks and proper gauge operation.

---

10 Blower motor and circuit - check, removal and component replacement

Blower motor

Check

Refer to illustrations 10.3 and 10.4

1   If the blower motor speed does not correspond to the setting selected on the blower switch, or the blower motor does not operate at all, the problem could be a bad fuse, relay, switch, blower motor resistor, blower motor or blower motor circuit wiring.

2   Before checking the blower motor or circuit, always check the fuse and relay (if equipped) first (see Chapter 12).

3   Remove the glove compartment and dash trim (see Chapter 11) to gain access to the heater case and blower motor (see illustration).

4   With the ignition key in the ON position, turn the blower switch to the faulty position(s) and, using a test light or voltmeter, check the voltage at the motor electrical connector (see

illustration). If the motor is receiving voltage but not operating, either the motor ground is bad (on these models the blower switch and resistor are part of the ground circuit) or the motor itself is faulty or the fan is binding.

5   To check for a bad ground, disconnect the electrical connector from the blower motor, connect a jumper wire between the ground wire terminal on the blower motor and a good ground, then connect a fused jumper wire between the battery positive terminal and the positive terminal on the blower motor. If the motor now operates properly, the ground circuit or resistor is bad. If the motor does not operate, the fan is either binding or faulty. Proceed to Step 6.

6   If you suspect the blower motor fan is binding, remove the blower motor (see step 7) to check for free operation of the fan.

Replacement

7   Disconnect the battery cable from the negative battery terminal. **Warning:** *On airbag-equipped models wait at least ten minutes after the ignition has been turned off and the battery disconnected before starting work on the vehicle. The supplemental inflatable restraint (airbag) system has electrical capacitors that must bleed down to avoid the possibility of airbag deployment.* **Caution:** *If the stereo in your vehicle is equipped with an anti-theft system, make sure you have the correct activation code before disconnecting the battery.*

8   Unplug the electrical connector at the blower motor **(see illustration 10.3).**

9   Remove the three blower unit retaining screws **(see illustration 10.3)** and lower the unit from the housing.

10   If you are replacing the motor, detach the fan and transfer it to the new motor.

11   Installation is the reverse of removal. Run the blower and check for proper operation.

Blower motor resistor

Check

Refer to illustrations 10.12 and 10.14

12   Remove the passenger side interior trim panel, which includes the glovebox, (see Chapter 11). Locate the electrical connector and wire for the heater blower motor resistor **(see illustration),** usually attached to a

3

10.3 Blower motor mounting details - to remove the blower motor, unplug the electrical connector (left arrow), remove the screws (arrows) and pull the assembly from the housing

10.4 Test for voltage at the blower motor plug

10.12 The blower motor resistor (arrow) is usually mounted on the blower case or nearby ductwork

10.14 Heater blower motor resistor - continuity check

Fan switch

LEVER POSITION TERMINAL	OFF	1	2	3	4
1					O
2	O				O
3		O			
4			O		
5	O	O	O	O	
6	O	O	O	O	
7	O	O	O	O	
8	O				
9	O				

Illumination lamp

10.16a Blower speed control switch continuity check - early model

heating/air conditioning duct or blower motor case.

13   Verify that the resistor is getting current from the blower motor:

a) *If the resistor is not getting current, check the wires and the connectors between the resistor and the motor. Check for loose or corroded connections and damaged wires.*

b) *If the wires and connectors are good and the blower switch is getting current, verify current is flowing out of the blower speed control switch to ground. If it is not go to step 15.*

14   Check the blower resistor for continuity **(see illustration)** as shown. If any checks indicate infinite resistance, replace the blower resistor.

Blower speed control switch

Refer to illustration 10.16a and 10.16b

15   Pull the control unit out from the dash enough to access the rear of the fan switch (see Section 12).

16   Unplug the electrical connector from the blower switch and check the continuity

Lever control type

LEVER POSITION TERMINAL	OFF	1	2	3	4
24					O
25				O	
26			O		
27		O			
12		O	O	O	O
23		O	O	O	O

10.16b Blower speed control switch continuity check - later model

across the switch terminals, as shown, with an ohmmeter **(see illustrations)**.

17   If continuity isn't as specified, replace the relay.

11   Heater core - removal and installation

Refer to illustrations 11.4, 11.6, 11.7, 11.11, 11.14, 11.15a and 11.15b

Warning 1: *Wait until the engine is completely cool before beginning this procedure.*

1   If the vehicle is equipped with air conditioning, have the air conditioning system discharged at a dealer service department or service station. **Warning 2:** *The air conditioning system is under high pressure. Do not loosen any fittings or remove any components until after the system has been discharged by a dealer service department or service station. Always wear eye protection when disconnecting refrigerant fittings.*

2   Disconnect the battery cable from the negative battery terminal. **Warning:** *On all airbag-equipped models wait at least ten minutes after the ignition has been turned off and the battery disconnected before starting work on the vehicle. The supplemental inflatable restraint (airbag) system has electrical capacitors that must bleed down to avoid the possibility of airbag deployment.*

Caution: *If the stereo in your vehicle is equipped with an anti-theft system, make sure you have the correct activation code before disconnecting the battery.*

3   Turn the heater control setting to HOT. Drain the cooling system (see Chapter 1). If the coolant is relatively new, or tests in good condition (see Section 2), save it and re-use it. **Warning:** *Do not allow antifreeze to come in contact with your skin or painted surfaces of the vehicle. Rinse off spills immediately with plenty of water. Antifreeze is highly toxic if ingested. Never leave antifreeze lying around in an open container or in puddles on the floor; children and pets are attracted by it's sweet smell and may drink it. Check with local authorities about disposing of used antifreeze. Many communities have collection centers which will see that antifreeze is disposed of safely. Never dump used anti-freeze on the ground or into drains.*

4   Working in the engine compartment, disconnect the heater hoses where they enter the firewall **(see illustration)**. **Caution:** *If the heater hoses are stuck firmly, it is better to cut off the hoses than to twist them with pliers and risk breaking the heater core tubes.*

5   Remove the rubber grommets where the heater core tubes go through the firewall **(see illustration 11.4)**.

6   Disconnect the air conditioning refrigerant lines and rubber grommet from the evaporator core if the vehicle is so equipped **(see illustration)**. **Warning:** *Always wear eye*

11.4 Disconnect the heater hoses at the firewall by loosening the hose clamps (arrows) and sliding them off the tubes, then remove the grommets (arrows)

11.6 Disconnect the two air conditioning refrigerant lines (arrows) that go through the firewall to the evaporator

1 Suction tube   2 Liquid tube

11.7 Access to the blower motor and ducts on late models requires removing the glove box and this metal support brace

11.11 Remove the control cables (arrows) attached to the heater unit

11.14 Removing the heater unit

11.15a Unhook the water control rod from the top of the heating unit

11.15b Slide the heater core from the heater unit

protection when disconnecting air conditioning system fittings.

7   Remove the glove box door, glove box and metal glove box support frame (see illustration). Note: On many early models with air conditioning, the glove box attachment plate must be removed, and a section of instrument panel cut out with a hacksaw and discarded (see Section 17). Before cutting, cover the blower motor vent holes with a rag to keep debris out.

8   Remove the left and right lower dash panels, center dash fascia, and center dash surround (see Chapter 11). Note: The amount of ducting and fasteners to remove for heater core access varies greatly with the year and model. A 1994 model is shown - earlier models may not require as much work, but heater core removal is difficult on many cars. Take your time and don't use excessive force - there may be fasteners you haven't found yet.

9   Remove the air conditioning/heater controls (see Section 12). Be sure to mark the locations of the cable clamps on the cables to ensure correct adjustment upon installation.

10   Remove the cooling unit (if equipped with air conditioning) or passenger side heater duct on models without air conditioning.

11   Remove the control cables connected to the left of the heater unit (see illustration).

12   Remove heater register center duct.

13   Remove bolts/nuts securing the heater unit to the firewall.

14   Pull down and back on the heater unit, making sure that all fasteners have been removed. Some twisting is required to separate the heater unit from the upper ducts (see illustration).

15   Remove the heater core from the heater unit (see illustrations).

16   Reassemble the heater unit and check the operation of the control flaps. If any parts bind, correct the problem before installation.

17   Reinstall the remaining parts in the reverse order of removal.

18   Refill the cooling system (see Chapter 1), reconnect the battery and run the engine. Check for leaks and proper system operation.

12 Air conditioner and heater control assembly - removal and installation

Refer to illustrations 12.8a, 12.8b and 12.8c

1   Disconnect the cable from the negative battery terminal. Warning: On airbag-equipped models wait at least ten minutes after the ignition has been turned off and the battery disconnected before starting work on the vehicle. The supplemental inflatable restraint (airbag) system has electrical capacitors that must bleed down to avoid the possibility of airbag deployment. Caution: If the stereo in your vehicle is equipped with an anti-theft system, make sure you have the correct activation code before disconnecting the battery.

2   Remove the center cluster trim panel which surrounds the radio and heater control assembly (see Chapter 11).

3   Remove the control mounting screws (see Chapter 11).

4   Carefully pull and tilt the unit out of the dash.

5   Check the outer sheath of the cables for indentations where the clamps grip them. Mark the cable sheath with paint if no indentation is visible. Remove the clamps and detach the control cables.

6   Unplug the electrical connectors and lift the control from the vehicle.

7   Installation is the reverse of removal.

8   Connect and/or adjust the heater control assembly cables as shown (see illustrations).

13 Air conditioning and heating system - check and maintenance

Refer to illustrations 13.1a, 13.1b, 13.9 and 13.10

Warning: The air conditioning system is under high pressure. Do not loosen any fittings or remove any components until after

12.8a Intake door control adjustment - set the control levers as shown (recirc. position), then push the door lever and cable outer toward the clamp and secure the clamp

12.8b Temperature control adjustment - set the control levers as shown (COLD position), then push the air-mix door and cable outer in direction of arrow and secure the clamp - on 1991 to 1994 models, set the lever to maximum HOT and pull the door lever *back*, then secure the clamp

12.8c Air control cable adjustment - set the control levers as shown (DEF position), then push the link and lever back toward the clamp and secure the clamp

the system has been discharged. Air conditioning refrigerant should be properly discharged into an EPA-approved container at a dealer service department or an automotive air conditioning repair facility. Always wear eye protection when disconnecting air conditioning system fittings.

1   The following maintenance checks should be performed on a regular basis to ensure that the air conditioning system **(see illustration)** continues to operate at peak efficiency.

 a) Check the compressor drivebelt. If it's worn or deteriorated, replace it (see Chapter 1).

 b) Check the drivebelt tension and, if necessary, adjust it (see Chapter 1).

 c) Check the system hoses. Look for cracks, bubbles, hard spots and deterioration. Inspect the hoses and all fittings for oil bubbles and seepage. If there's any evidence of wear, damage or leaks, replace the hose(s).

 d) Inspect the condenser fins for leaves, bugs and other debris. Use a "fin comb" or compressed air to clean the condenser.

 e) Make sure the system has the correct refrigerant charge.

 f) Check the evaporator housing drain tube for blockage **(see illustration)**.

2   It's a good idea to operate the system for about 10 minutes at least once a month, particularly during the winter. Long term non-use can cause hardening, and subsequent failure, of the seals.

3   Because of the complexity of the air conditioning system and the special equipment necessary to service it, in-depth troubleshooting and repairs are not included in this manual. However, simple checks and component replacement procedures are provided in this Chapter. For more complete information on the air conditioning system, refer to the Haynes *Automotive Heating and Air Conditioning Manual*.

4   The most common cause of poor cooling is simply a low system refrigerant charge. If a noticeable drop in cool air output occurs, one of the following quick checks will help you determine if the refrigerant level is low.

5   Warm the engine up to normal operating temperature.

6   Place the air conditioning temperature selector at the coldest setting and put the blower at the highest setting. Open the doors (to make sure the air conditioning system doesn't cycle off as soon as it cools the passenger compartment).

7   With the compressor engaged - the clutch will make an audible click and the center of the clutch will rotate - inspect the sight glass. **Note:** *The sight glass is normally located in the top of the receiver/drier* **(see illustration 14.2)**. If the refrigerant looks foamy, it's low, and must be recharged.

8   If there's no sight glass, feel the inlet and outlet pipes at the compressor. One side should be much colder the other. If there's no perceptible difference between the two pipes, there's something wrong with the compressor or system. It might be a low charge - it might be something else. Take the vehicle to a dealer service department or other qualified shop.

9   If the compressor clutch doesn't engage when the air conditioning is turned on, check the air conditioning relay for continuity. The air conditioning relay is located:

 a) on 1984 to 1986 models, up front on the passenger side of the radiator

 b) on 1987 and 1988 models, on the firewall, passenger side

 c) on 1989 and 1990 models, on the firewall, driver's side

13.1a An overall view of the air conditioning system (typical)

13.1b The air conditioning evaporator core drain tube (arrow) is located above the right side steering gear boot -check that it is not blocked

13.9 The air conditioning relay (arrow) is generally found in the main relay box

13.10 Air conditioning relay continuity check

14.2 The receiver/drier (arrow) is mounted to the left of the condenser on some models

d) on 1991 and later models, in the main relay box next to the battery (see illustration).

10 Inspect the air conditioning relay for continuity using an ohmmeter (see illustration). Apply battery voltage to the relay coil terminals - there should be continuity between the other two terminals. If continuity isn't as specified, replace the relay.

14 Air conditioning receiver/drier - removal and installation

Refer to illustration 14.2
Warning: *The air conditioning system is under high pressure. Do not loosen any fittings or remove any components until after the system has been discharged. Air conditioning refrigerant should be properly discharged into an EPA-approved container at a dealer service department or an automotive air conditioning repair facility. Always wear eye protection when disconnecting air conditioning system fittings.*
1 Have the refrigerant discharged at a dealer service department or an automotive air conditioning repair facility.
2 The receiver/drier, which acts as a reservoir and filter for the refrigerant, is located at the driver's side of the air conditioning condenser on some models and near the driver's side of the firewall on other models.(see illustration).
3 Detach the two refrigerant lines from the receiver/drier.
4 Immediately cap the open fittings to prevent the entry of dirt and moisture.

5 Unbolt the receiver/drier mounting bolt, at the clamp, and lift it from the vehicle.
6 Install new O-rings on the lines and lubricate them with clean refrigerant oil.
7 Installation is the reverse of removal.
Note: *Do not remove the sealing caps until you are ready to reconnect the lines. Do not mistake the inlet (marked IN) and the outlet connections.*
8 If a new receiver/drier is installed, add 0.2 US fluid ounces (6 cc) of refrigerant oil to the system. **Caution:** *When replacing entire components, additional refrigerant oil should be added equal to the amount that is removed with the component being replaced. Refrigerant oils, just like refrigerant R-12 vs. R-134a, are not compatible. Be sure to read the can before adding any oil to the system, to make sure it is compatible with the type of system being repaired.*
9 Have the system evacuated, charged and leak tested by the shop that discharged it.

15 Air conditioning compressor - removal and installation

Refer to illustrations 15.3, 15.4 and 15.6
Warning: *The air conditioning system is under high pressure. Do not loosen any fittings or remove any components until after the system has been discharged. Air conditioning refrigerant should be properly discharged into an EPA-approved container at a dealer service department or an automotive air conditioning repair facility. Always wear eye protection when disconnecting air conditioning system fittings.*

Caution: *When replacing entire components, additional refrigerant oil should be added equal to the amount that is removed with the component being replaced. Refrigerant oils, just like refrigerant R-12 vs. R-134a, are not compatible. Be sure to read the can before adding any oil to the system, to make sure it is compatible with the type of system being repaired.*
1 Have the refrigerant discharged at a dealer service department or an automotive air conditioning repair facility.
2 Disconnect the cable from the negative battery terminal and remove the battery. **Warning:** *On all airbag-equipped models wait at least ten minutes after the ignition has been turned off and the battery disconnected before starting work on the vehicle. The supplemental inflatable restraint (airbag) system has electrical capacitors that must bleed down to avoid the possibility of airbag deployment.* **Caution:** *If the stereo in your vehicle is equipped with an anti-theft system, make sure you have the correct activation code before disconnecting the battery.*
3 Detach the refrigerant lines from the compressor (see illustration) and immediately cap the open fittings to prevent the entry of dirt and moisture.
4 Disconnect the clutch wire from the compressor (see illustration).
5 Remove the accessory drivebelt (see Chapter 1).
6 Remove the compressor mounting bolts (see illustration) and remove the

15.3 Unbolting the refrigerant lines from the compressor

15.4 Disconnect the electrical connector (arrow) for the magnetic clutch

15.6 Once the refrigerant lines and electrical connections have been separated from the compressor, remove the mounting bolts (arrows) and the compressor from the mounting bracket

3

16.6 Remove the mounting bolts and brackets, then pull the condenser from the vehicle

17.5 A section of instrument panel support must be removed on some early models for AC and heater unit access

compressor from the engine compartment. **Note:** *Keep the compressor level during handling and storage. If the compressor seized or you find metal particles in the refrigerant lines, the system must be flushed out by an air conditioning technician and the receiver/drier must be replaced (see Section 14).*

7   Prior to installation, turn the center of the clutch six times to disperse any oil that has collected in the head.

8   Install the compressor in the reverse order of removal.

9   If you are installing a new compressor, the cycling clutch assembly may have to be transferred to the new compressor. **Note:** *The removal of the clutch assembly will require the use of several special tools. You may want to have the clutch assembly transferred to the new compressor by an air conditioning shop or dealer service department. Refer to the manufacturer's instructions for adding refrigerant oil to the system.* **Caution:** *When replacing entire components, additional refrigerant oil should be added equal to the amount that is removed with the component being replaced. Refrigerant oils, just like refrigerant R-12 vs. R-134a, are not compatible. Be sure to read the can before adding any oil to the system, to make sure it is compatible with the type of system being repaired.*

10   Have the system evacuated, charged and leak tested by the shop that discharged it.

16   Air conditioning condenser - removal and installation

Refer to illustration 16.6
Warning: *The air conditioning system is under high pressure. Do not loosen any fittings or remove any components until after the system has been discharged. Air conditioning refrigerant should be properly discharged into an EPA-approved container at a dealer service department or an automotive air conditioning repair facility.*

Always wear eye protection when disconnecting air conditioning system fittings.

1   Have the refrigerant discharged at a dealer service department or an automotive air conditioning repair facility.

2   Remove the grille (see Chapter 11) for access to condenser mounts on early models.

3   Disconnect the refrigerant lines from the condenser. Be sure to use a back-up wrench to avoid twisting the lines (if equipped with two nuts).

4   Immediately cap the open fittings to prevent the entry of dirt and moisture.

5   Unbolt the condenser mounts.

6   Unbolt the radiator mounts and pull the radiator and fan assembly toward the rear of the engine compartment until there is room to pull up the condenser **(see illustration)** and lift it out of the vehicle. Store it upright to prevent oil loss. **Caution:** *Place a towel or section of cardboard between the radiator and condenser while removing the condenser, to prevent damage to the radiator fins.*

7   Installation is the reverse of removal.

8   If a new condenser was installed, add 2.5 ounces (75 cc) of refrigerant oil to the system. **Caution:** *When replacing entire components, additional refrigerant oil should be added equal to the amount that is removed with the component being replaced. Refrigerant oils, just like refrigerant R-12 vs. R-134a, are not compatible. Be sure to read the can before adding any oil to the system, to make sure it is compatible with the type of system being repaired.*

9   Have the system evacuated, charged and leak tested by the shop that discharged it.

17   Air conditioning evaporator and expansion valve - removal and installation

Refer to illustration 17.5
Warning: *The air conditioning system is under high pressure. Do not loosen any fittings or remove any components until after*

the system has been discharged. Air conditioning refrigerant should be properly discharged into an EPA-approved container at a dealer service department or an automotive air conditioning repair facility. Always wear eye protection when disconnecting air conditioning system fittings.

1   Have the refrigerant discharged at a dealer service department or an automotive air conditioning repair facility.

2   Disconnect the cable from the negative battery terminal. **Warning:** *On all airbag-equipped models wait at least ten minutes after the ignition has been turned off and the battery disconnected before starting work on the vehicle. The supplemental inflatable restraint (airbag) system has electrical capacitors that must bleed down to avoid the possibility of airbag deployment.* **Caution:** *If the stereo in your vehicle is equipped with an anti-theft system, make sure you have the correct activation code before disconnecting the battery.*

3   Working in the engine compartment, disconnect the suction and liquid tubes **(see illustration 11.6)**, use a back-up wrench to avoid twisting and damaging the lines.

4   Immediately cap the open fittings to prevent the entry of dirt and moisture and remove the inlet and outlet grommets.

5   Remove the glove box (see Chapter 11) and dash panel below glove box. **Note:** *On many early models with air conditioning, the glove box attachment plate must be removed, and a section of instrument panel cut out with a hacksaw and discarded* **(see illustration)**. *Before cutting, cover the blower motor vent holes with a rag to keep debris out.*

6   Disconnect all electrical connectors and tubing from the assembly, remove the mounting nuts and bolts and pull the unit free.

7   To remove the evaporator disconnect all connectors, unfasten the retaining clips holding the two halves of the housing, and separate the housing halves.

8   Check the evaporator fins for blockage; if they are dirty clean them with compressed air - never use water for this purpose!

9   Check fittings for cracks and signs of wear; replace parts as necessary.

10   Installation is the reverse of the removal procedure. Be sure to replace all O-rings removed during disassembly with new ones.

11   If a new evaporator was installed, add 2.5 ounces (75 cc) of refrigerant oil to the system. **Caution:** *When replacing entire components, additional refrigerant oil should be added equal to the amount that is removed with the component being replaced. Refrigerant oils, just like refrigerant R-12 vs. R-134a, are not compatible. Be sure to read the can before adding any oil to the system, to make sure it is compatible with the type of system being repaired.*

12   Have the system evacuated, charged and leak tested by the shop that discharged it.

Chapter 4 Part A
Fuel and exhaust systems - carbureted engines

Contents

4A

Specifications

Fuel pressure	2 to 8 psi
Curb idle speed	See Chapter 1
Fast idle speed	
1982 and 1983	
E15	2,400 to 3,200 rpm
E16	
USA (except California)	
Manual transaxle	2,400 to 3,200 rpm
Automatic transaxle	2,700 to 3,500 rpm
California	
Manual transaxle	2,600 to 3,400 rpm
Automatic transaxle	2,900 to 3,700 rpm
Canada	
Manual transaxle	1,900 to 2,700 rpm
Automatic transaxle	2,400 to 3,200 rpm
1984 and 1985	
California	
Manual transaxle	2,600 to 3,400 rpm
Automatic transaxle	2,900 to 3,700 rpm
Canada	
Manual transaxle	1,900 to 2,700 rpm
Automatic transaxle	2,400 to 3,200 rpm
1986 and 1987	
Manual transaxle	1,800 to 2,600 rpm
Automatic transaxle	2,300 to 3,100 rpm

Torque Specifications

Air/fuel ratio control solenoid mounting screws	36 in-lbs

1   General information

The fuel system on all carbureted models consists of a fuel tank mounted in various locations on the chassis, a mechanically operated fuel pump and a carburetor. A combination of metal and rubber fuel hoses is used to connect these components.

The electric assist choke system consists of a thermostatic spring and cover (choke assembly), temperature sensing switch and a ceramic (positive temperature coefficient) heater. At temperatures below 60 degrees, the switch is open and no current is supplied to the ceramic heater located within the thermostatic spring. At temperatures above 60 degrees F, the temperature sensing switch closes and current is supplied to the ceramic heater. As the heater warms, it causes the spring to pull the choke plate open within 1 to 1 1/2 minutes.

The carburetor is either a Hitachi or Nikki two barrel type, depending on engine displacement and year of production. USA models are equipped with electronic feedback carburetors. These carburetors are linked with a variety of sensors and output actuators to help control the emissions output.

The fuel system is interrelated with the emissions control systems on all vehicles produced for sale in the United States. Components of the emissions control systems are described in Chapter 6.

2   Fuel pump/fuel pressure check

Warning: *Gasoline is extremely flammable, so take extra precautions when you work on any part of the fuel system. Don't smoke or allow open flames or bare light bulbs near the work area, and don't work in a garage where a natural gas-type appliance (such as a water heater or a clothes dryer) with a pilot light is present. Since gasoline is carcinogenic, wear latex gloves when there's a possibility of being exposed to fuel, and, if you spill any fuel on your skin, rinse it off immediately with soap and water. Mop up any spills immediately and do not store fuel-soaked rags where they could ignite. When you perform any kind of work on*

the fuel system, wear safety glasses and have a Class B type fire extinguisher on hand.
Note: *It is a good idea to check the fuel pump and lines for any obvious damage or fuel leakage. Also check all hoses from the tank to the pump, particularly the suction hoses at the fuel tank and pump which, if they have cracked, may not allow fuel to the fuel pump. It is also possible for the fuel pump diaphragm to rupture internally and leak fuel into the crankcase. If you have excess fuel consumption or fuel smell, and you can't find any external leaks, check the condition of the engine oil for any signs of fuel mixing with the engine oil; the oil level will usually be abnormally high and the oil will be thinned out and have a fuel smell.*
Refer to illustration 2.1

1   Disconnect the fuel line from the carburetor **(see illustration)** and install a T-fitting. Connect a fuel pressure gauge to the T-fitting with a section of fuel hose that is no longer than six inches.

2   Start the engine and allow it to idle. The pressure on the gauge should be 2 to 8 psi. It should remain constant and return to zero slowly when the engine is shut off. **Note:** *If the engine will not start, crank the engine until you get a reading on the gauge.*

3   An instant pressure drop indicates a faulty outlet valve and the fuel pump must be replaced.

4   If the pressure is too high, check the air vent to see if it is plugged before replacing the pump.

5   If the pressure is too low, be sure the fuel hoses and lines are in good shape and not plugged, then replace the pump.

3   Fuel lines and fittings - repair and replacement

Warning: *Gasoline is extremely flammable, so take extra precautions when you work on any part of the fuel system. Don't smoke or allow open flames or bare light bulbs near the work area, and don't work in a garage where a natural gas-type appliance (such as a water heater or a clothes dryer) with a pilot light is present. Since gasoline is carcinogenic, wear latex gloves when there's a possibility of being exposed to fuel, and, if you spill any fuel on your skin, rinse it off immediately with soap and*

water. Mop up any spills immediately and do not store fuel-soaked rags where they could ignite. When you perform any kind of work on the fuel system, wear safety glasses and have a Class B type fire extinguisher on hand.

Inspection
Refer to illustrations 3.2a and 3.2b

1   Once in a while, you will have to raise the vehicle to service or replace some component (an exhaust pipe hanger, for example). Whenever you work under the vehicle, always inspect the fuel lines and fittings for possible damage or deterioration.

2   Check all hoses and pipes for cracks, kinks, deformation or obstructions **(see illustrations).**

3   Make sure all hose and pipe clips attach their associated hoses or pipes securely to the underside of the vehicle.

4   Verify all hose clamps attaching rubber hoses to metal fuel lines or pipes are snug enough to assure a tight fit between the hoses and the metal pipes.
Replacement

5   If you must replace any damaged sections, use hoses approved for use in fuel systems or pipes made from steel only (it's best to use an original-type pipe from a dealer that's already flared and pre-bent). Do not install substitutes constructed from inferior or inappropriate material, as this could result in a fuel leak and a fire.

6   Always, before detaching or disassembling any part of the fuel line system, note the routing of all hoses and pipes and the orientation of all clamps and clips to assure that replacement sections are installed in exactly the same manner.

7   Before detaching any part of the fuel system, be sure to relieve the fuel tank pressure by removing the fuel filler cap.

8   Always use new hose clamps after loosening or removing them.

9   While you're under the vehicle, it's a good idea to check the following related components:

a) *Check the condition of the fuel filter - make sure that it's not clogged or damaged (see Chapter 1).*

b) *Inspect the evaporative emission control (EVAP) system. Verify that all hoses are attached and in good condition (see Chapter 6).*

2.1 Install a fuel pressure gauge onto a T-fitting and connect the assembly between the fuel pump and the carburetor bowl inlet valve at the carburetor

3.2a Check carefully for damaged fuel lines at the carburetor inlet

3.2b Carefully inspect the fuel lines that extend from the fuel pump to the fuel tank

4.3 Some fuel tanks are equipped with a drain plug (arrow)

4   Fuel tank - removal and installation

Refer to illustrations 4.3, 4.5a, 4.5b, 4.6, 4.9, 4.11a and 4.11b

Warning: *Gasoline is extremely flammable, so take extra precautions when you work on any part of the fuel system. Don't smoke or allow open flames or bare light bulbs near the work area, and don't work in a garage where a natural gas-type appliance (such as a water heater or a clothes dryer) with a pilot light is present. Since gasoline is carcinogenic, wear latex gloves when there's a possibility of being exposed to fuel, and, if you spill any fuel on your skin, rinse it off immediately with soap and water. Mop up any spills immediately and do not store fuel-soaked rags where they could ignite. When you perform any kind of work on the fuel system, wear safety glasses and have a Class B type fire extinguisher on hand.*

Note: *The following procedure is much easier to perform if the fuel tank is empty. Some tanks have a drain plug for this purpose. If the tank does not have a drain plug, drain the fuel into an approved fuel container using a commercially available siphoning kit (NEVER start a siphoning action by mouth) or wait until the fuel tank is nearly empty, if possible.*

1   Remove the fuel tank filler cap to relieve fuel tank pressure.

2   Detach the cable from the negative terminal of the battery.

3   If the tank still has fuel in it, you can drain it at the fuel feed line after raising the vehicle. If the tank has a drain plug (**see illus-**

4.5a Typical fuel tank and fuel level sending unit details

4.5b Scrape the mud and undercoating off the filler tube retainer to uncover the mounting bolts (arrows)

4.6 Loosen the clamp and remove the inlet hose and vapor line (arrow) from the fuel tank and the body

tration) remove it and allow the fuel to collect in an approved gasoline container.

4   Raise the vehicle and place it securely on jackstands.

5   Disconnect the fuel filler tube from the body of the vehicle (**see illustrations**).

6   Disconnect the fuel lines and the vapor return line (**see illustration**). **Note:** *The fuel feed and return lines and the vapor return line are three different diameters, so reattachment is simplified. If you have any doubts, however, clearly label the three lines and the fittings. Be sure to plug the hoses to prevent leakage and contamination of the fuel system.*

7   If there is still fuel in the tank, siphon it out from the fuel feed port. Remember - NEVER start the siphoning action by mouth!

Use a siphoning kit, which can be purchased at most auto parts stores.

8   Support the fuel tank with a floor jack. Position a wood block between the jack head and the fuel tank to protect the tank.

9   If equipped, remove the bolts from the heat shield located on the front side of the fuel tank (**see illustration**).

10   If equipped, disconnect the electrical connectors for the fuel pump and/or fuel level sending unit located under the rear seat (see Chapter 4B for additional details on fuel injected models).

11   Remove the bolts that retain the fuel tank to the chassis (**see illustrations**).

12   Remove the tank from the vehicle.

13   Installation is the reverse of removal.

4.9 Remove the heat shield from the front of the fuel tank

4.11a First, remove the forward mounting bolts (arrows) and then . . .

4.11b . . . remove the rear mounting bolts (arrows) from the fuel tank

4A

6.4 Remove the fuel pump from the engine

6.5 Install the gasket(s) to the engine block before installing the fuel pump

7.3a Remove the mounting bolts and lift the access cover from the body

5   Fuel tank cleaning and repair - general information

1   All repairs to the fuel tank or filler neck should be carried out by a professional who has experience in this critical and potentially dangerous work. Even after cleaning and flushing of the fuel system, explosive fumes can remain and ignite during repair of the tank.
2   If the fuel tank is removed from the vehicle, it should not be placed in an area where sparks or open flames could ignite the fumes coming out of the tank. Be especially careful inside garages where a natural gas-type appliance is located, because the pilot light could cause an explosion.

6   Fuel pump - removal and installation

Refer to illustrations 6.4 and 6.5
Warning: *Gasoline is extremely flammable, so take extra precautions when you work on any part of the fuel system. Don't smoke or allow open flames or bare light bulbs near the work area, and don't work in a garage where a natural gas-type appliance (such as a water heater or a clothes dryer) with a pilot light is present. Since gasoline is carcinogenic, wear latex gloves when there's a possibility of being exposed to fuel, and, if you spill any fuel on your skin, rinse it off immediately with soap and water. Mop up any spills immediately and do not store fuel-soaked rags where*

they could ignite. When you perform any kind of work on the fuel system, wear safety glasses and have a Class B type fire extinguisher on hand.
1   The fuel pump is located on the front side of the engine near the bottom of the block next to the engine mounts.
2   Place rags under the fuel pump to catch any gasoline which may be spilled during removal.
3   Carefully unscrew the fuel line fittings and detach the lines from the pump. A flare-nut wrench along with a backup wrench should be used on the pressure-side fitting to prevent damage to the line fittings.
4   Unbolt and remove the fuel pump **(see illustration)**.
5   Before installation, coat both sides of the gasket surface with gasket sealant, position the gasket and fuel pump against the block **(see illustration)** and install the bolts, tightening them securely.
6   Attach the lines to the pump and tighten the pressure fitting securely (use a flare-nut wrench, if one is available, to prevent damage to the fittings).
7   Run the engine and check for leaks.

7   Fuel level sending unit - check and replacement

Refer to illustrations 7.3a, 7.3b, 7.4a, 7.4b, 7.6, 7.10, 7.11, 7.12 and 7.13
Warning: *Gasoline is extremely flammable, so take extra precautions when you work on any*

part of the fuel system. Don't smoke or allow open flames or bare light bulbs near the work area, and don't work in a garage where a natural gas-type appliance (such as a water heater or a clothes dryer) with a pilot light is present. Since gasoline is carcinogenic, wear latex gloves when there's a possibility of being exposed to fuel, and, if you spill any fuel on your skin, rinse it off immediately with soap and water. Mop up any spills immediately and do not store fuel-soaked rags where they could ignite. When you perform any kind of work on the fuel system, wear safety glasses and have a Class B type fire extinguisher on hand.
Note: *Carbureted engines are equipped with a two-wire fuel level sending unit located in the tank. TBI models are equipped with a fuel pump/fuel level sending unit assembly. MPFI models are equipped with a separate fuel level sending unit and fuel pump that are accessible from the single opening at the top of the tank.*

Check

1   Before performing any tests on the fuel level sending unit, completely fill the tank with fuel.
2   Raise the vehicle and support it securely with jackstands.
3   Lift the rear seat and remove the access cover plate **(see illustrations)** to locate the fuel level sending unit electrical connector positioned on the fuel tank.
4   Position the ohmmeter probes into the electrical connector **(see illustrations)** and check the resistance. Use the 200-ohm or low scale on the ohmmeter.
5   With the fuel tank completely full, the resis-

7.3b Carbureted models are equipped with a two-wire sending unit

7.4a Measure the resistance of the fuel level sending unit. It should read approximately 73 to 88 ohms EMPTY and 4 to 5 ohms FULL

7.4b TBI models are equipped with a fuel pump/fuel level sending unit assembly. Check the resistance of the sending unit on terminals E and G

tance should be approximately 4.0 to 8.0 ohms. With the tank half full, the resistance should be approximately 27.0 to 35.0 ohms. With the fuel tank empty, the resistance of the sending unit should be approximately 73 to 88.0 ohms.

6   If the readings are incorrect, replace the sending unit. **Note:** *A more accurate check of the sending unit can be made by removing it (fuel level sending unit or assembly) from the fuel tank and checking its resistance while manually operating the float arm* **(see illustration).**

7   If the readings are incorrect, replace the sending unit.

Replacement

8   Remove the rear seat from the vehicle (see Chapter 11).

9   If necessary, carefully peel back the insulation material from the top of the fuel tank without damaging it.

10   On carbureted models, use a brass punch and hammer and tap the inside sending unit cover until the tabs align with the indents on the fuel tank retaining ring. On MPFI engines, remove the mounting screws **(see illustration).**

11   Lift the sending unit from the tank **(see illustration).** Carefully angle the sending unit out of the opening without damaging the fuel level float located at the bottom of the assembly. **Note:** *On TBI models, lift the fuel level sending unit/fuel pump assembly from the tank.*

12   On MPFI models, disconnect the fuel pump electrical connector from the sending unit **(see illustration).**

13   On MPFI models, remove the fuel lines from the sending unit **(see illustration).**

14   Installation is the reverse of removal.

---

8   Air filter housing - removal and installation

Refer to illustration 8.2

1   Remove the air filter element from the air filter housing (see Chapter 1).

2   Disconnect any vacuum hose, electrical connectors and mounting bolts **(see illustration)** that are attached to the housing and

7.6 Probe the terminals of the sending unit and manually move the float from empty to full and observe the change in resistance. The transition should be smooth without "dead spots" or "damaged areas"

7.10 Remove the mounting bolts arrows) from the fuel level sending unit assembly

FEEDBACK CARBURETED MODELS

Lock plate

Fuel tank gauge unit

O-ring

TBI MODELS

Fuel pump assembly

O-ring

Fuel check valve

7.11 Fuel level sending unit details on feedback carbureted and TBI models

7.12 Unplug the electrical connector and lift the sending unit from the fuel tank

7.13 On models equipped with MPFI, remove the fuel lines that attach the fuel sending unit to the fuel pump

8.2 Remove the air filter assembly mounting bolts

4A

9.1 Remove the accelerator cable from the carburetor bracket (arrow) and linkage

9.4 Typical accelerator linkage assembly on carbureted models

mark them with paint or marked pieces of tape for reassembly purposes.

3   Lift the air filter housing from the engine compartment.

4   Installation is the reverse of removal.

9   Accelerator cable - removal, installation and adjustment

Refer to illustrations 9.1 and 9.4

Removal

1   Remove the accelerator cable from the mounting bracket **(see illustration)**.

2   Rotate the throttle valve and remove the cable end from the recess.

3   Detach the screws and the clips retaining the lower instrument trim panel on the driver's side and remove the trim piece (see Chapter 11).

4   Pull the cable end out and then up from the accelerator pedal recess **(see illustration)**.

5   To disconnect the cable at the firewall, push the cable assembly through the firewall from inside the passenger compartment.

Installation

6   Installation is the reverse of removal. **Note:** *To prevent possible interference, flexible components (hoses, wires, etc.) must not be routed within two inches of moving parts, unless routing is controlled.*

7   Operate the accelerator pedal and check for any binding condition by completely opening and closing the throttle.

8   If necessary, at the engine compartment side of the firewall, apply sealant around the accelerator cable to prevent water from entering the passenger compartment.

Adjustment

9   The cable housing can be adjusted to allow for freeplay in the cable. Loosen the cable bracket screw (see Illustration 9.1) and move the cable housing up or down to allow for more or less cable freeplay (slack). The throttle valve should be able to completely close (idle) without hindrance.

10   Carburetor - diagnosis and overhaul

Warning: *Gasoline is extremely flammable, so take extra precautions when you work on any part of the fuel system. Don't smoke or allow open flames or bare light bulbs near the work area, and don't work in a garage where a natural gas-type appliance (such as a water heater or a clothes dryer) with a pilot light is present. Since gasoline is carcinogenic, wear latex gloves when there's a possibility of being exposed to fuel, and, if you spill any fuel on your skin, rinse it off immediately with soap and water. Mop up any spills immediately and do not store fuel-soaked rags where they could ignite. When you perform any kind of work on the fuel system, wear safety glasses and have a Class B type fire extinguisher on hand.*

Diagnosis

1   A thorough road test and check of carburetor adjustments should be done before any major carburetor service. Specifications for some adjustments are listed on the *Vehicle Emissions Control Information* (VECI) label found in the engine compartment.

2   Carburetor problems usually show up as flooding, hard starting, stalling, severe backfiring and poor acceleration. A carburetor that's leaking fuel and/or covered with wet looking deposits definitely needs attention.

3   Some performance complaints directed at the carburetor are actually a result of loose, out-of-adjustment or malfunctioning engine or electrical components. Others develop when vacuum hoses leak, are disconnected or are incorrectly routed. The proper approach to analyzing carburetor problems should include the following items:

a) *Inspect all vacuum hoses and actuators for leaks and correct installation (see Chapters 1 and 6).*

b) *Tighten the intake manifold and carburetor mounting nuts/bolts evenly and securely.*

c) *Perform a compression test and vacuum test (see Chapter 2B).*

d) *Clean or replace the spark plugs as necessary (see Chapter 1).*

e) *Check the spark plug wires (see Chapter 1).*

f) *Inspect the ignition primary wires.*

g) *Check the ignition timing (follow the instructions printed on the Emissions Control Information label).*

h) *Check the fuel pump pressure/volume (see Section 2).*

i) *Check the heat control valve in the air filter assembly for proper operation (see Chapter 1).*

j) *Check/replace the air filter element (see Chapter 1).*

k) *Check the PCV system (see Chapter 6).*

l) *Check/replace the fuel filter (see Chapter 1). Also, the strainer in the tank could be restricted.*

m) *Check for a plugged exhaust system.*

n) *Check EGR valve operation (see Chapter 6).*

o) *Check the choke - it should be completely open at normal engine operating temperature (see Chapter 1).*

p) *Check for fuel leaks and kinked or dented fuel lines (see Chapters 1 and 4).*

q) *Check accelerator pump operation with the engine off (remove the air filter assembly cover and operate the throttle as you look into the carburetor throat - you should see a stream of gasoline enter the carburetor).*

r) *Check for incorrect fuel or bad gasoline.*

s) *Check the valve clearances (if applicable) and camshaft lobe lift (see Chapters 1 and 2)*

t) *Have a dealer service department or repair shop check the electronic engine and carburetor controls.*

4   Diagnosing carburetor problems may require that the engine be started and run with the air filter assembly off. While running the engine without the air filter assembly, backfires are possible. This situation is likely to occur if the carburetor is malfunctioning, but just the removal of the air filter assembly can lean the fuel/air mixture enough to produce an engine backfire. **Warning:** *Do not position any part of your body, especially your face, directly over the carburetor during inspection and servicing procedures. Wear eye protection!*

Overhaul

Refer to illustrations 10.7a and 10.7b

5   Once it's determined that the carburetor needs an overhaul, several options are available. If you're going to attempt to overhaul the carburetor yourself, first obtain a good-quality carburetor rebuild kit (which will include all necessary gaskets, internal parts, instructions and a parts list). You'll also need some special solvent and a means of blowing out the internal passages of the carburetor with compressed air.

6   An alternative is to obtain a new or rebuilt carburetor. They are readily available from dealers and auto parts stores. Make absolutely sure the exchange carburetor is identical to the original. A tag is usually attached to the top of the carburetor or a number is stamped on the float bowl. It will help determine the exact type of carburetor you have. When obtaining a rebuilt carburetor or a rebuild kit, make sure the kit or carburetor matches your application exactly. Seemingly insignificant differences can make a large difference in engine performance.

7   If you choose to overhaul your own carburetor, allow enough time to disassemble it carefully, soak the necessary parts in the cleaning solvent (usually for at least one-half day or according to the instructions listed on the carburetor cleaner) and reassemble it, which will usually take much longer than disassembly **(see illustrations)**. When disassembling the carburetor, match each part

4A

10.7a Exploded view of the typical feedback carburetor on USA models (except California)

11.2 Align the bi-metal cover index mark with the center mark on the choke housing

10.7b Exploded view of the typical feedback carburetor on California and Canada models

11.3 With the engine not running, check for continuity between terminals A and B. Continuity should exist

1   *Ignition relay*
2   *Automatic choke relay*
3   *Automatic choke heater*
4   *Alternator L terminal*

with the illustration in the carburetor kit and lay the parts out in order on a clean work surface. Overhauls by inexperienced mechanics can result in an engine which runs poorly or not at all. To avoid this, use care and patience when disassembling the carburetor so you can reassemble it correctly.

8   Because carburetor designs are constantly modified by the manufacturer in order to meet increasingly more stringent emissions regulations, it isn't feasible to include a step-by-step overhaul of each type. You'll receive a detailed, well illustrated set of instructions with the carburetor overhaul kit.

11   Electric choke heater - testing

Refer to illustrations 11.2, 11.3 and 11.5
Caution: *If there is any loss of electrical current to the choke heater, operation of any type, including idling, should be avoided. Loss of power to the choke will cause the choke to remain partly closed during engine operation. A very rich air-to-fuel mixture will be created and result in abnormally high exhaust system temperatures, which may cause damage to the catalytic converter or other underbody parts of the vehicle.*
1   With the engine cold, connect a jumper wire from the choke heater wire to the positive battery terminal. The choke heater housing should begin becoming hot and the choke plate in the carburetor should slowly open after some time. Be sure it opens completely in about five minutes or replacement is necessary. **Note:** *As the heater is heating the choke coil, occasionally tap the accelerator to allow the choke to open.* **Note:** *The electric assist choke system consists of a thermostatic spring and cover (choke assembly), choke heater and a choke*

relay. The automatic choke relay opens and closes current to the heater. As the heater warms, it causes the spring to pull the choke plate open within 1 to 1-1/2 minutes.
2   If the choke heater tests okay, but the choke valve does not open in normal operation, check to make sure the bi-metal cover index mark lines up with the choke housing index mark **(see illustration)**.
3   With the engine not running, check for continuity on terminals A and B of the 12 pin Function Check connector **(see illustration)**. Continuity should exist. If continuity does not exist, check the heater circuit.
4   With the engine running at idle, check for voltage on terminals A and B of the 12 pin Function Check connector. The voltage should be approximately 12 volts (battery voltage). If voltage does not exist, check for an open circuit or a faulty choke heater relay.
5   Check the choke heater relay terminals

11.5 Use an ohmmeter and follow the correct pin terminals to check the choke heater relay

for continuity using an ohmmeter at the following connections (see illustration):

a Terminals 5 to 4 - no continuity
b Terminals 6 to 3 - continuity
c Apply battery voltage to terminals 1 and 2
d Terminals 5 to 4 - continuity
e Terminals 6 to 3 - no continuity

6   If the results are not as specified, replace the choke heater relay.

12 Anti-dieseling solenoid valve - check and replacement

Check

1   The anti-dieseling solenoid prevents excess engine idle and surges after the ignition switch has been turned off. The solenoid extends a plunger into the idle circuit within the carburetor when the ignition is turned OFF, immediately shutting off fuel to the idle circuit.
2   Turn the ignition key ON (engine not running) and using a voltmeter, check for battery voltage at the anti-dieseling solenoid. There should be approximately 12 volts.

12.5 Remove the anti-dieseling solenoid (arrow) from the carburetor

3   Touch the electrical connector to the solenoid and listen for a distinct "click" from the solenoid. If necessary, remove the solenoid from the carburetor and watch the solenoid plunger move as voltage is applied. If there is no movement from the plunger, replace it with a new part.

Replacement

Refer to illustration 12.5
4   Disconnect the electrical connector from the anti-dieseling solenoid.
5   Remove the solenoid from the carburetor (see illustration) using an open end wrench.
6   Installation is the reverse of removal.

13 Carburetor adjustments

Note : These carburetor adjustments are strictly in-vehicle adjustments. During overhaul, refer to the instructions included in the overhaul kit for complete procedures and any additional adjustments that are required.

Choke plate opening

Refer to illustration 13.3
1   The choke plate opening is a critical carburetor adjustment directly involved with cold-running conditions and choke

13.5 Checking the vacuum break adjustment

R = 1/16 to 7/64 inch

13.3 Checking the setting of the choke unloader

C (E15 engine) = 3/32 inch
C (E16 engine) = 1/8 inch

enrichment during cranking. The choke unloader is a mechanical device that partially opens the choke valve at wide open throttle to eliminate choke enrichment during hard acceleration.
2   Engines which have been stalled or flooded by excessive choke enrichment can be cleared by the use of the choke unloader. With the throttle valve at wide open throttle, the choke plate should be slightly open to allow a sufficient amount of intake air into the carburetor venturi.
3   Turn the throttle lever until the primary throttle valve is fully open. If it is not, bend the tongue on the unloader to compensate for the necessary adjustment on clearance C (see illustration).

Vacuum break

Refer to illustrations 13.5 and 13.6
4   The choke vacuum break is a double acting diaphragm which opens the choke valve plate immediately after cold starting to create a suitable air/fuel mixture during warm-up. With the engine cold, remove the air filter assembly and close the choke plate manually.
5   Depress the diaphragm rod fully and then check the clearance R (see illustration). The clearance is measured between the edge of the valve plate and the wall of the carburetor.
6   To adjust the vacuum break, bend the choke lever (see illustration).

13.6 Vacuum break diaphragm

4A

13.11 Valve plate interlock setting

G = 1/4 inch

13.15 Dashpot adjusting screw location

Fast idle speed

7   Install a tachometer according to the manufacturer's instructions.

8   Make sure the automatic choke housing cover index mark is opposite the center mark on the carburetor body **(see illustration 11.2)**.

9   Position the fast idle speed screw onto the second step on the fast idle cam. Start the engine and monitor the engine rpm. Adjust the fast idle to the speed listed in this Chapter's Specifications. Turn the fast idle cam adjusting screw IN to increase the rpm or OUT to decrease the rpm. **Note:** *Make sure the fast idle speed adjusting screw remains positioned onto the middle step of the cam.*

10   Adjust the engine idle speed (see Chapter 1).

Valve plate interlock

Refer to illustration 13.11

11   Manually turn the throttle valve until the throttle arm contacts the lock lever at point A **(see illustration)**.

12   Measure the clearance between the throttle valve and throttle bore (G). If not as specified, bend the throttle arm tongue to adjust.

Dashpot

Refer to illustration 13.15

13   The dashpot system prevents engine stall resulting from quick application of the brake or from quick release of the accelerator pedal.

14   Warm the engine to normal operating temperature.

15   Manually operate the throttle lever on the carburetor. With the engine running, have an assistant record the exact rpm range of the engine at the point the dashpot makes contact with the stop lever **(see illustration)**. If the speed is not between 1800 and

2600 rpm, release the locknut and turn the dashpot rod until the correct engine speed is attained.

16   Double-check the action of the dashpot by observing that the engine speed drops from 2,000 rpm to 1,000 rpm in three seconds after releasing the throttle lever.

14   Carburetor - removal and installation

Warning: *Gasoline is extremely flammable, so take extra precautions when you work on any part of the fuel system. Don't smoke or allow open flames or bare light bulbs near the work area, and don't work in a garage where a natural gas-type appliance (such as a water heater or a clothes dryer) with a pilot light is present. Since gasoline is carcinogenic, wear latex gloves when there's a possibility of being exposed to fuel, and, if you spill any fuel on your skin, rinse it off immediately with soap and water. Mop up any spills immediately and do not store fuel-soaked rags where they could ignite. When you perform any kind of work on the fuel system, wear safety glasses and have a Class B type fire extinguisher on hand.*

Removal

Refer to illustration 14.8

1   Remove the fuel filler cap to relieve fuel tank pressure.

2   Remove the air filter assembly from the carburetor. Be sure to label all vacuum hoses attached to the air filter housing.

14.8 The carburetor mounting nuts locations (arrows)

3   Disconnect the accelerator cable from the throttle valve (see Section 9).

4   If the vehicle is equipped with an automatic transaxle, disconnect the kickdown cable from the throttle valve.

5   Clearly label all vacuum hoses and fittings, then disconnect the hoses.

6   Disconnect the fuel line from the carburetor.

7   Label the wires and terminals, then unplug all the electrical connectors.

8   Remove the mounting fasteners **(see illustration)** and detach the carburetor from the intake manifold. Remove the carburetor mounting gasket. Stuff a rag into the intake manifold openings.

Installation

9   Use a gasket scraper to remove all traces of gasket material and sealant from the intake manifold (and the carburetor, if it's being reinstalled), then remove the shop rag from the manifold openings. Clean the mating surfaces with lacquer thinner or acetone.

10   Place a new gasket on the intake manifold.

11   Position the carburetor on the gasket and install the mounting fasteners.

12   To prevent carburetor distortion or damage, tighten the fasteners to approximately 16 ft-lbs in a criss-cross pattern, 1/4-turn at a time.

13   The remaining installation steps are the reverse of removal.

14   Check and, if necessary, adjust the idle speed (see Chapter 1).

15   If the vehicle is equipped with an automatic transaxle, refer to Chapter 7B for the kickdown cable adjustment procedure.

16   Start the engine and check carefully for fuel leaks.

15   Electronic feedback carburetor systems - general information

Refer to illustration 15.1

1   The electronically-controlled carburetor (ECC) emission system or most commonly called the electronic feedback carburetor system relies on an electronic signal, which is generated by an exhaust gas oxygen sensor, to control a variety of devices and keep emissions within limits **(see illustration)**. The system works in conjunction with a three-way catalyst to control the levels of carbon monoxide, hydrocarbons and oxides of nitrogen. The feedback carburetor system also works in conjunction with the computer. The two systems share certain sensors and output actuators; therefore, diagnosing the feedback carburetor system will require a thorough check of all the feedback carburetor components (refer to Chapter 6 for additional information).

2   The system operates in two modes: open loop and closed loop. When the engine is cold, the air/fuel mixture is controlled by

Air fuel ratio solenoid valve: ON

⇦ : Air
⬅ : Fuel
⬱ : Additional fuel

Air fuel ratio solenoid valve: OFF

⇦ : Air
⬅ : Fuel
⬱ : Additional air

15.1 The electronically-controlled carburetor (ECC) system incorporates a computer that controls the air/fuel ratio control solenoid thereby adjusting the air/fuel mixture electronically

the computer in accordance with a program designed in at the time of production. The air/fuel mixture during this time will be richer to allow for proper engine warm-up. When the engine is at operating temperature, the system operates in closed loop and the air/fuel mixture is varied depending on the information supplied by the exhaust gas oxygen sensor.

3   Here is a list of the various sensors and

output actuators involved with these feedback carburetor systems:

Coolant temperature sensor
Oxygen sensor
Crank Angle sensor
Air/fuel ratio solenoid valve
Computer
Throttle switch
Vacuum sensor
Air temperature sensor

4   Refer to Section 16 and also Chapter 6 for the diagnostic checks for the feedback carburetor system components.

16 Electronic feedback carburetor information sensors and output actuators - check and replacement

Note: *This section covers only a select few of the output actuators incorporated onto the carburetor. Refer to Chapter 6, Section 11 for additional information on the information sensors such as coolant temperature sensor, oxygen sensor, etc.*

Air/fuel ratio control solenoid
Check
Refer to illustrations 16.2a, 16.2b, 16.7, 16.8 and 16.10

1   The function of the air/fuel ratio control solenoid is to provide limited regulation of the air/fuel ratio of a feedback carburetor in response to the electronic signals sent by the computer. This is accomplished by metering the main fuel jets in the carburetor with the use of a fuel metering pintle that extends into the fuel passage and shuts the fuel off (lean) and on (rich), allowing the fuel/air mixture ratio to change. By controlling the duration of this voltage signal, the ratio of power ON-time versus the power OFF-time is called the duty cycle.

2   Maintain an engine speed of 1,500 rpm. Disconnect the air/fuel ratio control solenoid connector from the carburetor (**see illustrations**). Average engine speed should increase a minimum of 50 rpm. Reconnect the air/fuel ratio control solenoid connector. The engine speed should slowly return to 1,500 rpm. If rpm does not change as specified, there's a problem in the feedback carburetor system, although the oxygen sensor is usually the cause. First check for battery voltage to the air/fuel ratio control solenoid electrical connector, then check the oxygen sensor. If the oxygen sensor is OK and all connections are OK, the air/fuel ratio control solenoid is bad.

4A

16.2a The air/fuel ratio control solenoid electrical connector is part of the throttle switch electrical connector. Remove the retaining clip and pull out the correct wires for the solenoid harness

16.2b Some models are equipped with a specialized harness for the air/fuel ratio solenoid that is mounted on the side of the air filter assembly

16.7 Remove the mounting screws and pull the air/fuel ratio control solenoid up

16.8 Be sure to install a new grommet onto the solenoid assembly

16.10 Install a new O-ring onto the outer section of the solenoid

16.14 Using jumper wires, connect the corresponding terminals for the anti-dieseling solenoid to allow the engine to operate for testing

16.15 Check for continuity working on the carburetor side of the throttle switch harness

3   Another quick check on the air/fuel ratio control solenoid is to measure the resistance on the electrical connector terminals. The resistance should be approximately 30 to 50 ohms.

Replacement

4   Disconnect the cable from the negative battery terminal.

5   Disconnect the electrical connector from the air/fuel ratio control solenoid **(see illustrations 16.2a and 16.2b)**.

6   Remove the carburetor top from the carburetor.

7   Remove the mounting bolts for the solenoid **(see illustration)**.

8   Install a new air/fuel ratio control solenoid grommet onto the solenoid and apply silicon grease to the O-ring **(see illustration)**.

9   Tighten the mounting bolts to the torque listed in this Chapter's Specifications.

10   Install outer O-ring and apply slight amount of silicon grease **(see illustration)**.

11   The remainder of installation is the reverse of removal.

Vacuum sensor (manual transaxle models)

General description

12   The vacuum sensor monitors the intake manifold pressure changes resulting from

changes in engine load and speed. The vacuum sensor operates the same as the MAP sensor in later models. Refer to Chapter 6, Section 11 for the diagnostic procedures.

Throttle switch

General description

Refer to illustrations 16.14, 16.15, and 16.19

13   The throttle switch is located on the end of the throttle shaft on the carburetor body. This switch monitors the engine speed and signals the computer when the speed is below 1,000 to 1,700 rpm.

Check

14   To check the throttle switch, turn the ignition switch to OFF and disconnect the harness electrical connector. Using jumper wires, connect the terminals that power the anti-dieseling solenoid **(see illustration)**. This will allow the engine to be tested while running. **Note:** *Be careful when backprobing the electrical connector. Do not damage the wiring harness or pull on any connectors to make clean contact. Be sure the probes are placed in the correct position.*

15   Working on the carburetor side, check that continuity does not exist between the throttle valve switch terminals **(see illustration)**.

16   Start the engine and increase the engine speed to approximately 2000 rpm. Verify that

continuity exists between the throttle valve switch terminals.

17   Decrease the engine speed slowly to 1200 rpm while watching the ohmmeter, continuity should break at that point causing the ohmmeter to indicate an open circuit. If the test results are incorrect, adjust the switch.

Adjustment

18   Hold the engine speed steady at 1200 rpm.

19   Bend the plate until the ohmmeter indicates an open circuit **(see illustration)**.

16.19 Adjust the clearance by bending the plate

16.21 Schematic of the idle speed control system

20   Recheck the adjustment and adjust the idle speed if necessary (see Chapter 1).

Idle speed control motor (non California models)

General Information

Refer to illustration 16.21

21   The idle speed is controlled by the ECC computer **(see illustration)**. The computer senses the idle condition from information received from the coolant temperature sensor, the gear selection, air conditioning system operation, etc. and thereby provides the electrical signal to change the idle speed.

The vacuum control modulator transforms the electrical signal to the vacuum signal. The idle speed control actuator controls the idle speed by the vacuum signal from the modulator. The control vacuum produced in the vacuum control modulator goes to the control diaphragm chamber in the idle speed actuator. Therefore, the position of the valve is determined by the strength of the control vacuum and the intake manifold vacuum in the power diaphragm chamber.

Check

Refer to illustrations 16.23 through 16.26

22   Warm up the engine to normal

operating temperatures. Turn the ignition key off.

23   Remove the computer without disconnecting the harness electrical connector (see Chapter 6) and turn the diagnosis start switch to the ON position **(see illustration)**.

24   Disconnect the coolant temperature sensor harness **(see illustration)** and connect a jumper wire between the terminals.

25   Start the engine and check the vacuum between the vacuum control modulator and idle speed actuator. It should be between 2.56 to 4.13 in-Hg **(see illustration)**.

26   If the vacuum is not as specified, check

16.23 With the engine turned OFF, engage the diagnostic start switch to ON

16.24 Disconnect the coolant temperature sensor electrical connector and jump the terminals with a wire

16.25 Install a vacuum gauge between the vacuum control modulator and the idle speed actuator and check for vacuum

the air filters for clogging **(see illustration)**. Check all the vacuum hoses to the vacuum switches and solenoids for breaks, damage or misrouting. Refer to the vacuum schematics in Chapter 6 for complete diagram information.

27   Further diagnostics will have to be performed by a dealer service department or other qualified repair facility.

17   Exhaust system - servicing and general information

Refer to illustrations 17.1a, 17.1b and 17.4

Warning: *Inspection and repair of exhaust system components should be done only after enough time has elapsed after driving the vehicle to allow the system components to cool completely. Also, when working under the vehicle, make sure it is securely supported on jackstands.*

1   The exhaust system consists of the exhaust manifold(s), the catalytic converter(s), the muffler, the tailpipe and all connecting pipes, brackets, hangers and clamps **(see illustrations)**. The exhaust system is attached to the body with mounting brackets and rubber hangers. If any of the parts are improperly installed, excessive noise and vibration will be transmitted to the body.

16.26 Check the filters for plugging or damage

2   Conduct regular inspections of the exhaust system to keep it safe and quiet. Look for any damaged or bent parts, open seams, holes, loose connections, excessive corrosion or other defects which could allow exhaust fumes to enter the vehicle. Deteriorated exhaust system components should not be repaired; they should be replaced with new parts.

3   If the exhaust system components are extremely corroded or rusted together, welding equipment will probably be required to remove them. The convenient way to accomplish this is to have a muffler repair shop remove the corroded sections with a cutting torch. If, however, you want to save money by doing it yourself (and you don't have a welding outfit with a cutting torch), simply cut off the old components with a hacksaw. If you have compressed air, special pneumatic cutting chisels can also be used. If you do decide to tackle the job at home, be sure to wear safety goggles to protect your eyes from metal chips and work gloves to protect your hands.

4   Here are some simple guidelines to follow when repairing the exhaust system:

  a) *Work from the back to the front when removing exhaust system components.*
  b) *Apply penetrating oil to the exhaust system component fasteners to make them easier to remove* **(see illustration)**.
  c) *Use new gaskets, hangers and clamps when installing exhaust system components.*
  d) *Apply anti-seize compound to the threads of all exhaust system fasteners during reassembly.*
  e) *Be sure to allow sufficient clearance between newly installed parts and all points on the underbody to avoid overheating the floor pan and possibly damaging the interior carpet and insulation. Pay particularly close attention to the catalytic converter and heat shield.*

17.1a Catalytic converter hanger and mounting brackets

17.1b Muffler hanger and mounting brackets

17.4 Spray the exhaust nuts (arrows) with penetrating lubricant before attempting to remove them from the exhaust flange on the exhaust manifold

Chapter 4 Part B
Fuel and exhaust systems - fuel injected engines

Contents

Specifications

Fuel pressure

TBI
Fuel system pressure (at idle)

1987 and 1988	14 psi
1989 and 1990	34 psi

MPFI
Fuel system pressure (at idle)

Vacuum hose attached	32 to 38 psi
Vacuum hose detached	38 to 46 psi
Fuel system hold pressure (after 5 minutes)	30 to 40 psi
Fuel pump pressure (maximum)	65 psi
Fuel pump hold pressure	50 psi

Injector resistance

TBI	1 to 2 ohms
MPFI	10 to 14 ohms

Torque specifications

Ft-lbs (unless otherwise indicated)

Throttle body mounting bolts (TBI)	21 to 26
Injector cover mounting screws (TBI)	
Small center screw	48 to 60 in-lbs
Large set screws	36 to 43 in-lbs
Fuel pressure mounting screws (TBI)	48 to 60 in-lbs
Air intake plenum mounting bolts (MPFI)	156 to 180 in-lbs
Throttle body mounting bolts (MPFI)	156 to 192 in-lbs
EGR valve-to-throttle body (MPFI)	72 to 108 in-lbs
EGR base mounting assembly to air intake plenum (MPFI)	15 to 20
Air regulator to intake manifold (MPFI)	72 to 108 in-lbs
Fuel rail mounting bolts (MPFI)	70 to 105 in-lbs
Exhaust pipe-to-exhaust manifold bolts	15 to 25

1 General information

The fuel system on fuel injected engines consists of a fuel tank, an electric fuel pump (located in the fuel tank), a fuel pump relay, fuel injector(s), an air filter assembly and a throttle body unit. Fuel-injected engines appeared in 1987 with Throttle Body Injection (TBI) (1987 models are equipped with either the feedback carburetor or TBI). 1991 models were equipped with the Multi Port Fuel Injection (MPFI) system. The two systems are easily distinguished. The TBI system uses a large throttle body unit with a single injector, mounted on the intake manifold just like a carburetor, while MPFI uses separate injectors positioned over the intake valves, mounted in the intake manifold.

Throttle Body Injection (TBI) system

The Throttle Body Injection system incorporates a single injector mounted in a throttle body similar to that of a conventional carburetor. This system produces greatly improved fuel metering in all running conditions and since most of the control mechanism is electronic, TBI reduces maintenance and minor repair problems.

The Engine Control Module (ECM) automatically adjusts the air/fuel mixture according to engine load and performance. A fuel pressure regulator mounted in the fuel charging assembly regulates the electric pump-generated fuel pressure at a constant value. The injector consists of a solenoid activated pintle valve and a small inline fuel filter. It is energized by time-modulated electronic pulses from the ECM (computer).

Multi Port Fuel Injection (MPFI) system

Multi Port Fuel Injection uses timed impulses to inject the fuel directly into the intake port of each cylinder. The injectors are controlled by the Engine Control Module (ECM). The ECM monitors various engine parameters and delivers the exact amount of fuel required into the intake ports. The throttle body serves only to control the amount of air passing into the system. Because each cylinder is equipped with its own injector, much better control of the fuel/air mixture ratio is possible.

Fuel pump and lines

Fuel is circulated from the fuel tank to the fuel injection system, and back to the fuel tank, through a pair of metal lines running along the underside of the vehicle. An electric fuel pump is located inside the fuel tank. A vapor return system routes all vapors back to the fuel tank through a separate return line.

The fuel pump will operate as long as the engine is cranking or running and the ECM is receiving ignition reference pulses from the electronic ignition system. If there are no reference pulses, the fuel pump will shut off after two or three seconds.

Exhaust system

The exhaust system includes an exhaust manifold fitted with an exhaust oxygen sensor, a catalytic converter, an exhaust pipe, and a muffler.

The catalytic converter is an emission control device added to the exhaust system to reduce pollutants. A single-bed converter is used in combination with a three-way (reduction) catalyst. Refer to Chapter 6 for more information regarding the catalytic converter.

2 Fuel pressure relief procedure

Refer to illustrations 2.1a, 2.1b and 2.4
Warning: *Gasoline is extremely flammable, so take extra precautions when you work on any part of the fuel system. Don't smoke or allow open flames or bare light bulbs near the work area, and don't work in a garage where a natural gas-type appliance (such as a water heater or a clothes dryer) with a pilot light is present. Since gasoline is carcinogenic, wear latex gloves when there's a possibility of being exposed to fuel, and, if you spill any fuel on your skin, rinse it off immediately with soap and water. Mop up any spills immediately and do not store fuel-soaked rags where they could ignite. The fuel system is under constant pressure, so, if any fuel lines are to be disconnected, the fuel pressure in the system must be relieved first. When you perform any kind of work on the fuel system, wear safety glasses and have a Class B type fire extinguisher on hand.*
Note: *After the fuel pressure has been relieved. it's a good idea to lay a shop towel over any fuel connection to be disassembled, to absorb the residual fuel that may leak out when servicing the fuel system.*

1   Remove the fuel pump fuse from the fuse panel **(see illustrations)**.
2   Start the engine and allow it to run until it stops. This should take only a few seconds. Disconnect the cable from the negative terminal of the battery before working on the fuel system.
3   The fuel system pressure is now relieved. When you're finished working on the fuel system, simply install the fuel pump fuse back into the fuse panel and connect the negative cable to the battery.
4   It is a good idea to double-check by relieving the fuel pressure directly at the fuel filter using a shop rag to catch fuel that might spill out **(see illustration)**.

3 Fuel pump/fuel pressure - check

Warning: *Gasoline is extremely flammable, so take extra precautions when you work on any part of the fuel system. Don't smoke or allow open flames or bare light bulbs near the work area, and don't work in a garage where a natural gas-type appliance (such as a water heater or a clothes dryer) with a pilot light is present. Since gasoline is carcinogenic, wear latex gloves when there's a possibility of being exposed to fuel, and, if you spill any fuel on your skin, rinse it off immediately with soap and water. Mop up any spills immediately and do not store fuel-soaked rags where they could ignite. The fuel system is under constant pressure, so, if any fuel lines are to be disconnected, the fuel pressure in the system must be relieved first (see Section 2 for more information). When you perform any kind of work on the fuel system, wear safety glasses and have a Class B type fire extinguisher on hand.*

2.1a Location of the fuel pump fuse on a 1988 model

2.1b Location of the fuel pump fuse on a 1994 model. Use a fuse removal tool to avoid damaging the fuse panel

2.4 Loosen the clamp on the fuel filter and catch any residue fuel in a shop rag

3.3a Check for battery voltage on the fuel pump relay connector located in the engine compartment near the battery on 1991 through 1994 MPFI models

Note: *To perform the fuel pressure test, you will need to obtain a fuel pressure gauge and adapter set (fuel line fittings).*

Preliminary inspection

Refer to illustrations 3.3a, 3.3b, 3.4a and 3.4b

1   Should the fuel system fail to deliver the proper amount of fuel, or any fuel at all, inspect it as follows. Remove the fuel filler cap. Have an assistant turn the ignition key to the On position (engine not running) while you listen at the fuel filler opening. You should hear a whirring sound that lasts for a couple of seconds.

2   If you don't hear anything, check the fuel pump fuse (see Section 2). If the fuse is blown, replace it and see if it blows again. If it does, trace the fuel pump circuit for a short. If it isn't blown, check the fuel pump relay.

3   Remove the relays and check for battery voltage to the fuel pump relay connector and the EFI relay connector (see illustrations). If there is battery voltage present, have the relay(s) tested at a dealer service department or other qualified automotive repair shop.

4   If battery voltage is present, remove the rear seat and check for battery voltage at the fuel pump harness connector (see illustrations). If there is no voltage, check the fuel pump circuit. If there is voltage present, replace the pump (see Section 4).

Operating pressure check

Refer to illustrations 3.6a, 3.6b, 3.10, 3.11 and 3.13

5   Relieve the fuel system pressure (see Section 2). Detach the cable from the negative battery terminal.

6   Remove the fuel line from the fuel filter and attach a fuel pressure gauge (see illustrations) between the fuel filter and the fuel rail. Tighten the hose clamps securely.

7   Attach the cable to the negative battery terminal. Start the engine.

8   Note the fuel pressure and compare it with the pressure listed in this Chapter's Specifications.

TBI models

9   If the pressure is not as listed in this Chapter's Specifications, refer to Steps 13 and 14. Also confirm that the fuel pressure rises considerably when the vacuum hose at

3.3b Check for battery voltage on the fuel pump relay connector located in the driver's side dash area on 1987 through 1990 TBI models

the bottom of the regulator is detached. If it doesn't, replace the regulator.

MPFI models

10   Disconnect the vacuum hose from the fuel pressure regulator and hook up a hand-held vacuum pump (see illustration) to the port on the fuel pressure regulator.

11   Read the fuel pressure gauge with vacuum applied to the pressure regulator and also with no vacuum applied (see illustration). The fuel pressure should decrease

3.6a Install the fuel pressure gauge between the fuel filter and the throttle body assembly on TBI models

3.10 On MPFI engines, connect a hand-held vacuum pump to the fuel pressure regulator

3.4a Remove the rear seat from the vehicle and check for battery voltage to the fuel pump (MPFI model shown)

3.4b With the electrical harness disconnected, check for battery voltage to the fuel pump on terminal A (TBI model shown)

4B

3.6b Install the fuel pressure gauge between the fuel filter and the fuel rail on MPFI models

3.11 As vacuum is applied, the fuel pressure should decrease

as vacuum increases (and increase as vacuum decreases). Compare your readings with the values listed in this Chapter's Specifications.

12   Reconnect the vacuum hose to the regulator and check the fuel pressure at idle, comparing your reading with the value listed in this Chapter's Specifications. Disconnect the vacuum hose and watch the gauge - the pressure should jump up considerably as soon as the hose is disconnected. If it doesn't, check for a vacuum signal to the fuel pressure regulator (see Step 15).

13   If the fuel pressure is low, pinch the fuel return line shut **(see illustration)** and watch the gauge. If the pressure doesn't rise, the fuel pump is defective or there is a restriction in the fuel feed line. If the pressure rises sharply, replace the pressure regulator.

14   If the fuel pressure is too high, turn the engine off. Disconnect the fuel return line and blow through it to check for a blockage. If there is no blockage, replace the fuel pressure regulator.

15   Connect a vacuum gauge to the pressure regulator vacuum hose. Start the engine and check for vacuum. If there isn't vacuum present, check for a clogged hose or vacuum port. If the amount of vacuum is adequate, replace the fuel pressure regulator.

16   If the system fuel pressure is less than specified:

a) Inspect the system for a fuel leak. Repair any leaks and recheck the fuel pressure.

b) If the fuel pressure is still low, replace the fuel filter (it may be clogged) and recheck the fuel pressure.

c) If the pressure is still low, check the fuel pump output pressure (see below) and/or the fuel pressure regulator

17   If the pressure is higher than specified:

a) Check the fuel return line for an obstruction.

b) Replace the fuel pressure regulator

18   Turn the ignition switch to Off, wait five minutes and recheck the pressure on the gauge. Compare the reading with the hold pressure listed in this Chapter's Specifications. If the hold pressure is less than specified:

a) The fuel lines may be leaking.

b) The fuel pressure regulator may be allowing the fuel pressure to bleed through to the return line

c) A fuel injector (or injectors) may be leaking.

d) The fuel pump may be defective.

Fuel pump output pressure check

Warning: For this test it is necessary to use a fuel pressure gauge with a bleeder valve in order to relieve the fuel pressure after the test is completed (the normal procedure for pressure relief will not work because the gauge is connected directly to the fuel pump).

19   Relieve the system fuel pressure (see Section 2).

3.13 Place a rag on the fuel return line and using a pair of pliers, carefully squeeze the line and observe the fuel pressure gauge (be sure to wrap a rag around the hose to prevent damage)

20   Detach the cable from the negative battery terminal.

21   Attach a fuel pressure gauge directly to the fuel feed line at the fuel tank.

22   Attach the cable to the negative battery terminal.

23   Using a jumper wire from the battery, disconnect the fuel pump electrical connector and apply battery voltage to the fuel pump.

24   Note the pressure reading on the gauge and compare the reading to the value listed in this Chapter's Specifications.

25   If the indicated pressure is less than specified, inspect the fuel line for leaks between the pump and gauge. If no leaks are found, replace the fuel pump.

26   Remove the jumper wire and wait five minutes. Note the reading on the gauge and compare it to the hold pressure listed in this Chapter's Specifications. If the hold pressure is less than specified, check the fuel line between the pump and gauge for leaks. If no leaks are found, replace the fuel pump.

27   Open the bleeder valve on the gauge and allow the pressurized fuel drain into an approved fuel container. Remove the gauge and reconnect the fuel line.

4   Fuel pump - removal and installation

Warning: *Gasoline is extremely flammable, so take extra precautions when you work on any part of the fuel system. Don't smoke or allow open flames or bare light bulbs near the work area, and don't work in a garage where a natural gas-type appliance (such as a water heater or a clothes dryer) with a pilot light is present. Since gasoline is carcinogenic, wear latex gloves when there's a possibility of being exposed to fuel, and, if you spill any fuel on your skin, rinse it off immediately with soap and water. Mop up any spills immediately and do not store fuel-soaked rags where they could ignite. The fuel system is under constant pressure, so, if any fuel lines are to be disconnected, the fuel pressure in the system must be relieved first (see Section 2*

for more information). When you perform any kind of work on the fuel system, wear safety glasses and have a Class B type fire extinguisher on hand.

1   Unless the vehicle has been driven far enough to completely empty the tank, it's a good idea to siphon the residual fuel out before removing the fuel pump from the vehicle. **Warning:** *DO NOT start the siphoning action by mouth! Use a siphoning kit (available at most auto parts stores).*

2   Relieve the fuel pressure (see to Section 2).

3   Detach the cable from the negative terminal of the battery.

4   Remove the rear seat from the vehicle (see Chapter 11).

5   Remove the access cover for the fuel pump/fuel level sending unit assembly (see Chapter 4A, Section 7).

6   Disconnect the fuel pump/fuel level sender electrical connector.

TBI models

7   Remove the six screws securing the fuel pump/level sending unit to the tank.

8   Carefully pull the fuel pump/sending unit assembly from the tank.

9   Remove the old gasket and discard it.

10   If you're planning to reinstall the original fuel pump/sending unit, remove the strainer by prying it off with a screwdriver, wash it in clean solvent, then push it back onto the metal pipe on the end of the pump. If you're installing a new pump/sending unit, the assembly will include a new strainer.

11   To separate the fuel pump from the assembly, remove the clamp and disconnect the electrical connector from the fuel pump.

12   Installation is the reverse of removal.

MPFI models

Refer to illustrations 4.14, 4.15, 4.16 and 4.17

13   Remove the six screws securing the fuel pump/level sending unit to the tank. Lift the unit out part way, detach the hoses and electrical connector from the cover, then remove the sending unit assembly **(see illustrations 7.12 and 7.13 in Chapter 4A).**

14   Reach into the fuel tank opening and squeeze the tab that retains the fuel pump to the mounting assembly **(see illustration).**

4.14 Reach inside the fuel pump access hole on top of the fuel tank and press the tab (1) forward, releasing the fuel pump from the housing and . . .

4.15 ... lift the pump from the fuel tank

4.16 Press the tab (left hand) and separate the holder with the right hand

4.17 Lift the fuel pump from the holder

15   Lift the fuel pump from the fuel tank **(see illustration)**.
16   To remove the fuel pump from the holder, squeeze the locking tab while pulling the case to separate the holder **(see illustration)**.
17   Separate the fuel pump from the holder **(see illustration)**.
18   Installation is the reverse of removal.

5   Air filter assembly - removal and installation

Refer to illustrations 5.3, 5.4, 5.5 and 5.6
1   Detach the cable from the negative terminal of the battery.

2   Remove the air filter from the air filter housing (see Chapter 1).
3   On TBI models, remove the mounting bolts from the air filter housing **(see illustration)**.
4   On MPFI models, loosen the clamp on the air intake duct **(see illustration)** and separate the duct from the air filter housing.
5   On MPFI models, unclip the upper half of the air filter housing assembly and remove it **(see illustration)**.
6   On MPFI models, remove the mounting bolts from the air filter housing **(see illustration)**.
7   Remove the air filter housing from the engine compartment.
8   Installation is the reverse of removal.

6   Accelerator cable - removal, installation and adjustment

Removal
Refer to illustrations 6.2, 6.4, 6.5 and 6.9

1   On TBI models, remove the air filter assembly (see Section 5).
2   Detach the accelerator cable from the throttle lever **(see illustration)**.
3   If equipped, remove the cruise control cable from the cable bracket.
4   Separate the accelerator cable from the cable bracket **(see illustration)**.
5   Detach the nylon collar from the upper

4B

5.3 Remove the mounting bolts (arrows) from the air filter housing (TBI model shown)

5.4 Loosen the clamp that retains the air intake duct to the air filter assembly (MPFI model shown)

5.5 Lift the air filter upper section from the engine compartment (MPFI model shown)

5.6 Remove the air filter assembly mounting bolts (arrows)

6.2 Rotate the throttle lever and detach the cable end

6.4 Unscrew the nut nearest the exposed cable, then pass the cable through the bracket

6.5 Exploded view of the accelerator pedal and cable

end of the accelerator pedal arm **(see illustration).**

6   Remove the cable through the firewall from the engine compartment.

Installation

7   Installation is the reverse of removal. Be sure the cable is routed correctly.

8   If necessary, at the engine compartment side of the firewall, apply sealant around the accelerator cable to prevent water from entering the passenger compartment.

Adjustment

9   To adjust the cable **(see illustration):**

a) *Lift up on the cable to remove any slack.*
b) *Turn the adjusting nut until it is 1/8-inch away from the cable bracket.*
c) *Tighten the locknut and check cable deflection at the throttle linkage. Deflection should be 3/8 to 1/2-inch. If deflection is not within specifications, loosen the locknut and turn the*

adjusting nut until the deflection is as specified.
d) *After you have adjusted the throttle cable, have an assistant help you verify that the throttle valve opens all the way when you depress the accelerator pedal to the floor and that it returns to the idle position when you release the accelerator. Verify the cable operates smoothly. It must not bind or stick.*
e) *If the vehicle is equipped with an automatic transaxle, adjust the transaxle throttle valve cable (see Chapter 7B).*

---

7   Electronic fuel injection system - general information

Throttle Body Injection (TBI)

Refer to illustration 7.1

The Throttle Body Injection (TBI) system **(see illustration on opposite page)** uses a single point, pulse time modulated injection system. Fuel is metered into the air intake stream in accordance with engine demands by a single solenoid injection valve mounted in a throttle body on the intake manifold.

Fuel is supplied from the fuel tank by a low pressure, electric fuel pump mounted in the fuel tank. The fuel is filtered and sent to the air throttle body, where a regulator maintains the fuel delivery pressure of 14 psi. An injector nozzle is mounted vertically above the throttle plate and connected in series with

the fuel pressure regulator. Excess fuel supplied by the pump but not needed by the engine is returned to the fuel tank by a steel fuel return line.

The fuel charging assembly consists of five individual com-ponents which perform the fuel and air metering function. The throttle body assembly is attached to the conventional carburetor mounting flange on the intake manifold and houses the air control system, fuel injector, fuel pressure regulator, airflow meter, Idle Speed Control (ISC) valve and throttle switch and sensor.

Air-flow to the engine is controlled by a single butterfly valve mounted in a two piece, die-cast aluminum housing called a throttle body. The butterfly valve is identical in configuration to the throttle plates of a conventional carburetor and is actuated by a similar pedal and linkage arrangement.

The fuel injector is mounted vertically above the throttle plate and is an electro-mechanical device which meters and atomizes the fuel delivered to the engine. The injector valve body consists of a solenoid actuated ball and seat valve assembly.

An electric control signal from the ECM (computer) activates the solenoid, causing the ball to move off the seat and allowing fuel to flow. The injector flow orifice is fixed and the fuel supply is constant. Therefore, fuel flow to the engine is controlled by how long the solenoid is energized.

The pressure regulator is integral to the fuel charging main body. The regulator is located so as to nullify the effects of the supply line pressure drops. Its design is such that it is not sensitive to back pressure in the return line to the tank.

A second function of the pressure regulator is to maintain fuel supply pressure upon fuel pump shutdown. The regulator functions as a downstream check valve and traps the fuel between itself and the fuel pump. The constant fuel pressure level after engine shutdown precludes fuel line vapor formation and allows for rapid restarts and stable idle operation immediately thereafter.

The ISC valve is a rotary solenoid valve. It receives a pulse signal from the ECM and adjusts the bypass air quantity by opening or closing a slider (door) within the ISC valve. The ISC valve operates in conjunction with other systems to control idle speed. During cold start, feedback control, air conditioning and power steering changes and deceleration vacuum control.

The throttle switch and sensor has two functions. It contains an idle switch and a throttle sensor. The idle switch closes when the throttle valve is at idle and is open at all other positions. The throttle sensor is a potentiometer that that transforms throttle position into a output voltage and feeds the signals into the ECM. The throttle switch also determines when the throttle lever has contacted the actuator, signaling the need to control engine rpm.

6.9 Accelerator cable adjusting nut location on a TBI model

7.1 Component location diagram for the Throttle Body Injection (TBI) system

Multi Port Fuel Injection (MPFI)

Refer to illustration 7.12

The Multi Port Fuel Injection (MPFI) system **(see illustration)** is a multi-point, pulse timed, speed density controlled fuel injection system. On the MPFI system, fuel is metered into each intake port in accordance with engine demand through injectors mounted on the intake manifold. The two-piece air intake manifold includes an air intake plenum.

This system incorporates an on-board Engine Control Module (ECM) computer that accepts inputs from various engine sensors to compute the required fuel flow rate necessary to maintain a prescribed air/fuel ratio throughout the entire engine operational range. The computer then outputs a command to the fuel injectors to meter the approximate quantity of fuel. The system automatically senses and compensates for changes in altitude, load and speed. **Note:** *The computer terminology has changed from Engine Control Module (ECM) to the Powertrain Control Module (PCM) on later models due to standardization of the self-diagnosis system within the automotive industry.*

The fuel delivery system includes an electric in-tank fuel pump which forces pressurized fuel through a series of metal and plastic lines and an inline fuel filter to the fuel charging manifold assembly.

A constant fuel pressure drop is maintained across the injector nozzles by a pressure regulator. The regulator is positioned downstream from the fuel injectors. Excess fuel passes through the regulator and returns to the fuel tank through a fuel return line.

7.12 Component location for the Multi Port Fuel Injection (MPFI) system

8.6 Install a special TBI "noid light" into the harness connector and confirm that it blinks when the engine is cranked

8.7 Check the TBI system injector for a conical shaped spray pattern while the engine is running. Raise the engine rpm and watch carefully for breaks, hesitations or uneven spray patterns

8.8 Clean the interior of the throttle body using carburetor spray and shop towels

8.9 Use a stethoscope to determine if the injectors are working properly - they should make a steady clicking sound that rises and falls with engine speed changes

8 Electronic fuel injection system - check

Warning: *Gasoline is extremely flammable, so take extra precautions when you work on any part of the fuel system. Don't smoke or allow open flames or bare light bulbs near the work area, and don't work in a garage where a natural gas-type appliance (such as a water heater or a clothes dryer) with a pilot light is present. Since gasoline is carcinogenic, wear latex gloves when there's a possibility of being exposed to fuel, and, if you spill any fuel on your skin, rinse it off immediately with soap and water. Mop up any spills immediately and do not store fuel-soaked rags where they could ignite. The fuel system is under constant pressure, so, if any fuel lines are to be disconnected, the fuel pressure in the system must be relieved first (see Section 2 for more information). When you perform any kind of work on the fuel system, wear safety glasses and have a Class B type fire extinguisher on hand.*
Note: *The following procedure is based on the assumption that the fuel pump is working and the fuel pressure is adequate (see Section 3).*

Preliminary checks

1 Check all electrical connectors that are related to the system. Loose electrical connectors and poor grounds can cause many problems that resemble more serious malfunctions.
2 Check to see that the battery is fully charged, as the control unit and sensors depend on an accurate supply voltage in order to properly meter the fuel.
3 Check the air filter element - a dirty or partially blocked filter will severely impede performance and economy (see Chapter 1).
4 If a blown fuse is found, replace it and see if it blows again. If it does, search for a grounded wire in the harness to the fuel pump (see Chapter 12).

System checks

Refer to illustrations 8.6, 8.7, 8.8, 8.9, 8.10 and 8.11

5 Check the condition of the vacuum hoses connected to the intake manifold.

Throttle Body Injection (TBI) systems

6 First, purchase a special injector test light (sometimes called a "noid" light) and install it into the injector electrical connector **(see illustration)**. Crank the engine and check to see if the noid light flashes. If it does, the injector is receiving proper voltage. If it doesn't flash, further diagnosis should be performed by a dealer service department or other repair shop.
7 Install a timing light, according to the manufacturer's instructions, and point the light into the TBI unit while the engine is running **(see illustration)**. Watch the conical shaped spray pattern from the injector. Make sure it is even and constant. Vary the idle speed and watch also. There should not be any intermittent breaks or weak spray patterns. **Caution:** *Make sure all timing light wires are carefully tucked away to avoid any accidental contact with the drivebelts or fan blades during testing.*

Multi Port Fuel Injection (MPFI) systems

8 Remove the air intake duct from the throttle body and check for dirt, carbon or other residue build-up in the throttle body, particularly around the throttle plate. If it's dirty, clean it with aerosol carburetor cleaner, a rag and a toothbrush, if necessary **(see illustration)**.
9 With the engine running, place an

automotive stethoscope against each injector, one at a time, and listen for a clicking sound, indicating operation **(see illustration)**. If you don't have a stethoscope, you can place the tip of a long screwdriver against the injector and listen through the handle.
10 If an injector isn't functioning (not clicking), purchase a special injector test light (sometimes called a "noid" light) and install it into the injector electrical connector **(see illustration)**. Start the engine and check to see if the noid light flashes. If it does, the injector is receiving proper voltage. If it doesn't flash, further diagnosis should be performed by a dealer service department or other repair shop.
11 With the engine OFF and the fuel injector electrical connectors disconnected, measure the resistance of each injector **(see illustration)**. Compare your measurements

8.10 Install the noid light into the fuel injector electrical connector and confirm that it blinks when the engine is running

8.11 Measure the resistance of each injector. It should be within Specifications

4B

with the injector resistance listed in this Chapter's Specifications. If any injector is open or has an abnormally high resistance, replace it with a new one.

9   Throttle Body Injection (TBI) system - component check and replacement

Warning: *Gasoline is extremely flammable, so take extra precautions when you work on any part of the fuel system. Don't smoke or allow open flames or bare light bulbs near the work area, and don't work in a garage where a natural gas-type appliance (such as a water heater or a clothes dryer) with a pilot light is present. Since gasoline is carcinogenic, wear latex gloves when there's a possibility of being exposed to fuel, and, if you spill any fuel on your skin, rinse it off immediately with soap and water. Mop up any spills immediately and do not store fuel-soaked rags where they could ignite. The fuel system is under constant pressure, so, if any fuel lines are to be disconnected, the fuel pressure in the system must be relieved first (see Section 2). When you perform any kind of work on the fuel system, wear safety glasses and have a Class B type fire extinguisher on hand.*
Note: *Refer to Chapter 6, Section 11 for checking procedures on the vacuum sensor and the air temperature sensor*

TBI assembly
Refer to illustrations 9.1 and 9.10

1   When buying replacement parts **(see illustration)** for the TBI assembly, always check the number on the identification tag on the side of the TBI assembly to make sure that you are getting the right parts.
2   Relieve the fuel system pressure (see Section 2). Detach the cable from the negative terminal of the battery.
3   Remove the air filter housing assembly (see Section 5).
4   Detach the accelerator cable and, if equipped, cruise control cable fitting from the throttle lever (see Section 6).
5   If your vehicle is equipped with an automatic transmission, detach the kickdown rod.
6   Disconnect the electrical connectors to the fuel injector, the Idle Speed Control (ISC) valve and the Throttle Position (TP) switch and sensor.
7   Remove the fuel line bracket bolt.
8   Using a backup wrench, detach the fuel feed and return lines. **Note:** *If either line proves difficult to pull out, carefully wiggle it up and down - do not strike the lines with a tool or attempt to pry them loose or you may dent them.*
9   Detach the PCV hose.
10   Remove the four mounting nuts **(see illustration)**.
11   Installation is the reverse of removal.

Idle Speed Control (ISC) valve (1987 and 1988 models)
Refer to illustrations 9.12, 9.13 and 9.17

Check
12   Disconnect the electrical connector from the ISC valve and probe the indicated terminals of the ISC valve with an ohmmeter **(see illustration)**. The ISC valve resistance should be:

> 9.5 to 10.5 ohms
>   between terminals A and B
> 8.5 to 9.5 ohms
>   between terminals B and C

13   Turn the ignition key ON (engine not running) and check for battery voltage at

9.1 Exploded view of the throttle body unit

9.10 Remove the four large Allen head bolts (arrows) to remove the throttle body from the intake manifold

9.12 Check the ISC valve resistance with an ohmmeter

9.13 Remove the ISC valve connector and check for battery voltage with the ignition key ON (engine not running)

9.17 Tighten the ISC valve bolts to 43 in-lbs - first tightening A then B then C

terminal B of the engine harness side of the connector **(see illustration)**.
14 With the engine idling, disconnect the electrical connector from the ISC valve and confirm a change in rpm. If the idle is not affected, have the ISC diagnosed at a dealer service department or other qualified repair facility.

Replacement
15 Detach the cable from the negative terminal of the battery and disconnect the electrical connector from the ISC valve.
16 Remove the two mounting bolts and detach the ISC valve.
17 Installation is the reverse of removal. Be sure to tighten the ISC bolts in the correct pattern **(see illustration)**.

Auxiliary Air Control (AAC) valve (1989 and 1990 models)
Refer to illustration 9.18

Check
18 Disconnect the electrical connector from the AAC valve. Using an ohmmeter, probe the terminals of the AAC valve connector **(see illustration)**.
19 The resistance of the AAC valve should be approximately 10 ohms. If not as specified, replace the valve.
20 Verify that there is battery voltage between terminal A (gray wire) of the engine harness side of the connector and ground. If battery voltage is not present, repair the open circuit in the gray wire.

21 Connect the AAC valve harness connector, start the engine and warm it up to normal operating temperature. Using a voltmeter, backprobe terminal B (red/white wire) of the AAC valve connector. There should be approximately 4 to 8 volts at terminal B with the engine idling. If the specified voltage is not present, have the ECM diagnosed by a dealership service department or other qualified repair facility.

Replacement
22 Disconnect the electrical connector at the AAC valve.
23 Remove the screws retaining the AAC valve to the throttle body and remove the valve.
24 Installation is the reverse of removal.

Throttle valve switch/sensor
Refer to illustrations 9.28a and 9.28b

General description
25 The throttle valve switch and sensor has two functions. It contains an idle switch and a throttle sensor. The idle switch closes when the throttle valve is at idle and is open at all other positions. The throttle sensor is a potentiometer that transforms throttle position into an output voltage and feeds the signals into the ECM. The throttle switch also determines when the throttle lever has contacted the actuator, signaling the need to control engine rpm.

Check
26 To check the throttle valve switch, warm the engine to normal operating temperature.
27 Check the idle speed and adjust it if necessary (see Chapter 1).
28 Turn the ignition key OFF and disconnect the throttle valve switch connector and the throttle sensor connector **(see illustration)** and connect the probes of an ohmmeter to the throttle valve switch terminals **(see illustration)**.
29 Start the engine and manually open the throttle until the engine speed reaches:
   Manual transaxle:
      900 to 1,200 rpm
   Automatic transaxle:
      820 to 1,120 rpm
Make sure the idle contacts turn from ON to OFF (breaks continuity).
30 If the throttle valve switch opens before or after the correct specification, adjust the throttle valve switch (see Steps 37 through 39).
31 To check the throttle sensor, first disconnect the electrical connector to the sensor and check for battery voltage between terminals D and F of the engine harness connector with the key On (engine not running). Place the positive probe of the voltmeter on terminal F (red wire on 1987 and 1988 models or outside white wire on 1989 and 1990 models) and the negative probe on terminal D (black wire). If battery voltage is not present, check the harness between the throttle sensor and the ECM for opens or shorts. If the circuits are good, have the ECM diagnosed by a dealer service department or other qualified repair facility.

4B

9.18 On 1989 and 1990 models, check the resistance across the AAC valve terminals

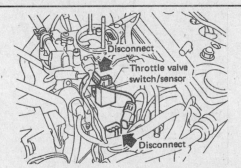

9.28a Disconnect the throttle valve switch and the throttle sensor connectors (arrows)

9.28b Use an ohmmeter and probe the throttle switch terminals and observe any change in continuity

9.42a Remove the Allen head bolts and set screw from the injector cover (arrows)

9.42b Lift the injector cover from the throttle body

Pull upward

9.43 Place a rag on the injector and lift the injector out of the recess with a pair of pliers

32   Connect the electrical connector to the throttle sensor and backprobe terminal E (white wire, middle terminal) with the positive probe of the voltmeter. Connect the negative probe to a good body ground. With the key On (engine not running), check the voltage as you rotate the throttle by hand from closed to open throttle. The voltage should read approximately 0.5 volt at closed throttle to 5.0 volts at wide-open throttle. If the readings are not as specified or if there isn't a smooth transition from closed to wide-open throttle, replace the throttle switch/sensor.

Replacement

33   Detach the cable from the negative terminal of the battery.
34   Disconnect the wire harness electrical connector from the throttle valve connector.
35   Remove the throttle valve retaining screws.
36   Slide the throttle position sensor off the throttle shaft. Installation is the reverse of removal.

Adjustment

37   Start the engine.
38   With the throttle valve bolts in place and slightly loose, rotate the throttle valve until the switch breaks continuity within the correct rpm range (see steps 28 and 29).
39   Tighten the adjustment bolts.

Fuel injector

Check

40   See Section 8 for the fuel injector opera-

tional check. If the injector is receiving adequate voltage but doesn't spray fuel, unplug the electrical connector and measure the resistance across the terminals of the injector. Compare your reading with the value listed in this Chapter's Specifications.

Replacement

Refer to illustrations 9.42a, 9.42b, 9.43 and 9.46

41   Relieve the fuel pressure (see Section 2).
42   Remove the injector cover assembly from the top of the throttle body **(see illustrations)**.
43   Place a rag on the injector and pull the injector straight up **(see illustration)**.
44   Discard the old O-rings and replace them with new ones. Use a light grade oil to lubricate the new O-rings before installing them.
45   Installation is the reverse of removal.
46   Push the injector into the recess using a 1/2-inch or 13 mm socket **(see illustration)**.
47   Install the injector cover and tighten the screws to torque listed in this Chapter's Specifications.

Airflow meter

Check

Refer to illustration 9.49

48   Disconnect the electrical connector from the airflow meter harness connector.
49   Use jumper wires and apply battery voltage to terminals C (negative) and terminal E (positive) **(see illustration)**.
50   Check for voltage at terminals A (positive) and D (negative). It should be 1.5 to 2.0 volts.
51   Remove the airflow sensor from the throttle body and using compressed air, apply a steady stream of air across the sensor element. The voltage should increase to 2.5 to 4.0 volts.
52   If the readings are incorrect, replace the sensor.

Replacement

Refer to illustration 9.55

53   Detach the cable from the negative battery terminal.
54   Disconnect the harness electrical connector.
55   Remove the mounting bolts and lift the airflow meter from the throttle body **(see illustration)**.

Fuel pressure regulator

Note: *Refer to Section 3 for the fuel pressure regulator checking procedure.*

Replacement

Refer to illustration 9.58

56   Relieve the fuel pressure (see Section 2).

Push — 13 mm socket head

9.46 Install the injector into the throttle body using a 1/2-inch socket

AIR

A
B
C
D
E
F

Battery

9.49 The voltage should increase when air is directed over the sensor element

Apply silicone grease
Sensor portion
Plug portion
Pull straight.
Air flow meter

9.55 Remove the airflow meter from the TBI unit

9.58 Remove the mounting screws (arrows) from the TBI unit and separate the fuel pressure regulator from the assembly

57   Disconnect the vacuum hose from the bottom of the regulator.

58   Remove the bolts that retain the pressure regulator to the TBI unit **(see illustration)**.
59   Installation is the reverse of removal. Be sure to use new O-rings.

---

10   Multi Port Fuel Injection (MPFI) system - component check and replacement

Air intake plenum with throttle bodyF

Refer to illustrations 10.2, 10.8a, 10.8b and 10.8c

Removal

1   Detach the cable from the negative terminal of the battery.

2   Disconnect the electrical connectors at the AAC valve, throttle position sensor (TPS), AIV control solenoid and EGR/EVAP canister control solenoid **(see illustration)**.
3   Detach the accelerator cable (see Section 6) and transmission linkage (see Chapter 7) from the throttle body assembly.
4   Remove the accelerator cable from the intake manifold (see Section 6).
5   Clearly label, then detach, the vacuum lines from air intake plenum, the EGR valve, the BPT valve and the fuel pressure regulator.
6   Detach the PCV system by disconnecting the hose from the fitting on the intake plenum.
7   If equipped, detach the canister purge line or lines from the throttle body.
8   Remove the upper air intake plenum

4B

1 Fuel injector
2 Pressure regulator
3 Intake manifold
4 EGR tube
5 Exhaust gas temperature sensor
6 EGR control valve
7 AIV control solenoid valve
8 BPT valve
9 Intake manifold collector
10 Rod
11 Accelerator drum unit
12 Throttle sensor
13 Throttle chamber
14 Air regulator
15 AAC valve

10.2 Exploded view of the air intake plenum and related components (SR20 model shown)

10.8a Remove the upper bolts from the air intake plenum

10.8b Remove the plenum mounting bolt directly beneath the AAC valve

10.8c Remove the mounting bracket bolt directly in front of the throttle body

retaining bolts **(see illustration)** and the lower (side) retaining bolts **(see illustrations)**.

9   Remove the upper intake manifold and throttle body as an assembly from the lower intake manifold.

Installation

10   Be sure to clean and inspect the mounting faces of the lower intake manifold (see Chapter 2A) and the air intake plenum before positioning the new gasket(s) onto the lower intake mounting face. Install the air intake plenum and throttle body assembly onto the intake manifold. Ensure the gasket remains in place. Install the upper intake manifold retaining bolts and tighten them to the torque listed in this Chapter's Specifications. The remainder of installation is the reverse of removal.

Throttle body

Removal

Refer to illustration 10.15

11   Detach the cable from the negative terminal of the battery.

12   Detach the Throttle Position Sensor (TPS) connector.

13   Disconnect the accelerator cable (see Section 6) from the throttle body.

14   Carefully mark and remove the vacuum hoses from the throttle body.

15   Remove the four throttle body mounting nuts **(see illustration)**.

16   Remove and discard the gasket between the throttle body air intake plenum.

Installation

17   Clean the gasket mating surfaces. If scraping is necessary, be careful not to damage the gasket surfaces or allow material to drop into the manifold. Installation is the reverse of removal. Be sure to tighten the throttle body mounting nuts to the torque listed in this Chapter's Specifications.

Throttle Position Sensor (TPS)

18   Refer to Chapter 6, Section 7 for the check and replacement procedures for the TPS.

Fuel rail assembly

Refer to illustration 10.23 and 10.24

Removal

19   Relieve the fuel pressure (see Section 2).

20   Detach the cable from the negative terminal of the battery.

21   Remove the air intake plenum assembly (see Steps 1 through 9).

22   Disconnect the fuel feed and return lines from the fuel rail assembly.

23   Remove the fuel rail assembly retaining bolts **(see illustration)**.

24   Disconnect each fuel injector electrical connector. Carefully lift the fuel rail and fuel injectors from the engine **(see illustration)**. **Note:** *Remove the injectors with the fuel rail as an assembly.*

25   If necessary, remove the injectors from the fuel rail (see Steps 43 and 44).

Installation

Note: *It's a good idea to replace the injector O-rings whenever the fuel rail is removed.*

26   Ensure that the injector caps are clean and free of contamination.

27   Install the fuel injectors on the fuel rail, if removed. Ensure that the injectors are well seated in the fuel rail assembly.

28   Install the fuel rail and injector assembly onto the engine and secure the fuel rail assembly with the retaining bolts. Tighten the bolts to the torque listed in this Chapter's Specifications.

29   The remainder of installation is the reverse of removal.

Fuel pressure regulator

Check

Note: *This procedure assumes the fuel filter is in good condition.*

30   Check the fuel pressure and perform the necessary steps to diagnose problems with the pressure regulator (see Section 3).

31   Start the engine and check for leakage around the fuel rail, fuel lines and the fuel pressure regulator.

32   If the fuel pressure regulator is faulty or leaking, replace it with a new part.

Replacement

Refer to illustration 10.37

33   Relieve the fuel pressure from the system (see Section 2).

34   Disconnect the cable from the negative terminal of the battery.

10.15 Remove the four nuts (arrows) from the throttle body

10.23 Remove the fuel rail mounting bolts (arrows)

10.24 Remove the fuel rail and fuel injector assembly from the engine as a single unit

10.37 Remove the fuel pressure regulator mounting bolts, loosen the hose clamp on the fuel return line, then detach the regulator from the fuel rail and the hose

10.43 Remove the fuel injector assembly screws (arrows)

10.44 Carefully wiggle the fuel injector from the fuel rail recess

35 Remove the fuel rail from the engine (see Steps 19 through 24).

36 Clean any dirt from around the fuel pressure regulator.

37 Loosen the hose clamp and remove the bolts from the fuel pressure regulator **(see illustration)**. Detach the regulator from the fuel rail.

38 Install new O-rings on the pressure regulator and lubricate them with a light coat of oil.

39 Installation is the reverse of removal. Tighten the pressure regulator mounting bolts and the hose clamp securely.

Fuel injectors

Refer to illustrations 10.43, 10.44 and 10.45

Removal

40 Relieve the system fuel pressure (see Section 2).

41 Remove the air intake plenum assembly (see Steps 1 through 9).

42 Remove the fuel rail assembly (see Steps 19 through 24).

43 Remove the screws that retain the injector in the fuel rail **(see illustration)**.

44 Grasping the injector body, pull up while gently rocking the injector from side-to-side **(see illustration)**.

45 Inspect the injector O-rings (two per injector) for signs of deterioration **(see illustration)**. Replace as required. **Note:** *As long*

as you have the fuel rail off it's a good idea to replace the O-rings.

46 Inspect the injector plastic "hat" (covering the injector pintle) and washer for signs of deterioration. Replace as required. If the hat is missing, look for it in the intake manifold.

Installation

47 Lubricate the new O-rings with light grade oil and install two on each injector. **Caution:** *Do not use silicone grease. It will clog the injectors.*

48 Using a light twisting motion, install the injector(s).

49 The remainder of installation is the reverse of removal.

Auxiliary Air Control (AAC) valve

Refer to illustrations 10.51a, 10.51b, 10.52, 10.54a and 10.54b

General Information

50 The AAC valve is attached to the air intake plenum. The ECM (computer) actuates the AAC valve by an on/off pulse signal. The longer the on-duty signal is left on, the larger the amount of air that will be allowed to flow through the AAC valve. This valve works in conjunction with the Fast Idle Control Device (FICD) solenoid.

Check

51 With the engine running, disconnect the AAC valve electrical connector **(see illustrations)** and confirm that the idle speed drops immediately. If it does not, continue checking the idle control system.

52 First, check the AAC valve resistance **(see illustration)**. Probe the terminals of the AAC valve with an ohmmeter and record the resistance. It should be between 6 to 15 ohms. If the AAC valve resistance is out of range, replace it.

53 Next, remove the valve and check the pintle for excessive carbon deposits. If necessary, clean it with carburetor cleaner spray. Also clean the valve housing to remove any deposits.

10.45 Remove the O-rings from the fuel injector (arrows)

4B

10.51a Disconnect the harness connector from the AAC valve and observe a drop in the engine rpm (GA16-DE engine)

10.51b The AAC valve (arrow) is located behind the electrical connectors on the SR20-DE engine

10.52 Check the resistance of the AAC valve. It should be between 6 and 15 ohms

10.54a Apply battery voltage to the FICD solenoid and listen for a distinct "click" as the solenoid activates (GA16-DE engine)

10.54b FICD location on the SR20-DE engine

10.66 Remove the two air regulator mounting bolts from the intake manifold (air intake plenum removed for clarity)

54   Also, check the FICD solenoid. Using jumper wires from the battery terminals, apply battery voltage to the FICD solenoid. There should be a distinct "click" (see illustrations). Listen carefully for the solenoid activation. If there is no sound, replace the FICD.

Removal

55   Disconnect the electrical connector from the AAC valve and the FICD solenoid.
56   Remove the valve attaching screws and separate the assembly from the air intake plenum.
57   Check the condition of the gasket seal. Replace it with a new gasket.
58   Clean the sealing surface and the bore of the throttle body assembly to ensure a good seal. **Caution:** *The AAC valve itself is an electrical component and must not be soaked in any liquid cleaner, as damage may result.*

Installation

59   Install a new gasket on the AAC valve assembly.
60   Install the AAC valve and tighten the screws securely.
61   Plug in the electrical connector to the AAC valve assembly.

Air regulator

General information

62   The air regulator provides air bypass when the engine is cold for fast idle. It consists of a bi-metal heater and rotary shutter. When the temperature of the bi-metal is low, the shutter opens and allows air to bypass from the air intake duct into the intake manifold. As the engine warms, the shutter closes and does not allow any air to circulate into the intake manifold. This condition continues until the engine is stopped and the temperature of the engine block cools down.

Check

63   With the engine completely cold, start the engine and check for the presence of battery voltage on the harness electrical connector. Battery voltage should be present.
64   Allow the engine to warm up to normal operating temperature, turn the ignition key OFF and remove the air regulator. Check to make sure the shutter has been activated and is completely closed (no air flow). If the shutter is open, replace the air regulator.

Replacement

Refer to illustration 10.66

65   Detach the air regulator electrical connector and disconnect the two hoses.
66   Remove the air regulator mounting bolts **(see illustration)**.
67   Lift the assembly from the intake manifold.
68   Installation is the reverse of removal.

Chapter 5 Engine electrical systems

Contents

Specifications

Battery voltage
Engine off ... 12-volts
Engine running ... 14-to-15 volts

Firing order ... See Chapter 2

Ignition coil-to-distributor cap wire resistance ... 5,000 ohms per foot

Ignition coil resistance
1982 through 1986
 Primary resistance ... 1.04 to 1.27 ohms
 Secondary resistance ... 7.3 to 11.0 K-ohms
1987 through 1990
 Primary resistance ... 0.84 to 1.02 ohms
 Secondary resistance ... 8.2 to 12.4 K-ohms
1991 through 1994
 GA16DE
  Primary resistance ... 0.9 ohms
  Secondary resistance ... 13.0 K-ohms
 SR20DE
  Primary resistance ... 1.0 ohms
  Secondary resistance ... 10 K-ohms

Air gap ... 0.012 to 0.020 inch

Ignition coil primary winding-to-case resistance ... 10 M-ohms

Alternator brush length
New ... 1/2 inch
Minimum ... 1/4 inch

1   General information

The engine electrical systems include all ignition, charging and starting components. Because of their engine-related functions, these components are considered separately from chassis electrical devices like the lights, instruments, etc.

Be very careful when working on the engine electrical components. They are easily damaged if checked, connected or handled improperly. The alternator is driven by an engine drivebelt which could cause serious injury if your hands, hair or clothes become entangled in it with the engine running. Both the starter and alternator are connected directly to the battery and could arc or even cause a fire if mishandled, overloaded or shorted out.

Never leave the ignition switch on for long periods of time with the engine off. Don't disconnect the battery cables while the engine is running. Correct polarity must be maintained when connecting battery cables from another source, such as another vehicle, during jump starting. Always disconnect the negative cable first and hook it up last or the battery may be shorted by the tool being used to loosen the cable clamps.

Additional safety related information on the engine electrical systems can be found in *Safety first* near the front of this manual. It should be referred to before beginning any operation included in this Chapter.

2   Battery - removal and installation

Refer to illustration 2.1

1   Disconnect both cables from the battery terminals **(see illustration)**. **Caution:** *Always disconnect the negative cable first and hook it up last or the battery may be shorted by the tool being used to loosen the cable clamps.*

2   Locate the battery hold-down clamp straddling the top of the battery. Remove the nuts and the hold-down clamp.

3   Lift out the battery. Use the special straps that attach to the battery posts - lifting and moving the battery is much easier if you use one.

4   Installation is the reverse of removal.

2.1 Detach the battery cables (arrows) (negative first) then remove the nuts from the battery hold-down clamps

3   Battery - emergency jump starting

Refer to the *Booster battery (jump) starting* procedure at the front of this manual.

4   Battery cables - check and replacement

1   Periodically inspect the entire length of each battery cable for damage, cracked or burned insulation and corrosion. Poor battery cable connections can cause starting problems and decreased engine performance.

2   Check the cable-to-terminal connections at the ends of the cables for cracks, loose wire strands and corrosion. The presence of white, fluffy deposits under the insulation at the cable terminal connection is a sign that the cable is corroded and should be replaced. Check the terminals for distortion, missing mounting bolts and corrosion.

3   When replacing the cables, always disconnect the negative cable first and hook it up last or the battery may be shorted by the tool used to loosen the cable clamps. Even if only the positive cable is being replaced, be sure to disconnect the negative cable from the battery first.

4   Disconnect and remove the cable. Make sure the replacement cable is the same length and diameter.

5   Clean the threads of the relay or ground connection with a wire brush to remove rust and corrosion. Apply a light coat of petroleum jelly to the threads to prevent future corrosion.

6   Attach the cable to the relay or ground connection and tighten the mounting nut/bolt securely.

7   Before connecting the new cable to the battery, make sure that it reaches the battery post without having to be stretched. Clean the battery posts thoroughly and apply a light coat of petroleum jelly to prevent corrosion.

8   Connect the positive cable first, followed by the negative cable.

5   Ignition system - general information

Refer to illustrations 5.3, 5.6 and 5.8

1   The ignition system is designed to ignite the fuel/air charge entering each cylinder at just the right moment. It does this by producing a high voltage spark between the electrodes of each spark plug.

2   The types of ignition systems installed onto these vehicles evolved through the years to accommodate more strict emissions standards adapted by major automotive manufacturers. Some of the changes in the ignition systems overlapped in certain years and others changed with certain models depending upon geographical location (Canada, California, etc.). Here is a general listing of the various systems.

Breakerless ignition system

3   Early electronic (breakerless) ignition systems **(see illustration)** were equipped on all 1982 and 1983 models and 1984 through 1986 California and Canada models. These ignition systems are a solid state electronic design consisting of an ignition module, coil, distributor, the spark plug wires and the spark plugs. Mechanically, the system is similar to a breaker point system, except that the distributor cam and ignition points are replaced by a stator and a magnetic pick-up unit (pick-up coil). The coil primary circuit is controlled by an amplifier module (IC ignition unit).

4   When the ignition is switched on, the ignition primary circuit is energized. When the distributor armature "teeth" or "spokes" approach the magnetic coil assembly, a

5.3 Diagram of the breakerless type ignition system

5.6 Diagram of the Spark Timing Control system

5.8 Crank angle sensor distributor details

voltage is induced which signals the amplifier to turn off the coil primary current. A timing circuit in the amplifier module turns the coil current back on after the coil field has collapsed.

5   When it's on, current flows from the battery through the ignition switch, the coil primary winding, the amplifier module and then to ground. When the current is interrupted, the magnetic field in the ignition coil collapses, inducing a high voltage in the coil secondary windings. The voltage is conducted to the distributor where the rotor directs it to the appropriate spark plug. This process is repeated continuously. **Note:** *All 1982 and 1983 models and 1984 through 1986 California and Canada models are equipped with an IC ignition control unit (amplifier module) that is built into the distributor along with the stator (pick-up coil).*

Spark timing control systems

6   On this system, equipped onto 1984 through 1986 USA (except California) models and all 1987 and later models, the computer and the crank angle sensor located inside the distributor controls the spark timing advance characteristics **(see illustration)**. Vacuum advance and vacuum hoses have been eliminated from the design.

7   The crank angle sensor is the basis of this computer controlled system. It monitors engine speed and piston position and relays this data to the computer which in turn controls the fuel injection duration (fuel injector on/off time) and ignition timing. The

crank angle sensor has a rotor plate and a wave forming circuit. The rotor plate has 360 slits for each degree or one percent signal (engine speed signal) and four slits for the 180 degree crank angle signal. Light Emitting Diodes (LED) and photo diodes are built into the wave forming circuit. When the rotor plate passes the space between the LED and the photo diode, the slits on the rotor plate continually cut the beam of light sent to the photo diode from the LED. They are then converted into on-off pulses by the wave forming circuit and then sent to the ECM (computer).

8   The crank angle sensor type distributor must be replaced as a complete unit. There are no replacement parts available for the distributor except the cap, rotor and seal cover **(see illustration)**.

6   Ignition system - check

Refer to illustration 6.1
Warning: *Because of the high voltage generated by the ignition system, extreme care should be taken whenever an operation is performed involving ignition components. This not only includes the coil, distributor and spark plug wires, but related components such as plug connectors, tachometer and other test equipment also.*

1   If the engine turns over but won't start, disconnect the spark plug wire from any spark plug and attach it to a calibrated tester (available at most auto parts stores). Connect

the clip on the tester to a bolt or metal bracket on the engine **(see illustration)**. If you're unable to obtain a calibrated ignition tester, remove the wire from one of the spark plugs and using an insulated tool, pull back the boot and hold the end of the wire about 1/4-inch from a good ground.

2   Crank the engine and watch the end of the tester or spark plug wire to see if bright blue, well-defined sparks occur.

3   If sparks occur, sufficient voltage is reaching the plug to fire it (repeat the check at the remaining plug wires to verify that the distributor cap and rotor are OK). However,

6.1 To use a calibrated ignition tester, simply disconnect a spark plug wire and connect it to the tester, clip the tester to a convenient ground (like a valve cover bolt) and operate the starter - if there is enough power to fire the plug, sparks will be visible between the electrode tip and the tester body

5

the plugs themselves may be fouled, so remove and check them as described in Chapter 1.

4   If no sparks or intermittent sparks occur, remove the distributor cap and check the cap and rotor as described in Chapter 1. If moisture is present, dry out the cap and rotor, then reinstall the cap and repeat the spark test.

5   If there's still no spark, detach the coil secondary wire from the distributor cap and hook it up to the tester (reattach the plug wire to the spark plug), then repeat the spark check. Again, if you don't have a tester, hold the end of the wire about 1/4-inch from a good ground.

6   If sparks now occur, the distributor cap, rotor or plug wire(s) may be defective.

7   If no sparks occur, check the primary wire connections at the coil to make sure they're clean and tight. Check for voltage to the coil. Check the coil (see Section 8).

8   Check the air gap (see Section 7) on models equipped with the IC ignition unit (breakerless) type distributors. On later systems, check the crank angle sensor (see Chapter 6). Make any necessary repairs, then repeat the check again.

9   If there's still no spark, the coil-to-cap wire may be bad (check the resistance with an ohmmeter and compare it to the ignition coil-to-distributor cap wire resistance found in this Chapter's Specifications.

10   If the coil-to-cap wire is good and there is still no spark, the IC unit may be defective.

7   Air gap - check and adjustment

Note: *All 1982 and 1983 models and 1984 through 1986 California and Canada models are equipped with an IC ignition control unit (amplifier module) that is built into the distributor along with the stator (pick-up coil). The air gap, the distance between the reluctor and the stator, must be adjusted periodically.*
Refer to illustration 7.2

1   Remove the distributor cap from the distributor (see Chapter 1).

2   Position a brass feeler gauge between the reluctor and stator **(see illustration)** and measure the distance. It should be between 0.012 to 0.020 inch.

8.2a Checking the coil secondary resistance on 1982 through 1986 models

7.2 Checking the air gap on a breakerless type distributor

3   If the measurement is incorrect, loosen the stator mounting screws **(see illustration 10.1)** and adjust the air gap.

8   Ignition coil - check and replacement

Check
Refer to illustrations 8.1a, 8.1b, 8.2a and 8.2b

Primary and secondary coil resistance
Caution: *On engines equipped with breakerless ignition systems, if the coil terminals touch a ground source, the coil and/or pick-up coil could be damaged.*

1   With the ignition off, disconnect the wires from the coil. Connect an ohmmeter across the coil primary (small wire) terminals **(see illustrations)**. The resistance should be as listed in this Chapter's Specifications for the primary resistance. If not, replace the coil.

2   Connect an ohmmeter between the negative primary terminal and the secondary terminal **(see illustrations)** (the one that the distributor cap wire connects to). The resistance should be as listed in this Chapter's Specifications for the secondary resistance. If not, replace the coil.

Ignition coil primary winding-to-case resistance
3   Measure the resistance from the positive primary terminal to the case of the ignition coil.

8.2b Checking the coil secondary resistance on 1991 through 1994 models

8.1a Checking the coil primary resistance on 1982 through 1986 models

8.1b Checking the coil primary resistance on 1991 through 1994 models

4   If the indicated resistance is less than the resistance listed in this Chapter's Specifications, replace the ignition coil.

5   Reconnect the ignition coil wires.

Replacement
Refer to illustration 8.9

6   Detach the cable from the negative terminal of the battery.

7   Detach the wires from the primary terminals on the coil (some coils have a single electrical connector for the primary wires).

8   Disconnect the coil secondary lead.

9   Remove both bracket bolts and detach the coil **(see illustration)**.

10   Installation is the reverse of removal.

8.9 To replace the ignition coil, detach the cable from the negative terminal of the battery, disconnect the coil primary connection, detach the coil secondary lead and remove both coil bracket bolts (1994 models shown)

9.5a Paint a mark on the perimeter of the distributor body that marks the position of the rotor (arrow)

9.5b Paint a distinct mark on the base of the distributor body and the engine block to clearly define the position of the distributor

9.6a Remove the distributor from the engine (1991 model shown)

9 Distributor - removal and installation

Removal

Refer to illustrations 9.5a, 9.5b, 9.6a and 9.6b

1 Disconnect the primary lead from the coil.
2 Disconnect the electrical connector for the module. Follow the wires as they exit the distributor to find the connector.
3 Note the raised "1" on the distributor cap. This marks the location for the number one cylinder spark plug wire terminal. **Note:** *Some distributor caps may have been replaced with aftermarket units that are not marked.*
4 Remove the distributor cap (see Chapter 1) and turn the engine over until the rotor is pointing toward the number one spark plug terminal (see the TDC locating procedure in Chapter 2).
5 Make a mark on the edge of the distributor base directly below the rotor tip and in line with it **(see illustration)**. Also, mark the distributor base and the engine block to ensure that the distributor is installed correctly **(see illustration)**.
6 Remove the distributor hold-down bolt and clamp, then pull the distributor straight up to remove it **(see illustrations)**. **Caution:** *DO NOT turn the engine while the distributor is removed, or the alignment marks will be useless.*

Installation

7 Insert the distributor into the engine in exactly the same relationship to the block that it was in when removed.
8 To mesh the helical gears on the camshaft and the distributor, it may be necessary to turn the rotor slightly. If the distributor doesn't seat completely. Recheck the alignment marks between the distributor base and the block to verify that the distributor is in the same position it was in before removal. Also check the rotor to see if it's aligned with the mark you made on the edge of the distributor base. **Note:** *If the crankshaft has been moved while the*

distributor is out, locate Top Dead Center (TDC) for the number one piston (see Chapter 2) and position the distributor and rotor accordingly.
9 Place the hold-down clamp in position and loosely install the bolt.
10 Install the distributor cap and tighten the cap screws securely.
11 Plug in the module electrical connector.
12 Reattach the spark plug wires to the plugs (if removed).
13 Connect the cable to the negative terminal of the battery.
14 Check and, if necessary, adjust the ignition timing (refer to Chapter 1) and tighten the distributor hold-down bolt securely.

10 Distributor centrifugal and vacuum advance system - check

General information

Refer to illustration 10.1

1 To provide the proper spark advance or retard during different speeds and throttle openings, breakerless type distributors are equipped with a vacuum advance and a centrifugal advance mechanism in the distributor **(see illustration on following page)**. These parts may stick, wear out or become defective after years of service. **Note:** *The vacuum advance unit governs ignition timing according to engine load, while the centrifugal advance unit governs ignition timing according to engine speed. Some models are equipped with dual diaphragm vacuum advance units that provide additional timing retard during engine cranking to aid in starting and also reduce emissions during idle and during coast down.*
2 Both the vacuum advance and the centrifugal advance systems can be tested using the timing light method. After the initial test to determine its working capabilities, the different systems must be checked separately.

Timing light test

3 Disconnect the vacuum hose to the vacuum advance unit, plug the hose and run the engine at approximately 1,200 rpm.

9.6b Removing the distributor on an early style breakerless ignition

4 Install a timing light and observe the paint mark on the pulley while slowly raising the engine speed to 4,000 rpm. The timing mark should move smoothly and without any hesitations or sudden movements. If the timing mark jumps around, it will be necessary to remove the distributor cap and check the centrifugal weights for binding, missing parts or defective parts (refer to Section 11).
5 Next, check the operation of the vacuum advance unit. Run the engine at a steady 1,200 rpm and point the timing light at the timing mark.
6 Note the exact position of the timing mark and raise the rpm while observing the mark. Connect the vacuum hose to the vacuum advance unit, when the vacuum hose is connected the timing mark should advance quickly and completely. Most systems will advance the timing approximately 35 degrees when opened to wide open throttle.

Centrifugal advance check

7 With the engine OFF and the distributor cap removed from the distributor, advance the timing plate manually using the rotor and release the mechanism. It should snap back to its original position very quickly and without hesitation. Try oiling the weights and springs with a spray lubricant (WD-40) and repeat the test several times to loosen the springs and weights if they show signs of sticking or binding.

5

Cap
Insulation resistance: More than 50 MΩ
Carbon point
Length: More than 10 mm (0.39 in)
Rotor head
Insulation resistance: More than 50 MΩ
Roll pin
Stator
Magnet
Reluctor
IC ignition unit
Spacer
Breaker plate
Vacuum advance
Housing
O-ring
Collar
Roll pin
Packing
Rotor shaft setting screw
Rotor shaft
Governor spring
Governor weight
Shaft
Harness

10.1 Exploded view of a breakerless type distributor

8   Repeat the test several more times until the timing can be advanced without trouble.

Vacuum advance check

9   The diaphragm assembly is attached to the distributor breaker plate. A vacuum line attaches the diaphragm housing to a ported vacuum source. As vacuum changes from idle to acceleration through deceleration and back to idle, the timing changes accordingly.
10   With the engine OFF check the condition of the vacuum hose from the distributor to the vacuum source. Make sure the hose is connected and the ends sealed.
11   Disconnect and plug the vacuum hose

to the distributor. Connect a vacuum pump to the vacuum diaphragm and apply between 15 to 20 in-Hg to the advance unit.
12   Make sure the vacuum advance diaphragm holds vacuum. If the vacuum bleeds down, replace the unit with a new vacuum advance.

Vacuum advance removal

Refer to illustration 10.14
13   Remove the distributor cap and the vacuum hose to the advance unit.
14   Remove the two screws that retain the vacuum advance unit to the distributor body **(see illustration)**.

Vacuum advance

10.14 Removing the vacuum advance unit from the distributor body

11.1 Use a voltmeter and check for power supply to the IC ignition unit on the black/white wire

11.3 Check the ignition primary circuit with a voltmeter at the blue wire

11.4 Check the distributor ground circuit

15   Remove the clip that holds the vacuum advance plate to the vacuum advance link. Be very careful not to drop it into the distributor.

16   Remove the old vacuum advance unit and replace it with a new part.

17   Installation is the reverse of removal.

11 IC ignition unit/power transistor - check and replacement

Caution: *The IC ignition unit/power transistor is a delicate and relatively expensive electronic component. Failure to follow the step-by-step procedures could result in damage to the module and/or other electronic devices, including the ECM microprocessor itself. Additionally, all devices under computer control are protected by a Federally mandated extended warranty. Check with your dealer concerning this warranty before attempting to diagnose and replace the unit yourself.*

Note: *All 1982 and 1983 models and 1984 through 1986 California and Canada models are equipped with an IC ignition control unit (amplifier module) that is built into the distributor along with the stator (pick-up coil). 1984 through 1986 USA (except California) models and all 1987 through 1994 models are equipped with a power transistor (amplifier module) that is attached to the ignition coil.*

IC ignition unit

Check

Refer to illustrations 11.1, 11.3 and 11.4

1   Using a voltmeter, disconnect the positive wire (black/white wire) from the IC ignition unit inside the distributor **(see illustration)** and check for voltage. With the ignition key ON (engine not running), there should be battery voltage. This test checks for power supply to the IC ignition unit.

2   Next, with the voltmeter probes still in place as in step 1, remove the coil wire at the distributor cap and ground it to the engine block. Crank the engine over and note the voltage. There should be between 8.6 and 10.6 volts (cranking volts).

3   Next, using a voltmeter, disconnect the negative wire (blue wire) from the IC ignition unit inside the distributor **(see illustration)** and check for voltage. With the ignition key ON (engine not running), there should be battery voltage. This test checks the ignition primary circuit.

4   Also, check the ground circuit. Install the voltmeter between the distributor base and the negative terminal of the battery **(see illustration)**. With the coil wire removed and grounded, crank the engine and observe the voltage. It should be 0.5 volt or less.

5   If all the tests are correct, the ignition coil tested good (see Section 8) and there still is no spark at the plugs, replace the IC ignition control unit.

Replacement

Refer to illustrations 11.10, 11.11 and 11.12

6   Detach the cable from the negative terminal of the battery.

7   Remove the distributor cap and rotor (see Chapter 1).

8   Disconnect the electrical connectors from the IC unit.

9   Remove the vacuum advance unit from the distributor **(see illustration 10.1).**

10   Carefully pry the reluctor off the distributor shaft using two flat bladed screwdrivers **(see illustration).**

11   Remove the breaker plate assembly **(see illustration).**

12   Remove the IC ignition unit and spacers **(see illustration).**

13   Installation is the reverse of removal.

Power transistor

Check

Refer to illustrations 11.16a, 11.16b, 11.16c and 11.16d

14   Detach the cable from the negative terminal of the battery.

15   Disconnect the electrical connector from the power transistor.

16   Using an ohmmeter, check for continuity

11.10 Carefully pry the reluctor off the distributor shaft using two flat bladed screwdrivers

11.11 Remove the breaker plate assembly

11.12 Separate the IC ignition unit from the breaker plate assembly

5

Ohmmeter Leads to Pins		Should Read
(+)	(−)	
Ground	A	Approx. 0Ω
A	Ground	Approx. ∞ Ω
A	B	Approx. ∞ Ω
B	A	Approx. 0Ω
Ground	B	Approx. 0Ω
B	Ground	Approx. 0Ω

11.16a Power transistor test chart for 1984 through 1986 USA (except California) models

Terminal No.	Tester polarity	Continuity
① or ③	+	No continuity
④	−	
① or ③	−	Continuity should exist.
④	+	
① or ③	+	No continuity
②	−	
① or ③	−	Continuity should exist.
②	+	

11.16b Power transistor test chart for 1987 and 1988 models

Terminal No.	Tester polarity	Continuity
ⓒ	+	No continuity
ⓓ	−	
ⓒ	−	Continuity should exist.
ⓓ	+	
ⓒ	+	No continuity
ⓔ	−	
ⓒ	−	Continuity should exist.
ⓔ	+	

11.16c Power transistor test chart for 1989 and 1990 models

⊕ termi-nal side	⊖ terminal side					
	Terminal ⓐ		Terminal ⓑ		Terminal ⓒ	
	Resis-tance Ω	Result	Resis-tance Ω	Result	Resis-tance Ω	Result
Terminal ⓐ	—	—	∞	OK	∞	OK
	—	—	Not ∞ or 0	NG	Not ∞ or 0	NG
	—	—	0	NG	0	NG
Terminal ⓑ	∞	NG	—	—	∞	NG
	Not ∞ or 0	OK	—	—	Not ∞ or 0	OK
	0	NG	—	—	0	NG
Terminal ⓒ	∞	NG	∞	NG	—	—
	Not ∞ or 0	OK	Not ∞ or 0	OK	—	—
	0	NG	0	NG	—	—

11.16d Power transistor test chart for 1991 through 1994 models

11.20 Location of the power transistor mounting bolts (arrows) on the SR20DE engine

across the designated terminals **(see illustrations)**. Follow the terminal designations as outlined in the charts.

17 If any of the test results are incorrect, replace the power transistor with a new part.

Replacement

Refer to illustration 11.20

18 Detach the cable from the negative terminal of the battery.

19 Disconnect the electrical connector from the power transistor.

20 Remove the bolts that retain the power transistor to the coil or firewall **(see illustration)** and lift the assembly from the engine compartment.

21 Installation is the reverse of removal.

12 Charging system - general information and precautions

Refer to illustrations 12.1a and 12.1b

The charging system includes the alternator, an internal voltage regulator **(see illustrations)**, a charge indicator or warning light, the battery, a fusible link and the wiring between all the components. The charging system supplies electrical power for the ignition system, the lights, the radio, etc. The alternator is driven by a drivebelt at the front of the engine.

The purpose of the voltage regulator is to limit the alternator's voltage to a preset value. This prevents power surges, circuit overloads, etc., during peak voltage output.

The fusible link is a short length of insulated wire integral with the engine compartment wiring harness. The link is several wire gauges smaller in diameter than the circuit it protects. Production fusible links and their identification flags are identified by the flag color. Refer to Chapter 12 for additional information on fusible links.

The charging system doesn't ordinarily require periodic maintenance. However, the drivebelt, battery and wires and connections should be inspected at the intervals outlined in Chapter 1.

12.1a Exploded view of a typical Mitsubishi alternator

12.1b Exploded view of a typical Hitachi alternator

Be very careful when making electrical circuit connections to a vehicle equipped with an alternator and note the following:

a) *When reconnecting wires to the alternator from the battery, be sure to note the polarity.*

b) *Before using arc welding equipment to repair any part of the vehicle, disconnect the wires from the alternator and the battery terminals.*

c) *Never start the engine with a battery charger connected.*

d) *Always disconnect both battery cables before using a battery charger (negative cable first, positive cable last).*

13 Charging system - check

Refer to illustration 13.1

1 If a malfunction occurs in the charging

5

13.1 Typical charging system electrical schematic (1986 model shown)

circuit **(see illustration)**, do not immediately assume that the alternator is causing the problem. First check the following items:

a) *The battery cables where they connect to the battery. Make sure the connections are clean and tight.*
b) *The battery electrolyte specific gravity. If it is low, charge the battery.*
c) *Check the external alternator wiring and connections.*
d) *Check the drivebelt condition and tension (see Chapter 1).*
e) *Check the alternator mounting bolts for tightness.*
f) *Run the engine and check the alternator for abnormal noise.*

2   Using a voltmeter, check the battery voltage with the engine off. It should be approximately 12-volts.
3   Start the engine and check the battery voltage again. It should now be approximately 14 to 15-volts.
4   If the indicated voltage reading is less or more than the specified charging voltage, the problem may be within the alternator.

5   Due to the special equipment necessary to test or service the alternator, it is recommended that if a fault is suspected the vehicle be taken to a dealer or a shop with the proper equipment. But if the home mechanic feels confident in the use of an ohmmeter, and in some cases a soldering iron, the component check and replacement procedures for the most common alternator type are included in Section 15.
6   Some models are equipped with an ammeter on the instrument panel that indicates charge or discharge - current passing in or out of the battery. With all electrical equipment switched ON, and the engine idling, the gauge needle may show a discharge condition. At fast idle or normal driving speeds the needle should stay on the charge side of the gauge, with the charged state of the battery determining just how far over (the lower the battery state of charge, the farther the needle should swing toward the charge side).
7   Some models are equipped with a voltmeter on the instrument panel that

indicates battery voltage with the key ON (engine not running), and alternator output when the engine is running.
8   The charge light on the instrument panel illuminates with the key ON and engine not running, and should go out when the engine runs.
9   If the gauge does not show a charge when it should or the alternator light (if equipped) remains on, there is a fault in the system. Before inspecting the brushes or replacing the alternator, the battery condition, alternator belt tension and electrical cable connections should be checked.

14   Alternator - removal and installation

Refer to illustrations 14.2 and 14.3
1   Detach the cable from the negative terminal of the battery.
2   Disconnect the electrical connectors from the alternator **(see illustration)**.
3   Loosen the alternator bolts **(see illustration)** and detach the drivebelt.
4   Remove the adjustment and pivot bolts and separate the alternator from the engine.
5   Installation is the reverse of removal.
6   After the alternator is installed, adjust the drivebelt tension (see Chapter 1).

15   Alternator components - check and replacement

Disassembly
Refer to illustrations 15.2, 15.3, 15.4a, 15.4b, 15.4c, 15.5a, 15.5b, 15.6a, 15.6b, 15.6c and 15.7
1   Remove the alternator from the vehicle (Section 14).
2   Scribe or paint marks on the front and rear end frame housings of the alternator to facilitate reassembly **(see illustration)**.
3   Remove the nut retaining the fan pulley

14.2 Disconnect the electrical connectors (arrows) from the rear of the alternator

14.3 Pivot bolts (arrows) located on the bottom of the alternator

15.2 Paint a mark across the front cover, stator and rear cover to aid in reassembly

15.3 Use an air tool (power wrench) to remove the pulley nut

15.4a Remove the four bolts from the rear cover (arrows)

15.4b Separate the front cover from the alternator body

15.4c Remove the rotor from the alternator assembly

15.5a Remove the mounting nuts (arrows)

15.5b Separate the rear cover from the stator and diode assembly

15.6a Remove the diode assembly mounting screws (arrows)

15.6b Remove the brush assembly holder from the diode assembly

15.6c Remove the voltage regulator

to the rotor shaft and remove the pulley **(see illustration)**.

4   Remove the four through-bolts holding the front and rear covers together, then separate the rear cover assembly from the front cover. Remove the rotor. **(see illustrations)**.

5   Remove the nuts retaining the stator, separate the stator and diode assembly from the end frame **(see illustrations)**.

6   Remove the screws attaching the regulator and the brush holder to the diode assembly and remove the brush holder and regulator **(see illustrations)**.

7   Remove the diode assembly from the stator **(see illustration)**. On some types of alternators it will be necessary to use a solder gun and heat sink to melt the solder joints that connect the stator leads to the diode assembly.

Component checks

Refer to illustrations 15.8a, 15.8b, 15.9 and 15.10

15.7 Remove the four set screws and lift the diode assembly from the stator

8   Check the rotor for an open between the two slip rings **(see illustration)**. There should be continuity between the slip rings. Check

15.8a Continuity should exist between the rotor slip rings

5

15.8b No continuity should exist between the slip ring(s) and rotor shaft

15.9 Check for continuity on each stator lead. There should be no breaks in the windings, therefore continuity should exist between each terminal

for grounds between each slip ring and the rotor shaft **(see illustration)**. There should be no continuity (infinite resistance) between the rotor shaft and either slip ring. If the rotor fails either test, or if the slip rings are excessively worn, the rotor is defective.

9   Check for opens between the center terminal and each end terminal of the stator windings **(see illustration)**. If either reading is high (infinite resistance), the stator is defective. Check for a grounded stator winding between each stator terminal and the frame. If there's continuity between any stator winding and the frame the stator is defective.

10   Start the checks on the diode assembly by touching one probe (positive +) of the ohmmeter on the diode plate and the other probe on one of the other designated diode terminals (negative −) **(see illustration)**. Then reverse the probes and check again. Follow the chart carefully. The diode should have continuity with the ohmmeter one way and no continuity when the probes are reversed. Check each of the terminals in this manner. If any of the diodes fail the test, the diode assembly is defective.

| | Ohmmeter probes | | Continuity |
	Positive ⊕	Negative ⊖	
Diodes check (Positive side)	Positive diode plate	Diode terminals	Yes
	Diode terminals	Positive diode plate	No
Diodes check (Negative side)	Negative diode plate	Diode terminals	No
	Diode terminals	Negative diode plate	Yes

[MITSUBISHI make]

[HITACHI make]

15.10 Check each diode to make sure continuity exists only in ONE direction

11 To check the sub diodes, install the probes of the ohmmeter onto the sub diode terminals and check for continuity in the same way as the previous diode checks. Be sure to probe only the sub diode terminals. If any sub diode fails the test, the diode assembly is defective.

12 Measure the length of the brushes and replace them if they are at or near the minimum brush length found in this Chapter's Specifications. **Note:** *On some models the brush leads are soldered onto the voltage regulator assembly.*

Reassembly

Refer to illustration 15.14

13 Install the components in the reverse order of removal, noting the following:

14 Before installing the brush holder, push the brushes into the holder and slip a straightened paper clip or other suitable pin through the hole in the brush holder to hold the brushes in a retracted position. After the front and rear end frames have been bolted together remove the paper clip **(see illustration)**.

16 Starting system - general information and precautions

1 The function of the starting system is to crank the engine to start it. The system is composed of the starter motor, starter solenoid, battery, ignition switch, clutch start switch (manual transaxle models), neutral start switch (automatic transaxle models), diode box and connecting wires.

2 Turning the ignition key to the Start position actuates the starter relay through the starter control circuit. The starter solenoid then connects the battery to the starter. The battery supplies the electrical energy to the starter motor, which does the actual work of cranking the engine.

3 All vehicles are equipped with a starter/solenoid assembly that is mounted to the transmission bellhousing.

4 All vehicles are equipped with a clutch start switch or a neutral start switch in the

starter control circuit, which prevents operation of the starter unless the shift lever is in Neutral or Park (automatic) or the clutch is depressed (manual).

5 Never operate the starter motor for more than 15 seconds at a time without pausing to allow it to cool for at least two minutes. Excessive cranking can cause overheating, which can seriously damage the starter.

17 Starter motor and circuit - in-vehicle check

Note: *Before diagnosing starter problems, make sure the battery is fully charged.*

General check

1 If the starter motor doesn't turn at all when the switch is operated, make sure the shift lever is in Neutral or Park or the clutch is fully depressed.

2 Make sure the battery is charged and that all cables at the battery and starter solenoid terminals are secure.

3 If the starter motor spins but the engine doesn't turn over, then the drive assembly in the starter motor is slipping and the starter motor must be replaced (see Section 18).

4 If, when the switch is actuated, the starter motor doesn't operate at all but the starter solenoid operates (clicks), then the problem lies with either the battery, the starter solenoid contacts or the starter motor connections.

5 If the starter solenoid doesn't click when the ignition switch is actuated, either the starter solenoid circuit is open or the solenoid itself is defective. Check the starter solenoid circuit (see the wiring diagrams at the end of this book) or replace the solenoid (see Section 19).

6 To check the starter solenoid circuit, remove the push-on connector from the solenoid wire. Make sure that the connection is clean and secure and the relay bracket is grounded. If the connections are good, check the operation of the solenoid with a jumper wire. To do this, place the transmission in

Park or Neutral and apply the parking brake. Remove the push-on connector from the solenoid. Connect a jumper wire between the battery positive terminal and the exposed terminal on the solenoid. If the starter motor now operates, the starter solenoid is okay. The problem is in the ignition switch, Neutral start switch or in the starting circuit wiring (look for open or loose connections).

7 If the starter motor still doesn't operate, replace the starter solenoid (see Section 19).

8 If the starter motor cranks the engine at an abnormally slow speed, first make sure the battery is fully charged and all terminal connections are clean and tight. Also check the connections at the starter solenoid and battery ground. Eyelet terminals should not be easily rotated by hand. Also check for a short to ground. If the engine is partially seized, or has the wrong viscosity oil in it, it will crank slowly.

Starter cranking circuit test

Note: *To determine the location of excessive resistance in the starter circuit, perform the following simple series of tests.*

9 Disconnect the ignition coil wire from the distributor cap and ground it on the engine.

10 Connect a remote control starter switch from the battery terminal of the starter solenoid to the S terminal of the solenoid.

11 Connect a voltmeter positive lead to the starter motor terminal of the starter solenoid, then connect the negative lead to ground.

12 Actuate the ignition switch and take the voltmeter readings as soon as a steady figure is indicated. Do not allow the starter motor to turn for more than 15 seconds at a time. A reading of 9-volts or more, with the starter motor turning at normal cranking speed, is normal. If the reading is 9-volts or more but the cranking speed is slow, the motor is faulty. If the reading is less than 9-volts and the cranking speed is slow, the solenoid contacts are probably burned.

18 Starter motor - removal and installation

Refer to illustration 18.3

1 Detach the cable from the negative terminal of the battery.

2 Raise the vehicle and support it securely on jackstands.

3 Disconnect the large cable from the terminal on the starter motor and the solenoid terminal connections **(see illustration)**.

4 Remove the starter motor mounting bolts and detach the starter from the engine. Depending upon the year and engine type, the starter/solenoid assembly may be mounted above the transaxle or below the intake manifold.

5 If necessary, turn the wheels to one side to provide removal access.

6 Installation is the reverse of removal.

15.14 Install a paper clip into the backside of the alternator to hold the brushes in place during installation - after installation, simply pull the paper clip out

18.3 Disconnect the electrical connectors from the starter solenoid (arrows)

5

19   Starter solenoid - replacement

Refer to illustrations 19.2a and 19.2b

1   Remove the nut and disconnect the lead wire from the solenoid electrical terminal.

2   Remove the two bolts from the solenoid and separate the solenoid from the starter assembly **(see illustrations).**

3   Installation is the reverse of removal.

19.2a   Gear reduction type starter/solenoid assembly (1986 model shown)

19.2b   Direct drive type starter/solenoid assembly (1986 model shown)

Chapter 6
Emissions and engine control systems

Contents

1   General information

Refer to illustrations 1.1a, 1.1b, 1.1c and 1.7a through 1.7n

To prevent pollution of the atmosphere from incompletely burned and evaporating gases, and to maintain good driveability and fuel economy, a number of emission control systems are incorporated (see illustrations). They include the:

Spark Timing Control (TCS)
Air Injection Valve (AIV) system
Fuel shut-off system
Mixture heating system

Throttle Open Control (TOCS) system (Canadian models only)
High Altitude compensation system
EGR with vacuum amplifier
Automatic choke system
Heated air inlet system
Feedback carburetors
Evaporative Emission Control (EVAP) system
Throttle Body Injection (TBI) system
Multi Port Fuel Injection (MPFI) system
Positive Crankcase Ventilation (PCV) system
Exhaust Gas Recirculation (EGR) system (electronic)
Catalytic converter

All of these systems are linked, directly or indirectly, to the emission control system.

The Sections in this Chapter include general descriptions, checking procedures within the scope of the home mechanic and component replacement procedures (when possible) for each of the systems listed above.

Before assuming that an emissions control system is malfunctioning, check the fuel and ignition systems carefully. The diagnosis of some emission control devices requires specialized tools, equipment and training. If checking and servicing become too difficult or if a procedure is beyond your

6

1.1a Emission and engine control system component locations on the Multi-Port Fuel Injected engine (GA16DE engine)

1 Fast Idle Control Device (FICD) solenoid
2 Auxiliary Air Control (AAC) valve
3 Air intake plenum
4 EGR valve (under plenum)
5 TPS
6 Charcoal canister
7 MAF sensor
8 Fuel pump relay
9 Crank Angle sensor
10 Oxygen sensor
11 Fuel injector
12 Fuel pressure regulator

1.1b Emission and engine control system component locations on the Multi-Port Fuel Injected engine (SR20DE engine)

1 Fast Idle Control Device (FICD) solenoid
2 Auxiliary Air Control (AAC) valve
3 Air intake plenum
4 TPS electrical connector
5 TPS
6 Charcoal canister
7 MAF sensor
8 Fuel pump relay
9 Crank Angle sensor
10 Oxygen sensor
11 Fuel pressure regulator
12 Fuel injector

1.1c Emission and engine control system component locations on the Throttle-Body Injected (TBI) engine

1 Airflow meter
2 Throttle switch and sensor
3 ISC valve
4 Fuel pressure regulator
5 Charcoal canister
6 Power transistor
7 Crank Angle sensor
8 BPT valve
9 EGR valve
10 Fuel injector

ability, consult a dealer service department or other qualified repair facility. Remember, the most frequent cause of emissions problems is simply a loose or broken vacuum hose or wire, so always check the hose and wiring connections first.

This doesn't mean, however, that emission control systems are particularly difficult to maintain and repair. You can quickly and easily perform many checks and do most of the regular maintenance at home with common tune-up and hand tools. **Note:** *Because of a Federally-mandated extended warranty which covers the emission control system components, check with your dealer about warranty coverage before working on any emissions-related systems. Once the warranty has expired, you may wish to perform some of the component checks*

and/or replacement procedures in this Chapter to save money.

Pay close attention to any special precautions outlined in this Chapter. It should be noted that the illustrations of the various systems may not exactly match the system installed on the vehicle you're working on because of changes made by the manufacturer during production or from year-to-year.

A Vehicle Emissions Control Information (VECI) label is located in the engine compartment (see illustrations). This label contains important emissions specifications and adjustment information, as well as a vacuum hose schematic with emissions components identified. When servicing the engine or emissions systems, the VECI label in your particular vehicle should always be checked for up-to-date information.

1.7a The Vehicle Emission Control Information (VECI) label on some models is located in the engine compartment under the hood and contains information on the emission devices on your vehicle, vacuum line routing, etc.

1.7c Vacuum hose routing diagram for 1982 California models (1983 and 1984 similar)

1.7b Vacuum hose routing diagram for the 1982 feedback carburetor models

6

1.7e Vacuum hose routing diagram for 1982 Canada models (1983 and 1984 similar)

1.7d Vacuum hose routing diagram for 1982 USA (except California) models (1983 similar)

1.7g Vacuum hose routing diagram for 1984 through 1986 USA (except California) models

1.7f Vacuum hose routing diagram for 1985 and 1986 California models

6

1.7i   Vacuum hose routing diagram for 1987 and 1988 TBI models

1.7h   Vacuum hose routing diagram for 1985 and 1986 Canada models

1.7k Vacuum hose routing diagram for 1987 California and Canada TBI models

1.7j Vacuum hose routing diagram for 1987 49 states TBI models

6

1.7m Vacuum hose routing diagram for 1991 through 1994 MPFI models with the GA16DE engine

1.7l Vacuum hose routing diagram for 1989 and 1990 TBI models

1.7n Vacuum hose routing diagram for 1991 through 1994 MPFI models with the SR20DE engine

1   Three-way connector to vacuum gallery
2   AIV to vacuum tube
3   Vacuum tube to AIV control solenoid valve
4   Pressure regulator to three way connector
5   Air duct to vacuum gallery
6   Charcoal canister to vacuum gallery

7   Purge line to intake manifold
8   Throttle body to EGR and canister control solenoid valve
9   EGR and canister control valve to vacuum gallery
10 EGR and canister control solenoid valve to vacuum gallery

11 Intake manifold to vacuum gallery
12 AIV control solenoid valve to vacuum gallery
13 BPT valve to EGR tube
14 BPT valve to vacuum gallery
15 EGR control valve to BPT valve
16 AIV control solenoid valve to three-way connector

2.1 Schematic of the Spark Timing Control (TCS) system

2   Spark Timing Control (TCS) system

General information

Refer to illustration 2.1

1   The spark timing control (TCS) system is designed to control the vacuum advance on the distributor during varying engine load and speed conditions **(see illustration)**. This system ultimately controls the HC and NOx emissions output. This system consists of a thermal vacuum valve (TVV) which controls vacuum to the distributor according to temperature and a vacuum delay valve which prevents rapid vacuum change in the vacuum advance line. **Note:** *The Spark Timing Control (TCS) system, 1984 and later USA (except California) models, is equipped with a crank angle sensor built into the distributor. This system does not operate on vacuum but instead uses electronic voltage signals to the ECM to change the ignition timing. Refer to Chapter 5 for more information on the crank angle sensor and the power transistor.*

Check

Thermal vacuum valve (TVV)

Refer to illustration 2.3

2   Remove the thermal vacuum valve (TVV) from the intake manifold. Be sure to drain approximately two quarts of coolant from the radiator (see Chapter 1) before removing the valve.

3   Place the TVV in a pan of heated water and closely monitor the temperature using a thermometer. Use a hand held vacuum pump to apply vacuum to the top (intake) port of the TVV and note the operation at the indicated temperatures **(see illustration):**

Temperature below 50 degrees F	Valve closed
Temperature between 50 to 122 degrees F	Valve open
Temperature above 122 degrees F	Valve closed

4   If the TVV valve does not respond correctly, replace it with a new part.

6

2.3 Be sure all the ports of the TVV are covered by vacuum hose and plugged to avoid allowing water to enter inside the valve when testing

3.1a Schematic of the AIV system for Canada models

3.1b Schematic of the AIV system for USA (except California) models

3.4 Disconnect the hose from the air cleaner and place a finger over the outlet

3.6 Apply vacuum to the air injection control valve and observe that air flows through the air injection valve into the exhaust manifold

Vacuum delay valve

5   The vacuum delay valve is designed for one-way operation. Blow air from the intake manifold side of the valve and observe that the air flows through the valve and can be detected at the distributor side of the vacuum line.

6   Reverse the position and blow from the distributor side. No air pressure should pass through the valve.

7   If the vacuum delay valve tests are incorrect, replace the valve with a new part.

3   Air Injection Valve (AIV) system

General description

Refer to illustrations 3.1a and 3.1b

1   The air injection valve (AIV) system (see illustrations) reduces carbon monoxide and hydrocarbon content in the exhaust gases by directing fresh air (intake air) into the hot exhaust gases leaving the exhaust ports. When fresh air is mixed with hot exhaust gases, oxidation is increased, reducing the concentration of hydrocarbons and carbon monoxide and converting them into harmless carbon dioxide and water.

2   Many of the early models are equipped with either an AB valve (Canada) or a vacuum switching valve (USA - except California). Both systems are basically the same. The AB valve is actuated by intake manifold vacuum to prevent after-burning in the exhaust system during initial deceleration. The air injection control valve controls secondary air at many different levels.

Checking

Air bypass valve (Canada)

Refer to illustration 3.4

3   Warm-up the engine to normal operating temperature.

4   With the engine idling, disconnect the hose from the air cleaner and place a finger over the outlet (see illustration).

5   Run the engine at 3,000 rpm without load then quickly return the engine to idle. If there is a pull or suction feeling, the AB valve is working properly. If no suction is felt, replace the AB valve.

Air injection control valve (USA - except California)

Refer to illustration 3.6

6   Remove the vacuum line from the air injection control valve and install a hand held vacuum pump (see illustration).

7   Apply vacuum to the air injection control valve, start the engine and observe that secondary air is allowed to pass through the air injection valve into the exhaust manifold. Remove the hose from the air injection valve to detect air flow (pressure) from the intake system.

8   If no pressure is felt, replace the air injection control valve.

Air injection valve (all models)

9   Remove the air cleaner assembly from the engine (see Chapter 4).
10   Blow compressed air directly behind the air injection valve and make sure airflow can be felt passing through the valve.
11   If there is a restriction, remove the valve from the air cleaner and replace it with a new part.

Component replacement

12   To replace the air bypass valve, air injection control valve or air injection valve, clearly label, then disconnect, the hoses leading to them, replace the faulty component and reattach the hoses to the proper ports. Make sure the hoses are in good condition. If not, replace them with new ones.

4   Fuel shut-off system

General information

Refer to illustration 4.1

1   The fuel shut-off system cuts off the flow of fuel during deceleration at high speeds when manifold vacuum increases simultaneously with the rpm **(see illustration)**. This system operates in conjunction with the carburetor and fuel system to economize fuel mileage.
2   An anti-dieseling solenoid valve is attached to the carburetor with its needle valve facing the fuel passage in the primary slow circuit. When voltage is applied to the valve, the needle retracts and fuel flows. Fuel is shut off when power is removed from the circuit. This system also shares a speed sensor with the feedback carburetor system (see Section 10 in this chapter and also Chapter 4A for additional information). A vacuum switch located in the intake manifold detects changes in the manifold vacuum during deceleration. A signal is sent through the anti-dieseling valve which in turn deactivates the flow of fuel. A neutral switch (mounted on the transaxle) and a clutch switch (mounted on the pedal assembly) controls deactivation also. A special fuel shut-off relay is mounted to the relay bracket assembly to control the actual circuit voltage.

Checks

Refer to illustrations 4.4, 4.5, 4.6 and 4.8

3   Visually check the system for broken wires, defective switches or missing components. Repair any wiring problems or replace defective components.
4   Remove the fuel shut-off relay **(see illustration)** and using a voltmeter, check for battery voltage at terminal G/R of the Function Check Connector with the ignition key ON (engine not running). With the clutch pedal pressed, there should be 12 volts. With the clutch pedal free (engaged) there should be zero voltage.
5   Also, check the voltage with the transaxle selector in Neutral (12 volts) or in gear (zero voltage). These tests check the

4.1 Schematic of the fuel shut-off system

4.4 Location of the fuel shut-off relay

condition of the clutch switch **(see illustration)** and the neutral switch.
6   Install the fuel shut-off relay and disconnect the vacuum hose and the electrical connector at the vacuum switch. Apply vacuum to the vacuum switch using a hand held vacuum pump and check for continuity under the following vacuum conditions **(see illustration):**

Above 22 in-Hg.	C to NC should be infinite resistance
Above 22 in-Hg.	C to NO should be zero resistance
Below 22 in-Hg.	C to NC should be zero resistance
Below 22 in-Hg.	C to NO should be infinite resistance

4.5 Location of the clutch switch

4.6 Apply vacuum to the vacuum switch and check for continuity through the correct terminals

4.8 Disconnect the electrical connector from the anti-dieseling solenoid and observe that the engine stalls

7   Reconnect the vacuum switch hose and electrical connector. Start the engine and run it until it reaches operating temperatures.

8   Disconnect the anti-dieseling solenoid valve **(see illustration)** and make sure the engine stalls. If the engine continues to run, the solenoid is defective. Replace the part with a new one.

9   If any of the above test results are incorrect, replace the particular component(s) with a new part.

---

5   Mixture heating system

General information

Refer to illustration 5.1

1   The mixture heating system **(see illustration)** incorporates a Positive Temperature Coefficient (PTC) heater between the carburetor and the intake manifold that warms the fuel mixture as it passes through. This heated fuel/air mixture improves driveability during cold engine operation.

Checks

Coolant temperature switch

Refer to illustration 5.3

2   Check to make sure the coolant temperature switch deactivates at the proper temperature. Using an ohmmeter, observe a change in resistance as the temperature switch is warmed up to the correct deactivating temperature. It may be necessary to install a special radiator thermometer to monitor the change in coolant temperature:

California models

Below 99 degrees F	*Activated*
Above 99 degrees F	*Deactivated*

USA (except California) models

Below 122 degrees F	*Activated*
Above 122 degrees F	*Deactivated*

Mixture heater

3   Using an ohmmeter, check the mixture heater for an open circuit. Remove the electrical connector and install the probes of the ohmmeter onto the terminals **(see illustration)**. Continuity should exist.

Mixture heater relay

4   Remove the mixture heater relay from the relay panel and with the ignition key ON (engine not running), check for the presence of battery voltage. If battery voltage exists, have the relay checked at the dealer parts department or qualified repair facility.

5   If there is no voltage present, check the wiring harness for the mixture heating system (see Chapter 12 wiring diagrams) for shorts, damaged electrical harness or blown fuses.

Canada models

U.S.A. models

5.1   Schematics of the mixture heating systems (1984 models shown)

5.3 Disconnect the electrical connector from the mixture heater (between carburetor and intake manifold) and check for continuity. The heating grid should not contain any breaks or shorts, therefore continuity should exist

6   Heated air inlet system

General description

Refer to illustrations 6.1, 6.3 and 6.4

1   The inlet air temperature control system (carbureted models) **(see illustration)** provides heated intake air during warm-up, then maintains the inlet air temperature within a 100 degrees F to 130 degrees F operating range by mixing warm and cool air. This allows leaner fuel/air mixture settings for the carburetor system, which reduces emissions and improves driveability.

2   Two fresh air inlets - one warm and one cold - are used. The balance between the two is controlled by intake manifold vacuum, a temperature sensor and a vacuum motor. A vacuum motor, which operates a heat duct valve in the air cleaner, is controlled by the temperature sensor.

3   When the underhood temperature is cold, warm air radiating off the exhaust manifold is routed by a shroud which fits over the manifold up through a hot air inlet tube and into the air cleaner **(see illustration)**. This provides warm air for the carburetor, resulting in better driveability and faster warm-up. As the underhood temperature rises, a heat duct valve is gradually closed by a vacuum motor and the air cleaner draws air through a cold air duct instead. The result is a consistent intake air temperature.

4   A temperature vacuum switch **(see illustration)** mounted on the air cleaner housing monitors the temperature of the inlet air heated by the exhaust manifold.

5   The vacuum motor regulates the duct valve allowing warm air to pass through when the engine is cold and reversely shuts the flow of warm air and opens the cold air duct after the engine has reached operating temperature.

Checking

Note: *Make sure that the engine is cold before beginning this test.*

6   Check the vacuum source and the integrity of all vacuum hoses between the source and the vacuum motor before beginning the test. Do not proceed until they're okay.

6.1 Heated air inlet systems

7   Apply the parking brake and block the wheels.

8   Remove the air filter (see Chapter 1).

9   Use a hand held vacuum pump and apply vacuum to the vacuum motor. The duct valve should move. Watch carefully, it may be binding or sticking. Make sure that it's not rusted in an open or closed position by attempting to move it by hand. If it's rusted, it can usually be freed by cleaning and oiling the hinge. If it fails to work properly after servicing, replace it.

10   If the vacuum motor door is okay but the motor still fails to operate correctly, check carefully for a leak in the hose leading to it. Check the vacuum source to and from the sensor and the vacuum motor as well. If no leak is found, replace the vacuum motor.

11   Check the temperature sensor. Monitor the vacuum using a vacuum gauge first, when the engine is cold (start-up) and then finally when the engine has reached operating temperature. There should be vacuum when the engine is cold and then gradually shut down when the engine warms up.

Component replacement

Temperature sensor

12   Clearly label, then detach both vacuum hoses from the temperature sensor (one is coming from the vacuum source at the manifold and the other is going to the vacuum motor underneath the air cleaner housing).

13   Remove the air cleaner housing cover assembly (see Chapter 4A).

14   Remove the bolts that retain the sensor to the bottom of the air cleaner housing.

15   Remove the temperature sensor.

16   Installation is the reverse of removal.

Vacuum motor

17   Remove the air cleaner housing assembly (see Chapter 4A) and place it on a workbench.

18   Detach the vacuum hose from the motor.

19   Drill out the vacuum motor retaining strap rivet.

20   Remove the motor.

21   Installation is the reverse of removal. Use a sheet metal screw of the appropriate size to replace the rivet.

6

6.3 Location of the warm air duct leading from the exhaust manifold to the air cleaner

6.4 The temperature sensor is located in the air cleaner housing

7.1 Schematic of the Throttle Opener Control (TOCS) system for Canada

8.1 Schematic of the high-altitude compensation system

7   Throttle Open Control (TOCS) system (Canadian models only)

General Information

Refer to illustration 7.1

1   The Throttle Open Control (TOCS) system **(see illustration)** controls the throttle valve on the carburetor while the vehicle is decelerating. During deceleration, the manifold vacuum rises and the quantity of fuel mixture in the engine (manifold and combustion chambers) is inadequate and consequently large amounts of unburned HC are emitted from the tailpipe. The TOCS system allows gradual decrease of the fuel mixture to allow the combustion process to continue without drastic emissions problems.

Checks

2   Working on the Function check connector, use an ohmmeter and check for continuity between G/R and B terminals with the ignition key OFF **(see illustration 7.1)**. If continuity does not exist, solenoid may be faulty.
3   With the ignition key ON (engine not running), check for voltage across G/R and B terminals under the following conditions:

Manual transaxles

Remove the speedometer cable (see Chapter 12) and spin the cable with the fingers until the speedometer reads more than 16 mph. The voltage on the G/R and B terminals should change:

| Above 16 mph | zero volts |
| Below 16 mph | 12 volts |

Automatic transaxles

Check the voltage with the transmission gear selector in the following positions:

| Neutral or Park | 12 volts |
| Other positions | zero volts |

4   Check the condition of the throttle opener servo diaphragm. Apply vacuum to the diaphragm using a hand held vacuum pump and observe that the unit holds vacuum. If leaks are detected, replace the throttle opener servo diaphragm with a new part.
5   This system must coincide the angle and time of the throttle opening along with engine vacuum. Adjustments to the TOCS system should be performed by a dealer service department or other qualified repair facility.

8   High-altitude compensation system

General Information

Refer to illustration 8.1

1   Vehicles that are operated at high altitude, where the air is thinner (and the air/fuel mixture ratio and manifold vacuum boost vary and the amount of emissions increase) require a special system to compensate for the atmospheric changes **(see illustration)**.

9.3 To start the self diagnosis system inspection, connect the exhaust gas sensor test harness together

9.4 Observe that the inspection light on the dash is on; if not, replace the bulb

Checks

2   Check all the vacuum hoses and fittings for leaks, cuts or damage that would hinder the proper amount of engine vacuum to reach the components.
3   Check the EGR system to make sure it is functioning properly (see Section 12).

9   Electronic engine control systems and trouble codes

Feedback carburetor systems

Refer to illustrations 9.3, 9.4 and 9.11

General information

1   Feedback carburetor systems installed onto 1982 through 1986 Sentras have limited diagnostic capabilities. The diagnostic codes along with the inspection light located on the dash allow for a basic oxygen sensor check (see Chapter 1) and simple checks on various sensors and output actuators. Although this system is more simplified than later TBI and MPFI systems, the checks allow the home mechanic to narrow down the possibilities and identify the most common problems.

Self diagnosis

1982 and 1983 E15 and E16 models and 1984 through 1986 California models

2   Make sure the harness connector for the ECC system is disconnected (see illustration 9.3).
3   Connect the harness connector for the exhaust gas sensor (oxygen sensor) inspection (see illustration).
4   Turn the ignition key ON (engine not running) and make sure the inspection light on the instrument panel is on (see illustration). If the light is off, replace the bulb.
5   Start the engine and warm to operating temperature. The inspection light should go off after the engine rpm have exceeded 200. After warming the engine completely, run the engine at 2,000 rpm for approximately five minutes.

6   Recheck the inspection light. If the light remains off, there are no trouble codes stored. If the light is on, continue with the code extraction process.
7   Turn the ignition OFF and connect the harness connector for the ECC inspection. Be sure to leave connected the exhaust gas sensor inspection connector.
8   Start the engine and allow it to idle. Watch the inspection light to determine the correct code. There are only two possibilities:

1) The light will come ON and then OFF for a second and then back ON. This pattern will proceed exactly the same as initially; the light ON period will be slightly longer than the light OFF interval. Watch carefully to make this distinction. The possible faults are:

a Air fuel ratio solenoid defective (see Chapter 4A)
b Anti-dieseling solenoid faulty (see Chapter 4A)
c Vacuum switching solenoid (E15 engine only) (see a dealer service dept.)

2) The light will be OFF and then come ON for a second and then back OFF. This pattern will proceed exactly the same as initially; the light OFF period will be slightly longer than the light ON interval. Watch carefully to make this distinction. The possible faults are:

a Exhaust gas sensor defective (see Section 11)
b Coolant temperature sensor faulty (see Section 11)

1984 through 1986 USA (except California) models

9   Remove the computer from under the passenger seat but do not disconnect the electrical harness. For additional information on removing the computer, refer to Section 10.
10   Start the engine and warm it up until it reaches normal operating temperature. Turn the engine OFF.
11   Select the diagnosis start switch to off (see illustration).
12   After warming the engine completely, run the engine at 2,000 rpm for approximately five minutes.
13   With the engine running at 2,000 rpm, check that the green LED light on the computer goes on and off more than five times within a 10 second period. If not, check the oxygen sensor and harness (see Section 10).
14   Turn the engine OFF and select the diagnosis start switch on the computer to on. Turn the ignition key ON and check the Red

9.11 On USA (except California) models, select the self diagnosis start switch OFF to begin extracting the codes

and Green LED on the computer for the lighting interval(s).

1) The Red light will remain ON while the Green light will be OFF and then come ON for a second and then back OFF. This pattern will proceed exactly the same as initially; the Green light OFF period will be slightly longer than the Green light ON interval. Watch carefully to make this distinction. In both cases, the Green light will flash while the Red light is constant. The possible faults are:

a Vacuum sensor defective (see Section 11)
b Coolant temperature sensor problem (see Section 11)
c Air temperature sensor faulty (see Section 11)
d Barometric pressure sensor (see a dealer service department)

2) The Red light will remain ON while the Green light will be ON and then OFF for a second and then back ON. This pattern will proceed exactly the same as initially; the Green light ON period will be slightly longer than the Green light OFF interval. Watch carefully to make this distinction. The possible faults are:

a Mixture heater relay defective (see Section 5)
b Air/fuel ratio solenoid valve (see Chapter 4A)
c Richer solenoid valve (see a dealer service department)
d Anti-dieseling solenoid valve (see Chapter 4A)
e Air Injection Control solenoid valve (see Section 3)
f Duty cycle valve (see a dealer service department)

6

Electronic fuel injection systems (TBI and MPFI)

Refer to illustrations 9.25a and 9.25b

General information

15   The Electronic Fuel Injection (TBI and MPFI) controls the fuel injection system, the spark advance system, the self diagnosis system, the cooling fans, etc. by means of the Engine Control Module (ECM).

16   The ECM receives signals from various sensors which monitor changing engine operations such as intake air volume, intake air temperature, coolant temperature, engine RPM, acceleration/deceleration, exhaust temperature, etc. These signals are utilized by the ECU to determine the correct injection duration and ignition timing.

17   The Sections in this Chapter include general descriptions and checking procedures, within the scope of the home mechanic and component replacement procedures (when possible). Before assuming the fuel and ignition systems are malfunctioning check the emission control system thoroughly. The emission system and the fuel system are closely interrelated but can be checked separately. The diagnosis of some of the fuel and emission control devices requires specialized tools, equipment and training. If checking and servicing become too difficult or if a procedure is beyond your ability, consult a dealer service department or other qualified repair facility. Remember, the most frequent cause of fuel and emissions problems is simply a loose or broken vacuum hose or wire, so always check the hose and wiring connections first.
Note: *Because of federally-mandated extended warranty which covers the emission control system components (and any other components which have a primary purpose other than emission control but have significant effects on emissions), check with your dealer about warranty coverage before working on any emission related systems. Once the warranty has expired, you may wish to perform some of the component checks and/or replacement procedures in this Chapter to save you money.*

Precautions

18   Always disconnect the power by either turning off the ignition switch or disconnecting the battery terminals before disconnecting EFI wiring connectors.

19   When installing a battery, be particularly careful to avoid reversing the positive and negative cables.

20   Do not subject EFI or emission related components to severe impact during removal or installation.

21   Do not be careless during troubleshooting. Even slight terminal contact can invalidate a testing procedure and even damage one of the numerous transistor circuits.

22   Never attempt to work on the ECM or open the ECM cover. The ECM is protected by a government mandated extended warranty that will be nullified if you tamper with it.

23   If you are inspecting electronic control system components during rainy weather, make sure water does not enter any part. When washing the engine compartment, do not spray these parts or their connectors with water.

Self diagnosis

24   The self diagnosis mode is useful to diagnose malfunctions in major sensors and actuators of the Electronic Fuel Injection system. On TBI systems, there are five different modes available for diagnosing driveability problems. Only Mode III is used by home mechanics. On MPFI systems, Mode II is used for self diagnosis. It is important to know that several other modes are used strictly for testing the bulbs and inspection lights involved with the self diagnosis system. Sometimes it will be necessary to double-check these conditions before proceeding with the actual self diagnostics.

TBI systems

There are five modes in the self diagnosis system.

Mode I - Mixture ratio feedback control monitor A - During a closed loop condition (when the engine is warm), the green inspection lamp turns ON indicating a lean condition or OFF for a rich condition. During an open loop condition (when the engine is cold) the green lamp remains OFF.

Mode II - Mixture ratio feedback control monitor B - During closed loop operation, the red inspection lamp turns ON and OFF simultaneously with the green inspection lamp when the mixture ratio is controlled within the specified value. During the open loop condition, the red lamp remains OFF.

Mode III - Self diagnosis - This mode stores all malfunctioning diagnostic items in its memory. It will be stored in the ECM memory until the starter is operated fifty times, or until the power supply to the ECM is interrupted.

9.25a First turn the diagnostic selector completely clockwise, wait for three flashes and turn the selector completely counterclockwise and watch carefully for the red and green flashes from the computer (small arrow) (TBI engine shown)

Mode IV - Switches ON/OFF diagnosis - During this mode, the inspection lamp monitors the idle switch portion of the throttle valve switch, the starter switch, vehicle speed sensor and other switches with an ON/OFF condition.

Mode V - Real time diagnosis - The moment the malfunction is detected, the display will be presented. This is the mode in which the malfunction can be observed during a road test, as it occurs.

MPFI systems

There are two modes in the self diagnosis system. Mode I is slightly different for various models:

Mode I - Bulb check - In this mode, the red LED in the ECM and the CHECK ENGINE light on the dash will come ON when the ignition key is turned to ON (engine not running). If either do not light, then the bulbs must be replaced.

Mode I (for California models) - Malfunction warning - In this mode, the engine is started and the CHECK ENGINE light remains ON while the engine is running. This indicates stored trouble codes in mode II.

Mode I (for USA - except California models) - Malfunction warning - In this mode, the engine is started and the CHECK ENGINE light remains ON while the engine is running. This indicates a defective ECM.

Mode II - Self diagnosis - This mode stores all malfunctioning diagnostic items in its memory. It will be stored in the ECM memory until the starter is operated fifty times, or until the power supply to the ECM is interrupted. This mode will be most commonly used for self diagnostic procedures.

25   To access the correct mode for self diagnosis, turn the ignition switch to the ON (engine not running) position. Turn the diagnostic mode selector on the ECM fully clockwise **(see illustrations)**:

On **TBI** systems, wait until the inspection lamps flash (at least two seconds). Count the number, and after three flashes, turn the diagnostic mode selector fully counterclockwise. This locks the computer into Mode III (self diagnostic capabilities).

9.25b Diagnostic selector on a MPFI model

Note: *Home mechanics use only Mode III. It is important to know that if the mode selector is turned prematurely, then the computer will access the wrong mode. For example, to access Mode I, wait for only a single flash and then turn the diagnostic mode selector fully counterclockwise. Wait for two flashes to access Mode II and so on.*

Carefully observe the lights on the ECM. If everything in the self diagnosis system is functioning properly, the computer will flash a code 44. This code will be represented by four flashes on the red LED followed by four flashes on the green LED. If the computer has actual trouble codes stored, carefully observe the flashes and record the exact number onto paper. For example, code 42 (throttle sensor or TPS) is indicated by four flashes on the red LED followed by two flashes on the green LED. Refer to the trouble

code chart below for the exact codes and component failures.

If the ignition key is turned OFF during the code extraction process and possibly turned back on, the diagnosis will automatically return to Mode I. Restart the procedure to extract the codes.

On **MPFI** systems, wait at least two seconds and then turn the diagnostic mode selector fully counterclockwise. Turn the mode selector clockwise again, wait two seconds and turn it counterclockwise. The ECM is now in Mode II and will begin displaying codes. Read the diagnosis code as indicated by the number of flashes of the "CHECK ENGINE " light on the dash. Normal system operation is indicated by Code No. 55 (no malfunctions) for all models. The "CHECK ENGINE" light displays a Code No. 55 by blinking five long flashes followed by a pause

and then five short flashes. While the CHECK ENGINE light is blinking, a red LED located on the computer will blink the exact same pattern. If in doubt, double-check the codes from the LED. Also, some codes are not programmed to flash on the CHECK ENGINE light but instead will flash only on the computer. Be sure to check the code chart for the necessary information.

Clearing codes

26 After the tests have been performed and the repairs completed, erase the memory by turning the diagnostic mode selector on the ECM fully clockwise. After the inspection lamps have flashed 4 times (TBI systems only), turn the diagnostic selector fully counterclockwise. This will erase any memory the ECM has stored concerning a particular component.

Throttle Body Injection (TBI) systems

Trouble codes	Circuit or system	Probable cause
Code 11 (1 red flash, 1 green flash)	Crank angle sensor/circuit	Check the crank angle sensor or circuit (see Section 11).
Code 12 (1 red flash, 2 green flashes)	Airflow meter/circuit	The air flow meter source or ground circuit(s) may be shorted or open. Check the airflow meter (Chapter 4B).
Code 13 (1 red flash, 3 green flashes)	Coolant temperature sensor	The sensor source or ground circuit(s) may be shorted or open. Check the temperature sensor and circuit (see Section 11).
Code 21 (2 red flashes, 1 green flash)	Ignition signal	The ignition signal in the primary circuit is missing during engine cranking or running. This repair must be performed by a dealer service department.
Code 22 (2 red flashes, 2 green flashes)	Idle speed control	The idle speed system is defective (see Chapter 4B).
Code 33 (3 red flashes, 3 green flashes)	Oxygen sensor	The oxygen sensor circuit is open (see Section 11).
Code 41 (4 red flashes, 1 green flash)	Air temperature sensor	The air temperature sensor circuit is open or shorted (see Section 11).
Code 42 (4 red flashes, 2 green flashes)	Throttle sensor circuit	The TPS or circuit is open or shorted (see Section 11).
Code 43 (4 red flashes, 3 green flashes)	Mixture ratio feedback	Possible clogged fuel injector (see Chapter 4B).
Code 44 (4 red flashes, 4 green flashes)	EFI system	Normal operation.

Multi Port Fuel Injection (MPFI) systems

Trouble codes	Circuit or system	Probable cause
Code 11* (1 long flash, 1 short flash)	Crank angle sensor/circuit	Check the crank angle sensor or circuit (see Section 11).
Code 12 (1 long flash, 2 short flashes)	Mass airflow sensor/circuit	The mass airflow sensor source or ground circuit(s) may be shorted or open. Check the mass airflow sensor or circuit (see Section 11).
Code 13 (1 long flash, 3 short flashes)	Coolant temperature sensor	The Coolant sensor or circuit may be shorted or open. Check the Coolant temperature sensor and circuit (see Section 10).
Code 14 (1 long flash, 4 short flashes)	Vehicle speed sensor.	The vehicle speed sensor signal circuit is open (see Section 11).
Code 21* (2 long flashes, 1 short flash)	Ignition signal	The ignition signal in the primary circuit is not entered during engine cranking or running (see a dealer service department).
Code 31 (3 long flashes, 1 short flash)	ECM control unit	The ECM input signal is beyond "normal" range (see a dealer service department).
Code 32 (3 long flashes, 2 short flashes)	EGR Function	The EGR control valve does not operate (see Section 12).
Code 33 (3 long flashes, 3 short flashes)	Oxygen sensor	The oxygen sensor circuit is open (see Section 11).
Code 34 (3 long flashes, 4 short flashes)	Knock sensor	The knock sensor circuit is open or shorted (see Section 11).
Code 35 (3 long flashes, 5 short flashes)	Exhaust gas temperature sensor	The exhaust gas temperature sensor circuit is open or shorted (see Section 11).
Code 43 (4 long flashes, 3 short flashes)	Throttle position sensor (TPS)	The TPS circuit is open or shorted (see Section 11).
Code 45 (4 long flashes, 5 short flashes)	Injector leak	The injector(s) have fuel leaks (see Chapter 4B, Section 17).
Code 55 (5 long flashes, 5 short flashes)	EFI system	Normal operation.

This code must be read by watching the red LED located on the computer as it flashes. Follow the same diagnostic procedure.

10.3 On TBI models, first remove the plastic cover located under the front seat

10.4 On MPFI models, remove the bracket bolts from the middle of the console

10.5 On TBI models, slide the computer assembly out and then remove the plastic cover

10   Engine Control Module (ECM) - removal and installation

Refer to illustrations 10.3, 10.4 and 10.5
Note: *The ECM (computer) is located in various places depending upon the year and model. On feedback carbureted models, the computer is located under the driver's front seat. On TBI models, the computer is located under the passenger's front seat. On MPFI models, the computer is located under the dash in the middle of the center console.*

1   The Engine Control Module (ECM) is located inside the passenger compartment. The retaining bracket and bolts must be removed from inside the passenger's compartment.
2   Disconnect the negative battery cable from the battery. **Warning:** *Some models have airbags. Always disconnect the negative battery cable, then the positive cable and wait ten minutes before working in the vicinity of the impact sensors, steering column or instrument panel to avoid the possibility of accidental deployment of the airbag, which could cause personal injury* (see Chapter 12).
3   Working in the passenger compartment, remove the bolt that retains the ECM plastic

cover to the body **(see illustration)**. Some models are not equipped with a plastic cover.
4   Remove the retaining nuts **(see illustration)** from the ECM.
5   Working inside the driver's compartment, carefully slide the ECM out far enough to clear the kick panel **(see illustration)**. **Caution:** *The ignition switch must be turned OFF when pulling out or plugging in the electrical connectors to prevent damage to the ECM.* **Note:** *Avoid any static electricity damage to the computer by using gloves and a special anti-static pad to store the ECM on once it is removed.*

11   Information sensors - check and replacement

Coolant temperature sensor

Refer to illustrations 11.2a, 11.2b, 11.2c and 11.3

General description

1   The coolant temperature sensor is a thermistor (a resistor which varies the value of its voltage output in accordance with

temperature changes). The change in the resistance values will directly affect the voltage signal from the coolant sensor. As the sensor temperature DECREASES, the resistance values will INCREASE. As the sensor temperature INCREASES, the resistance values will DECREASE. A failure in the coolant sensor circuit should set a Code 13. This code indicates a failure in the coolant temperature circuit, so in most cases the appropriate solution to the problem will be either repair of a wire or replacement of the sensor.

Check

2   Check the resistance value of the coolant temperature sensor while it is completely cold (50 to 65-degrees F = 2,300 to 3,000 ohms). Next, start the engine and warm it up until it reaches operating temperature **(see illustrations)**. The resistance should be lower (176 to 180-degrees F = 300 to 330 ohms). **Note:** *Access to the coolant temperature sensor makes it difficult to position electrical probes on the terminals. If necessary, remove the sensor and perform the tests in a pan of heated water to simulate the conditions.*
3   If the resistance values on the sensor are correct, check the signal voltage to the

11.2a Check the resistance of the coolant temperature sensor with the engine completely cold and then with the engine at operating temperature. Resistance should decrease as temperature increases (TBI model shown)

11.2b Checking the resistance of the coolant temperature sensor on a MPFI model (GA16DE engine)

11.2c Coolant temperature sensor location on a SR model (SR20DE engine)

11.3 Working on the harness side, check the voltage from the ECM to the coolant temperature sensor with the ignition key ON and the engine not running. It should be approximately 5.0 volts

11.7 Remove the vacuum hose from the vacuum sensor and attach a hand held vacuum pump

11.8 First check the signal voltage without vacuum applied and then with vacuum. The sensor should change voltage from 4.0 volts (without vacuum) to 0.5 volts (with vacuum)

sensor from the ECM (see illustration). It should be approximately 5.0 volts.

Replacement

4   Before installing the new sensor, wrap the threads with Teflon sealing tape to prevent leakage and thread corrosion.
5   Disconnect the electrical connector and remove the sensor. **Caution:** *Handle the coolant sensor with care. Damage to this sensor will affect the operation of the entire fuel injection system.* Install the sensor and tighten it securely.

Vacuum sensor (feedback carburetor models)

Refer to illustrations 11.7 and 11.8

General description

6   The vacuum sensor monitors the intake manifold pressure changes resulting from changes in engine load and speed and converts the information into a voltage output. The ECM uses the vacuum sensor to control fuel delivery and ignition timing. The ECM will receive information as a voltage signal. This signal can be detected using a voltmeter. The voltage will vary from 4.0 volts without engine vacuum to 0.5 volts with 25 in-Hg. vacuum.

Check

7   Remove the vacuum hose from the vacuum sensor and install a hand held vacuum pump (see illustration).
8   Disconnect the electrical connector from the vacuum sensor. Install jumper wires from the battery to the vacuum sensor designated terminals (see illustration). Using a voltmeter, check for signal voltage from the vacuum sensor.
9   Without vacuum, the sensor voltage should be approximately 4.0 volts.
10   Use the hand-held vacuum pump and apply 25 in-Hg of vacuum to the vacuum sensor and observe the voltage readings. The voltmeter should read approximately 0.5 volts.
11   If the test results are incorrect, replace the vacuum sensor.

Oxygen sensor

Refer to illustrations 11.14, 11.17 and 11.24

General information

12   The oxygen sensor, located in the exhaust manifold, monitors the oxygen content of the exhaust gas stream. The oxygen content in the exhaust reacts with the oxygen sensor to produce a voltage output which varies from 0.1-volt (high oxygen, lean mixture) to 0.9-volts (low oxygen, rich mixture). The ECM constantly monitors this variable voltage output to determine the ratio

of oxygen to fuel in the mixture. The ECM alters the air/fuel mixture ratio by controlling the pulse width (open time) of the fuel injector(s). A mixture ratio of 14.7 parts air to 1 part fuel is the ideal mixture ratio for minimizing exhaust emissions, thus allowing the catalytic converter to operate at maximum efficiency. It is this ratio of 14.7 to 1 which the ECM and the oxygen sensor attempt to maintain at all times. **Note:** *Some models are equipped with a single wire oxygen sensor but most are equipped with the heated oxygen sensor (three wire) type.*
13   The oxygen sensor produces no voltage when it is below its normal operating temperature of about 600-degrees F. During this initial period before warm-up, the ECM operates in open loop mode.

Check

14   Locate the oxygen sensor electrical connector and backprobe the oxygen sensor connector with a straight-pin (see illustration). Install the positive probe of a voltmeter onto the pin and the negative probe to ground. On heated oxygen sensor models, backprobe terminal B (see illustration 11.17) and observe the sensor voltage signal.
15   Monitor the voltage signal as the engine goes from cold to warm.
16   The oxygen sensor will produce a steady voltage signal at first (open loop) of approximately 0.1 to 0.2 volts with the engine cold. After a period of approximately two minutes, the engine will reach operating temperature and the oxygen sensor will start to fluctuate between 0.1 to 0.9 volts (closed loop). If the oxygen sensor fails to reach the closed loop mode or there is a very long period of time until it does switch into closed loop mode, replace the oxygen sensor with a new part.
17   Also inspect the oxygen sensor heater. Disconnect the oxygen sensor electrical connector and connect an ohmmeter between terminals A and C (see illustration). It should measure approximately 3.0 to 1,000 ohms.
18   Check for proper supply voltage to the heater. Measure the voltage on the harness side of the oxygen sensor electrical connector, terminal C. There should be

11.14 Backprobe the oxygen sensor and observe the millivolt signal the sensor produces as it goes from cold to fully warm

11.17 Install the probes of the ohmmeter onto terminals A and C and check the resistance of the oxygen sensor heater

6

battery voltage with the ignition key ON (engine not running). If there is no voltage, check the circuit between the EFI relay, the ECM and the sensor (see Chapter 12).

19   The proper operation of the oxygen sensor depends on four conditions:

a) *Electrical - The low voltages generated by the sensor depend upon good, clean connections which should be checked whenever a malfunction of the sensor is suspected or indicated.*

b) *Outside air supply - The sensor is designed to allow air circulation to the internal portion of the sensor. Whenever the sensor is removed and installed or replaced, make sure the air passages are not restricted.*

c) *Proper operating temperature - The ECM will not react to the sensor signal until the sensor reaches approximately 600-degrees F. This factor must be taken into consideration when evaluating the performance of the sensor.*

d) *Unleaded fuel - The use of unleaded fuel is essential for proper operation of the sensor. Make sure the fuel you are using is of this type.*

20   In addition to observing the above conditions, special care must be taken whenever the sensor is serviced.

a) *The oxygen sensor has a permanently attached pigtail and electrical connector which should not be removed from the sensor. Damage or removal of the pigtail or electrical connector can adversely affect operation of the sensor.*

b) *Grease, dirt and other contaminants should be kept away from the electrical connector and the louvered end of the sensor.*

c) *Do not use cleaning solvents of any kind on the oxygen sensor.*

d) *Do not drop or roughly handle the sensor.*

e) *The silicone boot must be installed in the correct position to prevent the boot from being melted and to allow the sensor to operate properly.*

21   If the oxygen sensor fails any of these tests, replace it with a new part.

Replacement

Note: *Because it is installed in the exhaust manifold or pipe, which contracts when cool, the oxygen sensor may be very difficult to loosen when the engine is cold. Rather than risk damage to the sensor (assuming you are planning to reuse it in another manifold or pipe), start and run the engine for a minute or two, then shut it off. Be careful not to burn yourself during the following procedure.*

22   Disconnect the cable from the negative terminal of the battery.

23   Raise the vehicle and place it securely on jackstands, if necessary on some models.

24   Carefully disconnect the electrical connector from the sensor (**see illustration**).

25   Carefully unscrew the sensor from the exhaust manifold. **Caution:** *Excessive force may damage the threads.*

26   Anti-seize compound must be used on the threads of the sensor to facilitate future removal. The threads of new sensors will already be coated with this compound, but if an old sensor is removed and reinstalled, recoat the threads.

27   Install the sensor and tighten it securely.

28   Reconnect the electrical connector of the pigtail lead to the main engine wiring harness.

29   Lower the vehicle and reconnect the cable to the negative terminal of the battery.

Throttle Position Sensor (TPS) (MPFI models only)

General description

Refer to illustrations 11.31a, 11.31b, 11.32, 11.33 and 11.34

Note: *Refer to Chapter 4B, Section 9 for the complete adjustment and replacement procedure for the throttle switch and sensor that is equipped onto TBI systems.*

30   The Throttle Position Sensor (TPS) is located on the end of the throttle shaft on the throttle body. By monitoring the output voltage from the TPS, the ECM can determine fuel delivery based on throttle valve angle (driver demand). A broken or loose TPS can cause intermittent bursts of fuel from the injector and an unstable idle

11.24 Remove the oxygen sensor using a special slotted socket

because the ECM thinks the throttle is moving. Any problems in the TPS or circuit will set a code 42 TBI systems or 43 MPFI systems.

Check

31   To check the TPS, turn the ignition switch to ON (engine not running) and install the probes of the voltmeter into the ground wire and signal wire on the backside of the electrical connector. This test checks for the proper signal voltage from the TPS (**see illustrations**). **Note:** *Be careful when backprobing the electrical connector. Do not damage the wiring harness or pull on any connectors to make clean contact.*

32   The sensor should read 0.50 to 1.0-volt at closed throttle. Have an assistant depress the accelerator pedal to simulate full throttle and the sensor should increase voltage to 4.0 to 5.0-volts (**see illustration**). If the TPS voltage readings are incorrect, replace it with a new unit.

33   Also, check the TPS reference voltage. With the ignition key ON (engine not running), install the positive (+) probe of the voltmeter (**see illustration**) onto the voltage reference wire. There should be approximately 5.0 volts sent from the ECM to the TPS.

Replacement

Refer to illustration 11.34

34   Remove the two retaining screws (**see**

11.31a Backprobe terminal A (signal wire) to check for signal voltage from the TPS and observe that the signal voltage is approximately 0.5 volts (GA16DE engine)

11.31b On SR20DE models, the TPS electrical connector (arrow) is mounted on the air intake plenum away from the TPS (arrow)

11.32 Open the throttle to wide open and observe that the signal voltage increases to approximately 4.0 volts

11.33 Check the reference voltage to the TPS with a voltmeter. Probe terminal C (red wire) (harness side) with the positive (+) probe of the voltmeter and make sure the reference voltage is approximately 5.0 volts

11.34 Remove the two screws (arrows) from the TPS and separate it from the throttle body

11.38 Probe terminal A with the positive (+) probe of the voltmeter and check for voltage fluctuations

illustration) and separate the TPS from the throttle body.

35   Install the new TPS leaving the mounting screws loose. Connect a voltmeter to the signal and ground wires as in Step 31. Rotate the sensor until the voltmeter reading is 0.45 to 0.55-volt. Tighten the screws securely.

Mass Airflow (MAF) sensor (MPFI models only)

Refer to illustrations 11.38 and 11.43

General Information

36   The Mass Airflow Sensor (MAF) is located on the air intake duct. This sensor uses a hot wire sensing element to measure the amount of air entering the engine. The air passing over the hot wire causes it to cool. Consequently, this change in temperature can be converted into an analog voltage signal to the ECM which in turn calculates the required fuel injector pulse width.

Check

37   Check for power to the MAF sensor. Disconnect the MAF sensor electrical connector. Working on the engine harness side, connect a voltmeter to terminal C **(see illustration 11.38)** and ground. There should be battery voltage on terminal C.

11.43 Remove the four bolts (arrows) and separate the MAF sensor from the air cleaner housing

38   Reconnect the electrical connector and backprobe the MAF sensor terminal A **(see illustration)** with the voltmeter and check the voltage. The voltage should be less than 1.0 volt with the ignition switch ON (engine not running).
39   Start the engine and raise the engine rpm. The signal voltage from the MAF sensor should increase to approximately 1.3 to 1.7 volts on 1991 and 1992 models or 0.7 to 1.1 volts on 1993 and 1994 models. If the MAF sensor voltage does not vary, replace the sensor.
40   If the voltage readings are correct, check the wiring harness for open circuits or a damaged harness (see Chapter 12).

Replacement

41   Disconnect the electrical connector from the MAF sensor.
42   Remove the air cleaner assembly (see Chapter 4B).
43   Remove the four bolts **(see illustration)** and lift the MAF sensor from the engine compartment.
44   Installation is the reverse of removal.

Airflow meter (TBI models only)

Note: *Refer to Chapter 4B, Section 9 for the complete checks and replacement procedures for the airflow meter on throttle body injected (TBI) models.*

Vehicle Speed Sensor (VSS)

General description

45   The Vehicle Speed Sensor (VSS) is located on the transaxle (see Chapter 7B). This sensor works in conjunction with a reed switch which is installed into the speedometer unit. The reed switch transforms vehicle speed into a pulsing voltage signal that is translated by the ECM and provided as information for other systems for fuel and transmission shift control. Any problems with the VSS will usually set a Code 14 on MPFI models. There are no VSS codes available for the TBI systems.

Check

46   To check the vehicle speed sensor,

remove the electrical connector in the wiring harness near the sensor. Using a voltmeter, check for power to the sensor. With the ignition key ON (engine not running), the supply wire should have 12 volts or more available. If there is no voltage available, have the ECM diagnosed by a dealer service department or other qualified repair shop.

Replacement

47   To replace the VSS, disconnect the electrical connector from the VSS.
48   Remove the retaining bolt and lift the VSS from the transaxle.
49   Installation is the reverse of removal.

Air temperature sensor (TBI models only)

Refer to illustration 11.54

General description

50   The air temperature sensor is located inside the air intake duct. This sensor acts as a resistor which changes value according to the temperature of the air entering the engine. Low temperatures produce a high resistance value (for example, at 68 degrees F the resistance is 2.3 to 2.7 K-ohms) while high temperatures produce low resistance values (at 176 degrees F the resistance is 300 to 330 ohms). The ECM supplies approximately 5-volts (reference voltage) to the air temperature sensor. The voltage will change according to the temperature of the incoming air. The voltage will be high when the air temperature is cold and low when the air temperature is warm. Any problems with the air temperature sensor will usually set a code 41 on TBI systems.

Check

51   To check the air temperature sensor, disconnect the two prong electrical connector and turn the ignition key ON but do not start the engine.
52   Measure the voltage (reference voltage). The voltmeter should read approximately 5-volts.
53   If the voltage signal is not correct, have the ECM diagnosed by a dealer service department or other repair shop.
54   Measure the resistance across the air

6

11.54 Location of the air temperature sensor and the harness connector on TBI models

11.55 Location of the power steering oil pressure switch

11.60 Disconnect the EGR gas temperature sensor harness connector and check the resistance cold and then with the engine completely warmed up to operating temperature

temperature sensor terminals **(see illustration)**. The resistance should be HIGH when the air temperature is LOW. Next, start the engine and let it idle (cold). Allow the engine to reach normal operating temperature. Turn the ignition OFF, disconnect the air temperature sensor and measure the resistance across the terminals. The resistance should be LOW when the air temperature is HIGH. If the sensor does not exhibit this change in resistance, replace it with a new part.

Power steering pressure switch

Refer to illustration 11.55

General description

55   Turning the steering wheel increases power steering fluid pressure and engine load. The pressure switch **(see illustration)** will close before the load can cause an idle problem. A pressure switch that will not open or an open circuit from the ECM will cause timing to retard at idle, affecting idle quality. A pressure switch that will not close or an open circuit may cause the engine to die when the power steering system is used heavily.

Check

56   Disconnect the electrical connector to the pressure switch.
57   Connect an ohmmeter across the terminals of the pressure switch. Start the

engine and check for continuity as the steering wheel is turned. There should be no continuity when the steering wheel is not being turned.
58   If the switch fails this test, replace the switch.

EGR gas temperature sensor

General Description

59   Some models are equipped with an EGR gas temperature sensor mounted near the EGR valve, installed into the EGR tube. This sensor detects the temperature of the exhaust as it moves through the EGR valve. The information is sent to the ECM and in turn the EGR on/off time is regulated precisely and more efficiently. Any malfunction with the EGR gas temperature sensor will set a code 35.

Check

Refer to illustration 11.60

60   Disconnect the harness connector for the EGR gas temperature sensor **(see illustration)** and measure the resistance of the sensor. Resistance should decrease as temperature increases and at 212 degrees F should measure 77 to 93 K-ohms.

Removal and installation

61   Disconnect the harness connector for the EGR gas temperature sensor and using and open-end wrench, remove the sensor from the intake manifold.
62   Installation is the reverse of removal.

Knock sensor

Refer to illustrations 11.64a and 11.64b

General description

63   The knock sensor is located in the engine block under the intake manifold. The knock sensor detects abnormal vibration in the engine. The sensor produces an AC output voltage which increases with the severity of the knock. The signal is fed into the ECM and the timing is retarded up to 10 degrees to compensate for severe detonation. Any problems with the knock sensor will set a code 34 in MPFI systems.

Check

64   Disconnect the electrical connector at the knock sensor. Using an ohmmeter set of the high scale, check for continuity between terminal A and ground **(see illustrations)**. If continuity doesn't exist replace the sensor.
65   Also check for a loose knock sensor. Tighten with an open end wrench if necessary.

Crank angle sensor

Refer to illustrations 11.72a, 11.72b, 11.72c and 11.72d

Note: *A description and replacement procedures of the crank angle sensor can be found in Chapter 5, Section 5.*

Check

66   Remove the distributor (see Chapter 5).
67   Remove the rotor retaining screw and pull the rotor off the shaft (see Chapter 5).
68   Remove the sensor dust cover retaining screws and lift off the cover.
69   Inspect the crank angle signal plate for damage and dirt intrusion. Blow any accumulated dust out of the distributor and reinstall the cover and rotor.
70   Inspect the electrical connections for damage and corrosion and correct any defects.
71   With the distributor removed, reconnect the electrical harness to the crank angle sensor, turn the ignition key ON (engine not running) and check the crank angle sensor.

11.64a Location of the knock sensor harness connector

11.64b Check for continuity between terminal A and ground of the knock sensor

72 Backprobe the electrical connector and check for battery voltage at the following terminals (see illustrations):

1988 and earlier; terminal B (red/black wire)
1989 and 1990;
   terminal C (black/white wire)
1991 and later;
   GA16DE - terminal 3 (orange/blue wire)
   SR20DE - terminal C (orange/blue wire)

If battery voltage is not present, check the circuit from the crank angle sensor to the EFI or ECC main relay for an open circuit or a defective relay.

73 Using an ohmmeter, check for continuity to ground on the following terminals:

1990 and earlier; terminal D (black wire)
1991 and later;
   GA16DE - terminal 4 (black wire)
   SR20DE - terminal B (black wire)

If no continuity exists, check for an open circuit from the crank angle sensor to ground.
74 Check for the 180-degree crankshaft position signal. This will be indicated by a fluctuation on the voltmeter from zero to five volts, two times for every complete rotation of the distributor shaft (360 degrees). Backprobe the following terminals and rotate the distributor shaft slowly, by hand:

1988 and earlier;
   terminal A (red/white wire)
1989 and 1990;
   terminal A (green/black wire)
1991 and later;
   GA16DE - terminal 1 (blue wire)
   SR20DE - terminal A (blue wire)

75 Next, check the one-degree timing signal. This will be indicated by a fluctuation on the voltmeter from zero to five volts, 360 times every complete rotation of the distributor. It will be necessary to rotate the distributor very slowly to detect these voltage changes. Backprobe the following terminals and rotate the distributor shaft very slowly, by hand:

1988 and earlier; terminal C (red/blue wire)
1989 and 1990;
   terminal B (green/yellow wire)
1991 and later;
   GA16DE - terminal 2 (yellow wire)
   SR20DE - terminal D (yellow wire)

76 If the crank angle sensor signal test results are incorrect, replace the distributor as a complete unit.

12 Exhaust Gas Recirculation (EGR) system

General description

Refer to illustrations 12.5, 12.6, 12.12 and 12.15

1 The EGR system is used to lower NOx (oxides of nitrogen) emission levels caused by high combustion temperatures. The EGR recirculates a small amount of exhaust gases into the intake manifold. The additional mixture lowers the temperature of combustion thereby reducing the formation of NOx compounds.

2 Early EGR systems are equipped with either a Thermal Vacuum Valve that receives a ported vacuum signal or a VVT (venturi vacuum transducer) valve which receives ported and venturi vacuum. The venturi vacuum system utilizes a vacuum tap at the throat of the carburetor venturi to provide the control signal. The ported vacuum control system uses a slot in the carburetor body which is exposed to an increasing percentage of manifold vacuum as the throttle valve is opened up during acceleration. **Note:** *Refer to illustrations 1.7a through 1.7n for schematics and component locations for the EGR systems.*

3 On the early systems, the venturi vacuum transducer monitors exhaust pressure and venturi vacuum in order to activate the EGR diaphragm. The VVT controls the carburetor throttle vacuum that is in turn applied to the EGR control valve. **Note:** *Later systems are similar but the VVT valve has been changed to the BPT valve.* The EGR system is also equipped with a thermal vacuum valve which detects coolant temperature and opens or closes the air passage from the air cleaner according to temperature. The vacuum delay valve reduces NOx emissions during rapid acceleration by restricting the airflow in the vacuum line when the throttle valve is rapidly opened (wide open throttle). This creates some delay time for the EGR valve to operate. When vacuum decreases, the EGR will respond normally because the valve operates one way. USA (except California) models are equipped with a vacuum switching valve that supplies vacuum from the vacuum reservoir tank to the EGR valve.

Check

4 Check all hoses for cracks, kinks, broken sections and proper connection. Inspect all system connections for damage, cracks and leaks.
5 To check the EGR system operation, bring the engine up to operating temperature and, with the transmission in Neutral (parking brake set and tires blocked to prevent movement), allow it to idle for 70 seconds. Open the throttle abruptly so the engine speed is between 2,000 and 3,000 rpm and then allow it to close. The EGR valve stem should move if the control system is working properly. The test should be repeated several times. Movement of the stem indicates the control system is functioning correctly (see illustration).

11.72a 1988 and earlier model crank angle sensor terminal locations

11.72c 1991 and later GA16DE crank angle sensor terminal locations

11.72b 1989 and 1990 model crank angle sensor terminal locations

11.72d 1991 and later SR20DE crank angle sensor terminal locations

12.5 Check to make sure the EGR diaphragm moves when slight pressure is applied to the valve

6

12.6 Use a hand-held vacuum pump to apply vacuum to the EGR valve

12.12 Close off one port of the BPT valve with a finger and apply vacuum. Check for leaks in the diaphragm

12.15 Check the resistance of the EGR vacuum switching solenoid. It should measure between 20 and 100 ohms

6   If the EGR valve stem does not move, check all of the hose connections to make sure they are not leaking or clogged. Disconnect the vacuum hose and apply ten inches of vacuum with a hand pump **(see illustration)**. If the stem still does not move, replace the EGR valve with a new one. If the valve does open, measure the valve travel to make sure it is approximately 1/8-inch. Also, the engine should run roughly when the valve is open. If it doesn't, the passages are probably clogged.

7   Apply vacuum with the pump and then clamp the hose shut. The valve should stay open for 30 seconds or longer. If it does not, the diaphragm is leaking and the valve should be replaced with a new one.

8   If the EGR valve is not receiving port or venturi vacuum, the carburetor or throttle body unit must be removed to check and clean the slotted port in the throttle bore and the vacuum passages and orifices in the throttle body. Use solvent to remove deposits and check for flow with light air pressure.

9   If the engine idles roughly and it is suspected the EGR valve is not closing, remove the EGR valve and inspect the poppet and seat area for deposits.

10   If the deposits are more than a thin film of carbon, the valve should be cleaned. To clean the valve, apply solvent and allow it to penetrate and soften the deposits, making sure that none gets on the valve diaphragm, as it could be damaged.

12.21 Remove the EGR flange nut from the EGR tube using a large open end wrench

11   Use a vacuum pump to hold the valve open and carefully scrape the deposits from the seat and poppet area with a tool. Inspect the poppet and stem for wear and replace the valve with a new one if wear is found.

12   Locate the VVT or BPT valve and plug one of the ports with a finger **(see illustration)**. Use a hand held vacuum pump and apply vacuum to the valve. Check for any sign of leaks.

13   With the engine running, check for a vacuum signal from the intake manifold. This test will determine if manifold vacuum is reaching the various valves and components of the EGR system.

14   Also apply vacuum to the port (vacuum hose) that is routed to the EGR valve. The gauge should hold vacuum. If not, check for broken hoses or ruptured diaphragms in the EGR valve.

15   Check the EGR solenoid (if equipped). Using a hand held vacuum pump apply vacuum and then apply battery voltage. The solenoid should activate and allow vacuum to pass through the solenoid **(see illustration)**.

16   Also remove the vacuum hose(s) from the solenoid and check for vacuum to the EGR valve.

Component replacement

EGR valve

Refer to illustration 12.21

17   When buying a new EGR valve, make sure that you have the right EGR valve. Use the stamped code located on the top of the EGR valve.

18   Detach the cable from the negative terminal of the battery.

19   Remove the air cleaner housing assembly (see Chapter 4A and 4B).

20   Detach the vacuum line from the EGR valve.

21   Raise the vehicle and support it securely on jackstands. Remove the EGR pipe from the exhaust manifold **(see illustration)**. Lower the vehicle.

22   Remove the EGR valve mounting bolts.

23   Remove the EGR valve and gasket from the manifold. Discard the gasket.

24   With a wire wheel, buff the exhaust

deposits from the EGR valve mounting surface on the manifold and, if you plan to use the same valve, the mounting surface of the valve itself. Look for exhaust deposits in the valve outlet. Remove deposit build-up with a screwdriver. **Caution:** *Never wash the valve in solvents or degreaser - both agents will permanently damage the diaphragm. Sand blasting is also not recommended because it will affect the operation of the valve.*

25   If the EGR passage contains an excessive build-up of deposits, clean it out with a wire wheel. Make sure that all loose particles are completely removed to prevent them from clogging the EGR valve or from being ingested into the engine.

26   Installation is the reverse of removal.

EGR vacuum control solenoid (MPFI models only)

27   Detach the cable from the negative terminal of the battery.

28   Remove the air intake duct from the air cleaner assembly (see Chapter 4).

29   Unplug the electrical connector from the solenoid.

30   Clearly label and detach both vacuum hoses.

31   Remove the solenoid mounting screw and remove the solenoid.

32   Installation is the reverse of removal.

13   Evaporative Emissions Control System (EVAP)

Refer to illustrations 13.2 and 13.14

General description

1   This system is designed to trap and store fuel vapors that evaporate from the fuel tank, throttle body and intake manifold.

2   The Evaporative Emission Control System (EVAP) consists of a charcoal-filled canister and the lines connecting the canister to the fuel tank, ported vacuum and intake manifold vacuum **(see illustration)**.

3   Fuel vapors are transferred from the fuel tank, throttle body and intake manifold to a canister where they are stored when the

13.2 Typical Evaporative Emission Control System

engine is not operating. When the engine is running, the fuel vapors are purged from the canister by a purge control solenoid and consumed in the normal combustion process.

Check

4   Poor idle, stalling and poor driveability can be caused by an inoperative purge control solenoid, a damaged canister, split or cracked hoses or hoses connected to the wrong tubes.
5   Evidence of fuel loss or fuel odor can be caused by fuel leaking from fuel lines or the TBI, a cracked or damaged canister, an inoperative bowl vent valve, an inoperative purge valve, disconnected, misrouted, kinked, deteriorated or damaged vapor or

control hoses or an improperly seated air cleaner or air cleaner gasket.
6   Inspect each hose attached to the canister for kinks, leaks and breaks along its entire length. Repair or replace as necessary.
7   Inspect the canister. If it is cracked or damaged, replace it.
8   Look for fuel leaking from the bottom of the canister. If fuel is leaking, replace the canister and check the hoses and hose routing.
9   Apply a short length of hose to the lower tube of the purge control valve and attempt to blow through it. Little or no air should pass into the canister (a small amount of air will pass because the canister has a constant purge hole).
10   With a hand-held vacuum pump, apply vacuum through the control vacuum signal tube near the throttle body to the EGR and canister control solenoid valve.
11   If the purge control solenoid does not hold vacuum for at least 20 seconds, the purge control solenoid is leaking and must be replaced.
12   If the diaphragm holds vacuum, apply battery voltage to the canister control solenoid and observe that vacuum (vapors) are allowed to pass through to the intake system.

Component replacement

13   Clearly label, then detach, all vacuum lines from the canister.

14   Loosen the canister mounting clamp bolt(s) (see illustration) and pull the canister out.
15   Installation is the reverse of removal.

14   Positive Crankcase Ventilation (PCV) system

Refer to illustration 14.1

1   The Positive Crankcase Ventilation (PCV) system reduces hydrocarbon emissions by scavenging crankcase vapors. It does this by circulating fresh air from the air cleaner through the crankcase, where it mixes with blow-by gases and is then rerouted through a PCV valve to the intake manifold (see illustration on following page).
2   The main components of the PCV system are the PCV valve, a fresh air filtered inlet and the vacuum hoses connecting these two components with the engine.
3   To maintain idle quality, the PCV valve restricts the flow when the intake manifold vacuum is high. If abnormal operating conditions arise, the system is designed to allow excessive amounts of blow-by gases to flow back through the crankcase vent tube into the air cleaner to be consumed by normal combustion.
4   Checking and replacement of the PCV valve and filter is covered in Chapter 1.

13.14 Typical charcoal canister mounting details - arrow indicates clamp bolt

6

Cruising

Acceleration or high load

P.C.V. valve

P.C.V. valve

| Engine not running or backfiring | Crusing |
| Idling or decelerating | Acceleration or high load |

⇨ : Fresh air
➡ : Blow-by gas

14.1 Gas flow in typical PCV system (MPFI engine shown)

15.1 Remove the heat shield mounting nuts (arrows) and lift the assembly to gain access to the catalytic converter

15   Catalytic converter

General description

Refer to illustration 15.1

1   The catalytic converter **(see illustration)** is an emission control device added to the exhaust system to reduce pollutants from the exhaust gas stream. A single-bed converter design is used in combination with a three-way (reduction) catalyst. The catalytic coating on the three-way catalyst contains platinum and rhodium, which lowers the levels of oxides of nitrogen (NOx) as well as hydrocarbons (HC) and carbon monoxide (CO).

Check

2   The test equipment for a catalytic converter is expensive and highly sophisticated. If you suspect that the converter on your vehicle is malfunctioning, take it to a dealer or authorized emissions inspection facility for diagnosis and repair.

3   Whenever the vehicle is raised for servicing of underbody components, check the converter for leaks, corrosion and other damage. If damage is discovered, the converter should be replaced.

Replacement

4   Because the converter part of the exhaust system, converter replacement requires removal of the exhaust pipe assembly (see Chapter 4A). Take the vehicle, or the exhaust system, to a dealer or a muffler shop.

Chapter 7 Part A
Manual transaxle

Contents

Specifications

Torque specifications

Ft-lbs (unless otherwise indicated)

Shift linkage
  1982 through 1986
    Rubber holder-to-body .... 78 to 104 in-lbs
    Control rod-to-transaxle .... 55 to 73 in-lbs
    Support rod-to-rear engine mounting .... 78 to 104 in-lbs
    Select stopper bolt .... 28 to 44 in-lbs
  1987 and later
    Control rod
      Control rod-to-transaxle bolt/nut .... 120 to 156 in-lbs
      Control rod-to-shift lever bolt/nut.......................... 156 to 204 in-lbs
    Support rod
      Support rod-to-support rod bracket nut .... 26 to 35
      Support rod-to-shift lever socket nuts .... 108 to 132 in-lbs
      Support rod-to-mass damper nut .... 192 to 264 in-lbs
    Holder bracket nuts .... 156 to 204 in-lbs
Engine-to-transaxle bolts
  1986 and earlier.. 12 to 16
  1987 and 1988 **(refer to illustration 6.24a)**
    Bolt No. 1 .... 12 to 16
    Bolt No. 2 .... 14 to 22
    Bolt No. 3 .... 12 to 16
    Bolt No. 4 .... 14 to 22
  1989 and 1990 **(refer to illustration 6.24b)**
    Bolt No. 1 .... 22 to 30
    Bolt No. 2 .... 22 to 30
    Bolt No. 3 .... 12 to 15
    Bolt No. 4 .... 12 to 15
  1991 and later
    GA engine **(refer to illustration 6.24c)**
      Bolt Nos. 1, 2 and 3.. 22 to 30
      Bolt No. 4 .... 12 to 15
    SR engine **(refer to illustration 6.24d)**
      Bolt Nos. 1 and 2 .... 51 to 59
      Bolt Nos. 3 and 4 .... 22 to 30

7A

2.4 Carefully pry out the driveaxle oil seal with a seal removal tool or a screwdriver; make sure you don't damage the seal bore or the new seal may leak

2.6 Use a seal installer, a large socket or a piece of pipe to install the new seal

2.9a To remove the speedometer pinion assembly on 1982 through 1993 models, disconnect the speedometer cable (arrow), remove the bolt (arrow) and remove the pinion gear from the transaxle

1   General information

The vehicles covered by this manual are equipped with either a 4-speed or a 5-speed manual transaxle, or a 3- or 4-speed automatic transaxle. Information on the manual transaxle is included in this Part of Chapter 7. Service procedures for the automatic transaxle are contained in Chapter 7, Part B.

The manual transaxle is a compact, two-piece, lightweight aluminum alloy housing containing both the transmission and differential assemblies.

Because of the complexity, difficulty in obtaining replacement parts and special tools necessary, internal repair procedures for the manual transaxle are beyond the scope of this manual. For readers who wish to tackle a transaxle rebuild, exploded views and a brief *Manual transaxle overhaul - general information* Section are provided. The bulk of information in this Chapter is devoted to removal and installation procedures.

2   Oil seal replacement

1   Oil leaks frequently occur due to wear of the driveaxle oil seals and/or the speedometer drive gear oil seal and O-rings. Replacement of these seals is relatively easy, since the repairs can usually be performed without removing the transaxle from the vehicle.

Driveaxle oil seals

Refer to illustrations 2.4 and 2.6

2   The driveaxle oil seals are located on the sides of the transaxle, where the inner ends of the driveaxles are splined into the differential side gears. If you suspect that a driveaxle oil seal is leaking, raise the vehicle and support it securely on jackstands. If the seal is leaking, you'll see lubricant on the side of the transaxle, below the seal.
3   Remove the driveaxle(s) (see Chapter 8).
4   Using a screwdriver or pry bar, carefully pry the oil seal out of the transaxle bore **(see illustration)**.
5   If the oil seal cannot be removed with a screwdriver or pry bar, a special oil seal removal tool (available at auto parts stores) will be required.
6   Using a large section of pipe or a large deep socket as a drift, install the new oil seal. Drive it into the bore squarely and make sure that it is completely seated **(see illustration)**. Lubricate the lip of the new seal with multi-purpose grease.
7   Install the driveaxle(s). Be careful not to damage the lip of the new seal.

Speedometer pinion/vehicle speed sensor O-ring

Refer to illustrations 2.9a, 2.9b and 2.10
8   The speedometer pinion assembly (1982 through 1993 models), or vehicle speed sensor (1994 models), is located on the transaxle housing. Look for lubricant around the housing to determine if the O-ring is leaking.
9   Disconnect the speedometer cable, or (on 1994 models) disconnect the electrical connector, remove the hold-down bolt **(see illustrations)** and remove the pinion assembly or vehicle speed sensor from the transaxle.
10   Using a scribe or a small screwdriver, remove the O-ring seal **(see illustration)**.
11   Install a new O-ring on the driven gear housing.
12   Installation is the reverse of removal.

3   Transaxle mount - check and replacement

Refer to illustration 3.2
1   Raise the vehicle and place it securely on jackstands.
2   Insert a large screwdriver or prybar between the mount and the bracket and pry up **(see illustration)**.

2.9b To remove the vehicle speed sensor on 1994 models, disconnect the electrical connector, remove the hold-down bolt (arrow) and remove the sensor from the transaxle

2.10 Remove the oil seal O-ring from the speedometer pinion gear assembly with a small hook tool or a small screwdriver; make sure you don't gouge the groove

3.2 To check a transaxle mount, place a large screwdriver or prybar between the mount and the bracket and try to lever the transaxle up and down; if it moves excessively, replace the mount

4.1 If the shift lever knob is difficult to loosen, break it loose with a pair of adjustable pliers, but be sure to protect the knob with a clean shop rag

3   The transaxle should not move excessively away from the mount. If it does, replace the mount.
4   To replace a mount, support the transaxle with a jack, remove the nuts and bolts and remove the mount. It may be necessary to raise the transaxle slightly to provide enough clearance to remove the mount.
5   Installation is the reverse of removal.

4   Shift linkage - removal and installation

1982 through 1986 models

Refer to illustrations 4.1, 4.3a, 4.3b, 4.4, 4.9, 4.10, 4.11 and 4.13

1   Remove the shift lever knob. If the knob is difficult to loosen, break it loose with a pair of adjustable pliers, but be sure to protect the knob with a clean shop rag (see illustration).
2   Raise the vehicle and place it securely on jackstands.
3   Remove the nuts and bolts and separate the control and support rods from the transaxle (see illustrations).
4   Remove the control rod bracket fasteners (see illustration) and remove the shift linkage assembly.
5   Remove the shift lever bracket, the bearing set spring ring, seat and spring (see illustration 4.3a).

4.3a An exploded view of a typical shift linkage assembly for 1982 through 1986 vehicles

4.3b To disconnect the control and support rods from the transaxle, remove these fasteners (arrows)

4.4 To remove the shift linkage assembly from a 1982 through 1986 vehicle, remove the control bracket retaining nuts (arrows)

6   Remove the flexible mountings, the dust cover and the shift lever bearing (see illustration 4.3a).
7   Drive out the old control rod rubber bushings with a bolt, nut, washers and a spacer. Drive in the new bushings with the same setup. Coat the new bushings with silicone grease before installing them.
8   Reassembly is the reverse of removal.

Be sure to apply silicone grease to the pivot and friction surfaces.
9   Always use a new cotter pin at the end of the control rod and make sure that its ends are bent round as shown (see illustration).
10   Adjust the clearance between the support rod and the flexible mounting backplate (see illustration).
11   Fit the dust cover securely (see illustration).

7A

4.9 Always use a new cotter pin at the end of the control rod and make sure that its ends are bent round as shown

4.10 Adjust the clearance between the support rod and the flexible mounting backplate to the specified dimension

Standard clearance 2 mm (0.08 in)

4.11 Make sure the shift lever dust cover is seated properly

4.13 Loosen these three stopper plate bolts (arrows) before adjusting the shift lever

12 The remainder of installation is the reverse of removal. Adjust the shift lever as follows:

13 Loosen, but do not remove, the select stopper plate bolts **(see illustration)**.

14 Move the shift lever to the first-gear position.

15 Move the stopper plate until a 0.039-inch gap is visible between the stopper plate and the shift lever.

16 Tighten the stopper bolts to the torque listed in this Chapter's Specifications. Verify that the shift lever and linkage operate properly in all gears.

17 Remove the jackstands and lower the vehicle.

1987 and later models

Refer to illustrations 4.20a, 4.20b, 4.21a, 4.21b, 4.21c and 4.22

18 Remove the shift lever knob. If the knob is difficult to loosen, break it loose with a pair of adjustable pliers, but be sure to protect the knob with a clean shop rag. Remove the dust boot.

19 Raise the vehicle and place it securely on jackstands.

20 Disconnect the support and control rod from the transaxle **(see illustrations)**.

21 Remove the nut and bolt that attach the control rod to the shift lever **(see illustration)**. Disconnect the return spring, remove the nuts that attach the support rod to the shift lever socket and mass damper **(see illustrations)** and remove the shift

1 Shift lever knob
2 Boot
3 Shift lever socket
4 Shift lever
5 Insulator
6 Seat
7 Bushing
8 O-ring
9 Dust boot
10 Base plate
11 Dust cover
12 Support rod
13 Washer
14 Collar
15 Bushing
16 Support rod bracket
17 Collar
18 Bushing
19 Control rod
20 Return spring
21 Return spring rubber
22 Holder bracket
23 Mass damper

4.20a An exploded view of a typical shift linkage assembly for 1987 and later vehicles

4.20b To disconnect the control and support rods from the transaxle, remove these fasteners (arrows)

4.21a To disconnect the control rod from the shift lever, remove this nut (arrow) and bolt

4.21b To disconnect the support rod from the shift lever socket, remove the nuts

4.21c To disconnect the support rod from the mass damper, remove this nut (center arrow); to replace the rubber mount, remove the two outer nuts (arrows)

4.22 To replace the large shift lever dust boot, remove the two front nuts (upper arrows) and the two rear nuts from below (not visible in this photo)

5.1 The back-up light switch (arrow) is located on the lower left side of the transaxle

linkage assembly. Inspect the condition of all the bushings at both ends of the support and control rods. If they're cracked or worn, replace them. Inspect the return spring rubber; replace it if it's cracked or torn. Also inspect the condition of the rubber insulator portion of the mass damper holder bracket. If the rubber is cracked or torn, replace the holder bracket.

22 Pull out the shift lever and slide off the dust boot, seat, insulator and shift lever socket. Inspect these parts for cracks and tears. Replace as necessary. The condition of the shift lever socket and the seat are especially important; if either of these parts is damaged, shifting will be difficult. Also inspect the condition of the large rubber shift lever boot (see illustration). If it's damaged, replace it.

23 Installation is the reverse of removal. Make sure you lubricate all friction surfaces - the spherical bearing surface of the shift lever, the inside of the shift lever socket and the inside of the seat - with silicone grease. Also be sure to lubricate all support and control rod bushings and collars with silicone

5.3 To check the back-up light switch, disconnect the connector, probe the terminals with an ohmmeter and verify that there's continuity when the transaxle is in Reverse, but no continuity in any other gear (the neutral switch, on the other side of the transaxle, is checked the same way, except that continuity should exist only in Neutral)

grease. Finally, make sure you tighten all fasteners to the torque listed in this Chapter's Specifications.

5 Back-up light and neutral switches - check and replacement

Check
Back-up light switch
Refer to illustrations 5.1 and 5.3
1 Raise the vehicle and place it securely on jackstands. The back-up light switch is located on the lower left side of the transaxle (see illustration).
2 Disconnect the switch electrical connector.
3 Place the transaxle into Reverse and verify that there's continuity between the two connector terminals (see illustration).
4 Verify that there's no continuity between the two terminals in any other gear.
5 If continuity isn't as specified, replace the back-up light switch (see below).

Neutral switch
Refer to illustration 5.6
6 Raise the vehicle and place it securely on jackstands. The neutral switch is located on the lower right side of the transaxle (see illustration).

5.6 The neutral switch (arrow) is located on the lower right side of the transaxle

7 Disconnect the switch electrical connector.
8 Put the transaxle into Neutral and verify that there's continuity between the two connector terminals (see illustration 5.3).
9 Verify that there's no continuity between the two terminals in any other gear.
10 If continuity isn't as specified, replace the neutral switch (see below).

Replacement
11 Disconnect the switch electrical connector.
12 Unthread the switch.
13 Install in the new switch and tighten it securely.
14 Connect the electrical connector.
15 Check the switch as described above to ensure it's working properly.
16 Remove the jackstands and lower the vehicle.

6 Transaxle - removal and installation

Removal
Refer to illustrations 6.7 and 6.14
1 Disconnect the negative cable from the battery. On 1987 through 1990 vehicles, remove the battery (see Chapter 5).
2 On 1991 and later vehicles, remove the air intake duct (see Chapter 4).
3 Disconnect the clutch cable (see Chapter 8).
4 On 1982 through 1993 vehicles, disconnect the speedometer cable from the pinion assembly. On 1994 vehicles, disconnect the electrical connector for the vehicle speed sensor (see illustrations 2.9a and 2.9b).
5 Disconnect the electrical connectors for the back-up light and the neutral switches (see Section 5). Disconnect all ground wires.
6 If the starter motor and solenoid are easier to remove from above, remove them now (see Chapter 5).

7A

6.7 Typical upper transaxle-to-engine bolts (arrows) (1991 and later GA engine shown, others similar)

6.14 To detach the lower part of the clutch cover from the transaxle bellhousing, remove the bolts (arrows) from the engine-to-transaxle braces

19   Make a final check that all wires and hoses have been disconnected from the transaxle.

20   Lower the left (driver's) end of the engine, then roll the transaxle and jack toward the side of the vehicle. Once the input shaft is clear of the splines in the clutch hub, lower the transaxle and remove it from under the vehicle. Try to keep the transaxle as level as possible.

21   The clutch components can now be inspected (see Chapter 8). In most cases, new clutch components should be routinely installed whenever the transaxle is removed.

Installation

Refer to illustrations 6.24a, 6.24b, 6.24c and 6.24d

22   If removed, install the clutch components (see Chapter 8).

23   With the transaxle secured to the jack as on removal, raise it into position and then carefully slide it forward, engaging the input shaft with the splines in the clutch hub. Do not use excessive force to install the transaxle - if the input shaft does not slide into place, readjust the angle of the transaxle so it is level and/or turn the input shaft so the splines engage properly with the clutch.

24   Install the transaxle-to-engine bolts **(see illustrations)**. Tighten all engine-to-transaxle bolts to the torque listed in this Chapter's Specifications.

25   Install the transaxle mount nuts and bolts. Tighten all nuts and bolts securely.

26   Remove the jacks supporting the transaxle and the engine.

27   Install the various items removed previously. Refer to Chapter 8 for the installation of the driveaxles and Chapter 4 for information regarding the exhaust system components.

28   Make a final check that all wires, hoses and the speedometer cable have been connected and that the transaxle has been filled with the specified lubricant to the proper level (see Chapter 1). Lower the vehicle.

29   Connect the negative battery cable. Road test the vehicle to check for proper transaxle operation and check for leakage.

7   Remove the upper transaxle-to-engine bolts **(see illustration)**.

8   Loosen the wheel lug nuts. Raise the vehicle and support it securely on jackstands. Remove the wheels.

9   On 1991 and later vehicles, remove the section of exhaust pipe underneath the engine/transaxle (see Chapter 4).

10   Drain the transaxle fluid (see Chapter 1).

11   Disconnect the shift support and shift control rods from the transaxle (see Section 4).

12   Remove the driveaxles (see Chapter 8).

13   Remove the starter motor, if you haven't already done so (see Chapter 5).

14   Remove the bolts from the engine-to-transaxle braces **(see illustration)**.

15   Support the engine. This can be done from above by using an engine hoist, or by placing a jack (with a block of wood as an insulator) under the engine oil pan. The engine should remain supported at all times while the transaxle is out of the vehicle.

16   Support the transaxle with a jack (preferably a special jack made for this purpose). If you're using a floor jack, be sure to place a wood block between the lifting pad and the transaxle to protect the cast aluminum housing. Safety chains will help steady the transaxle on the jack.

17   Raise the engine and transaxle slightly and disconnect the transaxle mounts.

18   Remove the remainder of the bolts securing the transaxle to the engine.

6.24a Transaxle-to-engine bolts (1987 and 1988 vehicles)

6.24b Transaxle-to-engine bolts (1989 and 1990 vehicles)

6.24c Transaxle-to-engine bolts (1991 and later vehicles with GA engine)

6.24d Transaxle-to-engine bolts (1991 and later vehicles with SR engine)

7   Transaxle overhaul - general information

Refer to illustrations 7.4a, 7.4b and 7.4c

1   Overhauling a manual transaxle is a difficult job for the do-it-yourselfer. It involves the disassembly and reassembly of many small parts. Numerous clearances must be precisely measured and, if necessary, changed with select fit spacers and snaprings. As a result, if transaxle problems arise, it can be removed and installed by a competent do-it-yourselfer, but overhaul should be left to a transmission repair shop. Rebuilt transaxles may be available - check with your dealer parts department and auto parts stores. At any rate, the time and money

involved in an overhaul is almost sure to exceed the cost of a rebuilt unit.

2   Nevertheless, it's not impossible for an inexperienced mechanic to rebuild a transaxle if the special tools are available and the job is done in a deliberate step-by-step manner so nothing is overlooked.

3   The tools necessary for an overhaul include internal and external snap-ring pliers, a bearing puller, a slide hammer, a set of pin punches, a dial indicator and possibly a hydraulic press. In addition, a large, sturdy workbench and a vise or transaxle stand will be required.

4   During disassembly of the transaxle, make careful notes of how each piece comes off, where it fits in relation to other pieces and what holds it in place. Exploded views are included **(see illustrations)** to show where the parts go - but actually noting how they are installed when you remove the parts will make it much easier to get the transaxle back together.

5   Before taking the transaxle apart for repair, it will help if you have some idea what area of the transaxle is malfunctioning. Certain problems can be closely tied to specific areas in the transaxle, which can make component examination and replacement easier. Refer to the *Troubleshooting* section at the front of this manual for information regarding possible sources of trouble.

7.4a An exploded view of the transaxle case components (typical)

7A

7.4b An exploded view of the transaxle gear components (typical)

7.4c An exploded view of the shift control components (typical)

Chapter 7 Part B
Automatic transaxle

Contents

Specifications

Throttle valve dimension "L"
1992 and earlier... 1-5/64 to 1-15/64 inches
1993 and later .... 1-37/64 to 1-21/32 inches

Torque specifications   **Ft-lbs** (unless otherwise indicated)

Driveplate-to-torque converter bolts
  1986 and earlier .... 36 to 51
  1987 through 1990 .... 29 to 36
  1991 through 1994
    RL3F01A .... 29 to 36
    RL4F03A and RE4F03V
      Bolt with flange .... 33 to 43
      Bolt without flange .... 29 to 36
Transaxle-to-engine bolts
  1982 through 1984
    8-mm bolts .... 144 to 192 in-lbs
    10-mm bolts .... 29 to 36
  1985 through 1988 .... 144 to 192 in-lbs
  1989 and 1990 .... 22 to 30
  1991 through 1994
    RL3F01A and RL4F03A
      Bolts No. 1 and 2 .... 22 to 30
      Bolt No. 3 .... 144 to 180 in-lbs]
      Front gusset-to-engine bolts .... 22 to 30
      Rear gusset-to-engine bolts .... 144 to 180 in-lbs
    RL4F03V and RE4F03V
      Bolts No. 1, 2 and 3 .... 51 to 59
      Bolts No. 4 and 5 .... 144 to 180 in-lbs

1   General information

All models covered by this manual are equipped with either a 4- or 5-speed manual transaxle or a 3- or 4-speed automatic transaxle. All information on the automatic transaxle is included in this Part of Chapter 7. Information for the manual transaxle can be found in Part A of this Chapter.

Because of the complexity of the automatic transaxles and the specialized equipment necessary to perform most service operations, this Chapter contains only those procedures related to general diagnosis, routine maintenance, adjustment and removal and installation.

If the transaxle requires major repair work, it should be left to a dealer service department or an automotive or transmission repair shop. You can, however, remove and install the transaxle yourself and save the expense, even if the repair work is done by a transmission shop.

The various model automatic transaxles used are as follows:

1990 and earlier	RL3F01A	3-speed
1991 and 1992 with GA16DE engine:		
DX model	RL3F01A	3-speed
All except DX	RL4F03V	4-speed
1991 and 1992 with SR20DE engine	RL4F03V	4-speed
1993 and 1994 with GA16DE engine	RL4F03A	4-speed
1993 and later with SR20DE engine	RE4F03V	4-speed

2   Diagnosis - general

Note: *Automatic transaxle malfunctions may be caused by five general conditions: poor engine performance, improper adjustments, hydraulic malfunctions, mechanical malfunctions or malfunctions in the computer or its signal network. Diagnosis of these problems should always begin with a check of the easily repaired items: fluid level and condition (see Chapter 1), shift linkage adjustment and throttle linkage adjustment. Next, perform a road test to determine if the problem has been corrected or if more diagnosis is necessary. If the problem persists after the preliminary tests and corrections are completed, additional diagnosis should be done by a dealer service department or transmission repair shop. Refer to the Troubleshooting section at the front of this manual for information on symptoms of transaxle problems.*

Preliminary checks

1   Drive the vehicle to warm the transaxle to normal operating temperature.
2   Check the fluid level as described in Chapter 1:

a) If the fluid level is unusually low, add enough fluid to bring the level within the designated area of the dipstick, then check for external leaks (see below).
b) If the fluid level is abnormally high, drain off the excess, then check the drained fluid for contamination by coolant. The presence of engine coolant in the automatic transmission fluid indicates that a failure has occurred in the internal radiator walls that separate the coolant from the transmission fluid (see Chapter 3).
c) If the fluid is foaming, drain it and refill the transaxle, then check for coolant in the fluid, or a high fluid level.

3   Check the engine idle speed. **Note:** *If the engine is malfunctioning, do not proceed with the preliminary checks until it has been repaired and runs normally.*
4   Check the throttle valve cable for freedom of movement. Adjust it if necessary (see Section 3). **Note:** *The throttle cable may function properly when the engine is shut off and cold, but it may malfunction once the engine is hot. Check it cold and at normal engine operating temperature.*
5   Inspect the shift cable (see Section 4). Make sure that it's properly adjusted and operates smoothly.

Fluid leak diagnosis

6   Most fluid leaks are easy to locate visually. Repair usually consists of replacing a seal or gasket. If a leak is difficult to find, the following procedure may help.
7   Identify the fluid. Make sure it's transmission fluid and not engine oil or brake fluid (automatic transmission fluid is a deep red color).
8   Try to pinpoint the source of the leak. Drive the vehicle several miles, then park it over a large sheet of cardboard. After a minute or two, you should be able to locate the leak by determining the source of the fluid dripping onto the cardboard.
9   Make a careful visual inspection of the suspected component and the area immediately around it. Pay particular attention to gasket mating surfaces. A mirror is often helpful for finding leaks in areas that are hard to see.
10   If the leak still cannot be found, clean the suspected area thoroughly with a degreaser or solvent, then dry it.
11   Drive the vehicle for several miles at normal operating temperature and varying speeds. After driving the vehicle, visually inspect the suspected component again.
12   Once the leak has been located, the cause must be determined before it can be properly repaired. If a gasket is replaced but the sealing flange is bent, the new gasket will not stop the leak. The bent flange must be straightened.
13   Before attempting to repair a leak, check to make sure that the following conditions are corrected or they may cause another leak. **Note:** *Some of the following*

conditions cannot be fixed without highly specialized tools and expertise. Such problems must be referred to a transmission shop or a dealer service department.

Gasket leaks

14   Check the pan periodically. Make sure the bolts are tight, no bolts are missing, the gasket is in good condition and the pan is flat (dents in the pan may indicate damage to the valve body inside).
15   If the pan gasket is leaking, the fluid level or the fluid pressure may be too high, the vent may be plugged, the pan bolts may be too tight, the pan sealing flange may be warped, the sealing surface of the transaxle housing may be damaged, the gasket may be damaged or the transaxle casting may be cracked or porous. If sealant instead of gasket material has been used to form a seal between the pan and the transaxle housing, it may be the wrong sealant.

Seal leaks

16   If a transaxle seal is leaking, the fluid level or pressure may be too high, the vent may be plugged, the seal bore may be damaged, the seal itself may be damaged or improperly installed, the surface of the shaft protruding through the seal may be damaged or a loose bearing may be causing excessive shaft movement.
17   Make sure the dipstick tube seal is in good condition and the tube is properly seated. Periodically check the area around the speedometer gear or sensor for leakage. If transmission fluid is evident, check the O-ring for damage.

Case leaks

18   If the case itself appears to be leaking, the casting is porous and will have to be repaired or replaced.
19   Make sure the oil cooler hose fittings are tight and in good condition.

Fluid comes out vent pipe or fill tube

20   If this condition occurs, the transaxle is overfilled, there is coolant in the fluid, the case is porous, the dipstick is incorrect, the vent is plugged or the drain-back holes are plugged.

3   Throttle valve (TV) cable - adjustment

1   If the throttle valve cable is adjusted too tightly, the transaxle will downshift too soon; If It's adjusted too loosely, the transaxle will downshift too late, or not at all. If you are experiencing either of these symptoms, adjust the throttle valve cable as follows.

1985 through 1990 models

Refer to illustrations 3.3, 3.4 and 3.6
2   Remove the air cleaner assembly (see Chapter 4).

3.3 Loosen the throttle valve cable double nuts "A" and "B" at the bracket adjacent to the throttle linkage on the carburetor or throttle body

3.4 Adjustment details for pre-1991 models

3.6 Stroke "L" for pre-1991 models

3.8 Throttle valve cable adjustment details for 1991 and later models

3   Loosen the throttle valve cable double nuts at the bracket adjacent to the carburetor throttle linkage **(see illustration)**.
4   Move the throttle drum to the fully-open position ("P1"), then move fitting "Q" in direction "T" and tighten nut "B" by hand until it contacts bracket "S" **(see illustration).**

5   Back off nut "B" 1 to 1-1/2 turns in direction "T," then tighten nut "A" securely while holding the throttle drum at "P1."
6   Make sure that the throttle valve cable stroke "L" **(see illustration)** is within the range listed in this Chapter's Specifications.
7   Tighten the double nuts securely.

1991 and later models

Refer to illustration 3.8

8   While pressing the lock plate, move the adjusting tube in direction "T" **(see illustration).**
9   Return the lock plate (the adjusting tube is locked at this time).
10 Quickly move the throttle drum from "P2" to "P1" (the adjusting tube moves in direction "U" - toward the engine - while depressing the lock plate). Make sure that the throttle cable stroke "L" is within the range listed in this Chapter's Specifications, between full throttle and idle.

4   Shift cable - check, adjustment and replacement

Check

1   Move the shift lever from the "P" position to the "1" position. You should be able to feel the detents in each range. If you can't feel the detents, or if the pointer

indicating the ranges is incorrectly aligned, adjust the shift cable.

Adjustment

1985 through 1990 models

Refer to illustrations 4.6, 4.7, 4.9 and 4.10

2   Raise the vehicle and place it securely on jackstands.
3   Place the shift lever in the "P" position. Move the shift lever from "P" to "1" and verify that it moves smoothly and without any sliding noise.
4   Place the shift lever in the "P" position again.
5   Make sure that the shift lever locks at the "P" range.
6   On 1985 and 1986 models, loosen shift cable adjusting nut "A" and trunnion nut "B" **(see illustration)**. Allow the shift cable to assume its natural position in relation to the trunnion, then tighten both nuts "A" and "B."
7   On 1987 through 1990 models, loosen locknuts "X" and "Y" **(see illustration)**. Screw locknut "X" until it touches the select rod end while holding the select rod horizontal, and tighten locknut "Y."
8   Move the shift lever from the "P position to the "1" position again and make sure that it moves smoothly and without any sliding noise.
9   On 1985 and 1986 models, apply silicone grease to the spring washer **(see illustration)**. On 1987 through 1990 models,

7B

4.6 On 1985 and 1986 models, loosen shift cable adjusting nut "A" and trunnion nut "B," then allow the shift cable to assume its natural position in relation to the trunnion, then tighten both nuts "A" and "B"

4.7 On 1987 through 1990 models, loosen locknuts "X" and "Y," screw locknut "X" until it touches the select rod end while holding the select rod horizontal, and tighten locknut "Y"

4.9 On 1985 and 1986 models, apply silicone grease to the spring washer

4.10 On 1985 and 1986 models, after adjusting the shift cable, check the spring pins at both ends of the cable and make sure they're aligned as shown; if not, reposition them as shown

apply grease to the contact areas of the shift lever and the select rod.

10　On 1985 and 1986 models, after adjusting the shift cable, check the spring pins at both ends of the cable and make sure they're aligned as shown **(see illustration)**. If not, reposition them as shown.

1991 and later models

Refer to illustrations 4.13a and 4.13b

11　Place the shift lever in the "P" position.
12　Loosen the shift cable locknut and place the manual lever in the "P" position.
13　Adjust the cable by pulling it in the direction of the arrow as shown **(see illustrations)**.
14　Return the cable in the opposite direction of the arrow 1/32-inch to 3/64-inch.
15　Tighten the shift cable locknut.
16　Move the shift lever from the "P" position to the "1" position and make sure that the shift lever moves smoothly and without any sliding noise.
17　Apply silicone grease to the contact areas of the shift lever and the shift cable.

Replacement

Refer to illustrations 4.18 and 4.19

18　At the transaxle end, loosen the locknut and disconnect the cable from the manual lever and disconnect the cable bracket from the transaxle **(see illustration)**.

4.18　To disconnect the shift cable from the manual lever, remove this nut (right arrow); to disconnect the cable from the transaxle, remove these two bracket bolts (arrows)

4.13a　Shift cable adjustment details (1991 and 1992 models)

19　Disconnect the cable housing from the underside of the body **(see illustration)**.
20　Remove the console (see Chapter 11).
21　Disconnect the cable from the shift lever.
22　Installation is the reverse of removal.
23　Be sure to adjust the cable when you're done.

5　Neutral start/back-up light switch - check, adjustment and replacement

Check

Refer to illustration 5.2

1　If the engine will start with the shift lever in any position other than Park or Neutral, check and adjust the neutral start switch.

1985 through 1992 models

2　Disconnect the switch electrical connector and check continuity as follows **(see illustration)**:

4.19　To disconnect the cable housing from the underside of the vehicle, remove these two bolts (arrows)

4.13b　Shift cable adjustment details (1993 and 1994 models)

a)　*With the shift lever in Neutral or Park, there should be continuity between terminals 1 and 2.*
b)　*With the shift lever in Reverse, there should be continuity between terminals 3 and 4.*

3　With the shift lever in Neutral, turn the manual lever an equal amount in both directions and verify whether the current flow ranges are about the same. Normally, current should begin to flow (continuity) before the manual lever reaches an angle of 1.5 degrees in either direction. If current flows outside the normal range, or if the normal flow range is out of specification, adjust the switch.

1993 and 1994 models

Refer to illustration 5.4

4　Disconnect the switch electrical connector and check continuity between terminals 1 and 2, and between terminals 3 and 4, 5, 6, 7, 8 and 9 while moving the shift lever through each range. Compare your results to the accompanying table **(see illustration)**. If the switch fails any of these continuity

Terminal No. Range	①	②	③	④
P, N	○——	——○		
R			○——	——○

5.2　Neutral start/back-up light switch continuity table and terminal guide

Lever position	Terminal No.								
	①	②	③	④	⑤	⑥	⑦	⑧	⑨
P	O—O		O—O						
R			O—		—O				
N	O—O				—O				
D			O—				—O		
2			O—					—O	
1			O—						—O

5.4 Neutral start/back-up light switch continuity table and terminal guide (1993 and 1994 models)

checks, disconnect the shift cable from the manual lever and retest the switch.

a) *If the switch passes all the continuity checks this time, reconnect the shift cable and adjust it, then retest the switch.*
b) *If the switch still fails any of the continuity tests, remove it from the transaxle and try testing it again on the bench.*

5.5 Aligning the manual lever and neutral start/back-up light switch

c) *If the switch passes all the continuity tests on the bench, install it and adjust it (see below.*
d) *If the switch still fails any of the continuity tests, replace it (see below).*

Adjustment

Refer to illustration 5.5

5   Disconnect the shift cable from the manual lever, loosen the switch retaining screws, set the manual lever at the Neutral position and insert a 0.098-inch diameter pin or drill bit (0.157-inch pin on 1993 and 1994 models) into the adjustment holes in both the switch and the lever **(see illustration)**. Make sure the pin is perpendicular to the switch and the lever. Tighten the screws securely.

6   Recheck the switch continuity as described in Steps 2 or 4. If switch continuity is not as specified, replace the switch.

Replacement

Refer to illustration 5.9

7   Disconnect the negative cable from the battery.

8   Shift the transaxle into Neutral.

5.9 To remove the neutral start/back-up light switch, remove the nut that attaches the manual lever to the switch (arrow), then remove the switch retaining screws (arrows)

9   Remove the nut and lift off the manual lever **(see illustration)**.

10   Disconnect the electrical connector.

11   Remove the switch retaining screws and lift the switch off the manual lever shaft.

12   Installation is the reverse of removal. Don't tighten the retaining screws until you have adjusted the switch as described in Step 5.

6   Shift lock system - description, check and component replacement

Description

1   The shift lock system, which is used on 1992 and later models, prevents the shift lever from being shifted out of Park or Neutral until the brake pedal is applied. On 1991 and 1992 models, the system components include a shift lock control unit, a shift lock solenoid, a shift detention switch, a key detention switch, a key interlock solenoid, a key switch and a brake light switch. On 1993 and 1994 models, a somewhat simplified system consists of a shift lock control unit, a shift lock solenoid, a detention switch and a brake light switch. Other than the following simple component checks, diagnosis of the shift lock system should be left to a dealer service department.

Check

Shift lock solenoid

Refer to illustrations 6.3a and 6.3b

2   Remove the floor console (see Chapter 11).

3   Disconnect the shift lock solenoid connector. On 1991 and 1992 models, apply battery voltage to terminals 1 and 9 **(see illustration)** and verify that there's an audible "click" from the solenoid. On 1993 and 1994 models, apply battery voltage to terminals 8 and 9 **(see illustration)** and verify that there's an audible "click" from the solenoid.

4   If the shift lock solenoid doesn't click when energized by the battery, replace it.

6.3a To test the shift lock solenoid on 1991 and 1992 models, apply battery voltage to terminals 1 and 9 and verify that there's an audible "click" from the solenoid

6.3b To test the shift lock solenoid on 1993 and 1994 models, apply battery voltage to terminals 8 and 9 and verify that there's an audible "click" from the solenoid

7B

6.5 1991 and 1992 model shift detention switch terminal guide

6.6 1991 and 1992 model key detention switch terminal guide

6.7 1993 and 1994 model detention switch terminal guide

6.8 1991 and 1992 model key lock solenoid terminal guide

6.10 1991 and 1992 model key switch terminal guide

6.11 Brake light switch terminal guide

Detention switch

Refer to illustrations 6.5, 6.6 and 6.7

5   To test the shift detention switch on 1991 and 1992 models, check continuity between terminals 5 and 11 of the shift lock electrical connector **(see illustration)** while moving the shift lever through the following positions:

a) *When the shift lever is in the Park position with the shift lever button depressed, or when the shift lever is in any position except Park, there should be continuity.*

b) *When the shift lever is in the Park position without the shift lever button depressed, there should be no continuity.*

6   To test the key detention switch on 1991 and 1992 models, check continuity between terminals 11 and 12 of the shift lock electrical connector **(see illustration)** while moving the shift lever through the following positions:

a) *When the shift lever is in the Park position with the shift lever button depressed, or when the shift lever is in any position except Park, there should be continuity.*

b) *When the shift lever is in the Park position without the shift lever button depressed, there should be no continuity.*

7   To test the detention switch on 1993 and 1994 models, check continuity between terminals 5 and 6 of the shift lock electrical connector **(see illustration)** while moving the shift lever through the following positions:

a) *When the shift lever is in the Park position with the shift lever button is released, there should be no continuity.*

b) *When the shift lever is in any position except the above, there should be continuity.*

Key interlock solenoid (1991 and 1992 models only)

Refer to illustration 6.8

8   To check the operation of the locking mechanism, apply battery voltage to terminals 10 and 8 of the key lock solenoid electrical connector **(see illustration)**. It should emit an audible "clicking" sound.

9   To check the operation of the unlocking mechanism, apply battery voltage to terminals 10 and 8 of the key lock solenoid electrical connector. It should emit an audible "clicking" sound.

Key switch (1991 and 1992 models only)

Refer to illustration 6.10

10   Check continuity between terminals 4 and 11 of the key switch electrical connector **(see illustration)**. When the key is inserted into the key lock cylinder, there should be continuity; when the key is removed from the key lock cylinder, there should be no continuity.

Brake light switch

Refer to illustration 6.11

11   To test the brake light switch, check continuity between terminals 1 and 2 of the brake light switch electrical connector **(see illustration)**. When the brake pedal is depressed, there should be continuity; when the brake pedal is released, there should be no continuity.

Component replacement

Shift lock solenoid/detention switch

Refer to illustrations 6.12 and 6.15

12   Remove the shift lever knob **(see illustration)**.

13   Remove the center console (see Chapter 11).

14   Remove the position indicator.

15   Disconnect the electrical connector for

6.12 **Details of the shift lock assembly (1991 and 1992 models)**

7B

6.15 Shift lock solenoid and detention switch installation details (1993 and 1994 models)

the shift lock solenoid or detention switch **(see illustration)**.

16 Remove the shift lock solenoid or detention switch.

17 Installation is the reverse of removal.

Key interlock solenoid/key switch

18 Refer to Chapter 12.

Brake light switch

19 Refer to Chapter 9.

7   Automatic transaxle - removal and installation

Removal

1 Detach the cable from the negative battery terminal.

2 Disconnect the neutral start/back-up light switch electrical connector (see Section 5).

3 Disconnect the speedometer cable or disconnect the vehicle speed sensor electrical connector.

4 Disconnect the throttle valve cable from the carburetor or throttle body.

5 Remove the starter (see Chapter 5).

6 Remove the upper transaxle-to-engine bolts.

7 Loosen the wheel lug nuts. Raise the vehicle and support it securely on jackstands. Remove the wheels.

8 Drain the transaxle/differential fluid (see Chapter 1).

9 Disconnect the oil cooler hoses. Plug the hoses to keep out dirt and moisture.

10 Remove the dipstick tube.

11 Disconnect the shift cable from the transaxle (see Section 4).

12 Remove the driveaxles (see Chapter 8).

13 Remove the torque converter cover.

14 Mark the relationship of the torque converter to the driveplate so they can be installed in the same position.

15 Remove the torque converter mounting bolts. Turn the crankshaft for access to each one in turn.

16 Support the engine using a hoist from above, or a jack and a wood block under the oil pan to spread the load.

17 Support the transaxle with a jack - preferably a special jack made for this purpose. Safety chains will help steady the transaxle on the jack.

18 Remove the mounting bolts from the transaxle mounting brackets.

19 Remove the lower engine-to-transaxle bolts.

20 Lower the transaxle slightly and disconnect and plug the transaxle cooler lines.

21 Move the transaxle to the side to disengage it from the engine block dowel pins and make sure the torque converter is detached from the driveplate. Secure the torque converter to the transaxle so that it will not fall out during removal. Lower the transaxle from the vehicle.

Installation

Refer to illustrations 7.26a, 7.26b and 7.26c

22 Make sure that the torque converter is securely engaged in the transaxle prior to installation.

23 With the transaxle secured to the jack, raise it into position. Be sure to keep it level so the torque converter does not slide forward. Connect the cooler lines.

24 Move the transaxle carefully into place until the dowel pins are engaged and the torque converter is engaged.

25 Turn the torque converter to line up the bolt holes with the holes in the driveplate. The match marks on the torque converter and driveplate, made during step 14, must line up.

26 Install the transaxle-to-engine bolts and nuts **(see illustrations)**. Tighten them to the torque listed in this Chapter's Specifications.

27 Install the torque converter-to-driveplate bolts. Tighten them to the torque listed in this Chapter's Specifications.

28 Install the transaxle/engine mounting bracket bolts and nuts. Tighten them securely.

29 Remove the jacks supporting the transaxle and the engine.

30 Install the dipstick tube.

31 Install the starter.

32 Connect the shift cable and throttle valve cable.

33 Plug in the electrical connectors for the neutral start/back-up light switch and, if equipped, the vehicle speed sensor.

34 Install the torque converter cover.

35 Connect the driveaxles to the transaxle (see Chapter 8).

36 Connect the speedometer cable, if equipped.

37 Adjust the throttle valve cable (see Section 3) and shift cable (see Section 4).

38 Lower the vehicle.

39 Fill the transaxle with the proper type and amount of fluid (see Chapter 1). Run the vehicle and check for fluid leaks.

7.26a RL3F01A transaxle-to-engine bolt torque guide (1991 and 1992 models)

7.26b RL4F03A transaxle-to-engine bolt torque guide (1991 through 1994 models)

7.26c RL4F03V and RE4F03V transaxle-to-engine bolt torque guide (1991 through 1994 models)

Chapter 8
Clutch and driveaxles

Contents

Specifications

Inner CV joint length (dimension "L" in illustration 10.10a)

1982	4-11/64 inches
1983 and 1984	
Tripod type	4-13/32 inches
Ball-and-cage type	3-5/16 inches
1985	
Left side	3-51/64 inches
Right side	4-11/32 inches
1986	3-51/64 inches
1987 through 1990	
Tripod type	
Coupe	4.00 inches
All others	3-13/16 inches
Ball-and-cage type	3-1/2 inches
1991 on	
Tripod type	4.00 inches
Ball-and-cage type	3-7/8 inches

Torque specifications

	Ft-lbs
Clutch pressure plate bolts	16 to 22
Driveaxle/hub nut	
1986 and earlier	87 to 145
1987 on	145 to 203
Support bearing bolts	
Inner and middle bolts	19 to 26
Outer bolt	32 to 43

8

Flywheel

Clutch disc

Clutch cover

2.1 An exploded view of a typical clutch assembly

1   General information

The information in this Chapter deals with the components from the rear of the engine to the front wheels, except for the transaxle, which is dealt with in Chapter 7A and 7B. For the purposes of this Chapter, these components are grouped into two categories: Clutch and driveaxles. Separate Sections within this Chapter offer general descriptions and checking procedures for both groups.

Since nearly all the procedures covered in this Chapter involve working under the vehicle, make sure it's securely supported on sturdy jackstands or a hoist where the vehicle can be easily raised and lowered.

2   Clutch - description and check

Refer to illustration 2.1

1   All vehicles with a manual transaxle use a single dry plate, diaphragm spring type clutch **(see illustration)**. The clutch disc has a splined hub which allows it to slide along the splines of the transaxle input shaft. The clutch and pressure plate are held in contact by spring pressure exerted by the diaphragm in the pressure plate.

2   The clutch release system is cable-operated. The release system consists of the clutch pedal, the clutch cable, the clutch release lever and the clutch release (or throw-out) bearing.

3   When pressure is applied to the clutch pedal to release the clutch, the cable transmits this movement to the clutch release lever. As the lever pivots, the shaft fingers push against the release bearing. The bearing pushes against the fingers of the diaphragm spring of the pressure plate assembly, which in turn releases the clutch plate.

4   Terminology can be a problem regarding the clutch components because common names have in some cases changed from that used by the manufacturer. For example, the driven plate is also called the clutch plate or disc, the pressure plate assembly is sometimes referred to as the clutch cover, and the clutch release bearing is sometimes called a throw-out bearing.

5   Other than replacing components that have obvious damage, some preliminary checks should be performed to diagnose a clutch system failure.

    a) *The first check should be the freeplay of the clutch cable (see Chapter 1). After adjusting the cable, retest the clutch operation.*

    b) *To check "clutch spin down time," run the engine at normal idle speed with the transaxle in Neutral (clutch pedal up - engaged). Disengage the clutch (pedal down), wait several seconds and shift the transaxle into Reverse. No grinding noise should be heard. A grinding noise would most likely indicate a problem in the pressure plate or the clutch disc.*

    c) *To check for complete clutch release, run the engine (with the parking brake applied to prevent movement) and hold the clutch pedal approximately 1/2-inch from the floor. Shift the transaxle between 1st gear and Reverse several times. If the shift is not smooth, component failure is indicated.*

    d) *Visually inspect the clutch pedal bushing at the top of the clutch pedal to make sure there is no sticking or excessive wear.*

    e) *Under the vehicle, check that the clutch release lever is solidly mounted on the ball stud.*

3   Clutch cable - removal and installation

Refer to illustrations 3.1, 3.2 and 3.3

1   Open the hood and loosen the clutch cable at the release lever by backing off the cable adjuster knob **(see illustration)**.

2   Disconnect the cable from the release lever **(see illustration)**.

3   Disconnect the cable housing from the firewall **(see illustration)**.

4   Remove the dash lower trim panel (see Chapter 11).

5   Disconnect the cable from the clutch pedal.

6   Installation is the reverse of removal. Adjust the clutch cable by following the procedure in Chapter 1, Section 10.

3.1 Loosen the clutch cable adjuster at the release lever

3.2 Disconnect the clutch cable from the release lever

3.3 To disconnect the clutch cable from the firewall, remove these nuts (arrows)

4.5 Mark the relationship of the pressure plate to the flywheel (in case you're going to re-use the same pressure plate)

4 Clutch components - removal, inspection and installation

Warning: *Dust produced by clutch wear and deposited on clutch components may contain asbestos, which is hazardous to your health. DO NOT blow it out with compressed air and DO NOT inhale it. DO NOT use gasoline or petroleum-based solvents to remove the dust. Brake system cleaner should be used to flush the dust into a drain pan. After the clutch components are wiped clean with a rag, dispose of the contaminated rags and cleaner in a labeled, covered container.*

Removal

Refer to illustrations 4.5, 4.7a and 4.7b

1 Access to the clutch components is normally accomplished by removing the transaxle, leaving the engine in the vehicle. If, of course, the engine is being removed for major overhaul, then the opportunity should always be taken to check the clutch for wear and replace worn components as necessary. However, the relatively low cost of the clutch components compared to the time and labor involved in gaining access to them warrants their replacement any time the engine or transaxle is removed, unless they are new or in near-perfect condition. The following

4.10 Examine the clutch disc for evidence of excessive wear, such as smeared friction material, chewed-up rivets, worn hub splines and distorted damper cushions or springs

4.7a Remove the pressure plate . . .

procedures assume that the engine will stay in place.

2 Remove the transaxle from the vehicle (see Chapter 7A). Support the engine while the transaxle is out. Preferably, an engine hoist should be used to support it from above. However, if a jack is used underneath the engine, make sure a piece of wood is used between the jack and oil pan to spread the load. **Caution:** *The pick-up for the oil pump is very close to the bottom of the oil pan. If the pan is bent or distorted in any way, engine oil starvation could occur.*

3 The release fork and release bearing can remain attached to the transaxle for the time being.

4 To support the clutch disc during removal, install a clutch alignment tool through the clutch disc hub.

5 Carefully inspect the flywheel and pressure plate for indexing marks. The marks are usually an X, an O or a white letter. If they cannot be found, scribe marks yourself so the pressure plate and the flywheel will be in the same alignment during installation **(see illustration).**

NORMAL FINGER WEAR

EXCESSIVE ─ WEAR

EXCESSIVE FINGER WEAR

BROKEN OR BENT FINGERS

4.12a Replace the pressure plate if any of these conditions are noted

4.7b . . . and the clutch disc

6 Slowly loosen the pressure plate-to-flywheel bolts. Work in a diagonal pattern and loosen each bolt a little at a time until all spring pressure is relieved.

7 Hold the pressure plate securely and completely remove the bolts, followed by the pressure plate and clutch disc **(see illustrations).**

Inspection

Refer to illustrations 4.10, 4.12a and 4.12b

8 Ordinarily, when a problem occurs in the clutch, it can be attributed to wear of the clutch driven plate assembly (clutch disc). However, all components should be inspected at this time.

9 Inspect the flywheel for cracks, heat checking, score marks and other damage. If the imperfections are slight, a machine shop can resurface it to make it flat and smooth. Refer to Chapter 2 for the flywheel removal procedure.

10 Inspect the lining on the clutch disc. There should be at least 1/16-inch of lining above the rivet heads. Check for loose rivets, distortion, cracks, broken springs and other obvious damage **(see illustration).** As mentioned above, ordinarily the clutch disc is replaced as a matter of course, so if in doubt about the condition, replace it with a new one.

11 The release bearing should be replaced along with the clutch disc (see Section 5).

12 Check the machined surface and the diaphragm spring fingers of the pressure plate **(see illustrations).** If the surface is

8

4.12b Examine the pressure plate friction surface for score marks, cracks and evidence of overheating (blue spots)

4.14 Center the clutch disc in the pressure plate with a clutch alignment tool, then tighten the pressure plate-to-flywheel bolts

grooved or otherwise damaged, replace the pressure plate assembly. Also check for obvious damage, distortion, cracking, etc. Light glazing can be removed with emery cloth or sandpaper. If a new pressure plate is indicated, new or factory rebuilt units are available.

Installation

Refer to illustration 4.14

13   Before installation, carefully wipe the flywheel and pressure plate machined surfaces clean. It's important that no oil or grease is on these surfaces or the lining of the clutch disc. Handle these parts only with clean hands.

5.2b Disengage the return spring from the release bearing

5.2c To remove the release bearing, grasp it firmly and pull it straight off the input shaft

5.2a An exploded view of a typical clutch release bearing and lever

Labels: Release lever; Return spring; Release fork; Bearing retainer *; * Pay attention to direction of bearing retainer; Clutch release bearing; Release pin

14   Position the clutch disc and pressure plate with the clutch held in place with an alignment tool **(see illustration)**. Make sure it's installed properly (most replacement clutch plates will be marked "flywheel side" or something similar - if not marked, install the clutch disc with the damper springs or cushion toward the transaxle).
15   Tighten the pressure plate-to-flywheel bolts only finger tight, working around the pressure plate.
16   Center the clutch disc by ensuring the alignment tool is through the splined hub and into the recess in the crankshaft. Wiggle the tool up, down or side-to-side as needed to bottom the tool. Tighten the pressure plate-to-flywheel bolts a little at a time, working in a crisscross pattern to prevent distortion of the cover. After all of the bolts are snug, tighten them to the torque listed in this Chapter's Specifications. Remove the alignment tool.
17   Using high-temperature grease, lubricate the inner groove of the release bearing (see Section 5). Also place grease on the release lever contact areas and the transaxle input shaft bearing retainer.

5.3 Before you can remove the release lever and the release fork, you'll have to knock out the two roll pins that lock the release lever and fork together; make sure you angle the pins so they're pointing toward the cavity in the clutch housing

18   Install the clutch release bearing (see Section 5).
19   Install the transaxle, clutch release cable and all components removed previously, tightening all fasteners to the proper torque specifications.

5   Clutch release bearing and lever - removal, inspection and installation

Warning: *Dust produced by clutch wear and deposited on clutch components may contain asbestos, which is hazardous to your health. DO NOT blow it out with compressed air and DO NOT inhale it. DO NOT use gasoline or petroleum-based solvents to remove the dust. Brake system cleaner should be used to flush it into a drain pan. After the clutch components are wiped clean with a rag, dispose of the contaminated rags and cleaner in a labeled, covered container.*

Removal

Refer to illustrations 5.2a, 5.2b, 5.2c and 5.3

1   Remove the transaxle (see Chapter 7).
2   Note how the return spring engages the release fork, then disconnect the spring **(see illustrations)**. Grasp the release bearing firmly and pull it off the input shaft **(see illustration)**.
3   Rotate the release lever and release fork so that the roll pins are pointing toward the cavity in the transaxle housing behind the release fork, then drive out the roll pins with a small punch **(see illustration)**. Separate the clutch release lever from the release fork.

Inspection

Refer to illustration 5.4

4   Hold the bearing by the outer race and rotate the inner race while applying pressure **(see illustration)**. If the bearing doesn't turn smoothly or if it's noisy, replace the bearing/hub assembly with a new one. Wipe the bearing with a clean rag and inspect it for

5.4 To check the condition of the bearing, hold it by the outer race and rotate the inner race while applying pressure - the bearing should turn smoothly - if it doesn't, replace it

5.5 Apply a light coat of high-temperature grease to the recess in the bore of the release bearing

5.7 Install the two roll pins to lock the release fork to the release lever; make sure the return spring is installed properly as shown

5.8 This is how the release bearing should look when the retainers (spring clips) and the return spring are properly engaged

damage, wear and cracks. Don't immerse the bearing in solvent - it's sealed for life and to do so would ruin it. Also check the release lever for cracks and bends.

Installation

Refer to illustrations 5.5, 5.7 and 5.8

5   Fill the inner groove of the release bearing with high-temperature grease. Also apply a light coat of the same grease to the transaxle input shaft splines **(see illustration)**.

6.   Lubricate the release lever bearing surfaces (where the lever seats and where it goes through the transaxle bellhousing), the tips of the release fork (where it contacts the release bearing) and the bearing retainers with high-temperature grease.

7   Install the release lever and slide on the return spring and release fork **(see illustration)**. Line up the holes in the release fork and the release lever and install the roll pins.

8   Slide the release bearing onto the transaxle input shaft and engage the retainers (spring clips) and return spring as shown **(see illustration)**.

9   Apply a light coat of high-temperature grease to the face of the release bearing where it contacts the pressure plate diaphragm fingers.

10   The remainder of installation is the reverse of the removal procedure.

6   Clutch start switch - check and replacement

Refer to illustration 6.1.

1   The clutch start switch **(see illustration)** is located at the top of the clutch pedal.

2   Verify that the engine will not start when the clutch pedal is released.

3   Verify that the engine will start when the clutch pedal is depressed all the way.

4   If the clutch start switch doesn't perform as described above, adjust the clutch pedal (see Chapter 1). The switch should now operate properly. If it doesn't, check switch continuity.

5   Verify that there is continuity between the clutch start switch terminals when the switch is On (pedal depressed).

6   Verify that no continuity exists between the switch terminals when the switch is Off (pedal released).

7   If the switch fails either of these continuity tests, replace it: loosen the nut near the body of the switch, then unscrew the switch. Unplug the electrical connector. Installation is the reverse of removal.

8   Adjust the clutch pedal (see Chapter 1).

9   Verify that the engine doesn't start when the clutch pedal is released.

7   Driveaxles - general information and inspection

Refer to illustration 7.1

1   Power is transmitted from the transaxle to the wheels through a pair of driveaxles **(see illustration on following page)**. The inner end of each driveaxle is splined into the differential side gears. The outer ends of the driveaxles are splined to the axle hubs and locked in place by a large nut.

2   The inner ends of the driveaxles are equipped with sliding constant velocity joints, which are capable of both angular and axial

6.1 The clutch start switch is located at the top of the clutch pedal; to replace it, unplug the electrical connector (arrow), loosen the locknut (above the bracket) and unscrew the switch

motion. Some inner joints consist of a tripod bearing and a joint housing (outer race) in which the joint is free to slide in and out as the driveaxle moves up and down with the wheel. These joints can be disassembled and cleaned in the event of a boot failure (see Section 10), but if any parts are damaged, the joints must be replaced as a unit. Other inner joints are the "double-offset" type, which consists of ball bearings running between an inner race and an outer cage. They can also be disassembled, cleaned and inspected, but they too must be replaced as a single unit if defective.

3   The outer CV joints are the "Rzeppa" (pronounced "sheppa") or "Birfield" type, which also consists of ball bearings running between an inner race and an outer cage. However, Rzeppa/Birfield joints are capable of angular - but not axial - movement. These outer joints should be cleaned, inspected and repacked whenever replacing an outer CV joint boot, but they cannot be disassembled. If an outer joint is damaged, it must be replaced.

4   The boots should be inspected periodically for damage and leaking lubricant. Torn CV joint boots must be replaced immediately or the joints can be damaged. Boot replacement involves removal of the driveaxle (see Section 10). **Note:** *Some auto parts stores carry "split" type replacement boots, which can be installed without removing the driveaxle from the vehicle. This is a convenient alternative; however, the driveaxle should be removed and the CV joint disassembled and cleaned to ensure the joint is free from contaminants such as moisture and dirt which will accelerate CV joint wear.* The most common symptom of worn or damaged CV joints, besides lubricant leaks, is a clicking noise in turns, a clunk when accelerating after coasting and vibration at highway speeds. To check for wear in the CV joints and driveaxle shafts, grasp each axle (one at a time) and rotate it in both directions while holding the CV joint housings, feeling for play indicating worn splines or sloppy CV joints. Also check the driveaxle shafts for cracks, dents and distortion.

8

Joint assembly (road wheel side)
Bellows band (large)
Bellows (wheel side)
Bellows band (small)

Transaxle side

Double offset joint

Snap ring (large)
Inner race
Cage
Ball

Bellows band (small)
Bellows (transaxle side)
Bellows band (large)
Snap ring (small)

Slide joint housing
Circlip

Circlip
Drive shaft

Road wheel side (rzeppa joint, birfield joint)

Tripod joint

Spider assembly
Slide joint cover

7.1 An exploded view of typical inner and outer CV joint assemblies

8.4 Remove the cotter pin and the nut lock

8.5 Use a large prybar to immobilize the hub while loosening the driveaxle/hub nut

8.9 Pull the steering knuckle out and slide the end of the driveaxle out of the hub

8 Driveaxles - removal and installation

Removal

Refer to illustrations 8.4, 8.5, 8.9, 8.10a and 8.10b

1   Disconnect the cable from the negative terminal of the battery.
2   Set the parking brake.
3   Loosen the front wheel lug nuts, raise the vehicle and support it securely on jackstands. Remove the wheel.
4   Remove the cotter pin and the bearing nut lock from the driveaxle/hub nut **(see illustrations)**.
5   Remove the driveaxle/hub nut and washer. To prevent the hub from turning, wedge a prybar between two of the wheel studs and allow the prybar to rest against the ground or the floorpan of the vehicle **(see illustration)**.
6   To loosen the driveaxle from the hub splines, tap the end of the driveaxle with a

soft-faced hammer or a hammer and a brass punch.
7   Remove the engine splash shields (see Chapter 1). Place a drain pan underneath the transaxle to catch the lubricant that may spill out when the driveaxles are removed.
8   Disconnect the control arm from the steering knuckle (see Chapter 10)
9   Pull out on the steering knuckle and detach the driveaxle from the hub **(see illustration)**.
10   Carefully pry the inner CV joint out of the transaxle **(see illustration)** and remove the driveaxle assembly. On some 1991 and later models, the inner CV joint housing on the right (passenger side) driveaxle terminates at a support bearing instead of the transaxle. The inner side of the housing has an extended shaft - instead of a short stub axle - that goes through the support bearing assembly and engages the right differential side gear. On these vehicles, insert the prybar between the inner CV joint housing and the bearing support assembly and pop the inner end of the extension shaft loose

from the side gear the same way you would any conventional inner CV joint, *then* unbolt the bearing support assembly from the block. Do not try to separate the driveaxle from the CV joint housing until you have the entire assembly on the bench (see Section 10).

8.10a To separate the inner end of the driveaxle from the transaxle, pry on the CV joint housing like this with a large screwdriver or prybar (you may need to give the prybar a sharp rap with a hammer)

8.10b If you can't pry the left driveaxle out on a model equipped with an automatic transaxle, remove the right driveaxle, insert a screwdriver through the differential side gears and tap the left driveaxle out

Note: *When removing the left (driver's) side driveaxle on models with an automatic transaxle, it may not be possible to pry the inner CV joint out of the transaxle. In this case, it will be necessary to remove the right side driveaxle and insert a screwdriver through the differential side gears and knock the left side shaft free* **(see illustration).**

11 Refer to Chapter 7 for the driveaxle oil seal replacement procedure.

Installation

12 Installation is the reverse of the removal procedure, but with the following additional points:

a) *When installing the left driveaxle, push the driveaxle sharply in to seat the retaining ring on the inner CV joint in the groove in the differential side gear.*
b) *Tighten the driveaxle hub nut to the torque listed in this Chapter's Specifications, then install the nut lock and a new cotter pin.*
c) *Install the wheel and lug nuts, lower the vehicle and tighten the lug nuts to the torque listed in the Chapter 1 Specifications.*
d) *Check the transaxle or differential lubricant and add, if necessary, to bring it to the proper level (see Chapter 1).*
e) *If you're installing the right driveaxle assembly on a vehicle using a support bearing and extension shaft, reattach the outer driveaxle assembly to the housing for the inner CV joint on the bench and install the outer driveaxle/support bearing/extension shaft as a single assembly. Be sure to tighten the support bearing bolts to the torque listed in this Chapter's Specifications.*

9 Support bearing assembly - removal, overhaul and installation

Refer to illustration 9.3

Note: *Some 1991 and later models use an extension shaft between the inner CV joint housing and the transaxle to give the right driveaxle the same length as the left unit. This extension shaft is hung from a support bearing assembly bolted to the block. The following procedure applies only to these models.*

1 Remove the right driveaxle/support bearing/extension shaft assembly (see Section 8).
2 Remove the boot clamps for the inner CV joint and slide the boot back out of the way.
3 Remove the large snap-ring **(see illustration)** and withdraw the axleshaft and bearing assembly from the outer housing.
4 Rotate the extension shaft and listen to the bearing. It should feel smooth. If the bearing is rough or noisy, take the support bearing assembly, a new bearing and three new dust shields **(refer to illustration 9.3)** to an automotive machine shop and have the old bearing pressed off and a new bearing installed.
5 Reattach the right driveaxle to its inner CV joint housing.
6 Installation is the reverse of removal (see Section 8).

9.3 An exploded view of a typical driveaxle assembly on 1991 and later models with equal-length driveaxles

1 Outer (Birfield/Rzeppa) CV joint assembly
2 Boot clamps
3 CV joint boot
4 Circlip
5 Axleshaft
6 Boot clamps
7 CV joint boot
8 Retaining ring
9 Snap-ring
10 Inner race
11 Cage
12 Ball
13 Snap-ring
14 Inner CV joint housing (left driveaxle)
15 Dust shield (left driveaxle)
16 Circlip (left driveaxle)
17 Inner CV joint housing and extension shaft (right driveaxle)
18 Snap-ring (right driveaxle)
19 Dust shield (right driveaxle)
20 Support bearing (right driveaxle)
21 Support bearing retainer (right driveaxle)
22 Bracket (right driveaxle)
23 Snap-ring
24 Dust shield

10 Driveaxle boot replacement and CV joint overhaul

Note: *If the CV joints must be overhauled (usually due to torn boots), explore all options before beginning the job. Complete rebuilt driveaxles are available on an exchange basis, which eliminates much time and work. Whichever route you choose to take, check on the cost and availability of parts before disassembling the vehicle.*

All units

1 Remove the driveaxle (see Section 8).

8

10.2a Pry up the retaining tabs on the boot clamps . . .

10.2b . . . then open the clamps and remove them from the boot

10.3 Once the boot is detached from the inner CV joint housing, the housing can be removed

10.4 Use a center punch to place marks (arrows) on the tripod and the driveaxle to ensure that they're properly reassembled

10.5 Remove the snap-ring from the groove in the end of the axleshaft

10.6 Drive the tripod joint from the axleshaft with a brass punch and hammer - make sure you don't damage the bearing surfaces or the splines on the shaft

Inner CV joint

Tripod type

Disassembly

Refer to illustrations 10.2a, 10.2b, 10.3, 10.4, 10.5 and 10.6

2   Remove the boot clamps **(see illustrations)**.

3   Pull the boot back from the inner CV joint and slide the joint housing off **(see illustration)**.

4   Use a center punch to mark the tripod and axleshaft to ensure that they are reassembled properly **(see illustration)**.

5   Remove the snap-ring from the end of the axleshaft with a pair of snap-ring pliers **(see illustration)**.

6   Use a hammer and a brass punch to drive the tripod joint from the driveaxle **(see illustration)**.

Check

7   Clean all components with solvent to remove the grease, and check for cracks, pitting, scoring and other signs of wear.

Reassembly

Refer to illustrations 10.8a, 10.8b, 10.10a, 10.10b, 10.10c and 10.10d

8   Slide the clamps and boot onto the

axleshaft. It's a good idea to wrap the axleshaft splines with tape to prevent damaging the boot **(see illustration)**. Place the tripod on the shaft **(see illustration)** and install the snap-ring. Apply grease to the tripod assembly, the inside of the joint housing and the inside of the boot.

9   Slide the boot into place, making sure both ends seat in their grooves.

10   Adjust the length of the joint **(see illustration)**, equalize the pressure in the boot **(see illustration)**, then tighten and secure the boot clamps **(see illustrations)**. Proceed to Step 30.

10.8a Wrap the splined area of the axleshaft with tape to prevent damage to the boots when installing them

10.8b Install the tripod with the chamfered (tapered) ends of the splines facing toward the axleshaft

10.10a Adjust the joint to the length indicated in the Specifications at the beginning of this Chapter, making sure the boot isn't distorted

10.10b Equalize the pressure inside the boot by inserting a small, DULL screwdriver between the boot and the CV joint housing

Double-offset (ball-and-cage) type

Disassembly

Refer to illustrations 10.11, 10.12, 10.13, 10.14 and 10.15

11   Remove both boot clamps (**see illustrations 10.2a and 10.2b**) and discard them. Slide the boot out of the way (**see illustration**).

12   Mark the shaft, the inner race, the cage and the outer race (housing) so they can be reassembled in the same way (**see illustration**).

13   Pry the wire ring bearing retainer from the housing (**see illustration**).

14   Pull the housing off the inner bearing assembly (**see illustration**).

15   Remove the snap-ring from the groove in the axleshaft with a pair of snap-ring pliers (**see illustration**).

16   Slide the inner race off the axleshaft.

17   Using a screwdriver or piece of wood, pry the ball bearings from the cage. Be careful not to scratch the inner race, the ball bearings or the cage.

18   Remove the cage.

Inspection

Refer to illustrations 10.19a and 10.19b

19   Clean the components with solvent to remove all traces of grease. Inspect the cage and races for pitting, score marks, cracks and other signs of wear and damage. Shiny, polished spots are normal and will not adversely affect CV joint performance (**see illustrations**).

10.10c To install the new clamps, bend the tang down . . .

10.11 Remove both boot clamps, then slide the boot down the axleshaft so it's out of the way

10.13 Pry the retainer from the housing with a small screwdriver

10.10d . . . and tap the tabs down to hold it in place

10.12 Mark the shaft, inner race, cage and outer race (housing) so they can be reassembled in the same relationship to each other

10.14 Slide the housing off the bearing assembly - some of the ball bearings may fall out when the race is removed, so be ready to catch them

10.15 Remove the snap-ring from the groove in the axleshaft with a pair of snap-ring pliers

10.19a Inspect the inner race lands and grooves for pitting, score marks, cracks and other signs of wear and damage

10.19b Inspect the cage for cracks, pitting and score marks (shiny, polished spots are normal and will not adversely affect CV joint performance)

8

10.25 Pack the inner race and cage assembly with grease, by hand, until grease is worked completely into the assembly (also note that the larger diameter side, or "bulge," is facing out)

Reassembly

Refer to illustration 10.25

20   Wrap the axleshaft splines with tape to avoid damaging the boot. Slide the small boot clamp and boot onto the axleshaft **(see illustration 10.8a)**, then remove the tape. Slide the large boot clamp over the boot.

21   Install the cage on the axleshaft with the smaller diameter side of the cage facing toward the boot.

22   Install the inner race onto the axleshaft with the matchmark on the race (or the larger diameter side) aligned with the mark on the end of the axleshaft.

23   Install the snap-ring in the groove. Make sure it's completely seated by pushing on the inner race.

24   Move the cage up over the inner race, aligning the match marks. Press the ball bearings into the cage windows with your thumbs. If they won't stay in place, apply CV joint grease to hold them.

25   Fill the outer race and boot with CV joint grease (normally included with the new boot kit). Pack the inner race and cage assembly with grease, by hand, until grease is worked completely into the assembly **(see illustration)**.

26   Slide the inner race, balls and cage into the CV joint housing and install the wire ring bearing retainer.

27   Wipe any excess grease from the axle

10.34 After the old grease has been rinsed away and the cleaning solvent has been blown out with compressed air, rotate the outer joint through its full range of motion and inspect the bearing surfaces for wear or damage - if any of the balls, the race or the cage look damaged, replace the outer joint assembly

boot groove on the outer race. Seat the small diameter of the boot in the recessed area on the axleshaft. Push the other end of the boot onto the CV joint housing and move the race in or out until there's no deformation (distortion or dents) in the boot.

28   Adjust the length of the joint **(see illustration 10.10a)**, then equalize the pressure in the boot by inserting a dull screwdriver between the boot and the outer race **(see illustration 10.10b)**. Don't damage the boot with the tool.

29   Install the boot clamps **(see illustrations 10.10c and 10.10d)**.

All inner CV joints

30   Install a new circlip on the inner CV joint stub axle.

31   Install the driveaxle (see Section 8).

Outer CV joint

Refer to illustrations 10.34, 10.38a and 10.38b

32   Remove the boot clamps **(see illustrations 10.2a and 10.2b)** and slide the boot back far enough to inspect the joint. If the axleshaft is rough and you're planning to re-use the same boot, wrap the axleshaft with tape to protect the boot from damage **(see illustration 10.8a)**.

33   Thoroughly wash the outer CV joint in clean solvent and blow dry it with compressed air, if available. The outer joint can't be disassembled, so it's difficult to wash away all the old grease and to rid the bearing of solvent once it's clean. But it's imperative that the job be done thoroughly, so take your time and do it right.

34   Bend the outer CV joint housing at an angle to the driveaxle to expose the bearings, inner race and cage **(see illustration)**. Inspect the bearing surfaces for signs of wear. If the joint is worn, replace it (see step 38).

35   If the boot is damaged but the joint is OK, remove the inner CV joint and boot (see Steps 2 through 6 for tripod and Steps 11 through 18 for double-offset). **Caution:** *The outer CV joint should only be removed if it is going to be replaced.* Proceed to the next step.

36   Slide the new outer boot onto the driveaxle. It's a good idea to wrap vinyl tape around the shaft splines to prevent damage to the boot **(see illustration 10.8a)**. When the boot is in position, add the specified amount of grease (included in the boot replacement kit) to the outer joint and the boot (pack the joint with as much grease as it will hold and put the rest into the boot). Slide the boot on the rest of the way, equalize the pressure inside the boot and install the new clamps **(see illustrations 10.10b, 10.10c and 10.10d)**.

37   Slide on the inner boot and install the inner CV joint (see Steps 8 through 10 for tripod and 20 through 29 for double-offset)

38   If the bearings are damaged or worn, replace the joint. This can be done by knocking the joint from the shaft using a hammer and punch, or by pulling the joint off with a slide hammer **(see illustration)**. Install the new joint by first sliding the new boot and clamps onto the axleshaft. Then thread the old driveaxle/hub nut onto the end of the shaft and assemble the joint onto the shaft splines. Drive the joint into place **(see illustration)**. Be sure to use a new driveaxle/hub nut when installing the driveaxle.

All units

39   Install the driveaxle (see Section 8).

10.38a The outer joint can be removed from the driveaxle shaft with a slide hammer

10.38b Drive the new joint onto the driveaxle shaft until the retaining ring in the joint seats in the groove in the shaft

Chapter 9   Brakes

Contents

Specifications

General
Brake fluid type.. See Chapter 1

Disc brakes
Minimum brake pad thickness .... See Chapter 1
Brake disc minimum thickness.............................. Refer to the marks cast into the disc
Maximum disc runout.. 0.0028 inch
Maximum disc thickness variation .... 0.0008 inch

Rear drum brakes
Maximum inside diameter .... Refer to the marks cast into the drum
Maximum out-of-round
  1982 .... 0.0006 inch
  1983 on .... 0.0012 inch
Maximum radial runout
  1982 .... 0.004 inch
  1983 on .... 0.0020 inch
Shoe friction material minimum thickness................... See Chapter 1

Brake pedal
Free height
  1982 .... 7-29/32 to 8-5/32 inches
  1983 on
    Manual transaxle
      1983 through 1986 .... 7-41/64 to 8-1/32 inches
      1987................................ 6-7/64 to 6-1/2 inches
      1988 through 1990 .... 6-19/64 to 6-39/64 inches
      1991 on............................ 5-53/64 to 6-7/32 inches
    Automatic transaxle
      1983 through 1986 .... 7-3/4 to 8-5/32 inches
      1987 through 1990 .... 6-1/2 to 6-27/32 inches
      1991 on............................ 6-3/16 to 6-9/16 inches

9

Brake pedal

Depressed height

  1982 through 1986 .... At least 3-11/32 inches

  1987 through 1990

    Manual transaxle .... At least 3-5/32 inches

    Automatic transaxle .... At least 3-11/32 inches

  1991 through 1993

    Manual transaxle

      GA16DE; SR20DE Coupe .... 2-61/64 inches

      SR20DE Sedan .... 3-5/32 inches

    Automatic transaxle

      GA16DE .... 3-5/32 inches

      SR20DE .... 3-11/32 inches

  1994

    Manual transaxle

      GA16DE .... 3-11/32 inches

      SR20DE .... 3-1/2 inches

    Automatic transaxle

      GA16DE .... 3-1/2 inches

      SR20DE .... 3-3/4 inches

Clearance between pedal stopper and brake light switch

  1982 through 1986 .... 0 to 1/32 inch

  1987 through 1990 .... 1/64 to 1/32 inch

  1991 on .... 0 to 1/64 inch

Pedal freeplay (1987 on) .... 3/64 to 1/8 inch

Power brake booster

Output rod length "A" (1982 and 1983 only) .... 13/32 inch

Input rod length "B" (1982 through 1984 only) .... 5-29/32 inches

Output rod length "A" (1991 on)

  M20 .... 3/16 to 13/64 inch

  M165T, M195T .... 13/32 inch

Torque specifications   **Ft-lbs** (unless otherwise indicated)

Brake booster-to-body mounting nuts

  1982 through 1990 .... 70 to 96 in-lbs

  1991 on .... 108 to 144 in-lbs

Brake caliper bolts (front)

  1982 through 1990 .... 16 to 23

  1991 on

    CL18VE .... 16 to 23

    AD18VE/AD22VF .... 23 to 30

Brake caliper torque plate (mounting bracket)

  Front .... 40 to 47

  Rear .... 28 to 38

Brake hose-to-caliper banjo bolt .... 144 to 168 in-lbs

Master cylinder-to-brake booster nuts .... 70 to 96 in-lbs

Wheel cylinder bolts .... 52 to 69 in-lbs

1   General information

The vehicles covered by this manual are equipped with hydraulically operated front and rear brake systems. The front brakes are disc type and the rear brakes are drum or disc type. Both the front and rear brakes are self adjusting. The disc brakes automatically compensate for pad wear, while the drum brakes incorporate an adjustment mechanism which is activated as the parking brake is applied.

Hydraulic system

The hydraulic system consists of two separate circuits. The master cylinder has separate reservoirs for the two circuits, and, in the event of a leak or failure in one hydraulic circuit, the other circuit will remain operative. A dual proportioning valve on the firewall provides brake balance between the front and rear brakes.

Power brake booster

The power brake booster, utilizing engine manifold vacuum and atmospheric pressure to provide assistance to the hydraulically operated brakes, is mounted on the firewall in the engine compartment.

Parking brake

The parking brake operates the rear brakes only, through cable actuation. It's activated by a lever mounted in the center console.

Service

After completing any operation involving disassembly of any part of the brake system, always test drive the vehicle to check for proper braking performance before resuming normal driving. When testing the brakes, perform the tests on a clean, dry, flat surface. Conditions other than these can lead to inaccurate test results.

Test the brakes at various speeds with both light and heavy pedal pressure. The vehicle should stop evenly without pulling to one side or the other. Avoid locking the brakes, because this slides the tires and diminishes braking efficiency and control of the vehicle.

Tires, vehicle load and wheel alignment are factors which also affect braking performance.

2 Anti-lock Brake System (ABS) - general information

Refer to illustration 2.1

1   The Anti-lock Brake System (ABS) **(see illustration)**, which was introduced in 1991, is designed to maintain vehicle steerability, directional stability and optimum deceleration under severe braking conditions and on most road surfaces. It does so by monitoring the rotational speed of each wheel and controlling the brake line pressure to each wheel during braking. This prevents the wheels from locking up.

Components

Actuator assembly

2   The actuator assembly consists of an electric hydraulic pump and four solenoid valves. The electric pump provides hydraulic pressure to charge the reservoirs in the actuator, which supplies pressure to the braking system. The solenoid valves modulate brake line pressure during ABS operation. The body contains four valves - one for each wheel. The pump, the reservoirs and the solenoid valves are all housed in the actuator assembly.

Speed sensors

3   The speed sensors, which are located at each wheel, generate small electrical pulsations when the toothed sensor rotors are turning, sending a variable voltage signal indicating wheel rotational speed to the ABS control unit.

4   The front speed sensors are mounted on the steering knuckles in close relationship to the toothed sensor rotors, which are integral with the outer constant velocity (CV) joints.

5   The rear wheel sensors are bolted to the axle carriers (rear knuckles). The sensor rotors are integral with the rear brake disc assemblies.

ABS computer

6   The ABS control unit, which is mounted behind the right (passenger side) kick panel, is the "brain" of the ABS system. The function of the control unit is to accept and process information received from the wheel speed

2.1 Anti-Lock Brake System (ABS) component locations

sensors to control the hydraulic line pressure, avoiding wheel lock up. The control unit also constantly monitors the system, even under normal driving conditions, to find faults within the system.

7   If a problem develops within the system, an "ABS" light will glow on the dashboard. A diagnostic code will also be stored in the control unit, which indicates the problem area or component.

Diagnosis and repair

Refer to illustrations 2.8a and 2.8b

8   If the ABS warning light on the dash comes on and stays on while the vehicle is in operation, the ABS system requires attention. Although no special tools other than a digital multimeter are necessary to troubleshoot the system, diagnosis is nevertheless quite complex, involving a number of lengthy diagnostic procedures, so we don't recommend attempting the fix the ABS system at home. However, if you're willing to do a little work, you can obtain a diagnostic trouble code - which will indicate the general area of the problem - as follows:

a) *Remove the passenger side kick panel in front of the right front door so you can see the LED light on the control unit.*

b) *Drive the vehicle above 19 mph for at least one minute.*

c) *Stop the vehicle but keep the engine running.*

d) *Count the number of flashes of the ABS LED light **(see illustration)**, then refer to the accompanying table **(see illustration on following page)**.*

e) *Turn off the engine.*

9   You can perform the following preliminary checks yourself:

a) *Check the brake fluid level in the reservoir.*

b) *Check that all electrical connectors are securely connected.*

c) *Check the fuses.*

d) *Check the brake system (see Chapter 1).*

e) *Check the brake pedal (see Chapter 1).*

f) *Check the brake pads (see Section 3).*

10   Start the engine again by slowly turning the ignition key (turning the key too quickly may cause the ABS warning light to stay on when there is nothing wrong).

2.8a The LED on the ABS control unit indicates a problem in a particular circuit by the number of flashes. For example, five flashes, separated by one second intervals, indicates a code 5, which means there's a problem in the left front wheel sensor circuit. There's a five to ten second pause at the end of a code, then the control unit repeats itself

No. of L.E.D. flashes	Malfunctioning parts or circuit
1	Left front actuator solenoid circuit
2	Right front actuator solenoid circuit
3	Both actuator solenoid circuits
5	Left front wheel sensor circuit
6	Right front wheel sensor circuit
7	Right rear wheel sensor circuit
8	Left rear wheel sensor circuit
9	Motor and motor relay
10	Solenoid valve relay
15	Sensor rotor
16	Control unit
Warning activates and L.E.D. "OFF"	Power supply and ground circuit

2.8b ABS diagnostic trouble code table

a) If the light stays on, take the vehicle to a dealer service department or other qualified repair shop and have the ABS system repaired.

b) If the light doesn't stay on, drive the vehicle above 19 mph for at least one minute and verify that the warning light on the dash doesn't come on again. If it does, take the vehicle to a dealer service department or other qualified repair shop and have the ABS system repaired.

3 Disc brake pads - replacement

Refer to illustrations 3.5 and 3.6a through 3.6jj

Warning: Disc brake pads must be replaced on both front wheels at the same time - never replace the pads on only one wheel. Also, the dust created by the brake system may contain asbestos, which is harmful to your health. Never blow it out with compressed air and don't inhale any of it. An approved filtering mask should be worn when working on the brakes. Do not, under any circum-

stances, use petroleum-based solvents to clean brake parts. Use brake system cleaner only!

1   Remove the cap from the brake fluid reservoir.

2   Loosen the front or rear wheel lug nuts, raise the front or rear of the vehicle and support it securely on jackstands. Block the wheels at the opposite end.

3   Remove the wheels. Work on one brake assembly at a time, using the assembled brake for reference if necessary.

4   Inspect the brake disc carefully as outlined in Section 5. If machining is necessary, follow the information in that Section to remove the disc, at which time the pads can be removed as well.

5   Push the piston back into its bore to provide room for the new brake pads. A C-clamp can be used to accomplish this **(see illustration)**. As the piston is depressed to the bottom of the caliper bore, the fluid in the master cylinder will rise. Make sure that it doesn't overflow. If necessary, siphon off some of the fluid. **Warning:** This procedure does not apply to rear caliper pistons; rear pistons use a ratcheting mechanism inside the caliper which will be damaged if you try to depress the piston with a C-clamp. Rear pistons are retracted with a pair of needle-nose pliers, as shown in the photo sequence for the rear pad replacement procedure.

6   Follow the accompanying photos **(see illustrations 3.6a through 3.6s)**, for the

3.5 Use a C-clamp to depress the piston into the caliper before removing the caliper and pads

1 Caliper pins
2 Pin boots
3 Torque plate bolts
4 Torque plate
5 Inner pad shim cover
6 Inner pad shim
7 Inner pad
8 Pad retainers
9 Outer pad
10 Outer pad shim
11 Brake hose-to-caliper banjo bolt
12 Copper washers
13 Caliper bolt
14 Bleeder valve
15 Caliper body
16 Piston seal
17 Piston
18 Piston boot

3.6a Exploded view of a CL18VD caliper assembly (1991 through 1994 models) (this is the unit shown in the following photo sequence)

3.6b Remove these two bolts (upper and lower arrows) to detach the caliper from the torque plate; the middle arrow points to the brake hose banjo bolt (which shouldn't be removed unless the caliper requires service)

3.6c Lift the caliper off the pads

3.6d Hang the caliper out of the way with a piece of coat hanger or wire

3.6e Remove the shim from the outer brake pad

3.6f Remove the outer pad

3.6g Remove the two shims from the inner brake pad

3.6h Remove the inner brake pad

3.6i Remove the lower pad retainer

3.6j Remove the upper pad retainer

3.6k Remove the caliper pins and the dust boots; inspect the boots for cracks and tears and replace them if they're damaged

3.6l Clean the caliper pins, inspect them for scoring and corrosion, and replace them if necessary; coat the pins with high-temperature grease before installing the caliper

3.6m Install the upper pad retainer

9

3.6n Install the lower pad retainer

3.6o Assemble the two inner pad shims; they fit together like this, with the smaller, darker shim underneath and the larger, lighter shim on top

3.6p The inner pad shims should look like this when installed correctly

3.6q Install the inner brake pad and shim

3.6r Install the outer brake pad and shim

3.6s Install the caliper and the caliper bolts, then tighten the caliper bolts to the torque listed in this Chapter's Specifications. Note: *If the caliper won't fit over the pads, use a C-clamp to push the piston into the caliper a little further*

3.6t An exploded view of an early CL18B caliper assembly (1982 through 1986 models)

actual front pad replacement procedure. Be sure to stay in order and read the caption under each illustration. **Note:** *The pad replacement procedure shown depicts one type of front brake caliper used on 1994 models. A number of different calipers have been used since 1982, but the pad replacement procedures are similar for all. Exploded views of other typical caliper assemblies are included* **(see illustrations 3.6t through 3.6x)** *to help you replace the pads or overhaul other calipers. If you're replacing rear brake pads, follow the second photo sequence* **(see illustrations 3.6y through 3.6jj).**

7   When reinstalling the caliper, be sure to tighten the mounting bolts to the torque listed in this Chapter's Specifications.

8   After the job has been completed, firmly depress the brake pedal a few times to bring the pads into contact with the disc. Check the level of the brake fluid, adding some if necessary. Check the operation of the brakes carefully before placing the vehicle into normal service.

Pad retainer
(Upper side)

Main pin

Torque
member

Pin boot

Inner shim

Copper
washer

Pad retainer
(Lower side)

Brake hose

Air bleeder

Pin bolt

Outer shim

Pad

Dust seal

Piston

Piston seal

Cylinder body

3.6u An exploded view of a later CL18B caliper assembly (1987 through 1990 models)

Main pin

Torque
member

Pin boot

Inner shim

Air bleeder

Brake hose

Banjo bolt

Copper washer

Main pin

Pad

Pin boot

Outer shim

Cylinder body

Dust seal
retainer

Dust
seal

Piston

Piston
seal

3.6v An exploded view of a an AD18V caliper assembly (1987 through 1990 models)

9

1 Pin boots
2 Torque plate bolts
3 Torque plate
4 Plug
5 Inner shim cover
6 Inner pad shim
7 Inner brake pad
8 Pad retainers
9 Outer brake pad
10 Outer pad shim
11 Banjo bolt
12 Copper washers
13 Caliper sliding pins
14 Bleeder valve
15 Caliper body
16 Piston seal
17 Piston
18 Piston boot
19 Piston boot retainer
20 Brake hose

3.6w An exploded view of an AD18VE caliper assembly (1991 through 1994 models)

1 Main pin bolts
2 Pin boots
3 Torque plate bolts
4 Torque plate
5 Pad retainers
6 Inner shim cover
7 Inner pad shim
8 Inner (right) and outer
(left) brake pads
9 Outer pad shim
10 Banjo bolt
11 Brake hose
12 Copper washers
13 Bleeder valve
14 Caliper body
15 Piston seal
16 Piston
17 Dust seal
18 Piston boot retainer

3.6x An exploded view of an AD22VF caliper assembly (1991 through 1994 models)

1 Washer
2 Spring
3 Toggle lever
4 Cam
5 Return spring
6 Cable guide
7 Banjo bolt
8 Copper washers
9 Bleeder valve
10 Rear caliper body
11 Strut
12 O-ring
13 Pushrod
14 Key plate
15 Spring
16 Spring cover
17 Snap-ring
18 Piston seal
19 Piston
20 Piston boot
21 Piston boot retainer
22 Inner shim
23 Inner pad
24 Outer pad
25 Outer shim
26 Torque plate
27 Retainer spring
28 Caliper pin

3.6y An exploded view of the AD7HA rear caliper assembly (1991 through 1994 models)

3.6z Remove the rear caliper pins (arrows)

3.6aa Remove the caliper and hang it out of the way with a piece of wire (see illustration 3.6d)

3.6bb Remove the outer pad and shim

3.6cc Remove the inner pad and shim

3.6dd Remove the pad retainer springs

9

3.6ee Remove the dust boots from the caliper ears, inspect them for cracks and tears and replace as necessary; clean out the old grease from the caliper pin bores in the ears and apply a fresh coat of new multi-purpose grease to both the caliper pin bores and the insides of the dust boots (greasing the pins themselves won't work - a lip inside the boots will scrape it off when the pin is inserted through the boot)

4   Disc brake caliper - removal, overhaul and installation

Warning: *The dust created by the brake system may contain asbestos, which is harmful to your health. Never blow it out with compressed air and don't inhale any of it. An approved filtering mask should be worn when working on the brakes. Do not, under any circumstances, use petroleum-based solvents to clean brake parts. Use brake system cleaner only!*

Removal

Refer to illustration 4.2

1   Loosen the front or rear wheel lug nuts, raise the front or rear of the vehicle and place it securely on jackstands. Block the wheels at the opposite end. Remove the front or rear wheel.
2   Remove the banjo bolt and discard the old copper washers **(see illustrations 3.6a or 3.6t through 3.6y)**. Disconnect the brake hose from the caliper. Plug the brake hose to keep contaminants out of the brake system and to prevent losing any more brake fluid than is necessary **(see illustration)**.
3   Refer to Section 3 for the caliper

3.6ff Install the pad retainer springs

3.6hh Install the outer pad, followed by the shim - make sure the pad ears are properly engaged with the retainer springs

removal procedure (it's part of brake pad replacement).

Overhaul

Refer to illustrations 4.4, 4.5, 4.7, 4.8 and 4.11
Note: *If an overhaul is indicated (usually because of fluid leakage), explore all options before beginning the job. New and factory rebuilt calipers are available on an exchange basis, which makes this job quite easy. If it's decided to rebuild the calipers, make sure a rebuild kit is available before proceeding. Always rebuild the calipers in pairs - never rebuild just one of them. Detailed exploded views of the front calipers are provided in illustrations 3.6a and 3.6t through 3.6x. Illus-*

3.6gg Install the inner pad and shim - make sure the ears on the inner pad are properly engaged with the retainer springs and the inner pad shim is installed correctly as shown

3.6ii Retract the piston by turning it clockwise with a pair of needle-nose pliers

tration 3.6y depicts a rear caliper; however, overhauling the rear caliper is extremely difficult without special tools, so if the rear caliper is leaking or otherwise defective, obtain a rebuilt unit or have it overhauled by a shop equipped with the proper tools.
4   If the dust boot is held in place by a retaining ring, remove it **(see illustration)**, then pry out the dust boot. If the boot does not have a retaining ring, you'll have to remove the piston first.
5   Place a wood block between the piston and the caliper frame to prevent damage as it is ejected. To remove the piston from the caliper, apply compressed air to the brake fluid hose connection on the caliper body

3.6jj Place the caliper over the pads, install the caliper pins and tighten them to the torque listed in this Chapter's Specifications

4.2 Using a piece of rubber hose of the appropriate size, plug the brake line

4.4 Using a screwdriver, remove the cylinder boot set ring (if equipped)

4.5 With the caliper padded to catch the piston, use compressed air to force the piston out of its bore - make sure your hands or fingers are not between the piston and caliper

4.7 To remove the seal from the caliper bore, use a plastic or wooden tool, such as a pencil

4.8 Push the sliding bushing on each side of the caliper up through the boot and pull it free, then remove the dust boots

(see illustration). Use only enough pressure to ease the piston out of its bore. **Warning:** *Be careful not to place your fingers between the piston and the caliper, as the piston may come out with some force.*

6   Inspect the mating surfaces of the piston and caliper bore wall. If there is any scoring, rust, pitting or bright areas, replace the complete caliper unit with a new one.

7   If these components are in good condition, remove the piston seal from the caliper bore using a wooden or plastic tool **(see illustration)**. Metal tools may damage the cylinder bore.

8   Push the sliding bushings, if equipped, out of the caliper ears **(see illustration)** and remove the dust boots from both ends.

9   Wash all the components with brake system cleaner.

10   Submerge the new piston seal in brake fluid and install it into the lower groove in the caliper bore, making sure it isn't twisted.

11   If the caliper doesn't use a retaining ring on the piston dust boot, install the boot in the upper groove in the caliper bore. Make sure the flange on the boot seats in the groove completely. Lubricate the piston with clean brake fluid, carefully slide it through the new boot **(see illustration)**, position it squarely in the caliper bore and apply firm (but not excessive) pressure to install it. Make sure the piston boot seats in the groove in the piston.

12   If the caliper uses a retaining ring for the piston dust boot, lubricate the piston with clean brake fluid and install the piston into the bore. Do not force the piston into the bore, but make sure it is squarely in place, then apply firm (but not excessive) pressure to install it. Install the new boot and retaining ring. Make sure the boot seats in the groove in the piston.

13   Install the new piston dust boot and set ring.

14   Lubricate the sliding bushings with silicone-based grease (supplied in the kit) and push them into the caliper ears. Install the dust boots.

Installation

15   Install the caliper by reversing the removal procedure. Don't forget to replace the copper washers at the brake hose-to-

caliper banjo bolts (new washers normally come with the rebuild kit).

16   Bleed the brake circuit according to the procedure in Section 11. Make sure there are no leaks from the hose connections. Test the brakes carefully before returning the vehicle to normal service.

5   Brake disc - inspection, removal and installation

Inspection

Refer to illustrations 5.3, 5.4a, 5.4b and 5.5

1   Loosen the wheel lug nuts, raise the vehicle and support it securely on jackstands. Remove the wheel and, on 1987 and later models, install two lug nuts to hold the disc in place.

2   Remove the brake caliper as outlined in Section 4. It isn't necessary to disconnect the brake hose. After removing the caliper bolts, suspend the caliper out of the way with a piece of wire **(see illustration 3.6d)**. Remove the two torque plate-to-steering knuckle bolts **(see illustrations 3.6a and 3.6t through 3.6x)** and detach the torque plate.

3   Visually inspect the disc surface for score marks and other damage. Light scratches and shallow grooves are normal after use and may not always be detrimental to brake operation, but deep scoring - over

5.3 The brake pads on this vehicle were obviously neglected, as they wore down to the rivets and cut deep grooves into the disc - wear this severe means the disc must be replaced

4.11 On calipers that don't use a boot retaining ring, install the dust boot flange in the upper groove of the cylinder, then insert the piston into the boot (NOT the bore) at an angle and, using a rotating motion, work the piston completely into the dust boot

0.039-inch (1.0 mm) - requires disc removal and refinishing by an automotive machine shop. Be sure to check both sides of the disc **(see illustration)**. If pulsating has been noticed during application of the brakes, suspect disc runout.

4   To check disc runout, place a dial indicator at a point about 1/2-inch from the outer edge of the disc **(see illustration)**. Set the indicator to zero and turn the disc. The indicator reading should not exceed the specified allowable runout limit. If it does, the disc should be refinished by an automotive machine shop. **Note:** *The discs should be resurfaced regardless of the dial indicator*

5.4a To check disc runout, mount a dial indicator as shown and rotate the disc

9

5.4b Using a swirling motion, remove the glaze from the disc surface with sandpaper or emery cloth

5.5 Use a micrometer to measure disc thickness

reading, as this will impart a smooth finish and ensure a perfectly flat surface, eliminating any brake pedal pulsation or other undesirable symptoms related to questionable discs. At the very least, if you elect not to have the discs resurfaced, remove the glaze from the surface with emery cloth using a swirling motion **(see illustration).**

5   It's absolutely critical that the disc not be machined to a thickness under the specified minimum allowable disc refinish thickness. The minimum wear (or discard) thickness is cast into the disc. The disc thickness can be checked with a micrometer **(see illustration).**

Removal

6   If you're working on a 1987 or later model, remove the lug nuts which you installed to hold the disc in place and remove the disc from the hub. If the disc is stuck to the hub and won't come off, install bolts of the proper diameter and thread pitch into the threaded holes between the wheel studs and tighten them, which will force the disc off the hub.

7   If you're working on a 1986 or earlier model, remove the hub and steering knuckle assembly. Due to the special tools and expertise required to press the hub and bearing from the steering knuckle, which must be done in order to remove the disc from the hub, this job should be left to a

professional mechanic. See Chapter 10 for the steering knuckle removal procedure.

Installation

8   If you're working on a 1987 or later model, place the disc in position over the threaded studs. If you're working on a 1986 or earlier model, refer to Chapter 10 and install the steering knuckle and hub assembly.

8   Install the torque plate and caliper assembly over the disc and position it on the steering knuckle. Tighten the torque plate bolts to the torque listed in this Chapter's Specifications.

9   Install the wheel, then lower the vehicle to the ground. Tighten the lug nuts to the torque listed in the Chapter 1 Specifications. Depress the brake pedal a few times to bring the brake pads into contact with the disc. Bleeding won't be necessary unless the brake hose was disconnected from the caliper. Check the operation of the brakes carefully before driving the vehicle.

---

6   Drum brake shoes - replacement

Refer to illustrations 6.2a, 6.2b, 6.4a through 6.4dd and 6.5

Warning: *Drum brake shoes must be replaced on both wheels at the same time -*

never replace the shoes on only one wheel. Also, the dust created by the brake system may contain asbestos, which is harmful to your health. Never blow it out with compressed air and don't inhale any of it. An approved filtering mask should be worn when working on the brakes. Do not, under any circumstances, use petroleum-based solvents to clean brake parts. Use brake system cleaner only!

Caution: *Whenever the brake shoes are replaced, the return and hold-down springs should also be replaced. Due to the continuous heating/cooling cycle the springs are subjected to, they lose tension over a period of time and may allow the shoes to drag on the drum and wear at a much faster rate than normal.*

1   Loosen the wheel lug nuts, raise the rear of the vehicle and support it securely on jackstands. Block the front wheels to keep the vehicle from rolling. Remove the wheels.

2   Release the parking brake and remove the brake drums. On 1982 through 1986 models, the drums also serve as the hubs for the inner and outer tapered wheel bearings; Refer to Chapter 1, Section 34, for the "Rear wheel bearing check, repack and adjustment" procedure. On 1987 and later models, the wheel bearings are sealed units and separate from the drums, but they must be removed from the spindles before the brake shoes can be replaced. Refer to Chapter 10, Section 15, for the "Hub and bearing assembly (rear) - removal and installation" procedure. If the brake drum is difficult to remove, remove the access plug from the backing plate, insert a small screwdriver through the hole, lift the adjuster lever off the adjusting wheel and turn the wheel with another screwdriver to back off the brake shoes **(see illustrations).** The drum should now come off.

3   **Note:** *All four rear brake shoes must be replaced at the same time, but to avoid mixing up parts, work on only one brake assembly at a time.*

4   Before disassembling anything, clean the brake assembly off with brake cleaner **(see illustration).** Follow the accompanying

6.2a If the brake drums are hanging up on the brake shoes because of excessive wear, remove the access plug from the backing plate, insert a pair of small screwdrivers (or a screwdriver and a brake adjuster tool, as shown) and retract the shoes

6.2b Lift the adjuster lever off the adjuster wheel with the screwdriver and rotate the adjuster wheel until the shoes are retracted sufficiently to allow drum removal (brake drum removed for clarity)

6.4a Before disassembling the brake, wash it thoroughly with brake system cleaner and allow it to dry - position a drain pan under the brake to catch the residue - DO NOT use compressed air to blow the brake dust off!

Plug

Back plate

Bleeder cup

Bleeder

Dust cover

Piston

Piston cup

Wheel cylinder body

Spring

(RG)

Toggle lever

Pin

Anti-rattle pin

Adjuster

Toggle lever spring

Shoe

Front

Washer

Clip

Return spring
(Model LT20A only)

Anti-rattle
spring

Spring seat

Retainer

Return spring (Coil type)

Return spring (Model LT18A only)

Retainer

6.4b An exploded view of the LT18/LT18A and LT20A rear drum brake assembly (1982 LT18, 1983 through 1984 LT18A and 1983 through 1990 LT20A)

6.4c To release the hold-down springs without a special brake spring tool, grip the edges of the spring retainer with a pair of pliers, depress it against spring pressure and rotate it 90-degrees, release the retainer . . .

6.4d . . . and remove the spring

6.4e Pry off the shoe return spring retainer

6.4f To remove the big U-shaped shoe return spring, grip one arm, lever it toward the other arm to release it from the hole in the shoe and pry it loose; place a rag over the spring to prevent it from accidentally flying off

6.4g Pull the upper ends of the shoes apart and remove the adjuster mechanism

6.4h Disconnect and remove the leading shoe and the lower shoe return spring. Before installing the shoes, refer to illustration 6.4s

9

6.4i To remove the parking brake and automatic adjuster levers, remove the clip, washers and pin that attach them to the old rear shoe (see illustration 6.4b) and install them on the new rear shoe; make sure the setup looks like this when you're done. To reassemble the brake, reverse the removal procedure

illustrations for the brake shoe replacement procedures. The first sequence depicts a typical earlier style brake (LT18/LT18A) **(see illustrations 6.4b through 6.4i)**. An exploded view of the other earlier unit is also included **(see illustration 6.4j)**. The second sequence depicts a later style unit (LT18C) **(see illustrations 6.4k through 6.4dd)**. Be sure to stay in order and read the caption under each illustration.

6.4j An exploded view of the LT23A rear drum brake assembly (1988 through 1990 models)

6.4k An exploded view of the LT18C rear drum brake assembly (1991 through 1994 models)

6.4l Remove the brake hold-down springs and retainers, then pull out the hold-down pins through the rear of the backing plate

6.4m Lift the brake assembly off the backing plate as a single assembly, then remove the upper and lower return springs

6.4n Disengage the adjuster and the adjuster spring (the one *behind* the adjuster) and remove the leading shoe

6.4o Disengage and remove the adjuster from the trailing shoe

6.4p Disengage and remove the adjuster lever from the trailing shoe

6.4q Remove the C-clip retainer from the parking brake lever pivot pin and disconnect the parking brake lever from the trailing shoe

6.4r Disengage the parking brake cable from the parking brake lever

6.4s Apply high-temperature grease to the friction surfaces on the brake backing plate

6.4t Install the parking brake lever on the new trailing shoe and secure it with a new C-clip retainer

6.4u Install the new trailing shoe; make sure it's properly engaged with the wheel cylinder

6.4v Insert the hold-down pin through the rear of the backing plate and install the trailing shoe hold-down spring and retainer

6.4w Attach the adjuster spring to the trailing shoe as shown; note that the spring is hooked into the hole from the *rear*

9

6.4x Attach the lower return spring to the trailing shoe as shown; note that the spring is hooked into the hole from the *front*

6.4y Attach the adjuster spring to the post on the backside of the leading shoe

6.4z Insert the adjuster between the two shoes

6.4aa Make sure the adjuster is properly engaged with both shoes

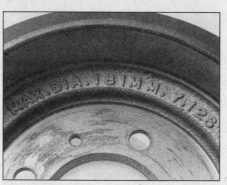

6.4bb Insert the hold-down pin through the rear of the backing plate and install the hold-down spring and retainer for the leading shoe

6.4cc Install the adjuster lever - make sure it's properly engaged with the pivot pin and the adjuster

5   Before reinstalling the drum, it should be checked for cracks, score marks, deep scratches and hard spots, which will appear as small discolored areas. If the hard spots cannot be removed with fine emery cloth or if any of the other conditions listed above exist, the drum must be taken to an automotive machine shop to have it resurfaced. **Note:** *Professionals recommend resurfacing the drums each time a brake job is done. Resurfacing will eliminate the possibility of out-of-round drums.* If the drums are worn so much that they can't be resurfaced without exceeding the maximum allowable diameter, which is stamped into the drum **(see illustration)**, then new ones will be required. At

6.4dd Hook the rear end of the return spring to the adjuster lever and the front end to the post on the leading shoe

the very least, if you elect not to have the drums resurfaced, remove the glaze from the surface with emery cloth using a swirling motion.
6   Install the brake drum. If the vehicle is a pre-1987 model with tapered roller bearings, refer to Chapter 1.
7   To make a preliminary adjustment of the brake, turn the adjuster star wheel until the brakes just begin to drag on the drum as it is turned, then back-off the star wheel until no dragging can be heard when you rotate the drum. Depress the brake pedal firmly several times, then rotate the drum to ensure that the brakes are not dragging. If they are, back off the star wheel a little more.

6.5 The brake drum maximum allowable inside diameter is cast inside the drum

8   Mount the wheel, install the lug nuts, then lower the vehicle. Tighten the wheel lug nuts to the torque listed in the Chapter 1 Specifications.
9   Make a number of forward and reverse stops and operate the parking brake to adjust the brakes until satisfactory pedal action is obtained.
10 Check the operation of the brakes carefully before driving the vehicle.

7   Wheel cylinder - removal, overhaul and installation

Note: *If an overhaul is indicated (usually because of fluid leaks or sticky operation), explore all options before beginning the job. New wheel cylinders are available, which makes this job quite easy. If it's decided to rebuild the wheel cylinder, make sure a rebuild kit is available before proceeding. Never overhaul only one wheel cylinder - always rebuild both of them at the same time.*

Removal

Refer to illustration 7.4

1   Raise the rear of the vehicle and support it securely on jackstands. Block the front wheels to keep the vehicle from rolling.
2   Remove the brake shoe assembly (see Section 6).

7.4 To remove the wheel cylinder, disconnect the brake line fitting (lower arrow), then remove the two wheel cylinder bolts (upper arrows)

1 Dust boot
2 Piston head
3 Piston
4 Piston cup
5 Wheel cylinder housing
6 Bleeder screw
7 Bleeder screw cap

7.7 Exploded view of the rear wheel cylinder

3   Remove all dirt and foreign material from around the wheel cylinder.

4   Disconnect the brake line **(see illustration)** with a flare-nut wrench, if available. Don't pull the brake line away from the wheel cylinder.

5   Remove the wheel cylinder mounting bolts.

6   Detach the wheel cylinder from the brake backing plate and place it on a clean workbench. Immediately plug the brake line to prevent fluid loss and contamination.

Overhaul

Refer to illustration 7.7

7   Remove the bleeder screw, cups, pistons, boots and spring assembly from the wheel cylinder body **(see illustration).**

8   Clean the parts with brake system cleaner. **Warning:** *Do not, under any circumstances, use petroleum-based solvents to clean brake parts!*

9   Use compressed air to dry the wheel cylinder and blow out the passages.

10   Check the bore for corrosion and score marks. Crocus cloth can be used to remove light corrosion and stains, but the cylinder must be replaced with a new one if the defects cannot be removed easily, or if the bore is scored.

11   Lubricate the new cups with brake fluid.

12   Assemble the wheel cylinder components. Make sure the cup lips face in.

Installation

13   Place the wheel cylinder in position and install the bolts finger tight. Connect the brake line to the cylinder, being careful not to cross-thread the fitting. Tighten the wheel cylinder bolts to the torque listed in this Chapter's Specifications.

14   Tighten the brake line securely and install the brake shoe assembly.

15   Bleed the brakes (see Section 11).

16   Check the operation of the brakes carefully before driving the vehicle.

8   Master cylinder - removal, overhaul and installation

Note: *Before deciding to overhaul the master cylinder, check on the availability and cost of a new or factory rebuilt unit and also the availability of a rebuild kit.*

Removal

Refer to illustrations 8.2 and 8.4

1   Disconnect the cable from the negative battery terminal.

2   Unplug the electrical connector for the fluid level warning switch **(see illustration).**

3   Remove as much fluid as possible from the reservoir with a syringe.

4   Place rags under the fittings and prepare caps or plastic bags to cover the ends of the lines once they're disconnected. **Caution:** *Brake fluid will damage paint. Cover all body parts and be careful not to spill fluid during this procedure.* Loosen the fittings at the ends of the brake lines where they enter the master cylinder **(see illustration).** To prevent rounding off the flats, use a flare-nut wrench, which wraps around the fitting hex.

5   Pull the brake lines away from the master cylinder and plug the ends to prevent contamination.

6   Remove the nuts attaching the master cylinder to the power booster **(see illustration 8.4).** Pull the master cylinder off the studs to remove it. Again, be careful not to spill the fluid as this is done. Remove and discard the old gasket between the master cylinder and the power brake booster.

Overhaul

Refer to illustrations 8.8, 8.9, 8.10, 8.11a, 8.11b and 8.15

7   Before attempting the overhaul of the master cylinder, obtain the proper rebuild kit,

8.2 Unplug the electrical connector (arrow) for the fluid level warning switch

8.4 Loosen the brake line fittings (arrows) with a flare-nut wrench and remove the master cylinder mounting nuts (arrows)

9

8.8 An exploded view of a typical master cylinder assembly (1991 and later model master cylinder shown)

Labels: Reservoir cap, Filter, Float, Reservoir tank, Seal, Primary piston assembly, Secondary piston assembly, Stopper cap, Piston cup, Piston cup, Spring seat, Secondary return spring, Dual proportioning valve (Do not disassemble)

8.9 To remove the stopper cap, pry open the two small tangs on the side with a small screwdriver

8.10 Depress the pistons and remove the snap-ring with a pair of snap-ring pliers

which will contain the necessary replacement parts and also any instructions which may be specific to your model.

8   Pull off the reservoir and remove the grommets **(see illustrations)**.

9   Place the cylinder in a vise. Remove the stopper cap **(see illustration)**. Use a punch or Phillips screwdriver to depress the pistons until they bottom against the other end of the master cylinder. Hold the pistons in this position and remove the stopper bolt or screw, if equipped, from the master cylinder.

10   Depress the pistons and remove the snap-ring at the end of the master cylinder **(see illustration)**.

11   The internal components can now be removed from the bore **(see illustrations)**.

Make a note of the proper order of the components so they can be returned to their original locations.

12   Carefully inspect the bore of the master cylinder. Any deep score marks or other damage will mean a new master cylinder is required. DO NOT attempt to hone the bore.

13   Replace all parts included in the rebuild kit, following any instructions in the kit. Clean all re-used parts with brake system cleaner. **Warning:** *Do not use any petroleum-based solvents. During reassembly, lubricate all parts liberally with clean brake fluid.*

14   Push the assembled components into

the bore, bottoming them against the end of the master cylinder, then install the stopper bolt, if applicable.

15   Install the new snap-ring, making sure it's seated properly in the groove. Install a new stopper cap **(see illustration)**.

16   Install the reservoir grommets and reservoir.

17   Before installing the master cylinder, it should be bench bled. Since you'll have to apply pressure to the master cylinder piston and, at the same time, control flow from the brake line outlets, the master cylinder should be mounted in a vise, with the jaws of the vise clamping on the mounting flange.

18   Insert threaded plugs into the brake line outlet holes and snug them down so no air will leak past them, but not so tight that they can't be easily loosened.

8.11a After the snap-ring has been removed, the primary piston assembly can be removed

8.11b Remove the cylinder from the vise and tap it against a block of wood until the secondary piston is exposed. Pull the piston assembly STRAIGHT OUT - if it becomes even slightly cocked, the bore may be damaged

8.15 Before installing the new stopper cap, make sure the two tangs bend inward

8.27 Have an assistant depress the brake pedal and hold it down, then loosen the fitting nut, allowing the air and fluid to escape; repeat this procedure on both fittings until the fluid is clear of air bubbles

19   Fill the reservoir with brake fluid of the recommended type (see Chapter 1).
20   Remove one plug and push the piston assembly into the bore to expel the air from the master cylinder. A large Phillips screwdriver can be used to push on the piston assembly.
21   To prevent air from being drawn back into the master cylinder, the plug must be replaced and snugged down before releasing the pressure on the piston.
22   Repeat the procedure until only brake fluid is expelled from the brake line outlet hole. When only brake fluid is expelled, repeat the procedure at the other outlet hole and plug. Be sure to keep the master cylinder reservoir filled with brake fluid to prevent the introduction of air into the system.
23   Since high pressure isn't involved in the bench bleeding procedure, an alternative to the removal and replacement of the plugs with each stroke of the piston assembly is available. Before pushing in on the piston assembly, remove the plug as described in Step 20. Before releasing the piston, however, instead of replacing the plug, simply put your finger tightly over the hole to keep air from being drawn back into the master cylinder. Wait several seconds for brake fluid to be drawn from the reservoir into the bore, then depress the piston again, removing your finger as brake fluid is expelled. Be sure to put your finger back over the hole each time before releasing the piston, and when the bleeding procedure is complete for that outlet, replace the plug and tighten it before going on to the other port.

Installation

Refer to illustration 8.27
24   Install the master cylinder over the studs on the power brake booster and tighten the nuts only finger-tight at this time. Don't forget to use a new gasket.
25   Thread the brake line fittings into the master cylinder. Since the master cylinder is still a bit loose, it can be moved slightly so the fittings thread in easily. Don't strip the threads as the fittings are tightened.
26   Tighten the mounting nuts and the brake line fittings.

9.1 A typical proportioning valve; to replace it, simply unscrew all the threaded fittings and disconnect and plug the brake lines, then remove the mounting bolt

27   Fill the master cylinder reservoir with fluid, then bleed the master cylinder (only if hasn't been bench bled) and the brake system (see Section 11). To bleed the master cylinder on the vehicle, have an assistant depress the brake pedal and hold it down. Loosen the fitting to allow air and fluid to escape **(see illustration)**. Tighten the fitting, then allow your assistant to return the pedal to its rest position. Repeat this procedure on both fittings until the fluid is free of air bubbles. Check the operation of the brake system carefully before driving the vehicle.

9   Proportioning valve - replacement

Refer to illustration 9.1
1   The proportioning valve **(see illustration)** is mounted on the firewall. Its purpose is to limit hydraulic pressure to the rear brakes under heavy braking conditions to prevent rear wheel lockup.
2   The valve is not serviceable; if you suspect it's malfunctioning, have it checked by a dealer service department or repair shop equipped with the necessary pressure gauges.
3   If the valve is leaking or has been determined to be defective, replace it by unscrewing the brake lines (using a flare-nut

10.3 Loosen the threaded fitting on the brake line; use a flare-nut wrench, if available, to protect the corners of the nut

wrench, if available) and unbolting the valve from its mounting bracket. After the new valve is installed, bleed the complete brake system as described in Section 12.

10   Brake hoses and lines - inspection and replacement

Inspection

1   About every six months, with the vehicle raised and supported securely on jackstands, the rubber hoses which connect the steel brake lines with the front and rear brake assemblies should be inspected for cracks, chafing of the outer cover, leaks, blisters and other damage. These are important and vulnerable parts of the brake system and inspection should be complete. A light and mirror will be helpful for a thorough check. If a hose exhibits any of the above conditions, replace it with a new one.

Replacement

Front brake hose

Refer to illustrations 10.3 and 10.4
2   Loosen the wheel lug nuts, raise the vehicle and support it securely on jackstands. Remove the wheel.
3   At the bracket, unscrew the brake line fitting from the hose **(see illustration)**. Use a flare-nut wrench to prevent rounding off the corners.
4   Remove the U-clip from the female fitting at the bracket with a pair of pliers **(see illustration)**, then pass the hose through the bracket.
5   At the caliper end of the hose, remove the banjo bolt, then separate the hose from the caliper. Note that there are two copper sealing washers on either side of the banjo fitting - they should be replaced with new ones during installation.
6   Remove the U-clip from the strut bracket, then detach the hose from the bracket.
7   To install the hose, pass the caliper fitting end through the strut bracket, then connect the fitting to the caliper with the banjo bolt and copper washers.

10.4 Pull off the U-clip with a pair of pliers

9

8   Make sure the hose isn't twisted between the caliper and the strut bracket.

9   Route the hose into the frame bracket, again making sure it isn't twisted, then connect the brake line fitting, starting the threads by hand. Install the U-clip, then tighten the fitting securely.

10   Bleed the caliper (see Section 11).

11   Install the wheel and lug nuts, lower the vehicle and tighten the lug nuts to the torque listed in the Chapter 1 Specifications.

Rear brake hose

12   The rear brake hose serves as the flexible connection between two rigid metal lines, one on the body and the other on the axle. Both ends of the hose are attached to these metal lines with threaded fittings and U-clips. Refer to Steps 2, 3 and 4. Be sure to bleed the wheel cylinder when you're done (see Section 11).

Metal brake lines

13   When replacing brake lines, be sure to use the correct parts. Don't use copper tubing for any brake system components. Purchase steel brake lines from a dealer or auto parts store.

14   Prefabricated brake line, with the tube ends already flared and fittings installed, is available at auto parts stores and dealer parts departments. These lines are also bent to the proper shapes.

15   When installing the new line, make sure it's securely supported in the brackets and has plenty of clearance between moving or hot components.

16   After installation, check the master cylinder fluid level and add fluid as necessary. Bleed the brake system (see Section 11) and test the brakes carefully before driving the vehicle in traffic.

---

11   Brake hydraulic system - bleeding

Refer to illustration 11.8

Warning: *Wear eye protection when bleeding the brake system. If the fluid comes in contact with your eyes, immediately rinse them with water and seek medical attention.*

Note: *Bleeding the hydraulic system is necessary to remove any air that manages to find its way into the system when it's been opened during removal and installation of a hose, line, caliper or master cylinder.*

1   You'll probably have to bleed the system at all four brakes if air has entered it due to low fluid level, or if the brake lines have been disconnected at the master cylinder.

2   If a brake line was disconnected only at a wheel, then only that caliper or wheel cylinder must be bled.

3   If a brake line is disconnected at a fitting located between the master cylinder and any of the brakes, that part of the system served by the disconnected line must be bled.

11.8 When bleeding the brakes, a hose is connected to the bleed screw at the caliper or wheel cylinder and then submerged in brake fluid - air will be seen as bubbles in the tube and container (all air must be expelled before moving to the next wheel)

4   Remove any residual vacuum from the brake power booster by applying the brake several times with the engine off.

5   Remove the master cylinder reservoir cover and fill the reservoir with brake fluid. Reinstall the cover. **Note:** *Check the fluid level often during the bleeding operation and add fluid as necessary to prevent the fluid level from falling low enough to allow air bubbles into the master cylinder.* If you're working on a 1994 model equipped with ABS, turn the ignition switch off and disconnect the electrical connector from the ABS actuator.

6   Have an assistant on hand, as well as a supply of new brake fluid, a clear plastic container partially filled with clean brake fluid, a length of 3/16-inch plastic, rubber or vinyl tubing to fit over the bleeder valve and a wrench to open and close the bleeder valve.

7   Beginning at the right rear wheel, loosen the bleeder valve slightly, then tighten it to a point where it's snug but can still be loosened quickly and easily.

8   Place one end of the tubing over the bleeder valve and submerge the other end in brake fluid in the container **(see illustration).**

9   Have the assistant pump the brakes slowly a few times to get pressure in the system, then hold the pedal down firmly.

10   While the pedal is held down, open the bleeder valve just enough to allow a flow of fluid to leave the valve. Watch for air bubbles to exit the submerged end of the tube. When the fluid flow slows after a couple of seconds, close the valve and have your assistant release the pedal.

11   Repeat Steps 9 and 10 until no more air is seen leaving the tube, then tighten the bleeder valve and proceed to the left front wheel, the left rear wheel and the right front wheel, in that order, and perform the same procedure. Be sure to check the fluid in the master cylinder reservoir frequently.

12   Never use old brake fluid. It contains moisture which will deteriorate the brake system components and could cause the fluid to boil, which could render the brake system inoperative.

13   Refill the master cylinder with fluid at the end of the operation. If you're working on a 1994 model with ABS, be sure to reconnect the electrical connector to the ABS actuator.

14   Check the operation of the brakes. The pedal should feel solid when depressed, with no sponginess. If necessary, repeat the entire process. **Warning:** *Do not operate the vehicle if you're in doubt about the effectiveness of the brake system.*

---

12   Power brake booster - check, removal and installation

Operating check

1   Depress the brake pedal several times with the engine off and make sure there's no change in the pedal reserve distance.

2   Depress the pedal and start the engine. If the pedal goes down slightly, operation is normal.

Airtightness check

3   Start the engine and turn it off after one or two minutes. Depress the brake pedal slowly several times. If the pedal depresses less each time, the booster is airtight.

4   Depress the brake pedal while the engine is running, then stop the engine with the pedal depressed. If there's no change in the pedal reserve travel after holding the pedal for 30 seconds, the booster is airtight.

Removal

Refer to illustration 12.7

5   Power brake booster units shouldn't be disassembled. They require special tools not normally found in most automotive repair stations or shops. They're fairly complex and, because of their critical relationship to brake performance, should be replaced with a new or rebuilt one.

6   To remove the booster, first remove the brake master cylinder (see Section 8).

7   Remove the steering column lower finish panel. Locate the pushrod clevis connecting the booster to the brake pedal **(see illustration).** It's accessible from inside the vehicle, under the dash on the driver's side.

8   Remove the clevis pin retaining clip with pliers and pull out the clevis pin.

9   Disconnect the hose leading from the engine to the booster. Be careful not to damage the hose when removing it from the booster fitting.

10   Remove the four nuts and washers holding the brake booster to the firewall **(see illustration 12.7);** you may need a light to see them.

11   Slide the booster straight out from the firewall until the studs clear the holes.

Installation

12   Installation procedures are basically the reverse of removal. However, be sure to make the following adjustments where necessary.

Clevis pin

Brake booster

12.7 An exploded view of a typical power brake booster assembly

B

12.14 Power brake booster input rod length "B" (1982 through 1984 models)

Adjustment

13   Measure and - where possible - adjust the following dimensions: The length of the input rod between the clevis and the booster, and the length of the booster output rod (pushrod) between the booster and the master cylinder primary piston.

Input rod length (1982 through 1984 models only)

Refer to illustration 12.14

14   On 1982 through 1984 models, measure the length of the input rod - length B - **(see illustration)** and compare your measurement to the dimension listed in this Chapter's Specifications.

15   If the input rod length isn't within specification, loosen the locknut and turn the clevis until the dimension is correct, then tighten the locknut securely.

16   On 1985 and later models, there is no adjustment for input rod length.

Output rod length

Refer to illustrations 12.17 and 12.19

17   On 1982 and 1983 models, measure the length of the portion of the output rod that protrudes from the booster - length A - **(see**

illustration)**. If this dimension is not within specification, replace the power brake booster assembly.

18   On 1984 through 1990 models, the pushrod does not need to be adjusted.

19   On 1991 and later models, apply approximately 20 in-Hg of vacuum to the brake booster with a hand-operated vacuum pump **(see illustration**, measure the length of the output rod **(see illustration 12.17)** and compare your measurement to the dimensions listed in this Chapter's Specification. If the rod length is outside specifications, replace the booster.

13   Parking brake - check and adjustment

Check

1   The parking brake lever, when properly adjusted, should travel up the following number of clicks when a moderate pulling force is applied:

a) *Six to seven clicks on 1982 through 1986 models*
b) *Seven to eleven clicks on 1987 through 1990 models*

c) *Five to seven clicks on 1991 models with rear drum brakes; seven to nine clicks on 1991 models with rear disc brakes.*
d) *Five to six clicks on 1991 models with rear drum brakes; seven to eight clicks on 1991 models with rear disc brakes.*

2   If the parking brake lever travels less than the specified minimum number of clicks, it might not be releasing completely and the shoes or pads could even be dragging against the drum or disc. If the lever can be pulled up more than the specified maximum number of clicks, the parking brake may not hold adequately on an incline, allowing the car to roll.

Adjustment

1982 through 1986 models

Refer to illustration 13.5

3   Release the parking brake lever.
4   Raise the vehicle and place it securely on jackstands.
5   Locate the adjuster nut in the rear cable between the equalizer and the right rear wheel **(see illustration)**. Turn the adjuster lock nut clockwise to tighten the cable and decrease the number of clicks at the parking brake lever, or turn it counterclockwise to loosen the cable and increase the number of clicks at the lever.

Output rod length "A"

12.17 Power brake booster output rod length "A" (1982 and 1983 and 1991 and later models)

12.19 On 1991 and later models, apply approximately 20 in-Hg of vacuum to the power brake booster before measuring output rod length

13.5 To adjust parking brake lever travel on 1982 through 1986 models, turn the locknut adjuster (arrow) clockwise to tighten the cable and decrease the number of clicks at the lever, or turn it counterclockwise to loosen the cable and increase the number of clicks

9

13.8 To adjust parking brake lever travel on 1987 and later models, turn the adjusting nut until the specified travel is obtained

6   Remove the jackstands and lower the vehicle.

1987 and later models

Refer to illustration 13.8

7   To gain access to the parking brake cable adjuster, remove the center console (see Chapter 11).

8   Loosen or tighten the adjusting nut **(see illustration)** until the desired travel is attained. Turn the nut clockwise to tighten the cable and decrease the number of clicks at the parking brake lever, or turn it counterclockwise to loosen the cable and increase the number of clicks at the lever.

9   Install the console (see Chapter 11).

14.4c On later models with rear disc brakes, the parking brake cable is attached to a bracket on the caliper by a lock plate which can be removed with a prybar . . .

14.4d . . . then unhook the cable end from the parking brake lever on the caliper

14.4a On earlier models, the parking brake cable ferrule is pushed into a reinforced tube welded to the backing plate; to remove it, pry it loose at the ferrule flange; to install it, guide the cable through the tube, then tap the flange on the flange until the ferrule is fully seated into the tube

14   Parking brake cables - replacement

1   Make sure the parking brake is completely released.

2   Loosen the rear wheel lug nuts, raise the rear of the vehicle and support it securely on jackstands. Block the front wheels. Remove the wheel.

Rear cables

Refer to illustrations 14.4a, 14.4b, 14.4c, 14.4d, 14.5a, 14.5b and 14.7

3   On models with rear drum brakes, remove the brake drums and the brake shoes, and disconnect the cable from the parking brake levers on both trailing shoes (see Section 6).

14.4b On later models, the parking brake cable ferrule is attached to the backing plate by these two nuts; to detach the cable housing from the backing plate, remove the nuts and pull the cable out of the plate

4   On models with rear drum brakes, disconnect the cable ferrules from the backing plates **(see illustrations)** and pull the cables through the plates. On models with rear disc brakes, remove the large lock plates that attach the cables to the brackets on the calipers **(see illustration)**, then disconnect the cables from the rear calipers **(see illustration)**.

5   Unbolt any cable brackets from the frame or the suspension pieces **(see illustrations)**.

6   On 1987 and later models, remove the exhaust pipe and catalytic converter heat shields.

7   To disconnect the rear cables on 1982 through 1986 models, unscrew the adjuster nut **(see illustrations 13.5 and 14.5a)** and disengage the cables from the equalizer. To disconnect the rear cables on 1987 and later models, remove the two cable housing nuts just behind the equalizer and disengage

14.5a An exploded view of the parking brake cable assembly on 1982 through 1986 models

14.5b An exploded view of the parking brake assembly on 1991 and later models

For disc brake

For drum brake

the cables from the equalizer **(see illustration)**.

8 Installation is the reverse of removal. Apply a light coat of grease to the portion of the cable end that engages with the equalizer.

9 Adjust the parking brake when you're done (see Section 13).

Front cable (1982 through 1986 models only)

Refer to illustration 14.11

10 Remove the center console (see Chapter 11).

11 Unplug the electrical connector for the parking brake light switch **(see illustration)**.

12 Remove the seat belt anchor bolts.

13 Remove the parking brake lever retaining bolts **(see illustration 14.11)** and the front cable bracket retaining screws **(see illustration 14.5a)**.

14 Raise the rear of the vehicle and place it securely on jackstands.

15 Disconnect the front cable from the equalizer **(see illustration 14.5a)**. Pull the cable through the hole in the floorpan.

16 You'll have to chisel off the clevis pin head **(see illustration 14.11)** to disconnect the front cable from the parking brake lever. The new cable can be attached with a clevis pin and cotter pin, which are available at the dealer parts department.

17 Installation is the reverse of removal. Apply a light coat of grease to the portion of the cable end that engages with the equalizer.

18 Adjust the parking brake lever when you're done (see Section 13).

15 Brake light switch - check and replacement

Check

Refer to illustration 15.1

1 The brake light switch is located on a bracket at the top of the brake pedal (see

14.7 To disconnect the rear parking brake cables from the equalizer on 1987 and later models, simply remove these bracket nuts (right arrows), slide the cables forward slightly and disengage the cable ends (left arrows) from the equalizer

14.11 To disconnect the front parking brake cable from the parking brake lever on 1982 through 1986 models, unplug the electrical connector (1) for the parking brake light switch, remove the two parking brake lever bolts (2) and cut off the head of the clevis pin (3) with a cold chisel

9

15.1 The brake light switch (arrow) is located at the top of the brake pedal

illustration). The switch activates the brake lights at the rear of the vehicle when the pedal is depressed.

2   To check the brake light switch, simply note whether the brake lights come on when the pedal is depressed and go off when the pedal is released. If they don't, adjust the switch as described in Chapter 1, Section 16 (adjusting the switch is part of brake pedal adjustment).

3   If the switch still doesn't work properly, either it's not getting voltage, or the switch itself is defective.

4   Use a voltmeter or test light to verify that there's voltage at the switch connector. With the pedal at rest, voltage should be present at one of the terminals of the switch. With the pedal depressed, voltage should be present at both terminals. If voltage isn't present at both terminals when the pedal is depressed, replace the switch.

Replacement

5   Disconnect the negative battery cable from the battery.

6   Unplug the electrical connector for the brake light switch.

7   Loosen the locknuts and unscrew the switch from the pedal bracket.

8   Installation is the reverse of removal.

9   Adjust the brake pedal and brake light switch (see Chapter 1, Section 16).

Chapter 10
Suspension and steering systems

Contents

Specifications

Torque specifications
Front suspension

	Ft-lbs (unless otherwise indicated)
Strut piston rod self-locking nut	
1982 through 1990	46 to 53
1991 through 1994	84 to 98
Strut upper mounting nuts	
1982 and 1983	132 to 204 in-lbs
1984 through 1986	23 to 31
1987 through 1994	18 to 22
Strut-to-steering knuckle bolts/nuts	
1982 and 1983	51 to 65
1984 through 1990	72 to 87
1991 through 1994	84 to 98
Lower balljoint	
1982 through 1986	
Balljoint-to-control arm nuts	40 to 47
Balljoint-to-steering knuckle nut	25 to 36
1987 through 1994	
Balljoint-to-steering knuckle nut	43 to 54
Control arm	
Pivot bolt nut	72 to 87
Bushing clamp bolts	
1982 and 1983	58 to 72
1984 through 1986	65 to 80
1987 through 1994	58 to 72
Pivot stud nut (1982 through 1986)	72 to 87
Stabilizer bar	
Link bolt nuts	
1985 and 1986	84 to 96 in-lbs
1987 through 1990	
Stabilizer-to-link nut	25 to 33
Link-to-control arm nut	144 to 192 in-lbs
1991 and 1992	
Stabilizer-to-link nut	34 to 38
Link-to-control arm nut	14 to 22
1993 and 1994	
Stabilizer-to-link nut	34 to 38
Link-to-control arm nut	12 to 16
Bushing clamp bolts	
1985 and 1986	84 to 96 in-lbs
1987 through 1990	144 to 180 in-lbs
1991 through 1994	23 to 31

10

Torque specifications (continued)   **Ft-lbs** (unless otherwise indicated)

Rear suspension

Shock absorber (1982 through 1986)	
Upper mounting nut	78 to 104 in-lbs
Lower mounting bolt	
1982 and 1983	26 to 35
1984 through 1986	51 to 65
Trailing arm pivot bolt nuts	
1982 and 1983	43 to 51
1984 through 1986	51 to 58
Strut assembly (1987 and later)	
Piston rod nut	46 to 53
Strut to body nuts	18 to 22
Strut-to-knuckle bolts/nuts	
1987 through 1990	72 to 87
1991 through 1994	72 to 98
Suspension arms (1987 and later)	
Parallel links	
Parallel links-to-body bolts	72 to 87
Parallel links-to-knuckle bolt/nut	72 to 87
Radius rod	
1987 through 1990	
Bushing clamp bolts	65 to 80
Radius rod-to-knuckle nut	47 to 61
1991 through 1994	
Radius rod-to-body	72 to 87
Radius rod-to-knuckle	72 to 87
Rear hub/bearing retainer nut (1987 and later)	137 to 188

Steering

Airbag module Torx bolts (T50H)	132 to 216 in-lbs
High pressure line-to-steering gear fitting	
1982 and 1983	14 to 22
1984 through 1994	132 to 216 in-lbs
High pressure line-to-pump banjo bolt	
1982 through 1986	22 to 36
1987 through 1993	36 to 51
1994	51 to 58
Pump pulley nut	
1982 through 1986	31 to 46
1987 and 1988	23 to 31
1989 through 1994	40 to 50
Steering gear mounting clamp bolts	
1982 through 1986	43 to 58
1987 through 1994	54 to 72
Steering shaft lower U-joint pinch-bolts	
1982 through 1986	22 to 29
1987 through 1994	17 to 22
Steering wheel nut	
1982	22 to 29
1983 through 1986	29 to 40
1987 through 1990	22 to 29
1991 through 1994	29 to 39
Tie-rod-to-steering knuckle nut	
1982 through 1986	22 to 36
1987 through 1994	22 to 29

1   General information

Refer to illustrations 1.1, 1.2, 1.3 and 1.4

The front suspension is a Macpherson strut design. The upper end of each strut is attached to the vehicle body. The lower end of the strut is connected to the upper end of the steering knuckle. The steering knuckle is attached to a balljoint mounted on the outer end of the control arm **(see illustrations)**. A stabilizer bar is used on 1985 and later models. The bar is attached to the body with a pair of clamps and to the control arms with link bolts.

The rear suspension on 1982 through 1986 models uses shock absorbers and coil springs with trailing arms. The upper end of each shock is attached to the vehicle body; the lower end is attached to the trailing arm **(see illustration)**.

The rear suspension on 1987 through 1990 models **(see illustration)** uses strut/coil spring assemblies and a pair of lateral suspension arms at each wheel (Nissan calls them "lateral links"). A stabilizer bar (Nissan calls it a "radius rod") is mounted in front of -

**1.1 Front suspension components
(1988 model shown, others similar)**

1 Steering gear assembly
2 Control arm front pivot bolt
3 Strut/coil spring assembly
4 Stabilizer bar
5 Stabilizer bar bushing/clamp
6 Control arm rear bushing/clamp
7 Control arm
8 Stabilizer bar-to-control link rod nut

**1.2 Rear suspension components
(1982 through 1986 models)**

1 Trailing arm
2 Shock absorber-to-trailing arm mounting
  bolt/nut
3 Trailing arm pivot bolt/nut

**1.3 Rear suspension components
(1987 through 1990 models)**

1 Lateral arm pivot bolt/nut
2 Lateral arm
3 Strut/coil spring assembly
4 Stabilizer bar
5 Knuckle
6 Stabilizer bar bushing/clamp
7 Lateral arm-to-knuckle through-bolt/nut

10

**1.4 Rear suspension components
(1991 and later models)**

1 Strut/coil spring assembly
2 Knuckle
3 Trailing arm
4 Forward lateral arm
5 Rear lateral arm
6 Left stabilizer bushing/clamp nuts
7 Right stabilizer bushing/clamp
8 Stabilizer bar

and is connected to - the suspension arms. In addition to its anti-roll function, the stabilizer bar positions the strut/knuckle/hub assembly longitudinally.

The rear suspension on 1991 and later models **(see illustration)** also uses strut/coil spring assemblies and a pair of lateral suspension arms at each wheel, except that the stabilizer bar ("radius rod") is replaced by a pair of conventional trailing arms (Nissan calls these arms "radius rods" too!). The trailing arms position the strut/knuckle/hub assembly longitudinally. The stabilizer bar is moved to the rear of the lateral arms.

The rack-and-pinion steering gear is located behind the engine/transaxle assembly at the bottom of the firewall (it's bolted to the lower rear crossmember on 1991 and later models) and actuates the tie-rods, which are attached to the steering knuckles. The inner ends of the tie-rods are protected by rubber boots which should be inspected periodically for secure attachment, tears and leaking lubricant.

The power assist system consists of a belt-driven pump and associated lines and hoses. The fluid level in the power steering pump reservoir should be checked periodically (see Chapter 1).

The steering wheel operates the steering shaft, which actuates the steering gear through universal joints. Looseness in the steering can be caused by wear in the steering shaft universal joints, the steering gear, the tie-rod ends and loose retaining bolts.

Frequently, when working on the suspension or steering system components, you may come across fasteners which seem impossible to loosen. These fasteners on the underside of the vehicle are continually subjected to water, road grime, mud, etc., and can become rusted or "frozen," making

them extremely difficult to remove. In order to unscrew these stubborn fasteners without damaging them (or other components), be sure to use lots of penetrating oil and allow it to soak in for a while. Using a wire brush to clean exposed threads will also ease removal of the nut or bolt and prevent damage to the threads. Sometimes a sharp blow with a hammer and punch will break the bond between a nut and bolt threads, but care must be taken to prevent the punch from slipping off the fastener and ruining the threads. Heating the stuck fastener and surrounding area with a torch sometimes helps too, but isn't recommended because of the obvious dangers associated with fire. Long breaker bars and extension, or "cheater," pipes will increase leverage, but never use an extension pipe on a ratchet - the ratcheting mechanism could be damaged. Sometimes tightening the nut or bolt first will help to break it loose. Fasteners that require drastic measures to remove should always be replaced with new ones.

Since most of the procedures dealt with in this Chapter involve jacking up the vehicle and working underneath it, a good pair of jackstands will be needed. A hydraulic floor jack is the preferred type of jack to lift the vehicle, and it can also be used to support certain components during various operations. **Warning:** *Never, under any circumstances, rely on a jack to support the vehicle while working on it. Whenever any of the suspension or steering fasteners are loosened or removed they must be inspected and, if necessary, replaced with new ones of the same part number or of original equipment quality and design. Torque specifications must be followed for proper reassembly and component retention. Never attempt to heat or straighten any*

suspension or steering components. Instead, replace any bent or damaged part with a new one.

---

2   Strut assembly (front) - removal, inspection and installation

Removal

Refer to illustrations 2.3 and 2.5

1   Loosen the front wheel lug nuts, raise the front of the vehicle and support it securely on jackstands. Remove the wheels.

2   Unclip the brake hose from the strut bracket and detach it from the bracket. If the vehicle is equipped with ABS, detach the speed sensor wiring harness from the strut by removing the clamp bracket bolt.

3   Remove the strut-to-knuckle nuts **(see illustration)** and knock the bolts out with a hammer and punch.

4   Separate the strut from the steering knuckle. Be careful not to overextend the inner CV joint.

2.3 To detach the strut assembly from the steering knuckle, remove the two nuts (arrows), then knock out the bolts with a hammer and punch

2.5 To detach the upper end of the strut assembly from the body, remove the upper mounting nuts (arrows). Warning: *Don't remove the center nut!*

3.3 Install the spring compressor according to the tool manufacturer's instructions and compress the spring until all pressure is relieved from the upper spring seat

3.4 Remove the damper shaft nut

5   Support the strut and spring assembly with one hand and remove the three strut-to-shock tower nuts **(see illustration)**. Remove the assembly out from the fenderwell.

Inspection

6   Check the strut body for leaking fluid, dents, cracks and other obvious damage which would warrant repair or replacement.
7   Check the coil spring for chips or cracks in the spring coating (this will cause premature spring failure due to corrosion). Inspect the spring seat for cuts, hardness and general deterioration.
8   If any undesirable conditions exist, proceed to the strut disassembly procedure (see Section 3).

Installation

9   Guide the strut assembly up into the fenderwell and insert the upper mounting studs through the holes in the shock tower. Once the studs protrude from the shock tower, install the nuts so the strut won't fall back through. This is most easily accomplished with the help of an assistant, as the strut is quite heavy and awkward.
10   Slide the steering knuckle into the strut flange and insert the two bolts. Install the nuts and tighten them to the torque listed in this Chapter's Specifications.
11   Guide the brake hose through its bracket in the strut and install the clip.
12   Install the wheel and lug nuts, then

lower the vehicle and tighten the lug nuts to the torque listed in the Chapter 1 Specifications.
13   Tighten the upper mounting nuts to the torque listed in this Chapter's Specifications.
14   Drive the vehicle to an alignment shop to have the front end alignment checked, and if necessary, adjusted.

3   Strut/coil spring assembly - replacement

1   If the struts or coil springs exhibit the telltale signs of wear (leaking fluid, loss of damping capability, chipped, sagging or cracked coil springs) explore all options before beginning any work. The strut/shock absorber assemblies are not serviceable and must be replaced if a problem develops. However, strut assemblies complete with springs may be available on an exchange basis, which eliminates much time and work. Whichever route you choose to take, check on the cost and availability of parts before disassembling your vehicle. **Warning:** *Disassembling a strut is a potentially dangerous undertaking and utmost attention must be directed to the job, or serious injury may result. Use only a high quality spring compressor and carefully follow the manufacturer's instructions furnished with the tool. After removing the coil spring from the strut assembly, set it aside in a safe, isolated area.*

Disassembly

Refer to illustrations 3.3, 3.4, 3.5, 3.6 and 3.7
2   Remove the strut and spring assembly following the procedure described in the previous Section. Mount the strut assembly in a vise. Line the vise jaws with wood or rags to prevent damage to the unit and don't tighten the vise excessively.
3   Following the tool manufacturer's instructions, install the spring compressor (which can be obtained at most auto parts stores or equipment yards on a daily rental basis) on the spring and compress it sufficiently to relieve all pressure from the upper spring seat **(see illustration)**. This can be verified by wiggling the spring.
4   Loosen the damper shaft nut **(see illustration)**.
5   Remove the nut and suspension support **(see illustration)**. Inspect the bearing in the suspension support for smooth operation. If it doesn't turn smoothly, replace the suspension support. Check the rubber portion of the suspension support for cracking and general deterioration. If there is any separation of the rubber, replace it.
6   Lift the spring seat and upper insulator from the damper shaft **(see illustration)**. Check the rubber spring seat for cracking and hardness, replacing it if necessary.
7   Carefully lift the compressed spring from the assembly **(see illustration)** and set

3.5 Lift the suspension support off the damper shaft

3.6 Remove the spring seat from the damper shaft

3.7 Remove the compressed spring assembly - keep the ends of the spring pointed away from your body

10

- Coil spring
- Bumper rubber
- Dust cover
- Strut mounting insulator case
- Strut mounting insulator
- Strut insulator bracket
- Thrust seat
- Dust seal
- Spring seat
- Spring rubber seat
- Stabilizer bar
- Stabilizer connecting rod
- Strut assembly (Non-disassembly type)
- Wheel hub assembly
- Transverse link
- Lower ball joint
- Cotter pin

3.10 An exploded view of the front suspension assembly (1987 through 1990 models shown, other similar)

it in a safe place. **Warning:** *Never place your head near the end of the spring!*

8 Slide the rubber bumper off the damper shaft.

9 Check the lower insulator (if equipped) for wear, cracking and hardness and replace it if necessary.

Reassembly

Refer to illustrations 3.10 and 3.11

10 If the lower insulator is being replaced, set it into position with the dropped portion seated in the lowest part of the seat. Extend the damper rod to its full length and install the rubber bumper **(see illustration)**.

11 Carefully place the coil spring onto the lower insulator, with the end of the spring resting in the lowest part of the insulator **(see illustration)**.

12 Install the upper insulator and spring seat.

13 Install the dust seal and suspension support to the damper shaft.

14 Install the nut and tighten it to the torque listed in this Chapter's Specifications.

15 Install the strut/shock absorber and coil spring assembly following the procedure described in Section 2.

4 Stabilizer bar (front) - removal and installation

Refer to illustrations 4.2 and 4.3

1 Loosen the wheel lug nuts, raise the front of the vehicle, support it securely on jackstands and remove the wheels.

2 Disconnect the stabilizer link nuts from both control arms **(see illustration)**.

3 Remove the stabilizer bar clamp bolts **(see illustration)**.

4 Remove the stabilizer assembly.

5 Inspect the clamp bushings and the link bushings. If they're cracked or torn, replace them.

6 Installation is the reverse of removal. Be sure to tighten all fasteners to the torque listed in this Chapter's Specifications.

3.11 When installing the spring, make sure the end fits into the recessed portion of the lower seat (arrow)

4.2 To disconnect the stabilizer link from the control arm on 1991 and later models, remove this nut (arrow)

4.3 To disconnect the stabilizer bar from the body on 1991 and later models, remove these two bushing clamp bolts (arrows) (left clamp shown, right clamp identical)

5.3 To remove the control arm on 1982 through 1986 models, remove the nuts (1) that attach the balljoint to the arm, the stabilizer bar link nut (2), the front pivot stud nut (3) and the rear bushing clamp bolts (4)

5.4a Remove the cotter pin . . .

5.4b . . . loosen the balljoint stud nut and back it off as far as it will go (without actually removing it) . . .

5.4c . . . then pop the balljoint stud loose with a "picklefork" (be sure to grease the pickle fork to protect the balljoint dust boot)

5.4d Separate the control arm from the steering knuckle by pulling down firmly

5 Control arm - removal, inspection and installation

Removal

Refer to illustrations 5.3, 5.4a, 5.4b, 5.4c, 5.4d, 5.5a and 5.5b

1 Loosen the wheel lug nuts on the side to be dismantled, raise the front of the vehicle, support it securely on jackstands and remove the wheel.

2 Disconnect the stabilizer link from the control arm (see Section 4).

3 On 1982 through 1986 models, remove the three nuts (see illustration) that attach the balljoint to the control arm.

4 On 1987 and later models, remove the cotter pin (see illustration), loosen the balljoint stud nut (see illustration) and separate the balljoint stud from the steering knuckle with a "picklefork"-type balljoint separator (see illustration). Be sure to grease the pickle fork to protect the rubber balljoint dust boot. Separate the arm from the steering knuckle (see illustration).

5 Remove the front pivot bolt nut and/or bolt. Remove the rear bushing clamp bolts (see illustrations). Remove the control arm.

Inspection

6 On 1982 through 1986 models, remove the rear bushing retaining nut to remove the rear bushing. Inspect the front and rear bushings for cracks and tears. If the front bushing is damaged or worn, have it pressed out and a new one pressed in at an automotive machine shop; if the rear bushing is damaged, you can replace it yourself. On 1987 and later models, the bushings are not replaceable; if either the front or rear bushing is worn or damaged, replace the control arm.

7 Inspect the control arm for straightness. If it's bent, replace it. Do not attempt to straighten a bent control arm.

5.5a On 1987 and later models, remove the front pivot bolt nut and the pivot bolt (arrows)

5.5b Remove the rear bushing clamp bolts (arrows) (1994 model shown, others similar)

10

Installation

8   Installation is the reverse of removal. Tighten all of the fasteners to the torque listed in this Chapter's Specifications.
9   Install the wheel and lug nuts, lower the vehicle and tighten the lug nuts to the torque listed in the Chapter 1 Specifications.
10   It's a good idea to have the front wheel alignment checked, and if necessary, adjusted after this job has been performed.

6   Balljoints - replacement

1   Loosen the wheel lug nuts, raise the vehicle and support it securely on jackstands. Remove the wheel.
2   Remove the control arm (see Section 5).
3   On 1982 through 1986 models, the balljoint can be removed from the control arm and a new balljoint installed. On 1987 and later models, the balljoint is an integral part of the control arm and cannot be replaced by itself. On these models, replace the control arm.
4   Installation is the reverse of removal. Be sure to tighten all fasteners to the torque listed in this Chapter's Specifications. Also be sure to install a new cotter pin. If the cotter pin hole doesn't line up with the slots on the nut, tighten the nut until the next hole in the nut lines up with the hole in the balljoint stud.
5   Install the wheel and lug nuts. Lower the vehicle and tighten the lug nuts to the torque listed in the Chapter 1 Specifications.
6   It's a good idea to have the front wheel alignment checked, and if necessary, adjusted after this job has been performed.

7   Steering knuckle and hub - removal and installation

Warning: *Dust created by the brake system may contain asbestos, which is harmful to your health. Never blow it out with compressed air and don't inhale any of it. Do not, under any circumstances, use petroleum-based solvents to clean brake parts. Use brake system cleaner only.*

Removal

1   Loosen the wheel lug nuts, raise the vehicle and support it securely on jackstands. Remove the wheel.
2   Remove the brake caliper and (on 1987 and later models) the brake disc, and disconnect the brake hose from the strut (see Chapter 9).
3   If the vehicle is equipped with ABS, disconnect and remove the wheel speed sensor.
4   Remove the strut-to-steering knuckle nuts, but don't remove the bolts yet (see Section 2).
5   Separate the tie-rod end from the steering knuckle arm (see Section 18).

9.3a An exploded view of the rear suspension assembly (1982 through 1986 models)

6   Separate the balljoint from the steering knuckle (see Sections 5 and 6).
7   Push the driveaxle from the hub as described in Chapter 8. Support the end of the driveaxle with a piece of wire.
8   Remove the strut-to-knuckle bolts and separate the knuckle from the strut.

Installation

9   Guide the knuckle and hub assembly into position, inserting the driveaxle into the hub.
10   Push the knuckle into the strut flange and install the bolts and nuts, but don't tighten them yet.
11   Attach the control arm to the steering knuckle (see Section 5).
12   Attach the tie-rod end to the steering knuckle arm (see Section 18). Tighten the strut-to-knuckle nuts to the torque listed in this Chapter's Specifications.
13   Place the brake disc on the hub (1987 and later models) and install the caliper as outlined in Chapter 9.
14   Install the driveaxle/hub nut and tighten it to the torque listed in the Chapter 8 Specifications.
15   Install the wheel and tighten the lug nuts but don't torque them yet.
16   Lower the vehicle and tighten the wheel lug nuts to the torque listed in the Chapter 1 Specifications.

8   Hub and bearing assembly (front) - removal and installation

Due to the special tools and expertise required to press the hub and bearing from the steering knuckle, this job should be left to a professional mechanic. However, the steering knuckle and hub may be removed and the assembly taken to a dealer service

department or other repair shop. See Section 7 for the steering knuckle and hub removal procedure.

9   Shock absorber (rear) - removal, inspection and installation

Note: *The following procedure applies to 1982 through 1986 models.*

Removal

Refer to illustrations 9.3a, 9.3b and 9.4
1   Loosen the rear wheel lug nuts, raise the rear of the vehicle and support it securely on jackstands. Remove the wheels.
2   Support the trailing arm with a floor jack.
Warning: *Because of the coil spring, failure to support the trailing arm with a floor jack could result in serious injury when the shock is unbolted from the arm.*
3   Remove the shock-to-trailing arm bolt and nut **(see illustrations)**.

9.3b To disconnect the lower end of the shock absorber from the trailing arm, remove this nut and bolt (arrow)

9.4 To detach the upper end of the shock absorber from the body, remove the upper mounting nut (arrow)

9.7 When you attach the upper end of the shock absorber to the body, make sure the bushings and washers are arranged in the order shown

4   Open the trunk or raise the hatch, remove the side trim and locate the upper nut **(see illustration)**.
5   Remove the upper mounting nut while an assistant supports the shock so it doesn't fall. Guide the shock out of the fenderwell.

Inspection

6   Check the shock absorber body for leaking fluid, dents, cracks and other obvious damage which would warrant repair or replacement. If the shock assembly is leaking, damaged or worn out, replace it.

Installation

Refer to illustration 9.7
7   Maneuver the shock and coil spring assembly up into the fenderwell and insert the mounting stud through the hole in the body. Make sure the bushings and washers are installed as shown **(see illustration)**. Install the nut, tightening it securely.
8   Connect the lower end of the shock to the trailing arm, install the bolt and nut, but don't tighten them yet.
9   Install the wheel and lug nuts, lower the

vehicle and tighten the lug nuts to the torque listed in the Chapter 1 Specifications.
10   Tighten the shock lower mounting nut/bolt to the torque listed in this Chapter's Specifications.
11   Install the side trim inside the trunk or hatch area.

10   Coil spring (rear) - removal and installation

Note: *The following procedure applies to 1982 through 1986 models only.*

Removal

1   Loosen the rear wheel lug nuts, raise the rear of the vehicle and support it securely on jackstands. Remove the wheels.
2   Support the trailing arm with a floor jack. **Warning:** *Failure to support the trailing arm with a floor jack could result in serious injury when the shock is unbolted from the arm.*
3   Chain the coil spring to the trailing arm to prevent it from popping out when the trailing arm is lowered.

11.2 To remove the trailing arm on 1982 through 1986 models, unclip the parking brake cable (1), remove the entire brake assembly, disconnect the lower end of the shock absorber (2) and remove the pivot bolts and nuts (3) at the forward end of the arm

4   Disconnect the lower end of the shock absorber from the trailing arm (see Section 9).
5   Slowly lower the floor jack, allowing the coil spring to extend fully. Remove the coil spring.

Inspection

6   Inspect the coil spring for chips or cracks in the spring coating (this will cause premature spring failure due to corrosion). Inspect the spring seat for cuts, hardness and general deterioration.
7   Inspect the rubber bumper for cracks or tears. If it's damaged or deteriorated, replace it.

Installation

8   Installation is the reverse of removal. Be sure to tighten the shock absorber lower mounting bolt/nut to the torque listed in this Chapter's Specifications after the vehicle is back on the ground.

11   Trailing arm (rear) - removal, inspection and installation

Note: *The following procedure applies to 1982 through 1986 models.*

Removal

Refer to illustration 11.2
1   Loosen the wheel lug nuts, raise the rear of the vehicle and place it securely on jackstands. Block the front wheels and remove the rear wheels.
2   Unbolt the parking brake cable from the underside of the trailing arm **(see illustration)**. Remove the rear brake drums (see Chapter 9). **Warning:** *Dust created by the brake system may contain asbestos, which is harmful to your health. Never blow it out with compressed air and don't inhale any of it. Do not, under any circumstances, use petroleum-based solvents to clean brake parts. Use brake system cleaner only.*
3   Disconnect the brake line from the wheel cylinder and disconnect the brake hose from the brake line (see Chapter 9). Plug the brake line to prevent moisture and contamination from entering the brake system.
4   Detach the brake backing plate from the trailing arm.
5   Support the trailing arm with a floor jack. Place a block of wood between the arm and the jack head to protect the arm.
6   Chain the coil spring to the lower arm to prevent it from popping out when the arm is lowered.
7   Disconnect the lower end of the shock absorber from the trailing arm (see Section 9).
8   Lower the jack and remove the coil spring.
9   Remove the pivot bolts and nuts from the forward end of the trailing arm **(see illustration 11.2)**.
10   Remove the trailing arm.

10

Inspection

11   Inspect the trailing arm bushings for cracks, deformation and wear. If they're damaged or worn out, take the trailing arm assembly to a dealer service department or an automotive machine shop to have the old ones pressed out and new ones pressed in.

Installation

12   Installation is the reverse of removal **(see illustration 9.3a)**. Be sure to tighten all fasteners to the torque listed in this Chapter's Specifications.
13   Lower the vehicle and tighten the lug nuts to the torque listed in the Chapter 1 Specifications.
14   Bleed the brakes (see Chapter 9).

12   Strut/coil spring assembly (rear) - removal, inspection and installation

Note: *The following procedure applies to 1987 and later models.*

Removal

Refer to illustrations 12.3a, 12.3b, 12.3c and 12.5

1   Loosen the rear wheel lug nuts, raise the rear of the vehicle and support it securely on jackstands. Remove the wheels.
2   Disconnect the brake hose from the wheel cylinder or caliper (see Chapter 9). Have some rags and a container handy to catch the brake fluid. Unclip the hose from the strut bracket and push it through. If the vehicle is equipped with ABS, detach the speed sensor wiring harness from the strut by removing the clamp bracket bolt.
3   Remove the strut-to-knuckle nuts **(see illustrations)** and knock the bolts out with a hammer and punch.
4   Separate the strut from the knuckle.
5   On 1987 through 1990 coupes and wagons, the upper strut mounting nuts are located under a small plastic access cover inside the cargo area; on sedans, you'll have to remove the back seat (see Chapter 11) to get at the upper mounting nuts. The upper strut nuts are behind the seat on all 1991 and later models. Have an assistant support the strut and spring assembly while you remove the three strut-to-shock tower nuts **(see illustration)**. Remove the assembly out from the fenderwell.

Inspection

6   Refer to Steps 6 and 7 in Section 2.
7   If any undesirable conditions exist, proceed to the strut disassembly procedure (see Section 3).

Installation

Refer to illustration 12.8

8   Guide the strut assembly up into the fenderwell and insert the upper mounting studs through the holes in the shock tower. On 1991 and later models, make sure the strut upper spring seat is aligned as shown **(see illustration)**. Once the studs protrude from the shock tower, install the nuts so the strut won't fall back through. This is most easily accomplished with the help of an assistant, as the strut is quite heavy and awkward.
9   Slide the steering knuckle into the strut flange and insert the two bolts. Install the bolts and nuts and tighten them to the torque listed in this Chapter's Specifications.
10   Guide the brake hose through its bracket in the strut, reconnect it to the wheel cylinder or caliper and bleed the brakes (see Chapter 9). If the vehicle is equipped with ABS, install the speed sensor wiring harness bracket.
11   Install the wheel and lug nuts, then

12.3a   An exploded view of the rear suspension assembly (1987 through 1990 models)

12.3b An exploded view of the rear suspension assembly (1991 and later models)

1 Clamp	6 Clamp	11 Strut mounting	14 Rubber bumper	18 Knuckle assembly
2 Bushing	7 Link rod	insulator	15 Coil spring	19 Adjusting bolt
3 Bracket	8 Cap	12 Upper seat	16 Rubber seat	20 Lateral arm
4 Stabilizer bar	9 Strut seal	13 Rubber seat	17 Strut assembly	21 Trailing arm
5 Bushing	10 Gasket			

12.3c To disconnect the strut assembly from the rear knuckle, remove these two bolts (arrows) and their corresponding nuts (not visible in this photo)

12.5 The strut upper mounting nuts (arrows) are located behind the seat on 1987 through 1990 sedans and on all 1991 and later models

12.8 On 1991 and later models, make sure the upper spring seat is aligned as shown

10

13.2a To disconnect the stabilizer bar from the rear knuckle on 1987 through 1990 models, remove this nut (arrow) from each end of the bar

13.2b To disconnect the stabilizer from the body, remove these clamp bolts (arrows)

13.3a To disconnect the stabilizer link from the rear strut on 1991 and later models, remove this nut (arrow)

13.3b To disconnect the rear stabilizer bushing clamps on 1991 and later models, remove these nuts (arrows)

lower the vehicle and tighten the lug nuts to the torque listed in the Chapter 1 Specifications.

12   Tighten the upper mounting nuts to the torque listed in this Chapter's Specifications.

13   Drive the vehicle to an alignment shop to have the wheel alignment checked, and if necessary, adjusted.

13   Stabilizer bar (rear) - removal and installation

Refer to illustrations 13.2a, 13.2b, 13.3a and 13.3b

Note: *The following procedure applies to 1987 and later models.*

1   Loosen the rear wheel lug nuts, raise the rear of the vehicle, support it securely on jackstands and remove the wheels.

2   On 1987 through 1990 models, remove the large nuts from both ends of the stabilizer bar **(see illustration)**, then remove the clamp bolts **(see illustration)** and remove the stabilizer.

3   On 1991 and later models, remove the nuts from the link rods that attach the stabilizer to the struts **(see illustration)**, then remove the clamp nuts **(see illustration)** and remove the stabilizer.

4   Inspect all clamp bushings. If they're cracked or torn, replace them.

5   Installation is the reverse of removal. Be sure to tighten all fasteners to the torque listed in this Chapter's Specifications.

14   Suspension arms (rear) - removal and installation

Note: *The following procedure applies to 1987 and later models.*

1   Loosen the rear wheel lug nuts, raise the rear of the vehicle, support it securely on jackstands and remove the wheels.

Lateral arms

Refer to illustrations 14.2a, 14.2b and 14.3

2   Mark the positions of the toe adjusters so the toe-in adjustment is maintained **(see illustration)**. Remove the inner pivot bolts and nuts **(see illustrations)**.

3   Remove the outer through-bolt and nut that attach the lateral arms to the knuckle **(see illustration)**.

4   Remove the arm(s).

5   Installation is the reverse of removal. Be sure to line up the toe adjusters on the inner pivot bolts and tighten all fasteners to the torque listed in this Chapter's Specifications. **Note:** *Raise the rear suspension with a floor jack to simulate normal ride height before tightening the fasteners.*

6   When you're done, drive the vehicle to an alignment shop and have the rear-wheel toe adjusted.

Suspension R.H.   Suspension L.H.

Stopper plate

Toe-out   Toe-in   Toe-in   Toe-out

Front view on vehicle

14.2a Mark the toe adjusters to ensure that the basic toe adjustment is restored when the lateral arms are installed again; however, it's still a good idea to have the toe adjusted anytime you remove the arms (viewed from the front on 1987 through 1990 models [shown] - the adjusters on 1991 and later models are on the rearmost set of arms)

14.2b To disconnect the inner ends of the lateral arms from the body on 1991 and later models, remove these nuts and pivot bolts (arrows)

14.3 To disconnect the outer ends of the lateral arms from the knuckle, remove this nut and through-bolt (arrows)

14.7 To disconnect the forward end of the trailing arm from the body, remove this nut and pivot bolt (arrows)

14.8 Remove the bolt (arrow) (and nut) that attaches the rear end of the trailing arm to the knuckle

15.3 Remove the hub/bearing grease cap with a hammer and chisel

15.4 Remove the retaining nut cotter pin

15.5 Remove the bearing/hub retaining nut

15.6 Remove the hub/bearing assembly

Trailing arms (1991 and later models only)

Refer to illustrations 14.7 and 14.8

7 Remove the pivot bolt and nut from the forward end of the trailing arm (see illustration).
8 Remove the bolt and nut that attach the rear end of the arm to the knuckle (see illustrations).
9 Remove the trailing arm.
10 Installation is the reverse of removal. Place a floor jack under the rear knuckle and raise the suspension to simulate normal ride height, then tighten the fasteners to the torque listed in this Chapter's Specifications.

All models

11 Install the wheels, tighten - but don't torque - the lug nuts, remove the jackstands, lower the vehicle and tighten the wheel lug nuts to the torque listed in the Chapter 1 Specifications.
12 When you're done, drive the vehicle to an alignment shop and have the rear-wheel toe adjusted.

15 Hub and bearing assembly (rear) - removal and installation

Refer to illustrations 15.3, 15.4, 15.5 and 15.6
Note: *The following procedure applies to 1987 and later models.*

1 Loosen the rear wheel lug nuts, raise the rear of the vehicle, support it securely on jackstands and remove the wheels.
2 Remove the brake drum or disc (see Chapter 9).
3 Pry off the grease cap (see illustration).
4 Remove the cotter pin (see illustration).
5 Remove the bearing retainer nut (see illustration).
6 Remove the hub and bearing assembly (see illustration).
7 Installation is the reverse of removal. Be sure to tighten all fasteners to the torque listed in this Chapter's Specifications.

16 Knuckle (rear) - removal and installation

Refer to illustration 16.6
Note: *The following procedure applies to 1987 and later models.*

1 Loosen the rear wheel lug nuts, raise the rear of the vehicle, support it securely on jackstands and remove the wheels.
2 Remove the brake drum (see Chapter 9).
3 Remove the hub and bearing assembly (see Section 15).
4 Remove the brake assembly (see Chapter 9).
5 Disconnect the brake line fitting at the wheel cylinder (see Chapter 9). Also disconnect the parking brake cable housing

bolts from the rear of the backing plate (see Chapter 9).
6 Remove the brake backing plate (see illustration).
7 Disconnect the stabilizer bar assembly from the knuckle (see Section 13).
8 Disconnect the suspension arms from the knuckle (see Section 14).
9 Disconnect the strut/coil spring assembly from the knuckle (see Section 12).
10 Remove the knuckle.
11 Installation is the reverse of removal. Be sure to tighten all fasteners to the torque listed in this Chapter's Specifications.

16.6 To remove the brake backing plate from the rear knuckle, remove these bolts (arrows); it's not necessary to remove the wheel cylinder, but you'll have to disconnect the brake line fitting at the back; and don't forget to disconnect the parking brake cable too

10

17.2a To remove the horn pad on 1982 through 1986 models, simply pry it off the steering wheel from the top like this

17.2b To remove the horn pad on 1987 through 1990 models, remove the two screws from the rear (dash side) of the steering wheel . . .

17.2c . . . remove the pad and disconnect the horn lead

17.2d On 1991 and later models with a two-spoke steering wheel, the horn pad is attached to the wheel with a single screw (arrow) and three clips (not visible); to remove the pad, remove the screw . . .

17.2e . . . then pry the pad off and disconnect the horn lead

17.2f On 1991 and later models with a three-spoke steering wheel, the horn pad is attached to the wheel with three clamps; to remove the pad, insert a screwdriver into the hole on the back of the lower spoke and pry up on the clamps

17 Steering wheel - removal and installation

Non-airbag models

Removal

Refer to illustrations 17.2a, 17.2b, 17.2c, 17.2d, 17.2e, 17.2f, 17.2g, 17.3 and 17.4

1   Disconnect the cable from the negative terminal of the battery.

2   Remove the horn pad. On 1982 through 1986 models, simply pry off the horn pad **(see illustration)**. On 1987 through 1990 models, the horn pad is attached to the steering wheel by a pair of screws which must be removed from the rear (the side facing the dash) of the steering wheel **(see illustrations)**. On 1991 and later models, the horn pad is attached to the wheel by various combinations of clips **(see illustrations)**.

3   Remove the steering wheel retaining nut, then mark the relationship of the steering shaft to the hub (if marks don't already exist

or don't line up) to simplify installation and ensure steering wheel alignment **(see illustration)**.

4   Use a puller to disconnect the steering wheel from the shaft **(see illustration)**.

Installation

Refer to illustration 17.5

5   Before installing the wheel, lubricate the horn-contact slip ring and the sliding portion

17.2g To remove the horn pad on 1991 and later models with a four-spoke steering wheel, insert a Phillips screwdriver into the hole on the lower side of the spoke and remove the clamps, then lift off the pad

17.3 Remove the steering wheel retaining nut and, on some models, the washer, then mark the relationship of the steering wheel to the shaft (arrows) *before removing the wheel*

17.4 If the steering wheel is difficult to remove from the shaft, use a steering wheel puller - DO NOT beat on the shaft

17.5 Before installing the steering wheel, lubricate the horn contact ring and the sliding portion of the turn-signal cancel pin with multi-purpose grease

17.11a An exploded view of an airbag-equipped steering wheel assembly

of the turn signal cancel pin with multi-purpose grease (see illustration).

6   To install the wheel, align the mark on the steering wheel hub with the mark on the shaft and slip the wheel onto the shaft. Install the nut and tighten it to the torque listed in this Chapter's Specifications.

7   Connect the horn wire and install the horn pad.

8   Connect the negative battery cable.

Airbag-equipped models

Warning: *Some later models are equipped with airbags. To prevent accidental deployment (and possible injury) when working near airbag components, disconnect the negative battery cable and wait at least 10 minutes before beginning work (the system has a back-up capacitor that must fully discharge). For more information see Section 27 in Chapter 12.*

Removal

Refer to illustrations 17.11a, 17.11b and 17.12

9   Disconnect the cable from the negative battery terminal and wait at least ten minutes before removing the steering wheel.

10   Turn the steering wheel so that the front wheels are pointing straight ahead.

11   Remove the small lid from the underside of the steering wheel (see illustration) and unplug the airbag module connector (see illustration).

12   Remove the side lids and remove the Torx bolts behind them (see illustration) with a T50H Torx bit. The Torx bolts are coated with a special bonding agent, so they must be discarded; be sure to replace them during reassembly.

13   Lift the airbag module off the steering wheel. **Warning:** *Handle the airbag module with care and store it in a safe location with the trim side facing up. See the precautions in Chapter 12.*

14   The remainder of steering wheel removal is identical with a non-airbag steering wheel (refer to Steps 3 and 4 above). **Warning:** *Do not turn the steering shaft while the steering wheel is removed.*

Installation

Refer to illustration 17.15

15   Verify that the front wheels are pointing straight ahead, then turn the spiral cable clockwise by hand until it becomes hard to turn, then rotate the spiral cable counterclockwise about two turns until the yellow alignment mark appears on the left gear (see illustration). Align the arrow mark of the spiral cable with this yellow mark.

16   Install the steering wheel. Make sure the

spiral cable pin guides are properly engaged with their corresponding holes in the back of the steering wheel and pull the spiral cable through.

17   Install the steering wheel retaining nut and tighten it to the torque listed in this Chapter's Specifications.

18   Plug in the horn connector and engage the spiral cable with the pawls in the steering wheel.

19   Install the airbag module and secure it with a couple of new Torx bolts. Do not reuse the old bolts. Install the side lids.

17.11b The airbag module connector is located inside a recess in the underside of the steering wheel; it can be accessed by removing a protective lid

17.12 The airbag module is attached to the steering wheel with a pair of Torx T50H bolts located on either side of the steering wheel; they can be accessed by removing the small side lids

17.15 To align the spiral cable with the neutral position, turn the cable clockwise until it becomes hard to turn, then back it off about two turns until the yellow mark appears on the left gear; align the arrow mark of the spiral cable with this yellow mark

10

18.2a Loosen the jam nut . . .

18.2b . . . then mark the position of the tie-rod end in relation to the threads

18.4 Disconnect the tie-rod end from the steering knuckle arm with a puller (the nut has been loosened, but left on, to prevent the tie-rod end from separating violently)

20 Plug in the airbag module connector. Install the lid.

21 Verify the airbag circuit is operational by turning the ignition key to the On or Start position. The "AIR BAG" warning light should illuminate for about seven seconds, then turn off.

18 Tie-rod ends - removal and installation

Removal

Refer to illustrations 18.2a, 18.2b and 18.4

1 Loosen the wheel lug nuts. Raise the front of the vehicle, support it securely on jackstands, block the rear wheels and set the parking brake. Remove the front wheel.

2 Loosen the jam nut enough to mark the position of the tie-rod end in relation to threads **(see illustrations)**.

3 Remove the cotter pin and loosen, but don't remove, the nut on the tie-rod end stud.

4 Disconnect the tie-rod end from the steering knuckle arm with a puller **(see illustration)**. Remove the nut and separate the tie-rod.

5 Unscrew the tie-rod end from the tie-rod end.

Installation

6 Thread the tie-rod end on to the marked

position and insert the tie-rod stud into the steering knuckle arm. Tighten the jam nut securely.

7 Install the castle nut on the stud and tighten it to the torque listed in this Chapter's Specifications. Install a new cotter pin.

8 Install the wheel and lug nuts. Lower the vehicle and tighten the lug nuts to the torque listed in the Chapter 1 Specifications.

9 Have the alignment checked by a dealer service department or an alignment shop.

19 Steering gear boots - replacement

Refer to illustrations 19.3a and 19.3b

1 Loosen the lug nuts, raise the vehicle and support it securely on jackstands. Remove the wheel.

2 Remove the tie-rod end and jam nut (see Section 18).

3 Remove the outer steering gear boot clamp **(see illustration)** with a pair of pliers. Cut off the inner boot clamp **(see illustration)** with a pair of diagonal cutters. Slide the boot off.

4 Before installing the new boot, wrap the threads on the end of the steering rod with a layer of tape so the small end of the new boot isn't damaged.

5 Slide the new boot into position on the

steering gear until it seats in the groove in the steering rod and install new clamps.

6 Remove the tape and install the tie-rod end (see Section 18).

7 Install the wheel and lug nuts. Lower the vehicle and tighten the lug nuts to the torque listed in the Chapter 1 Specifications.

20 Steering gear - removal and installation

Removal

Refer to illustrations 20.2, 20.3a, 20.3b, 20.5a and 20.5b

1 Loosen the front wheel lug nuts, raise the front of the vehicle and support it securely on jackstands. Apply the parking brake and remove the wheels. Remove the engine splash shields (see Chapter 1).

2 If equipped with power steering, place a drain pan under the steering gear. Detach the power steering pressure and return lines **(see illustration)** and cap the ends to prevent excessive fluid loss and contamination.

3 Remove the universal joint cover **(see illustration)**. Mark the relationship of the lower universal joint to the steering gear input shaft **(see illustration)**. Remove the lower intermediate shaft pinch bolt.

19.3a The outer ends of the steering gear boots are secured by spring-type clamps

19.3b The inner ends of the steering gear boots are retained by clamps which must be cut off and discarded

20.2 Disconnect the power steering line fittings (arrows)

20.3a Remove the U-joint cover nuts (arrows) and peel the cover down far enough to get at the U-joint clamp bolt

20.3b Mark the relationship of the universal joint to the steering gear input shaft, then remove the U-joint pinch bolt (arrow)

4   Separate the tie-rod ends from the steering knuckle arms (see Section 18).

5   Support the steering gear and remove the steering gear mounting bolts **(see illustrations)**. Separate the intermediate shaft from the steering gear input shaft and remove the steering gear assembly. **Warning:** *Do not turn the steering wheel while the steering gear is removed on a model equipped with an airbag. If the steering wheel is inadvertently turned, remove the steering wheel and center the spiral cable (see Section 17). To prevent the steering wheel from turning, loop the seat belt through the steering wheel and fasten it into its latch.*

6   Check the steering gear rubber mounts for excessive wear or deterioration, replacing them if necessary.

Installation

7   Raise the steering gear into position and connect the U-joint, aligning the marks.

8   Install the mounting brackets and bolts and tighten them to the torque listed in this Chapter's Specifications.

9   Connect the tie-rod ends to the steering knuckle arms (see Section 18).

10   Install the U-joint pinch bolt and tighten it to the torque listed in this Chapter's Specifications.

11   If equipped with power steering, connect the power steering pressure and return hoses to the steering gear and fill the power steering pump reservoir with the recommended fluid (see Chapter 1).

12   Lower the vehicle and if equipped with power steering, bleed the steering system (see Section 22).

21   Power steering pump - removal and installation

Removal

1   Disconnect the cable from the negative battery terminal.

2   Using a large syringe or suction gun, suck as much fluid out of the power steering fluid reservoir as possible. Place a drain pan under the vehicle to catch any fluid that spills out when the hoses are disconnected.

3   Loosen the clamp and disconnect the fluid return hose from the pump.

4   Remove the pressure line-to-pump fitting or banjo bolt, then detach the line from the pump. Remove and discard the copper sealing washers. They must be replaced when installing the pump.

5   Loosen the pivot and adjuster bolt and remove the drivebelt (see Chapter 1).

6   Remove the pivot, adjuster and mounting bolts, then remove the pump from the vehicle.

Installation

7   Installation is the reverse of removal. Be sure to tighten the pressure line fitting or banjo bolt to the torque listed in this Chapter's Specifications. Adjust the drivebelt tension following the procedure described in Chapter 1.

8   Top up the fluid level in the reservoir (see Chapter 1) and bleed the system (see Section 22).

22   Power steering system - bleeding

1   Following any operation in which the power steering fluid lines have been disconnected, the power steering system must be bled to remove all air and obtain proper steering performance.

2   With the front wheels in the straight ahead position, check the power steering fluid level and, if low, add fluid until it reaches the Cold mark on the dipstick.

3   Start the engine and allow it to run at fast idle. Recheck the fluid level and add more if necessary to reach the Cold mark on the dipstick.

4   Bleed the system by turning the wheels from side to side, without hitting the stops. This will work the air out of the system. Keep the reservoir full of fluid as this is done.

5   When the air is worked out of the system, return the wheels to the straight ahead position and leave the vehicle running for several more minutes before shutting it off.

6   Road test the vehicle to be sure the steering system is functioning normally and noise free.

7   Recheck the fluid level to be sure it is up to the Hot mark on the dipstick while the engine is at normal operating temperature. Add fluid if necessary (see Chapter 1).

20.5a To remove the steering gear assembly, remove the left retaining bolts (arrows) . . .

20.5b . . . and the right-side bolts (arrows)

10

23   Wheels and tires - general information

Refer to illustration 23.1

1   All vehicles covered by this manual are equipped with metric-sized fiberglass or steel belted radial tires **(see illustration)**. Use of other size or type of tires may affect the ride and handling of the vehicle. Don't mix different types of tires, such as radials and bias belted, on the same vehicle as handling may be seriously affected. It's recommended that tires be replaced in pairs on the same axle, but if only one tire is being replaced, be sure it's the same size, structure and tread design as the other.

2   Because tire pressure has a substantial effect on handling and wear, the pressure on all tires should be checked at least once a month or before any extended trips (see Chapter 1).

3   Wheels must be replaced if they are bent, dented, leak air, have elongated bolt holes, are heavily rusted, out of vertical symmetry or if the lug nuts won't stay tight. Wheel repairs that use welding or peening are not recommended.

4   Tire and wheel balance is important in the overall handling, braking and performance of the vehicle. Unbalanced wheels can adversely affect handling and ride characteristics as well as tire life. Whenever a tire is installed on a wheel, the tire and wheel should be balanced by a shop with the proper equipment.

24   Wheel alignment - general information

Refer to illustration 24.1

A wheel alignment refers to the adjustments made to the wheels so they are in proper angular relationship to the suspension and the ground. Wheels that are out of proper alignment not only affect vehicle control, but also increase tire wear. The front end angles normally measured are camber, caster and toe-in **(see illustration)**. Camber and caster are preset at the factory on the vehicle covered by this manual; toe-in is the only adjustable angle on these vehicles. On 1987 and later models the rear toe-in can also be adjusted (but the camber and caster cannot). However, camber and caster are usually measured to check for bent or worn suspension parts.

Getting the proper wheel alignment is a very exacting process, one in which complicated and expensive machines are necessary to perform the job properly. Because of this, you should have a technician with the proper equipment perform these tasks. We will, however, use this space to give you a basic idea of what is involved with a wheel alignment so you can better understand the process and deal intelligently with the shop that does the work.

Toe-in is the turning in of the wheels. The purpose of a toe specification is to ensure parallel rolling of the wheels. In a vehicle with zero toe-in, the distance between the front edges of the wheels will be the same as the distance between the rear edges of the wheels. The actual amount of toe-in is normally only a fraction of an inch. On the front end, toe-in is controlled by the tie-rod end position on the tie-rod. On the rear end, it's controlled by a cam on the inner end of the rear (number two) suspension arm. Incorrect toe-in will cause the tires to wear improperly by making them scrub against the road surface.

Camber is the tilting of the wheels from vertical when viewed from one end of the vehicle. When the wheels tilt out at the top, the camber is said to be positive (+). When the wheels tilt in at the top the camber is negative (-). The amount of tilt is measured in degrees from vertical and this measurement is called the camber angle. This angle affects the amount of tire tread which contacts the road and compensates for changes in the suspension geometry when the vehicle is cornering or traveling over an undulating surface.

Caster is the tilting of the front steering axis from the vertical. A tilt toward the rear is positive caster and a tilt toward the front is negative caster.

23.1 Metric tire size code

A = Section width   B = Section height

24.1 Camber, caster and toe-in angles

Chapter 11 Body

Contents

1 General information

These models feature a "unibody" construction, using a floor pan with front and rear frame side rails which support the body components, front and rear suspension systems and other mechanical components. Certain components are particularly vulnerable to accident damage and can be unbolted and repaired or replaced. Among these parts are the body moldings, bumpers, hood and trunk lids and all glass.

Only general body maintenance practices and body panel repair procedures within the scope of the do-it-yourselfer are included in this Chapter.

2 Body - maintenance

1   The condition of your vehicle's body is very important, because the resale value depends a great deal on it. It's much more difficult to repair a neglected or damaged body than it is to repair mechanical components. The hidden areas of the body, such as the wheel wells, the frame and the engine compartment, are equally important, although they don't require as frequent attention as the rest of the body.
2   Once a year, or every 12,000 miles, it's a good idea to have the underside of the body steam cleaned. All traces of dirt and oil will be removed and the area can then be inspected carefully for rust, damaged brake lines, frayed electrical wires, damaged cables and other problems. The front suspension components should be greased after completion of this job.
3   At the same time, clean the engine and the engine compartment with a steam cleaner or water soluble degreaser.
4   The wheel wells should be given close attention, since undercoating can peel away

and stones and dirt thrown up by the tires can cause the paint to chip and flake, allowing rust to set in. If rust is found, clean down to the bare metal and apply an anti-rust paint.
5   The body should be washed about once a week. Wet the vehicle thoroughly to soften the dirt, then wash it down with a soft sponge and plenty of clean soapy water. If the surplus dirt is not washed off very carefully, it can wear down the paint.
6   Spots of tar or asphalt thrown up from the road should be removed with a cloth soaked in solvent.
7   Once every six months, wax the body and chrome trim. If a chrome cleaner is used to remove rust from any of the vehicle's plated parts, remember that the cleaner also removes part of the chrome, so use it sparingly.

3 Vinyl trim - maintenance

Don't clean vinyl trim with detergents, caustic soap or petroleum-based cleaners. Plain soap and water works just fine, with a soft brush to clean dirt that may be ingrained. Wash the vinyl as frequently as the rest of the vehicle.

After cleaning, application of a high quality rubber and vinyl protectant will help prevent oxidation and cracks. The protectant can also be applied to weatherstripping, vacuum lines and rubber hoses (which often fail as a result of chemical degradation) and to the tires.

4 Upholstery and carpets - maintenance

1   Every three months remove the carpets or mats and clean the interior of the vehicle (more frequently if necessary). Vacuum the

upholstery and carpets to remove loose dirt and dust.
2   Leather upholstery requires special care. Stains should be removed with warm water and a very mild soap solution. Use a clean, damp cloth to remove the soap, then wipe again with a dry cloth. Never use alcohol, gasoline, nail polish remover or thinner to clean leather upholstery.
3   After cleaning, regularly treat leather upholstery with a leather wax. Never use car wax on leather upholstery.
4   In areas where the interior of the vehicle is subject to bright sunlight, cover leather seats with a sheet if the vehicle is to be left out for any length of time.

5 Body repair - minor damage

See photo sequence

Repair of minor scratches

1   If the scratch is superficial and does not penetrate to the metal of the body, repair is very simple. Lightly rub the scratched area with a fine rubbing compound to remove loose paint and built-up wax. Rinse the area with clean water.
2   Apply touch-up paint to the scratch, using a small brush. Continue to apply thin layers of paint until the surface of the paint in the scratch is level with the surrounding paint. Allow the new paint at least two weeks to harden, then blend it into the surrounding paint by rubbing with a very fine rubbing compound. Finally, apply a coat of wax to the scratch area.
3   If the scratch has penetrated the paint and exposed the metal of the body, causing the metal to rust, a different repair technique is required. Remove all loose rust from the bottom of the scratch with a pocket knife, then apply rust inhibiting paint to prevent the formation of rust in the future. Using a rubber

11

These photos illustrate a method of repairing simple dents. They are intended to supplement *Body repair - minor damage* in this Chapter and should not be used as the sole instructions for body repair on these vehicles.

1   If you can't access the backside of the body panel to hammer out the dent, pull it out with a slide-hammer-type dent puller. In the deepest portion of the dent or along the crease line, drill or punch hole(s) at least one inch apart . . .

2   . . . then screw the slide-hammer into the hole and operate it. Tap with a hammer near the edge of the dent to help 'pop' the metal back to its original shape. When you're finished, the dent area should be close to its original contour and about 1/8-inch below the surface of the surrounding metal

3   Using coarse-grit sandpaper, remove the paint down to the bare metal. Hand sanding works fine, but the disc sander shown here makes the job faster. Use finer (about 320-grit) sandpaper to feather-edge the paint at least one inch around the dent area

4   When the paint is removed, touch will probably be more helpful than sight for telling if the metal is straight. Hammer down the high spots or raise the low spots as necessary. Clean the repair area with wax/silicone remover

5   Following label instructions, mix up a batch of plastic filler and hardener. The ratio of filler to hardener is critical, and, if you mix it incorrectly, it will either not cure properly or cure too quickly (you won't have time to file and sand it into shape)

6   Working quickly so the filler doesn't harden, use a plastic applicator to press the body filler firmly into the metal, assuring it bonds completely. Work the filler until it matches the original contour and is slightly above the surrounding metal

7   Let the filler harden until you can just dent it with your fingernail. Use a body file or Surform tool (shown here) to rough-shape the filler

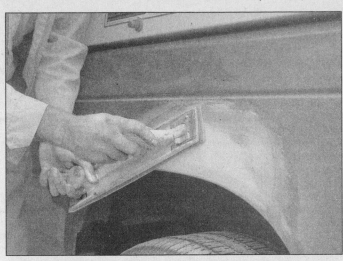

8   Use coarse-grit sandpaper and a sanding board or block to work the filler down until it's smooth and even. Work down to finer grits of sandpaper - always using a board or block - ending up with 360 or 400 grit

9   You shouldn't be able to feel any ridge at the transition from the filler to the bare metal or from the bare metal to the old paint. As soon as the repair is flat and uniform, remove the dust and mask off the adjacent panels or trim pieces

10   Apply several layers of primer to the area. Don't spray the primer on too heavy, so it sags or runs, and make sure each coat is dry before you spray on the next one. A professional-type spray gun is being used here, but aerosol spray primer is available inexpensively from auto parts stores

11   The primer will help reveal imperfections or scratches. Fill these with glazing compound. Follow the label instructions and sand it with 360 or 400-grit sandpaper until it's smooth. Repeat the glazing, sanding and respraying until the primer reveals a perfectly smooth surface

12   Finish sand the primer with very fine sandpaper (400 or 600-grit) to remove the primer overspray. Clean the area with water and allow it to dry. Use a tack rag to remove any dust, then apply the finish coat. Don't attempt to rub out or wax the repair area until the paint has dried completely (at least two weeks)

or nylon applicator, coat the scratched area with glaze-type filler. If required, the filler can be mixed with thinner to provide a very thin paste, which is ideal for filling narrow scratches. Before the glaze filler in the scratch hardens, wrap a piece of smooth cotton cloth around the tip of a finger. Dip the cloth in thinner and then quickly wipe it along the surface of the scratch. This will ensure that the surface of the filler is slightly hollow. The scratch can now be painted over as described earlier in this section.

Repair of dents

4   When repairing dents, the first job is to pull the dent out until the affected area is as close as possible to its original shape. There is no point in trying to restore the original shape completely as the metal in the damaged area will have stretched on impact and cannot be restored to its original contours. It is better to bring the level of the dent up to a point which is about 1/8-inch below the level of the surrounding metal. In cases where the dent is very shallow, it is not worth trying to pull it out at all.

5   If the back side of the dent is accessible, it can be hammered out gently from behind using a soft-face hammer. While doing this, hold a block of wood firmly against the opposite side of the metal to absorb the hammer blows and prevent the metal from being stretched.

6   If the dent is in a section of the body which has double layers, or some other factor makes it inaccessible from behind, a different technique is required. Drill several small holes through the metal inside the damaged area, particularly in the deeper sections. Screw long, self-tapping screws into the holes just enough for them to get a good grip in the metal. Now the dent can be pulled out by pulling on the protruding heads of the screws with locking pliers.

7   The next stage of repair is the removal of paint from the damaged area and from an inch or so of the surrounding metal. This is done with a wire brush or sanding disk in a drill motor, although it can be done just as effectively by hand with sandpaper. To complete the preparation for filling, score the surface of the bare metal with a screwdriver or the tang of a file, or drill small holes in the affected area. This will provide a good grip for the filler material. To complete the repair, see the subsection on filling and painting later in this Section.

Repair of rust holes or gashes

8   Remove all paint from the affected area and from an inch or so of the surrounding metal using a sanding disk or wire brush mounted in a drill motor. If these are not available, a few sheets of sandpaper will do the job just as effectively.

9   With the paint removed, you will be able to determine the severity of the corrosion and decide whether to replace the whole panel, if possible, or repair the affected area. New body panels are not as expensive as most people think and it is often quicker to install a new panel than to repair large areas of rust.

10   Remove all trim pieces from the affected area except those which will act as a guide to the original shape of the damaged body, such as headlight shells, etc. Using metal snips or a hacksaw blade, remove all loose metal and any other metal that is badly affected by rust. Hammer the edges of the hole in to create a slight depression for the filler material.

11   Wire brush the affected area to remove the powdery rust from the surface of the metal. If the back of the rusted area is accessible, treat it with rust inhibiting paint.

12   Before filling is done, block the hole in some way. This can be done with sheet metal riveted or screwed into place, or by stuffing the hole with wire mesh.

13   Once the hole is blocked off, the affected area can be filled and painted. See the following subsection on filling and painting.

Filling and painting

14   Many types of body fillers are available, but generally speaking, body repair kits which contain filler paste and a tube of resin hardener are best for this type of repair work. A wide, flexible plastic or nylon applicator will be necessary for imparting a smooth and contoured finish to the surface of the filler material. Mix up a small amount of filler on a clean piece of wood or cardboard (use the hardener sparingly). Follow the manufacturer's instructions on the package, otherwise the filler will set incorrectly.

15   Using the applicator, apply the filler paste to the prepared area. Draw the applicator across the surface of the filler to achieve the desired contour and to level the filler surface. As soon as a contour that approximates the original one is achieved, stop working the paste. If you continue, the paste will begin to stick to the applicator. Continue to add thin layers of paste at 20-minute intervals until the level of the filler is just above the surrounding metal.

16   Once the filler has hardened, the excess can be removed with a body file. From then on, progressively finer grades of sandpaper should be used, starting with a 180-grit paper and finishing with 600-grit wet-or-dry paper. Always wrap the sandpaper around a flat rubber or wooden block, otherwise the surface of the filler will not be completely flat. During the sanding of the filler surface, the wet-or-dry paper should be periodically rinsed in water. This will ensure that a very smooth finish is produced in the final stage.

17   At this point, the repair area should be surrounded by a ring of bare metal, which in turn should be encircled by the finely feathered edge of good paint. Rinse the repair area with clean water until all of the dust produced by the sanding operation is gone.

18   Spray the entire area with a light coat of primer. This will reveal any imperfections in the surface of the filler. Repair the imperfections with fresh filler paste or glaze filler and once more smooth the surface with sandpaper. Repeat this spray-and-repair procedure until you are satisfied that the surface of the filler and the feathered edge of the paint are perfect. Rinse the area with clean water and allow it to dry completely.

19   The repair area is now ready for painting. Spray painting must be carried out in a warm, dry, windless and dust free atmosphere. These conditions can be created if you have access to a large indoor work area, but if you are forced to work in the open, you will have to pick the day very carefully. If you are working indoors, dousing the floor in the work area with water will help settle the dust which would otherwise be in the air. If the repair area is confined to one body panel, mask off the surrounding panels. This will help minimize the effects of a slight mismatch in paint color. Trim pieces such as chrome strips, door handles, etc., will also need to be masked off or removed. Use masking tape and several thickness of newspaper for the masking operations.

20   Before spraying, shake the paint can thoroughly, then spray a test area until the spray painting technique is mastered. Cover the repair area with a thick coat of primer. The thickness should be built up using several thin layers of primer rather than one thick one. Using 600-grit wet-or-dry sandpaper, rub down the surface of the primer until it is very smooth. While doing this, the work area should be thoroughly rinsed with water and the wet-or-dry sandpaper periodically rinsed as well. Allow the primer to dry before spraying additional coats.

21   Spray on the top coat, again building up the thickness by using several thin layers of paint. Begin spraying in the center of the repair area and then, using a circular motion, work out until the whole repair area and about two inches of the surrounding original paint is covered. Remove all masking material 10 to 15 minutes after spraying on the final coat of paint. Allow the new paint at least two weeks to harden, then use a very fine rubbing compound to blend the edges of the new paint into the existing paint. Finally, apply a coat of wax.

6 Body repair - major damage

1   Major damage must be repaired by an auto body shop specifically equipped to perform unibody repairs. These shops have the specialized equipment required to do the job properly.

2   If the damage is extensive, the body must be checked for proper alignment or the vehicle's handling characteristics may be adversely affected and other components may wear at an accelerated rate.

3   Due to the fact that all of the major body components (hood, fenders, etc.) are

9.1 Before removing the hood, make marks around the hinge plate

9.10 Loosen the hood latch bolts, move the latch and retighten bolts, then close the hood to check the fit - repeat the procedure until the hood is flush with the fenders

9.11 Adjust the hood closing height by turning the hood bumpers in or out

separate and replaceable units, any seriously damaged components should be replaced rather than repaired. Sometimes the components can be found in a wrecking yard that specializes in used vehicle components, often at considerable savings over the cost of new parts.

7 Hinges and locks - maintenance

Once every 3000 miles, or every three months, the hinges and latch assemblies on the doors, hood and trunk should be given a few drops of light oil or lock lubricant. The door latch strikers should also be lubricated with a thin coat of grease to reduce wear and ensure free movement. Lubricate the door and trunk locks with spray-on graphite lubricant.

8 Windshield and fixed glass - replacement

Replacement of the windshield and fixed glass requires the use of special fast-setting adhesive/caulk materials and some specialized tools. It is recommended that these operations be left to a dealer or a shop specializing in glass work.

9 Hood - removal, installation and adjustment

Refer to illustrations 9.1, 9.10 and 9.11
Note: *The hood is heavy and somewhat awkward to remove and install - at least two people should perform this procedure.*

Removal and installation

1   Make marks around the bolt heads to ensure proper alignment during installation **(see illustration)**.
2   Use blankets or pads to cover the cowl area of the body and fenders. This will protect the body and paint as the hood is lifted off.

3   Disconnect any cables or wires that will interfere with removal.
4   Have an assistant support the hood. Remove the hinge-to-hood screws or bolts.
5   Lift off the hood.
6   Installation is the reverse of removal.

Adjustment

7   Fore-and-aft and side-to-side adjustment of the hood is done by moving the hinge plate slot after loosening the bolts or nuts.
8   Scribe a line around the entire hinge plate so you can judge the amount of movement **(see illustration 9.1)**
9   Loosen the bolts or nuts and move the hood into correct alignment. Move it only a little at a time. Tighten the hinge bolts and carefully lower the hood to check the position.
10   If necessary after installation, the entire hood latch assembly can be adjusted up-and-down as well as from side-to-side on the radiator support so the hood closes securely, flush with the fenders. To make the adjustment, scribe a line around the hood latch mounting bolts to provide a reference point, then loosen them and reposition the latch assembly, as necessary **(see illustration)**. Following adjustment, retighten the mounting bolts.
11   Finally, adjust the hood bumpers on the radiator support so the hood, when closed, is flush with the fenders **(see illustration)**.
12   The hood latch assembly, as well as the

hinges, should be periodically lubricated with white, lithium-base grease to prevent binding and wear.

10 Radiator grille - removal and installation

Refer to illustrations 10.1, 10.4a and 10.4b
Warning: *Some later models are equipped with airbags. The airbag is armed and can deploy (inflate) anytime the battery is connected. To prevent accidental deployment (and possible injury), disconnect the negative battery cable whenever working near airbag components. After the battery is disconnected, wait at least ten minutes before beginning work (the system has a back-up capacitor that must fully discharge).*

1990 and earlier models

1   Use a screwdriver to rotate the plastic retaining clips 45-degrees and disengage them **(see illustration)**.
2   Once all of the retaining clips are disengaged, pull the grille out and remove it.
3   Installation is the reverse of removal.

1991 and later models

4   Use a screwdriver to release the retaining clips while pulling out and detach the grille **(see illustrations)**.
5   Place the grille in position and press it into place until the clips click.

10.1 Rotate the clip 45-degrees with a screwdriver, then detach the grille

10.4a Use a screwdriver to release the clips while pulling out on the grille

11

10.4b Press on the top (arrow) of the clip to release it

11.3 Scribe a mark around the bolt heads or hinge plate to help with lid realignment on installation

11.9a Use a socket and extension to loosen the bolts, then adjust the trunk latch position

---

11 Trunk lid - removal, installation and adjustment

Refer to illustrations 11.3, 11.9a and 11.9b

1   Open the trunk lid and cover the edges of the trunk compartment with pads or cloths to protect the painted surfaces when the lid is removed.

2   Disconnect any cables or wire harness connectors attached to the trunk lid that would interfere with removal.

3   Make alignment marks around the hinge mounting bolts with a marking pen **(see illustration)**.

4   While an assistant supports the lid, remove the lid-to-hinge bolts on both sides and lift it off.

5   Installation is the reverse of removal. **Note:** *When reinstalling the trunk lid, align the lid-to-hinge bolts with the marks made during removal.*

6   After installation, close the lid and make sure it's in proper alignment with the surrounding panels.

7   Forward-and-backward and side-to-side adjustments are made by loosening the hinge-to-lid bolts and gently moving the lid into correct alignment.

8   Vertical adjustments to the lid are made by adding or removing the shims used on the hinge.

9   To adjust the lid so it is flush with the body when closed, loosen the mounting bolts

and move the lock and striker **(see illustration)**. On some later models finer adjustments can be made by turning the rubber bumpers **(see illustration)**.

---

12 Liftgate and support struts - removal, installation and adjustment

Note: *The following procedure applies only to station wagon hatchback models*

Support struts

1   Open the liftgate. Support the liftgate.

2   Loosen the locknut and then unscrew the stud or remove the mounting bolts and remove the strut from the liftgate.

3   Installation is the reverse of removal. Tighten all fasteners securely.

Liftgate

4   Open the liftgate and cover the upper body area around the opening with pads or cloths to protect the painted surfaces when the liftgate is removed.

5   Unplug all electrical connectors and pull the wire harness out of the liftgate (tie string or wire to the cables so they can be pulled back into the body when the liftgate is reinstalled).

6   Paint or scribe alignment marks around the liftgate hinge flanges.

7   While an assistant supports the liftgate, detach the support struts (see above).

8   Remove the hinge bolts and detach the liftgate from the vehicle.

9   Installation is the reverse of removal. Be extremely careful with the wire harness when threading it back into the liftgate or you could cut it on a metal edge.

10   After installation, close the liftgate and make sure it's in proper alignment with the surrounding body panels.

11   If the liftgate needs to be adjusted, loosen the hinge bolts slightly, gently close the liftgate and verify that it's centered between the two fenders (the striker should center it). Then carefully open the liftgate and retighten the hinge bolts.

---

13 Door trim panel - removal and installation

Refer to illustrations 13.2, 13.3a, 13.3b, 13.5 and 13.7

1   Disconnect the negative cable from the battery.

2   On manual window regulator equipped models, remove the window crank, using a hooked tool to remove the retainer clip **(see illustration)**. A special tool is available for this purpose, but it's not essential. With the clip removed, pull off the handle.

3   Use a hooked tool or a screwdriver to pry out any cover for access to the retainer and detach the clips, then lift it out **(see illustration)**.

11.9b On some models, screw the rubber bumper in or out to adjust the trunk lid closing height

13.2 Use a hooked tool like this to remove the window regulator retaining clip

13.3a Use a small screwdriver or hooked tool to remove the plastic screw covers

13.3b If you have access to a special tool like this one, use it to disengage the trim panel clips

13.5 The perimeter of the trim panel is secured to the door with clips

13.7 If the plastic watershield is peeled off carefully, it can be reused

Some plastic retaining clips are used on later models **(see illustration)**.

4   Remove the inside door handle (see Section 15) and any door trim panel retaining screws and door pull/armrest assemblies.

5   Insert a wide putty knife, a thin screwdriver or a special trim panel removal tool between the trim panel and door to disengage the retaining clips, then grasp the panel and pull out **(see illustration)**. Work around the outer edge until the panel is free.

6   Once all of the clips are disengaged, detach the trim panel, unplug any electrical connectors and remove the trim panel from the vehicle by gently pulling it up and out.

7   For access to the inner door remove the plastic watershield. Peel back the watershield, taking care not to tear it **(see illustration)**. To install the trim panel, first press

the watershield back into place. If necessary, add more sealant to hold it in place.

8   Prior to installation of the door panel, be sure to reinstall any clips in the panel which may have come out during the removal procedure and stayed in the door.

9   Plug in any electrical connectors and place the panel in position. Press it into place until the clips are seated and install any retaining screws and armrest/door pulls. Install the manual regulator window crank or power switch assembly.

14   Door - removal, installation and adjustment

Removal and installation

Refer to illustrations 14.3 and 14.4

1   Remove the door trim panel (see Section 13) and disconnect any electrical connectors and push them through the door opening so they won't interfere with removal.

2   Position a jack under the door or have an assistant on hand to support the door when the hinge bolts are removed. **Note:** *If a jack or stand is used, place a rag between it and the door to protect the door's paint.*

3   Remove the door stop strut center pin **(see illustration)**.

4   Scribe or draw a line around the door hinge bolts **(see illustration)**.

5   Remove the hinge-to-door bolts and carefully detach the door. Installation is the reverse of removal.

Adjustment

Refer to illustration 14.6

6   Following installation, make sure the door is aligned properly. Adjust it if necessary as follows:

a) *Up-and-down and forward-and-backward adjustments are made by loosening the hinge-to-body bolts and moving the door, as necessary. A special offset tool may be required to reach some of the bolts.*

b) *In-and-out and up-and-down adjustments are made by loosening the door side hinge bolts and moving the door, as necessary. A special offset tool may be required to reach some of the bolts.*

c) *The door lock striker can also be adjusted both up-and-down and sideways to provide a positive engagement with the locking mechanism. This is done by loosening the screws and moving the striker, as necessary* **(see illustration)**.

15   Door latch, lock cylinder and handles - removal and installation

1   Remove the door trim panel and the plastic watershield (see Section 13).

Door latch

Refer to illustrations 15.2 and 15.3

2   Reach behind inside the door panel and disconnect the control links from the latch **(see illustration)**.

14.3 Gently tap the pin for the door stop strut in the direction shown

14.4 Before loosening or removing them, draw around the door bolt locations with a marking pen

14.6 Adjust the door lock striker by loosening the mounting screws and gently tapping the striker in the desired direction

15.2 Detach the links on the two rods (arrows) leading to the latch

11

15.3 Remove the latch screws (arrows) from the end of the door

15.6 The two links and outside handle retention nuts (arrows) can be reached through access hole in the door frame

15.7 To remove the lock cylinder, detach the link and pry the retaining clip off

15.9 Remove the handle retaining screw

15.10 Rotate the handle out, then detach the control link

16.4 Remove the two mounting bolts (arrows), detach the glass and lift it out of the door - place a rag over the glass to help prevent scratching it

17.4a Early model equalizer mounting bolt locations (arrows)

17.4b Later model lower equalizer mounting bolts (arrows)

3   Remove the latch retaining screws from the end of the door **(see illustration)**.
4   Detach the door latch and (if equipped) the door lock solenoid.
5   Installation is the reverse of removal.

Lock cylinder and outside handle

Refer to illustrations 15.6 and 15.7

6   Disconnect the control link rods from the outside handle, remove the outside handle retention nuts and pull the handle from the door **(see illustration)**.
7   Detach the control link from the lock cylinder, use a screwdriver to pry the

retaining clip off and remove the lock cylinder from the door **(see illustration)**.
8   Installation is the reverse of removal.

Inside handle

Refer to illustrations 15.9 and 15.10

9   Remove the retaining screw **(see illustration)**.
10   Pull the handle free, disconnect the link(s) from the inside handle control and remove the handle from the door **(see illustration)**.
11   Installation is the reverse of removal.

16 Door window glass - removal and installation

Refer to illustration 16.4

1   Remove the door trim panel and the plastic watershield (see Section 13).
2   Lower the window glass.
3   Carefully pry the inner weatherstrip out of the door window opening.
4   Place a rag inside the door panel to help prevent scratching the glass and remove the two glass mounting bolts **(see illustration)**.
5   Remove the glass by pulling it up.
6   Installation is the reverse of the removal procedure.

17 Window regulator - removal and installation

Refer to illustrations 17.4a, 17.4b, 17.4c, 17.4d and 17.4e

1   Remove the door trim panel and the plastic watershield (see Section 13).
2   Remove the window assembly (see Section 16).
3   If so equipped, unclip the power window control connector from the panel and disconnect it.
4   Remove the equalizer arm bracket and the regulator mounting bolts **(see illustrations)**.
5   Pull the regulator through the service hole to remove it.
6   Installation is the reverse of removal.

17.4c Later model upper equalizer mounting bolts (arrows)

17.4d Early model regulator bolt locations

17.4e Later model regulator bolt locations

18.4a Typical front bumper details

18.4b Typical rear bumper details

18 Bumpers - removal and installation

Refer to illustrations 18.4a and 18.4b
Warning: *Some later models are equipped with airbags. The airbag is armed and can deploy (inflate) anytime the battery is connected. To prevent accidental deployment (and possible injury), disconnect the negative battery cable whenever working near airbag components. After the battery is disconnected, wait at least 10 minutes before beginning work (the system has a back-up capacitor that must fully discharge).*

1   Apply the parking brake, raise the vehicle and support it securely on jackstands
2   Disconnect the cable from the negative battery terminal and disconnect any wiring that would interfere with bumper removal.
3   Remove the bumper cover if equipped, taking care to avoid damaging the cover and the fender.
4   Working under the vehicle remove the bumper retention bolts **(see illustrations)**.
5   Detach the bumper assembly from the vehicle.
6   Installation is the reverse of the removal procedure.

19 Outside mirrors - removal and installation

Refer to illustrations 19.1 and 19.2
1   On manually operated mirrors, remove the control handle **(see illustration)**. Pry off the mirror cover.

19.1 The manual mirror handle is retained by a screw

11

19.2 Remove the three nuts securing the outside mirror to the door

20.3a Use a screwdriver to pry out the console screw covers

20.3b Remove the console screws

21.2a Remove the upper bezel screws (there are two)

21.2b Remove the screws along the base of the bezel

2   Remove the three retaining nuts and detach the mirror **(see illustration)**.
3   Installation is the reverse of removal.

20 Console - removal and installation

Refer to illustrations 20.3a and 20.3b
Warning: *Some later models are equipped with airbags. The airbag is armed and can deploy (inflate) anytime the battery is connected. To prevent accidental deployment (and possible injury), disconnect the negative battery cable whenever working near airbag components. After the battery is*

21.3 Detach the bezel and lift it off

disconnected, wait at least 10 minutes before beginning work (the system has a back-up capacitor that must fully discharge).
1   Disconnect the cable from the negative battery terminal.
2   Pull the parking brake on.
3   Remove retaining screws at the rear of the console **(see illustrations)**.
4   Remove the front console screws. On manual shift models, unscrew the shift knob.
5   Lift the console up over shift lever, unplug any electrical connections and remove the console from the vehicle.
6   Installation is the reverse of the removal procedure.

21 Instrument cluster bezel - removal and installation

Refer to illustrations 21.2a, 21.2b and 21.3
Warning: *Some later models are equipped with airbags. The airbag is armed and can deploy (inflate) anytime the battery is connected. To prevent accidental deployment (and possible injury), disconnect the negative battery cable whenever working near airbag components. After the battery is disconnected, wait at least 10 minutes before beginning work (the system has a back-up capacitor that must fully discharge).*

1   Disconnect the cable from the negative battery terminal.
2   Remove the upper and lower bezel retaining screws **(see illustrations)**. On some models it may be necessary to remove the dashboard center bezel as well (see Section 22).
3   Grasp the bezel securely and detach it **(see illustration)**.
4   Installation is the reverse of the removal procedure.

22 Dashboard trim panels - removal and installation

Refer to illustrations 22.2a, 22.2b and 22.2c
Warning: *Some later models are equipped with airbags. The airbag is armed and can deploy (inflate) anytime the battery is connected. To prevent accidental deployment (and possible injury), disconnect the negative battery cable whenever working near airbag components. After the battery is disconnected, wait at least 10 minutes before beginning work (the system has a back-up capacitor that must fully discharge).*
1   Disconnect the cable from the negative battery terminal.
2   Refer to the accompanying illustrations for information on removing and installing the dashboard trim panels **(see illustrations)**.

Heater control

Glove box

When removing,
pull out.

22.2a 1986 and earlier models dashboard panel details

Fuse block

Super multiple junction (SMJ)-Instrument harness

Mounting bolt

Metal clip (8 places)

Metal clip (3 places)

Coupe only

Pawl

Pawl

Pawl

Pawl (2 places for upper and lower surfaces)

Pawl

Pawl (6 places)

Pawl (4 places)

CE114

CE114

TYPE 1

Pawl

Pawl

TYPE 2

Pawl

Pawl

Metal clip

Slit (6 places)

22.2b 1987 through 1990 model dashboard panel details

22.2c 1991 and later model dashboard panel details

23.2a After removing the screws, detach the lock cylinder cover (later models) (steering wheel removed for clarity)

23 Steering column cover - removal and installation

Refer to illustrations 23.2a and 23.2b

1   Remove the steering column cover screws.
2   Separate the cover halves and detach them from the steering column **(see illustrations)**.
3   Disconnect any electrical connections and remove the covers.
4   Installation is the reverse of the removal procedure.

24 Instrument panel - removal and installation

1   Disconnect the cable from the negative battery terminal.
2   Remove the dashboard trim panels (see Section 22).
3   Remove the instrument panel **(see illustrations 22.2a, 22.2b and 22.2c)**.
4   Installation is the reverse of removal.

25 Seats - removal and installation

Refer to illustration 25.1

1   Remove the retaining bolts, detach any clips, unplug any electrical connectors and lift the seat from the vehicle **(see illustration)**.
2   Installation is the reverse of removal.

26 Seat belts - check

1   Check the seat belts, buckles, latch plates and guide loops for any obvious damage or signs of wear.
2   Make sure the seat belt reminder light comes on when the key is turned on.
3   The seat belts are designed to lock up during a sudden stop or impact, yet allow free movement during normal driving. The retractors should hold the belt against your chest while driving and rewind the belt when the buckle is unlatched.
4   If any of the above checks reveal problems with the seat-belt system, replace parts as necessary.

23.2b Separate the steering column cover halves (steering wheel removed for clarity)

25.1 Typical seat mounting details

11

Notes

Chapter 12
Chassis electrical system

Contents

1   General information

The electrical system is a 12-volt, negative ground type. Power for the lights and all electrical accessories is supplied by a lead/acid-type battery which is charged by the alternator.

This Chapter covers repair and service procedures for the various electrical components not associated with the engine. Information on the battery, alternator, distributor and starter motor can be found in Chapter 5.

It should be noted that when portions of the electrical system are serviced, the cable should be disconnected from the negative battery terminal to prevent electrical shorts and/or fires. **Warning:** *If equipped with airbags, see Section 27. Do not disconnect, test or service any airbag system components or the wiring which disconnects them.*

2   Electrical troubleshooting - general information

A typical electrical circuit consists of an electrical component, any switches, relays, motors, fuses, fusible links or circuit breakers related to that component and the wiring and electrical connectors that link the component to both the battery and the chassis. To help you pinpoint an electrical circuit problem, wiring diagrams are included at the end of this book.

Before tackling any troublesome electrical circuit, first study the appropriate wiring diagrams to get a complete understanding of what makes up that individual circuit. Trouble spots, for instance, can often be narrowed down by noting if other components related to the circuit are operating properly. If several components or circuits fail at one time, chances are the problem is in a fuse or ground connection, because several circuits are often routed through the same fuse and ground connections.

Electrical problems usually stem from simple causes, such as loose or corroded connections, a blown fuse, a melted fusible link or a bad relay. Visually inspect the condition of all fuses, wires and connections in a problem circuit before troubleshooting it.

If testing instruments are going to be utilized, use the diagrams to plan ahead of time where you will make the necessary connections in order to accurately pinpoint the trouble spot.

The basic tools needed for electrical troubleshooting include a circuit tester or voltmeter (a 12-volt bulb with a set of test leads can also be used), a continuity tester, which includes a bulb, battery and set of test leads, and a jumper wire, preferably with a circuit breaker incorporated, which can be used to bypass electrical components. Before attempting to locate a problem with test instruments, use the wiring diagram(s) to decide where to make the connections.

Voltage checks

Voltage checks should be performed if a circuit is not functioning properly. Connect one lead of a circuit tester to either the negative battery terminal or a known good ground. Connect the other lead to a electrical connector in the circuit being tested, preferably nearest to the battery or fuse. If the bulb of the tester lights, voltage is present, which means that the part of the circuit between the electrical connector and the battery is problem free. Continue checking the rest of the circuit in the same fashion. When you reach a point at which no voltage is present, the problem lies between that point and the last test point with voltage. Most of the time the problem can be traced to a loose connection. **Note:** *Keep in mind that some circuits receive voltage only when the ignition key is in the Accessory or Run position.*

Finding a short

One method of finding shorts in a circuit is to remove the fuse and connect a test light or voltmeter in its place to the fuse terminals. There should be no voltage present in the circuit. Move the wiring harness from side to side while watching the test light. If the bulb goes on, there is a short to ground somewhere in that area, probably where the insulation has rubbed through. The same test can be performed on each component in the circuit, even a switch.

Ground check

Perform a ground test to check whether a component is properly grounded. Disconnect the battery and connect one lead of a self-powered test light, known as a continuity tester, to a known good ground. Connect the other lead to the wire or ground connection being tested. If the bulb goes on, the ground is good. If the bulb does not go on, the ground is not good.

Continuity check

A continuity check is done to determine if there are any breaks in a circuit - if it is passing electricity properly. With the circuit off (no power in the circuit), a self-powered continuity tester can be used to check the circuit. Connect the test leads to both ends of the circuit (or to the "power" end and a good ground), and if the test light comes on the circuit is passing current properly. If the light

3.1a The interior fuse box is located under the left (driver's side) of the instrument panel, under a cover

3.1b The engine compartment fuse box is located in the left front corner of the engine compartment and can contain relays (A) as well as fuses (B) and fusible links (C)

3.3 The fuses on these models can be easily checked visually to see if they are blown

doesn't come on, there is a break somewhere in the circuit. The same procedure can be used to test a switch, by connecting the continuity tester to the power in and power out sides of the switch. With the switch turned On, the test light should come on.

Finding an open circuit

When diagnosing for possible open circuits, it is often difficult to locate them by sight because oxidation or terminal misalignment are hidden by the electrical connectors. Merely wiggling an electrical connector on a sensor or in the wiring harness may correct the open circuit condition. Remember this when an open circuit is indicated when troubleshooting a circuit. Intermittent problems may also be caused by oxidized or loose connections.

Electrical troubleshooting is simple if you keep in mind that all electrical circuits are basically electricity running from the battery, through the wires, switches, relays, fuses and fusible links to each electrical component (light bulb, motor, etc.) and to ground, from which it is passed back to the battery. Any electrical problem is an interruption in the flow of electricity to and from the battery.

3 Fuses - general information

Refer to illustrations 3.1a, 3.1b and 3.3

The electrical circuits of the vehicle are protected by a combination of fuses, circuit breakers and fusible links. The fuse blocks are located under the instrument panel on the left side of the dashboard, and on later models, in the engine compartment next to the battery **(see illustrations)**.

Each of the fuses is designed to protect a specific circuit, and the various circuits are identified on the fuse panel itself.

Miniaturized fuses are employed in the fuse blocks. These compact fuses, with blade terminal design, allow fingertip removal and replacement. If an electrical component fails, always check the fuse first. A blown fuse is easily identified through the clear

plastic body. Visually inspect the element for evidence of damage **(see illustration)**.

Be sure to replace blown fuses with the correct type. Fuses of different ratings are physically interchangeable, but only fuses of the proper rating should be used. Replacing a fuse with one of a higher or lower value than specified is not recommended. Each electrical circuit needs a specific amount of protection. The amperage value of each fuse is molded into the fuse body.

If the replacement fuse immediately fails, don't replace it again until the cause of the problem is isolated and corrected. In most cases, this will be a short circuit in the wiring caused by a broken or deteriorated wire.

4 Fusible links - general information

Refer to illustration 4.2

Some circuits are protected by fusible links. The links are used in circuits which are not ordinarily fused, such as the ignition circuit.

The fusible links on 1986 and earlier models are color-coded wires connected to the battery positive cable **(see illustration)**. On later models the fusible links are located in the engine compartment fuse block **(see illustration 3.1b)** and are similar to fuses.

4.2 On 1986 and earlier models, the fusible links plug onto the battery terminal

To replace a fusible link, first disconnect the positive cable from the battery. Unplug the burned-out link from the positive cable and wiring harness or fuse block and replace it with a new one (available from your dealer or auto parts store). Always determine the cause for the overload which melted the fusible link before installing a new one.

5 Circuit breakers - general information

On some models circuit breakers protect components such as power windows, power door locks and headlights.

Because on some models the circuit breaker resets itself automatically, an electrical overload in a circuit breaker protected system will cause the circuit to fail momentarily, then come back on. If the circuit does not come back on, check it immediately.

6 Relays - general information

Refer to illustrations 6.2a, 6.2b and 6.2c

Several electrical accessories in the vehicle use relays to transmit the electrical signal to the component. If the relay is defective, that component will not operate properly.

The various relays are mounted in engine compartment and several locations throughout the vehicle **(see illustrations)**.

If a faulty relay is suspected, it can be removed and tested by a dealer or other qualified shop. Defective relays must be replaced as a unit.

7 Turn signal/hazard flashers - check and replacement

Refer to illustration 7.1

Warning: *Some later models are equipped with airbags. To prevent accidental*

Vacuum sensor

Intermittent wiper amplifier

Dimmer relay (Black)
• Auto-choke relay
• Bulb check relay

Inhibitor relay

Mixture relay

E.C.C. main relay

Horn relay (Black)

Resistor (For tachometer)

Air conditioner relay (With air conditioner: Black)

Condenser fan relay (With air conditioner: Brown)

6.2a Relay locations - 1986 and earlier models (typical)

Wiper amplifier

Air conditioner relay (Black)

Condenser motor relay (Blue)

Wiper motor

Horn relay (Gray)

Inhibitor relay (Gray)

• Auto choke relay (Gray)
• Bulb check relay (Blue)

P.T.C. relay (Blue)

Radiator fan relay (Blue)

Ignition coil

Fusible link

Battery

6.2b Typical 1987 through 1990 model engine compartment relays

Relay box: SR engine models

Relay box: SR engine models
- Horn relay (Gray)
- Radiator fan relay-3 (Brown)

Relay box
Fuse, fusible link and relay box

Relay box
- Inhibitor relay: A/T models (Gray)
- Clutch relay: M/T models (Blue)
- Radiator fan relay-1
  A/T models with SR engine (Brown)
- Radiator fan main relay:
  Except A/T models with SR engine (Blue)
- Radiator fan relay-2
  A/T models with SR engine (Brown)
- Radiator fan main relay:
  A/T models with GA engine (Brown)
- Fuel pump relay (Green)
- Air conditioner relay (Blue)

Fuse, fusible link and relay box
- Fusible link: A/T models with SR engine
- Fusible link
- Fuse
- Horn relay: GA engine models (Gray)
- Fusible link
- FUSE

6.2c Typical 1991 and later model relay layout

7.1 1982 and 1983 models have separate flasher units for the turn signals and hazard flashers

- Hazard flasher unit
- Turn signal flasher unit
- Stop lamp switch
- Clutch switch (M/T models)

deployment (and possible injury) when working near airbag components, disconnect the negative battery cable and wait at least 10 minutes before beginning work (the system has a back-up capacitor that must fully discharge). For more information see Section 27.

1   1982 and 1983 models use separate flasher units for the turn signals and hazard flashers (see illustration). 1984 and later models use a single combination turn signal and hazard flasher unit.

2   When the flasher unit is functioning properly, an audible click can be heard during its operation. If the turn signals fail on one side or the other and the flasher unit does not make its characteristic clicking sound, a faulty turn signal bulb is indicated.

3   If both turn signals fail to blink, the problem may be due to a blown fuse, a faulty flasher unit, a broken switch or a loose or open connection. If a quick check of the fuse box indicates that the turn signal fuse has blown, check the wiring for a short before installing a new fuse.

4   To replace the flasher, disconnect the electrical connector and remove the flasher unit from its mounting bracket.

5   Make sure that the replacement unit is identical to the original. Compare the old one to the new one before installing it.

6   Installation is the reverse of removal.

8.4b On 1991 and later models, the combination switch is held in place by several screws

8.4a On 1990 and earlier models the combination switch is attached by one screw

8 Combination switch - removal and installation

Refer to illustrations 8.4a, 8.4b, 8.5a and 8.5b
Warning: *Some later models are equipped with airbags. The airbag is armed and can deploy (inflate) anytime the battery is connected. To prevent accidental deployment (and possible injury), disconnect the negative battery cable whenever working near airbag components. After the battery is disconnected, wait at least 10 minutes before beginning work (the system has a back-up capacitor that must fully discharge). For more information see Section 27.*

1   Disconnect the negative cable at the battery.

2   Remove the steering wheel (see Chapter 10).
3   Remove the dashboard lower finish panel and steering column cover (see Chapter 11).
4   Remove the combination switch retaining screw(s). Earlier models are retained by a collar with one screw at the base and later models have several screws holding the switch to the column (**see illustrations**).
5   Trace the wiring harness down the steering column to the connector. Release the wiring retainer clamps, if equipped and unplug the connector and slide the switch up off the column (**see illustrations**).
6   Installation is the reverse of removal. If equipped with an airbag, refer to Chapter 10 and center the spiral cable before installing the steering wheel.

9 Steering column switches - check and replacement

Refer to illustrations 9.4a, 9.4b, 9.4c and 9.7
Warning: *Some later models are equipped with airbags. The airbag is armed and can deploy (inflate) anytime the battery is*

connected. To prevent accidental deployment (and possible injury), disconnect the negative battery cable whenever working near airbag components. After the battery is disconnected, wait at least 10 minutes before beginning work (the system has a back-up capacitor that must fully discharge). For more information see Section 27.
1   Disconnect the negative cable from the battery.
2   Remove the dashboard lower finish panel and steering column cover (see Chapter 11).
3   Remove the combination switch (see Section 8).

Check

4   Using an ohmmeter, check for continuity between the indicated terminals with the various switches in each of the indicated positions (**see illustrations on the following pages**).
5   If the continuity is not as specified, replace the defective switch.

Replacement

6   Remove the combination switch (see Section 8). If equipped with an airbag, remove the four screws retaining the spiral cable and remove the spiral cable from the combination switch.
7   Remove the retaining screws from the

8.5a Unplug the electrical connector from the combination switch

8.5b Slip the combination switch off the steering column

9.4a Terminal guide and continuity table for 1986 and earlier model wiper/washer, turn signal and headlight switches

9.4b 1987 through 1990 model terminal guide and continuity table for the wiper/washer, turn signal, headlight and horn switches

9.4c Terminal guide and continuity table for 1991 and later model wiper/washer, cruise control (ASCD), turn signal and horn switches

9.7 The steering column switches can be removed from the combination switch base on most models

10.5 Ignition/key switch continuity charts

10.7 To remove the ignition/lock cylinder assembly, drill out the two retaining bolts (arrows)

switch being replaced and remove the defective switch from the switch body **(see illustration)**.

8   Insert the terminals from the new switch into the connector, pushing in until they are securely locked in place.

9   The remainder or installation is the reverse of removal. If equipped with an airbag, refer to Chapter 10 and center the spiral cable before installing the steering wheel.

10 Ignition switch and key lock cylinder - check and replacement

Warning: Some later models are equipped with airbags. The airbag is armed and can deploy (inflate) anytime the battery is connected. To prevent accidental deployment (and possible injury), disconnect the negative battery cable whenever working near airbag components. After the battery is disconnected, wait at least 10 minutes before beginning work (the system has a back-up capacitor that must fully discharge). For more information see Section 27.

Ignition switch

1   Disconnect the negative cable at the battery.
2   Remove the steering wheel (see Chapter 10).

3   Remove the steering column cover (see Chapter 11).

Check

Refer to illustration 10.5
4   Trace the wire from the switch to the connector and unplug the connector.
5   Use an ohmmeter to check for continuity at the indicated terminals with the switch in each indicated position **(see illustration)**.
6   Replace the switch if continuity is not as specified.

Replacement

Refer to illustration 10.7
7   Remove the shear-head bolts retaining the ignition switch/lock cylinder assembly and separate the bracket halves from the steering column. This can be accomplished by drilling out the screws or using a small chisel and hammer to make slots in the them so they can be unscrewed with a screwdriver **(see illustration)**.
8   Place the new switch assembly position, install the new shear-head bolts and tighten them until the heads snap off. If equipped with an airbag, make sure to center the spiral cable before installing the steering wheel.

11.4 Terminal guide and continuity check for the rear window defogger switch

11 Rear window defogger switch - check and replacement

Refer to illustration 11.4
Warning: Some later models are equipped with airbags. The airbag is armed and can deploy (inflate) anytime the battery is connected. To prevent accidental deployment (and possible injury), disconnect the negative battery cable whenever working near airbag components. After the battery is disconnected, wait at least 10 minutes before beginning work (the system has a back-up capacitor that must fully discharge). For more information see Section 27.
1   Detach the cable from the negative battery terminal.
2   Use a small screwdriver to detach the switch and pull it gently free.
3   Pull the defogger switch out and unplug the electrical connector.
4   Use an ohmmeter to check for continuity at the indicated terminals with the switch in the indicated position **(see illustration)**.
5   Replace the switch if the continuity is not as specified.

12 Rear window defogger - check and repair

Refer to illustrations 12.4, 12.5 and 12.7
1   The rear window defogger consists of a number of horizontal elements baked onto the glass surface.
2   Small breaks in the element can be repaired without removing the rear window.

Check

3   Turn the ignition switch and defogger system switches to On.
4   When measuring voltage during the next two tests, wrap a piece of aluminum foil

12

12.4 When measuring the voltage at the rear window defogger grid, wrap a piece of aluminum foil around the negative probe of the voltmeter and press the foil against the wire with your finger

12.5 To determine if a wire has broken, check the voltage at the center of each wire - if the voltage is 6-volts, the wire is unbroken if the voltage is 12-volts, the wire is broken between the center of the wire and the positive end; if the voltage is 0-volt, the wire is broken between the center of the wire and ground

12.7 To find the break, place the voltmeter positive lead against the defogger positive terminal, place the voltmeter negative lead with the foil strip against the heat wire at the positive terminal end and slide it toward the negative terminal end - the point at which the voltmeter deflects from zero to several volts is the point at which the wire is broken

around the tip of the voltmeter negative probe and press the foil against the wire with your finger **(see illustration)**.

5   Check the voltage at the center of each heat wire **(see illustration)**. If the voltage is 6-volts, the wire is okay (there is no break). If the voltage is 12-volts, the wire is broken between the center of the element and the positive end. If the voltage is 0-volts the wire is broken between the center of the element and ground.

6   Connect the negative lead to a good body ground. The reading should stay the same.

7   To find the break, place the voltmeter positive lead against the defogger positive terminal. Place the voltmeter negative lead with the foil strip against the heat wire at the positive terminal end and slide it toward the negative terminal end. The point at which the

voltmeter deflects from zero to several volts is the point at which the heat element is broken **(see illustration). Note:** *If the heat element is not broken, the voltmeter will indicate no voltage at the positive end of the heat element but gradually increase to about 12-volts.*

Repair

8   Repair the break in the element using a repair kit specifically recommended for this purpose, such as Dupont paste No. 4817 (or equivalent). Included in this kit is plastic conductive epoxy.

9   Prior to repairing a break, turn off the system and allow it to cool off for a few minutes.

10   Lightly buff the element area with fine steel wool, then clean it thoroughly with rubbing alcohol.

11   Use masking tape to mask off the area being repaired.

12   Thoroughly mix the epoxy, following the instructions provided with the repair kit.

13   Apply the epoxy material to the slit in the masking tape, overlapping the undamaged area about 3/4-inch on either end.

14   Allow the repair to cure for 24 hours before removing the tape and using the system.

13   Radio and speakers - removal and installation

Warning: *Some later models are equipped with airbags. The airbag is armed and can deploy (inflate) anytime the battery is connected. To prevent accidental deployment (and possible injury), disconnect the negative battery cable whenever working near airbag components. After the battery is disconnected, wait at least 10 minutes before beginning work (the system has a back-up capacitor that must fully discharge). For more information see Section 27.*

1   Disconnect the negative cable at the battery.

Radio

Refer to illustrations 13.2, 13.3a, 13.3b, 13.4a and 13.4b

2   Pull off the radio control knobs, then remove the retaining nuts **(see illustration)**.

3   Remove the mounting screws or bolts and pull the center trim panel housing out of the dash **(see illustrations)**.

4   Remove the screws or nuts, pull the radio out, then unplug the electrical connector and the antenna lead and lift the radio out **(see illustrations)**.

13.2 Pull off the knobs and remove the retaining nuts

13.3a Remove the screws and detach the dashboard center trim panel

13.3b Unplug the electrical connectors and remove the panel

13.4a Pull the radio out, then . . .

13.4b . . . unplug the connectors and remove the unit

13.7 Remove the screws (arrows), pull the speaker out and unplug it

14.1 Use a small wrench to unscrew the antenna mast

5   Installation is the reverse of removal.

Speakers

Refer to illustration 13.7

6   Remove the front door trim panel (see Chapter 11).
7   Remove the speaker retaining screws/nuts. Unplug the electrical connector and remove the speaker **(see illustration).**
8   Installation is the reverse of removal.

14 Antenna - removal and installation

Refer to illustration 14.1

1   Use a small wrench to unscrew the mast **(see illustration).**
2   Install the new antenna mast and tighten it securely with the wrench.

15 Headlights - replacement

Refer to illustrations 15.2, 15.7, 15.12, 15.13 and 15.14

Sealed-beam type

1   Remove the clearance light housing (see Section 18).

2   Remove the screws holding the headlight retainer in place then remove the retainer **(see illustration).** Don't disturb the adjustment screws.
3   Pull the headlight out, unplug the electrical connector and remove the headlight assembly.
4   Installation is the reverse of removal.

Composite bulb-type

Warning: *Some models are equipped with halogen gas-filled bulbs which are under pressure and may shatter if the surface is scratched or the bulb is dropped. Wear eye protection and handle the bulbs carefully, grasping only the base whenever possible. Do not touch the surface of the bulb with your fingers because the oil from your skin could cause it to overheat and fail prematurely. If you do touch the bulb surface, clean it with rubbing alcohol.*

Retaining ring-type

5   Open the hood and locate the bulb retaining ring on the back of the headlight housing.
6   Rotate the headlight retaining ring counterclockwise (viewed from the rear).
7   Withdraw the bulb assembly from the headlight housing **(see illustration).**
8   Unplug the bulb holder from the electrical connector.

15.2 On sealed-beam headlights, remove the four screws (arrows) and detach the retainer

9   Without touching the glass with your bare fingers, insert the new bulb assembly into the headlight housing, install and tighten the retaining ring.
10   Plug in the electrical connector. Test headlight operation, then close the hood.

Retaining clip-type

11   Open the hood and locate the bulb assembly on the back of the headlight housing.
12   Unplug the electrical connector and pull off the rubber boot (if equipped) **(see illustration).**
13   Detach the headlight retaining clip **(see illustration).**

15.7 Retaining ring-type headlight bulb details

15.12 Unplug the electrical connector and remove the rubber boot from the back of the headlight

15.13 Detach the wire clip

12

15.14 Pull the bulb assembly straight out of the housing

16.1 Sealed beam headlights have a horizontal adjusting screw on the side and a vertical adjuster and the bottom of the headlight (arrows)

16.2a 1987 through 1990 model headlight adjusting screw locations (arrows)

14   Withdraw the bulb assembly from the headlight housing **(see illustration)**.
15   Without touching the glass with your bare fingers, insert the new bulb assembly into the headlight housing and secure it with the clip.
16   Plug in the electrical connector and install the rubber boot. Test headlight operation, then close the hood.

16 Headlights - adjustment

Refer to illustrations 16.1, 16.2a, 16.2b and 16.2c
Note: *It is important that the headlights are aimed correctly. If adjusted incorrectly they could blind the driver of an oncoming vehicle and cause a serious accident or seriously reduce your ability to see the road. The headlights should be checked for proper aim every 12 months and any time a new headlight is installed or front end body work is performed. It should be emphasized that the following procedure is only an interim step which will provide temporary adjustment until the headlights can be adjusted by a properly equipped shop.*
1   Sealed beam-type headlights have an

adjusting screw on the top controlling up-and-down movement and one on the side controlling left-and-right movement **(see illustration)**.
2   Later models equipped with composite headlights also have two adjustment screws, one to the side controlling left-and-right movement and one below the light for up-and-down movement **(see illustrations)**. On 1991 and later models adjustment is made by turning the screws to center the level gauges located on top of the headlight housings.
3   On other models, there are several methods of adjusting the headlights. The simplest method requires a blank wall 25 feet in front of the vehicle and a level floor.
4   Position masking tape vertically on the wall in reference to the vehicle centerline and the centerlines of both headlights.
5   Position a horizontal tape line in reference to the centerline of all the headlights. **Note:** *It may be easier to position the tape on the wall with the vehicle parked only a few inches away.*
6   Adjustment should be made with the vehicle sitting level, the gas tank half-full and no unusually heavy load in the vehicle.
7   Starting with the low beam adjustment, position the high intensity zone so it is two inches below the horizontal line and two inches to the right of the headlight vertical

line. Twist the adjustment screws until the desired level has been achieved.
8   With the high beams on, the high intensity zone should be vertically centered with the exact center just below the horizontal line. **Note:** *It may not be possible to position the headlight aim exactly for both high and low beams. If a compromise must be made, keep in mind that the low beams are the most used and have the greatest effect on driver safety.*
9   Have the headlights adjusted by a dealer service department at the earliest opportunity.

17 Composite headlight housing - removal and installation

Refer to illustrations 17.5a and 17.5b
1   Disconnect the cable from the negative battery terminal.
2   Remove the headlight bulb (Section 15).
3   Remove the radiator grille (Chapter 11).
4   Remove the parking light housing (Section 18).
5   Remove the retaining nuts and bolts, detach the housing and withdraw it from the vehicle **(see illustrations)**.
6   Installation is the reverse of removal.

16.2b On 1991 and later models use a Phillips screwdriver to adjust the headlights - the adjuster closest to the outer fender controls the horizontal movement and the one closest to the radiator, vertical movement

16.2c Turn the adjusting screws to center the bubble in each level gauge (1991 and later models)

17.5a There are four headlight retaining bolts and nuts: Two bolts (arrows) are on the fender brace . . .

17.5b . . . and the two nuts (arrows) are accessible from behind the radiator brace

18.1 On 1990 and earlier models, the turn signal bulb is accessible after removing the lens

18.2 1986 and earlier front side marker light bulb details

18.3a 1986 and earlier front clearance light details

18.3b 1987 through 1990 front combination light bulb replacement details

18 Bulb replacement

Front parking, side marker and clearance/turn signal lights

Refer to illustrations 18.1, 18.2, 18.3a, 18.3b, 18. 4a and 18.4b

1   On 1990 and earlier models the turn signal is mounted in the front bumper. Remove the two screws retaining the lens and replace the bulb **(see illustration)**.
2   Remove the side marker lens housing from the fender. The bulb can then be pulled out of the socket and replaced. **(see illustration)**.
3   The clearance/turn signals on 1990 and earlier models are held in place by screws **(see illustrations)**. Remove the bulbs from the rear side of the housing.
4   On 1991 and later models, remove the turn signal housing screw and push the housing straight forward to remove it **(see illustration)**. Turn the bulb holder counterclockwise and remove it from the back of the housing **(see illustration)**. Push in and rotate the bulb counterclockwise to remove it from the holder.

Rear side marker, turn signal, brake, tail and back-up lights

Refer to illustrations 18.5a, 18.5b, 18.6a and 18.6b

5   On earlier models, remove the screws and detach the side marker light lens, then pull the bulb straight out **(see illustration)**. On later models, remove the screws, detach the housing and remove the holder and bulb from the back of the housing **(see illustration)**.
6   On earlier models, remove the tail light

18.4a On 1991 and later models, remove the screw (arrow) and push the turn signal housing straight forward

18.4b The bulb is removed by turning the holder counterclockwise, then pushing in and turning the bulb

18.5a On 1986 and earlier models, remove rear side marker light lens, then pull the bulb straight out

18.5b Typical later model rear side marker bulb details

housing cover (if equipped) and replace the bulbs **(see illustration)**. On later models remove the housing and turn it over for access to the bulbs **(see illustration)**. Refer to Step 8 for the 1987 through 1990 station wagon backup light bulb replacement procedure.

License plate light
Refer to illustrations 18.7a, 18.7b, 18.8a and 18.8b
7   On 1986 and earlier sedan models, remove the bulb holder from inside the trunk compartment **(see illustration)**. On station wagon models, the license plate light bulb can be replaced after removing the screws and lenses **(see illustration)**.
8   On 1987 and later sedan models,

18.8a 1987 and later license plate light bulb details

18.6a Remove the cover, then push in and rotate the tail light bulbs

remove the screws, detach the housing and replace the bulb **(see illustration)**. On 1987 and later station wagon models, the backup light and license light bulbs are located under a cover **(see illustration)**.

High-mounted brake light
Refer to illustrations 18.9a, 18.9b, 18.9c, 18.8d and 18.8e
9   The brake light covers are retained by screws. Remove the cover and replace the bulb **(see illustrations)**.

18.7a On 1986 and earlier sedan models, the license plate bulbs are accessible from inside the trunk

18.8b 1987 through 1990 station wagon license plate and backup light details

18.6b 1991 and later model tail light bulb replacement details

18.7b 1986 and earlier station wagon license plate light bulb details

18.9a 1986 model sedan high-mounted brake light details

18.9b 1986 model station wagon high-mounted brake light details

18.9c 1987 through 1990 model sedan high-mounted brake light details

18.9d 1987 through 1990 model station wagon high-mounted brake light details

Interior lights

Refer to illustrations 18.10a, 18.10b and 18.10c

10 Remove the lens and replace the bulb **(see illustrations).**

Instrument cluster illumination

Refer to illustration 18.11

11 To gain access to the instrument cluster illumination lights, the instrument cluster will have to be removed (see Section 21). The bulbs can then be removed and replaced from the rear of the cluster **(see illustration).**

18.9e 1991 and later model high-mounted brake light details

19 Daytime Running Lights (DRL) - general information

The Daytime Running Lights (DRL) system used on Canadian models turns the headlights on whenever the engine is started. The only exception is when the engine is turned on when the parking brake is engaged. Once the parking brake is released, the lights will remain on as long as the ignition switch is on, even if the parking brake is later applied.

The DRL system supplies reduced power to the headlights so they won't be too bright for daytime use while prolonging headlight life.

20 Wiper motor - removal and installation

Refer to illustrations 20.3, 20.7a, 20.7b, 20.8, 20.9 and 20.10

Warning: *Some later models are equipped with airbags. The airbag is armed and can deploy (inflate) anytime the battery is connected. To prevent accidental deployment (and possible injury), disconnect the negative battery cable whenever working near airbag components. After the battery is disconnected, wait at least 10 minutes before beginning work (the system has a back-up*

18.10a On some interior lights, pull off the lens, then detach the bulb from the terminals

18.10c On 1991 and later models, use a small screwdriver with a piece of cloth under it to pry the lens off

18.10b On other models, rotate the lens to remove it

18.11 To remove an instrument cluster light bulb, depress it and turn it counterclockwise to release it

12

capacitor that must fully discharge). For more information see Section 27.

1   Disconnect the cable from the negative battery terminal. The windshield wiper motor is located on the right (passenger) side of the underhood compartment and the rear wiper motor (some 1990 and earlier models) is mounted in the liftgate.

Check

Windshield/wiper switch

2   Refer to Section 9 for the wiper/washer switch check procedure.

Rear wiper switch

3   Use a small screwdriver to pry the switch out of the dash, then unplug it and check for continuity between the indicated terminals with the switch in each of the indicated positions (see illustration).
4   If the continuity is not as specified, replace the switch.

Wiper motor

5   If a motor doesn't work or doesn't park properly and the switch checks out okay, the relay or the motor must be replaced.

Replacement

Windshield wiper motor

6   Disconnect the cable from the negative battery terminal.
7   Pry off the cover for the wiper arm nut, then unscrew the nut and remove the arm

	WIPE. WASH	WIPE	OFF	WASH
1	○		○	○	○
2			○	
3		○		○
4	○	○	○	○○

20.3 Terminal guide and continuity table for the rear wiper switch

(see illustration). Remove the screws and detach the cowl cover and wiper motor shield (see illustration).
8   Remove the motor spindle nut (see illustration).
9   Remove the motor bracket retaining bolts, detach the wiper arm then lower the wiper motor and bracket assembly (see illustration).
10   Unplug the electrical connector and

remove the motor from the vehicle (see illustration).
11   Installation is the reverse of removal.

Rear wiper motor

12   Remove the wiper arm, then remove the shaft spindle nuts and washers.
13   Unplug the electrical connector, detach the wiper linkage, remove the retaining bolts and lower the motor through the liftgate access hole as an assembly.
14   Installation is the reverse of removal.

---

21   Instrument cluster - removal and installation

Refer to illustrations 21.3, 21.4a and 21.4b
Warning: Some later models are equipped with airbags. The airbag is armed and can deploy (inflate) anytime the battery is connected. To prevent accidental deployment (and possible injury), disconnect the negative battery cable whenever working near airbag components. After the battery is disconnected, wait at least 10 minutes before

20.7a Use a small screwdriver to pry off the wiper arm nut cover, then remove the nut and pull the arm straight off its splined shaft

20.7b Use needle-nose pliers to remove the watershield clips (later models)

20.8 Unscrew the spindle nut (arrow)

20.9 Detach the arm from the spindle and pull the motor out from the firewall

20.10 Unplug the electrical connector and remove the wiper motor

21.3 Remove the instrument cluster screws

PUSH TO CONNECT

PRESS TO DISCONNECT

21.4a On earlier models, detach the speedometer cable from the cluster by pressing the release lever (arrows)

21.4b Pull the cluster out of the dash and unplug the electrical connectors from the backside

beginning work (the system has a back-up capacitor that must fully discharge). For more information see Section 27.

1   Disconnect the cable from the negative battery terminal.

2   Remove the instrument cluster bezel (see Chapter 11).

3   Remove the retaining screws and pull the cluster forward (see illustration).

4   On earlier models, reach behind the cluster and disconnect the speedometer cable (see illustration). Unplug the electrical connectors and remove the cluster from the vehicle (see illustration).

5   Installation is the reverse of the removal procedure.

22 Horn - check and replacement

Refer to illustration 22.3

Note: Check the fuses before beginning electrical diagnosis.

1   Unplug the electrical connector from the horn.

2   To test the horn, connect battery voltage to the two terminals with a pair of jumper wires. If the horn doesn't sound, replace it. If it does sound, the problem lies in the switch, relay or the wiring between the components.

3   To replace the horn, unplug the

electrical connector and remove the bracket bolt (see illustration).

4   Installation is the reverse of removal.

23 Cruise control system - description and check

Refer to illustrations 23.5a, 23.5b and 23.6

1   The cruise control system maintains vehicle speed with a vacuum actuated servo motor located on the firewall in the engine compartment, which is connected to the throttle linkage by a cable. The system consists of the servo motor, brake switch, control switches, a relay and associated vacuum hoses. Some features of the system require special testers and diagnostic procedures which are beyond the scope of the home mechanic. Listed below are some general procedures that may be used to locate common problems.

2   Locate and check the fuse (see Section 3).

3   Have an assistant operate the brake lights while you check their operation (voltage from the brake light switch deactivates the cruise control).

4   If the brake lights don't come on or don't shut off, correct the problem and retest the cruise control.

5   Visually inspect the vacuum hose

22.3 Unplug the electrical connector, remove the bolt (arrows) and detach the horn

connected to the servo and check the control linkage between the cruise control servo and the throttle linkage and replace as necessary (see illustrations).

6   Cruise controls use a variety of speed sensing devices. On these models the speed sensor pick-up is located in the transaxle. Remove the bolt and detach the sensor, rotate the sensor and check it with a digital voltmeter while it's rotating (see illustration). If the resistance doesn't vary as the cable rotates, the sensor is defective.

7   Test drive the vehicle to determine if the cruise control is now working. If it isn't, take it to a dealer service department or an automotive electrical specialist for further diagnosis and repair.

23.5a The cruise control servo is located on the firewall - make sure the vacuum hose (arrow) is connected securely

25.3b Make sure the cruise control (A) and accelerator (B) linkage mounted on the throttle body are not damaged and that they operate smoothly together when the throttle is opened

Vehicle speed sensor

Approx. 0.5V (Alternating current (AC))

Voltmeter

23.6 Check the vehicle speed sensor to make sure the voltage varies as the gear is turned

12

24 Power window system - description and check

1   The power window system operates the electric motors mounted in the doors which lower and raise the windows. The system consists of the control switches, the motors (regulators), glass mechanisms and associated wiring.

2   Power windows are wired so they can be lowered and raised from the master control switch by the driver or by remote switches located at the individual windows. Each window has a separate motor which is reversible. The position of the control switch determines the polarity and therefore the direction of operation. Some systems are equipped with relays that control current flow to the motors.

3   Some vehicles are equipped with a separate circuit breaker for each motor in addition to the fuse or circuit breaker protecting the whole circuit. This prevents one stuck window from disabling the whole system.

4   The power window system will only operate when the ignition switch is ON. In addition, many models have a window lockout switch at the master control switch which, when activated, disables the switches at the rear windows and, sometimes, the switch at the passenger's window also. Always check these items before troubleshooting a window problem.

5   These procedures are general in nature, so if you can't find the problem using them, take the vehicle to a dealer service department.

6   If the power windows don't work at all, check the fuse or circuit breaker.

7   If only the rear windows are inoperative, or if the windows only operate from the master control switch, check the rear window lockout switch for continuity in the unlocked position. Replace it if it doesn't have continuity.

8   Check the wiring between the switches and fuse panel for continuity. Repair the wiring, if necessary.

9   If only one window is inoperative from the master control switch, try the other control switch at the window. **Note:** *This doesn't apply to the drivers door window.*

10   If the same window works from one switch, but not the other, check the switch for continuity.

11   If the switch tests OK, check for a short or open in the wiring between the affected switch and the window motor.

12   If one window is inoperative from both switches, remove the trim panel from the affected door and check for voltage at the motor while the switch is operated.

13   If voltage is reaching the motor, disconnect the glass from the regulator (see Chapter 11). Move the window up and down by hand while checking for binding and damage. Also check for binding and damage to the regulator. If the regulator is not

damaged and the window moves up and down smoothly, replace the motor. If there's binding or damage, lubricate, repair or replace parts, as necessary.

14   If voltage isn't reaching the motor, check the wiring in the circuit for continuity between the switches and motors. You'll need to consult the wiring diagram for the vehicle. Some power window circuits are equipped with relays. If equipped, check that the relays are grounded properly and receiving voltage from the switches. Also check that each relay sends voltage to the motor when the switch is turned on. If it doesn't, replace the relay.

15   Test the windows after you are done to confirm proper repairs.

25 Power door lock system - description and check

The power door lock system operates the door lock actuators mounted in each door. The system consists of the switches, actuators and associated wiring. Diagnosis can usually be limited to simple checks of the wiring connections and actuators for minor faults which can be easily repaired.

Power door lock systems are operated by bi-directional solenoids located in the doors. The lock switches have two operating positions: Lock and Unlock. These switches activate a relay which in turn connects voltage to the door lock solenoids. Depending on which way the relay is activated, it reverses polarity, allowing the two sides of the circuit to be used alternately as the feed (positive) and ground side.

Some vehicles may have keyless entry, electronic control modules and anti-theft systems incorporated into the power locks. If you are unable to locate the trouble using the following general steps, consult your a dealer service department. **Note:** *Some vehicles also have control switches connected to the key locks in the doors which unlock all the doors when one is unlocked.*

1   Always check the circuit protection first. Some vehicles use a combination of circuit breakers and fuses.

2   Operate the door lock switches in both directions (Lock and Unlock) with the engine off. Listen for the faint click of the relay operating.

3   If there's no click, check for voltage at the switches. If no voltage is present, check the wiring between the fuse panel and the switches for shorts and opens.

4   If voltage is present but no click is heard, test the switch for continuity. Replace it if there's not continuity in both switch positions.

5   If the switch has continuity but the relay doesn't click, check the wiring between the switch and relay for continuity. Repair the wiring if there's no continuity.

6   If the relay is receiving voltage from the switch but is not sending voltage to the

solenoids, check for a bad ground at the relay case. If the relay case is grounding properly, replace the relay.

7   If all but one lock solenoids operate, remove the trim panel from the affected door (see Chapter 11). and check for voltage at the solenoid while the lock switch is operated. One of the wires should have voltage in the Lock position; the other should have voltage in the Unlock position.

8   If the inoperative solenoid is receiving voltage, replace the solenoid.

9   If the inoperative solenoid isn't receiving voltage, check for an open or short in the wire between the lock solenoid and the relay. **Note:** *It's common for wires to break in the portion of the harness between the body and door (opening and closing the door fatigues and eventually breaks the wires).*

26 Electric rear view mirrors - description and check

1   Most electric rear view mirrors use two motors to move the glass; one for up and down adjustments and one for left-right adjustments.

2   The control switch has a selector portion which sends voltage to the left or right side mirror. With the ignition ON but the engine OFF, roll down the windows and operate the mirror control switch through all functions (left-right and up-down) for both the left and right side mirrors.

3   Listen carefully for the sound of the electric motors running in the mirrors.

4   If the motors can be heard but the mirror glass doesn't move, there's probably a problem with the drive mechanism inside the mirror. Remove and disassemble the mirror to locate the problem.

5   If the mirrors don't operate and no sound comes from the mirrors, check the fuse (see Chapter 1).

6   If the fuse is OK, remove the mirror control switch from its mounting without disconnecting the wires attached to it. Turn the ignition ON and check for voltage at the switch. There should be voltage at one terminal. If there's no voltage at the switch, check for an open or short in the wiring between the fuse panel and the switch.

7   If there's voltage at the switch, disconnect it. Check the switch for continuity in all its operating positions. If the switch does not have continuity, replace it.

8   Re-connect the switch. Locate the wire going from the switch to ground. Leaving the switch connected, connect a jumper wire between this wire and ground. If the mirror works normally with this wire in place, repair the faulty ground connection.

9   If the mirror still doesn't work, remove the mirror and check the wires at the mirror for voltage. Check with ignition ON and the mirror selector switch on the appropriate side. Operate the mirror switch in all its positions. There should be voltage at one of

the switch-to-mirror wires in each switch position (except the neutral "off" position).

10   If there's not voltage in each switch position, check the wiring between the mirror and control switch for opens and shorts.

11   If there's voltage, remove the mirror and test it off the vehicle with jumper wires. Replace the mirror if it fails this test.

27   Airbag system - general information

Refer to illustration 27.1

Later models are equipped with a Supplemental Restraint System (SRS), more commonly known as an airbag. This system is designed to protect the driver from serious injury in the event of a head-on or frontal collision. It consists of an airbag module in the center of the steering wheel, a crash sensor mounted at the front of the vehicle, a diagnostic/control unit and tunnel and safing sensors located inside the passenger compartment **(see illustration)**.

Airbag module

The airbag module contains a housing incorporating the cushion (airbag) and inflator unit. The inflator assembly is mounted on the back of the housing over a hole through which gas is expelled, inflating the bag almost instantaneously when an electrical

signal is sent from the system. The specially wound wire that carries this signal to the module is called a spiral cable. The spiral cable is a flat, ribbon-like electrically conductive tape which is wound many times so that it can transmit an electrical signal regardless of steering wheel position.

Sensors

The system has three sensors: a crash sensor at the front of the vehicle behind the bumper and tunnel and safing sensors in the center of the vehicle.

The front crash sensor is basically a pressure sensitive switch that completes an electrical circuit during an impact of sufficient G force. The electrical signal from the crash sensors is sent to the control unit and tunnel/safing sensors, which then completes the circuit and inflates the airbag.

Diagnostic/control unit and tunnel/safing sensors

The diagnostic/control unit contains an on-board microprocessor which monitors the operation of the system and tunnel/safing safing sensors. It checks this system every time the vehicle is started, causing the "AIRBAG" light to go on then off, if the system is operating properly. If there is a fault in the system, the light will go on and stay on and the unit will store fault codes indicating the nature of the fault. If the AIRBAG light

goes on and stays on, the vehicle should be taken to your dealer immediately for service.

Precautions

Warning: *Failure to follow these precautions could result in accidental deployment of the airbag and personal injury.*

Whenever working in the vicinity of the steering wheel, steering column or any of the other SRS system components, the system must be disarmed. To disarm the system:

a) *Point the wheels straight ahead and turn the key to the Lock position.*
b) *Disconnect the cable from the negative battery terminal.*
c) *Wait at least 10 minutes for the back-up power supply to be depleted*

Whenever handling an airbag module, always keep the airbag opening pointed away from your body. Never place the airbag module on a bench of other surface with the airbag opening facing the surface. Always place the airbag module in a safe location with the airbag opening facing up.

Never measure the resistance of any SRS component. An ohmmeter has a built-in battery supply that could accidentally deploy the airbag.

Never use electrical welding equipment on a vehicle equipped with an airbag without first disconnecting the yellow airbag connector, located under the steering column near the combination switch connector.

27.1 Airbag system component layout

Never dispose of a live airbag module. Return it to your dealer for safe deployment, using special equipment, and disposal.

28 Wiring diagrams - general information

Refer to illustration 28.3

Since it isn't possible to include all wiring diagrams for every year covered by this manual, the following diagrams are those that are typical and most commonly needed.

Prior to troubleshooting any circuits, check the fuse and circuit breakers (if equipped) to make sure they are in good condition. Make sure the battery is properly charged and has

clean, tight cable connections (see Chapter 1).

When checking the wiring system, make sure that all electrical connectors are clean, with no broken or loose pins. When unplugging an electrical connector, do not pull on the wires, only on the connector housings themselves. Refer to the accompanying chart for a key to the wiring diagram symbols **(see illustration).**

ELECTRICAL SYMBOLS AND ABBREVIATIONS

SYMBOLS

- Single filament bulb
- Dual filament bulb
- Fuse
- Fusible link
- Diode
- Motor
- Transistor
- Resistor
- Coil
- Variable resistor
- Thermistor
- Reed switch
- Circuit breaker
- Condenser

- Switch (Normally open)
- Switch (Normally closed)
- Ground
- No connection between wires
- Connection between wires

CONNECTORS

- Pin-type connector (Male)
- Pin-type connector (Female)
- Plain-type connector (Male)
- Plain-type connector (Female)
- Bullet connector (Female and male)
- Plain connector (Female and male)

WIRE COLOR CODING

B = Black	BR = Brown
W = White	OR = Orange
R = Red	P = Pink
G = Green	PU = Purple
L = Blue	GY = Gray
Y = Yellow	SB = Sky blue
LG = Light Green	

In case of color coding using a Stripe. Base Color is given first, followed by the Stripe Color:

Example: L/W = Blue with White Stripe

ABBREVIATIONS
- S : Sedan
- C : Coupe
- W : Wagon
- M : M/T models
- A : A/T models

28.3 Key to wiring diagrams

Typical 1986 and earlier power supply routing

Typical 1987 carbureted model power supply routing

Typical 1987 through 1990 EFI model power supply routing

Typical 1991 and later power supply routing (1 of 2)

Typical 1991 and later power supply routing (2 of 2)

Typical 1982 and 1983 starting system

Typical 1984 through 1986 starting system

Typical 1987 through 1990 manual transaxle model starting system

Typical 1987 through 1990 automatic transaxle model starting system

12

Typical 1991 and later manual transaxle model starting system

Typical 1991 and later automatic transaxle model starting system

Typical 1982 charging system

Typical 1983 through 1986 charging system

12

Typical 1987 through 1990 charging system

Typical 1991 and later charging system

Typical 1986 and earlier headlights

TM : With tachometer
WO : Without tachometer

Typical 1987 through 1990 headlights

Typical 1991 and later USA model headlights

12

Typical 1990 and earlier daytime running light system

Typical 1991 and later daytime running light system

Typical 1982 and 1983 taillights

Typical 1982 and 1983 brake lights

Typical 1982 and 1983 turn signal/hazard lights

Typical 1984 through 1986 taillights

Typical 1984 through 1986 brake lights

Typical 1984 through 1986 turn signal/hazard lights

12

Typical 1987 through 1990 taillights and brake lights

Typical 1987 through 1990 turn signal/hazard lights

12

Typical 1991 and later taillights and brake lights

Typical 1991 and later turn signal/hazard lights

12

Typical 1986 and earlier instrument panel lights

Typical 1987 through 1990 instrument panel lights

Typical 1991 and later instrument panel lights

Typical 1986 and earlier windshield wiper and washer

Typical 1986 and earlier rear window wiper and washer

Typical 1987 through 1990 windshield wiper and washer

12

Typical 1987 through 1990 rear window wiper and washer

Typical 1991 and later windshield wiper and washer

Typical 1991 and later rear window wiper and washer

Typical 1986 and earlier radio and speakers

Typical 1987 through 1990 radio and speakers

Typical 1991 and later radio and speakers

Notes

Index

Haynes Automotive Manuals

NOTE: New manuals are added to this list on a periodic basis. If you do not see a listing for your vehicle, consult your local Haynes dealer for the latest product information.

ACURA
12020	Integra '86 thru '89 & Legend '86 thru '90
12021	Integra '90 thru '93 & Legend '91 thru '95

AMC
	Jeep CJ - see JEEP (50020)
14020	Concord/Hornet/Gremlin/Spirit '70 thru '83
14025	(Renault) Alliance & Encore '83 thru '87

AUDI
15020	4000 all models '80 thru '87
15025	5000 all models '77 thru '83
15026	5000 all models '84 thru '88

AUSTIN
	Healey Sprite - see MG Midget (66015)

BMW
*18020	3/5 Series '82 thru '92
18021	3 Series including Z3 models '92 thru '98
18025	320i all 4 cyl models '75 thru '83
18050	1500 thru 2002 except Turbo '59 thru '77

BUICK
*19010	Buick Century '97 thru '02
	Century (FWD) - see GM (38005)
*19020	Buick, Oldsmobile & Pontiac Full-size (Front wheel drive) '85 thru '02
19025	Buick Oldsmobile & Pontiac Full-size (Rear wheel drive) '70 thru '90
19030	Mid-size Regal & Century '74 thru '87
	Regal - see GENERAL MOTORS (38010)
	Skyhawk - see GM (38030)
	Skylark - see GM (38020, 38025)
	Somerset - see GENERAL MOTORS (38025)

CADILLAC
21030	Cadillac Rear Wheel Drive '70 thru '93
	Cimarron, Eldorado & Seville - see GM (38015, 38030, 38031)

CHEVROLET
10305	Chevrolet Engine Overhaul Manual
*24010	Astro & GMC Safari Mini-vans '85 thru '02
24015	Camaro V8 all models '70 thru '81
24016	Camaro all models '82 thru '92
	Cavalier - see GM (38015)
	Celebrity - see GM (38005)
24017	Camaro & Firebird '93 thru '00
24020	Chevelle, Malibu, El Camino '69 thru '87
24024	Chevette & Pontiac T1000 '76 thru '87
	Citation - see GENERAL MOTORS (38020)
24032	Corsica/Beretta all models '87 thru '96
24040	Corvette all V8 models '68 thru '82
24041	Corvette all models '84 thru '96
24045	Full-size Sedans Caprice, Impala, Biscayne, Bel Air & Wagons '69 thru '90
24046	Impala SS & Caprice and Buick Roadmaster '91 thru '96
	Lumina '90 thru '94 - see GM (38010)
*24048	Lumina & Monte Carlo '95 thru '01
	Lumina APV - see GM (38035)
24050	Luv Pick-up all 2WD & 4WD '72 thru '82
	Malibu - see GM (38026)
24055	Monte Carlo all models '70 thru '88
	Monte Carlo '95 thru '01 - see LUMINA
24059	Nova all V8 models '69 thru '79
24060	Nova/Geo Prizm '85 thru '92
24064	Pick-ups '67 thru '87 - Chevrolet & GMC, all V8 & in-line 6 cyl, 2WD & 4WD '67 thru '87; Suburbans, Blazers & Jimmys '67 thru '91
24065	Pick-ups '88 thru '98 - Chevrolet & GMC, all full-size models '88 thru '98; C/K Classic '99 & '00; Blazer & Jimmy '92 thru '94; Suburban '92 thru '99; Tahoe & Yukon '95 thru '99
*24066	Pick-ups '99 thru '01 - Chevrolet Silverado & GMC Sierra '99 thru '01; Suburban/Tahoe/Yukon/Yukon XL '00 & '01
24070	S-10 & GMC S-15 Pick-ups '82 thru '93
*24071	S-10, GMC S-15 & Jimmy '94 thru '01
24075	Sprint '85 thru '88, Geo Metro '89 thru '01
24080	Vans - Chevrolet & GMC '68 thru '96

CHRYSLER
10310	Chrysler Engine Overhaul Manual
25015	Chrysler Cirrus, Dodge Stratus, Plymouth Breeze, '95 thru '98
25020	Full-size Front-Wheel Drive '88 thru '93
	K-Cars - see DODGE Aries (30008)
	Laser - see DODGE Daytona (30030)
25025	Chrysler LHS, Concorde & New Yorker, Dodge Intrepid, Eagle Vision, '93 thru '97
*25026	Chrysler LHS, Concorde, 300M, Dodge Intrepid '98 thru '03
25030	Chrysler/Plym. Mid-size '82 thru '95 Rear-wheel Drive - see DODGE (30050)
*25035	PT Cruiser all models '01 thru '03
*25040	Chrysler Sebring/Dodge Avenger '95 thru '02

DATSUN
28005	200SX all models '80 thru '83
28007	B-210 all models '73 thru '78
28009	210 all models '78 thru '82
28012	240Z, 260Z & 280Z Coupe '70 thru '78
28014	280ZX Coupe & 2+2 '79 thru '83
	300ZX - see NISSAN (72010)
28016	310 all models '78 thru '82
28018	510 & PL521 Pick-up '68 thru '73
28020	510 all models '78 thru '81
28022	620 Series Pick-up all models '73 thru '79
	720 Series Pick-up - NISSAN (72030)
28025	810/Maxima all gas models, '77 thru '84

DODGE
	400 & 600 - see CHRYSLER (25030)
30008	Aries & Plymouth Reliant '81 thru '89
30010	Caravan & Ply. Voyager '84 thru '95
*30011	Caravan & Ply. Voyager '96 thru '02
30012	Challenger/Plymouth Saporro '78 thru '83
	Challenger '67-'76 - see DART (30025)
30016	Colt/Plymouth Champ '78 thru '87
30020	Dakota Pick-ups all models '87 thru '96
*30021	Durango '98 & '99, Dakota '97 thru '99
30025	Dart, Challenger/Plymouth Barracuda & Valiant 6 cyl models '67 thru '76
30030	Daytona & Chrysler Laser '84 thru '89
	Intrepid - see Chrysler (25025, 25026)
*30034	Dodge & Plymouth Neon '95 thru '99
*30035	Omni & Plymouth Horizon '78 thru '90
30040	Pick-ups all full-size models '74 thru '93
*30041	Pick-ups all full-size models '94 thru '01
*30045	Ram 50/D50 Pick-ups & Raider and Plymouth Arrow Pick-ups '79 thru '93
30050	Dodge/Ply./Chrysler RWD '71 thru '89
30055	Shadow/Plymouth Sundance '87 thru '94
30060	Spirit & Plymouth Acclaim '89 thru '95
*30065	Vans - Dodge & Plymouth '71 thru '03

EAGLE
	Talon - see MITSUBISHI (68030, 68031)
	Vision - see CHRYSLER (25025)

FIAT
34010	124 Sport Coupe & Spider '68 thru '78
34025	X1/9 all models '74 thru '80

FORD
10355	Ford Automatic Transmission Overhaul
10320	Ford Engine Overhaul Manual
36004	Aerostar Mini-vans '86 thru '97
	Aspire - see FORD Festiva (36030)
36006	Contour/Mercury Mystique '95 thru '00
36008	Courier Pick-up all models '72 thru '82
*36012	Crown Victoria & Mercury Grand Marquis '88 thru '00
36016	Escort/Mercury Lynx '81 thru '90
36020	Escort/Mercury Tracer '91 thru '00
	Expedition - see FORD Pick-up (36059)
*36024	Explorer & Mazda Navajo '91 thru '01
36028	Fairmont & Mercury Zephyr '78 thru '83
36030	Festiva & Aspire '88 thru '97
36032	Fiesta all models '77 thru '80
*36034	Focus all models '00 and '01
36036	Ford & Mercury Full-size '75 thru '87
36040	Granada & Mercury Monarch '75 thru '80
36044	Ford & Mercury Mid-size '75 thru '86
36048	Mustang V8 all models '64-1/2 thru '73
36049	Mustang II 4 cyl, V6 & V8 '74 thru '78
36050	Mustang & Mercury Capri '79 thru '93
*36051	Mustang all models '94 thru '03
36054	Pick-ups and Bronco '73 thru '79
36058	Pick-ups and Bronco '80 thru '96
*36059	Pick-ups, Expedition & Lincoln Navigator '97 thru '02
*36060	Super Duty Pick-up, Excursion '99 thru '02
36062	Pinto & Mercury Bobcat '75 thru '80
36066	Probe all models '89 thru '92
36070	Ranger/Bronco II all models '83 thru '92
*36071	Ford Ranger '93 thru '00 & Mazda Pick-ups '94 thru '00
36074	Taurus & Mercury Sable '86 thru '95
*36075	Taurus & Mercury Sable '96 thru '01
36078	Tempo & Mercury Topaz '84 thru '94
36082	Thunderbird/Mercury Cougar '83 thru '88
36086	Thunderbird/Mercury Cougar '89 thru '97
36090	Vans all V8 Econoline models '69 thru '91
*36094	Vans full size '92 thru '01
*36097	Windstar Mini-van '95 thru '03

GENERAL MOTORS
10360	GM Automatic Transmission Overhaul
38005	Buick Century, Chevrolet Celebrity, Olds Cutlass Ciera & Pontiac 6000 '82 thru '96
*38010	Buick Regal, Chevrolet Lumina, Oldsmobile Cutlass Supreme & Pontiac Grand Prix front wheel drive '88 thru '02
38015	Buick Skyhawk, Cadillac Cimarron, Chevrolet Cavalier, Oldsmobile Firenza Pontiac J-2000 & Sunbird '82 thru '94
*38016	Chevrolet Cavalier/Pontiac Sunfire '95 thru '01
38020	Buick Skylark, Chevrolet Citation, Olds Omega, Pontiac Phoenix '80 thru '85
38025	Buick Skylark & Somerset, Olds Achieva, Calais & Pontiac Grand Am '85 thru '98
*38026	Chevrolet Malibu, Olds Alero & Cutlass, Pontiac Grand Am '97 thru '00
38030	Cadillac Eldorado & Oldsmobile Toronado '71 thru '85, Seville '80 thru '85, Buick Riviera '79 thru '85
*38031	Cadillac Eldorado & Seville '86 thru '91, DeVille & Buick Riviera '86 thru '93, Fleetwood & Olds Toronado '86 thru '92
38032	DeVille '94 thru '02, Seville '92 thru '02
38035	Chevrolet Lumina APV, Oldsmobile Silhouette & Pontiac Trans Sport '90 thru '96
*38036	Chevrolet Venture, Olds Silhouette, Pontiac Trans Sport & Montana '97 thru '01
	General Motors Full-size Rear-wheel Drive - see BUICK (19025)

GEO
	Metro - see CHEVROLET Sprint (24075)
	Prizm - see CHEVROLET (24060) or TOYOTA (92030)
40030	Storm all models '90 thru '93
	Tracker - see SUZUKI Samurai (90010)

GMC
	Vans & Pick-ups - see CHEVROLET

HONDA
42010	Accord CVCC all models '76 thru '83
42011	Accord all models '84 thru '89
42012	Accord all models '90 thru '93
42013	Accord all models '94 thru '97
*42014	Accord all models '98 thru '02
42020	Civic 1200 all models '73 thru '79
42021	Civic 1300 & 1500 CVCC '80 thru '83
42022	Civic 1500 CVCC all models '75 thru '79
42023	Civic all models '84 thru '91
42024	Civic & del Sol '92 thru '95
*42025	Civic '96 thru '00, CR-V '97 thru '00, Acura Integra '94 thru '00
	Passport - see ISUZU Rodeo (47017)
*42040	Prelude CVCC all models '79 thru '89

HYUNDAI
*43010	Elantra all models '96 thru '01
43015	Excel & Accent all models '86 thru '98

ISUZU
	Hombre - see CHEVROLET S-10 (24071)
*47017	Rodeo '91 thru '02, Amigo '89 thru '02, Honda Passport '95 thru '02
47020	Trooper '84 thru '91, Pick-up '81 thru '93

JAGUAR
49010	XJ6 all 6 cyl models '68 thru '86
49011	XJ6 all models '88 thru '94
49015	XJ12 & XJS all 12 cyl models '72 thru '85

JEEP
50010	Cherokee, Comanche & Wagoneer Limited all models '84 thru '00
50020	CJ all models '49 thru '86
*50025	Grand Cherokee all models '93 thru '00
50029	Grand Wagoneer & Pick-up '72 thru '91
*50030	Wrangler all models '87 thru '00

LEXUS
	ES 300 - see TOYOTA Camry (92007)

LINCOLN
	Navigator - see FORD Pick-up (36059)
*59010	Rear Wheel Drive all models '70 thru '01

MAZDA
61010	GLC (rear wheel drive) '77 thru '83
61011	GLC (front wheel drive) '81 thru '85
61015	323 & Protegé '90 thru '00
*61016	MX-5 Miata '90 thru '97
61020	MPV all models '89 thru '94
	Navajo - see Ford Explorer (36024)
61030	Pick-ups '72 thru '93
	Pick-ups '94 on - see Ford (36071)
61035	RX-7 all models '79 thru '85
61036	RX-7 all models '86 thru '91
61040	626 (rear wheel drive) '79 thru '82
61041	626 & MX-6 (front wheel drive) '83 thru '91
61042	626 '93 thru '01, & MX-6/Ford Probe '93 thru '97

MERCEDES-BENZ
63012	123 Series Diesel '76 thru '85
63015	190 Series 4-cyl gas models, '84 thru '88
63020	230, 250 & 280 6 cyl sohc '68 thru '72
63025	280 123 Series gas models '77 thru '81
63030	350 & 450 all models '71 thru '80

MERCURY
64200	Villager & Nissan Quest '93 thru '01
	All other titles, see FORD listing.

MG
66010	MGB Roadster & GT Coupe '62 thru '80
66015	MG Midget & Austin Healey Sprite Roadster '58 thru '80

MITSUBISHI
68020	Cordia, Tredia, Galant, Precis & Mirage '83 thru '93
68030	Eclipse, Eagle Talon & Plymouth Laser '90 thru '94
*68031	Eclipse '95 thru '01, Eagle Talon '95 thru '98
68040	Pick-up '83 thru '96, Montero '83 thru '93

NISSAN
72010	300ZX all models incl. Turbo '84 thru '89
72015	Altima all models '93 thru '01
72020	Maxima all models '85 thru '92
*72021	Maxima all models '93 thru '01
72030	Pick-ups '80 thru '97, Pathfinder '87 thru '95
*72031	Frontier Pick-up '98 thru '01, Xterra '00 & '01, Pathfinder '96 thru '01
72040	Pulsar all models '83 thru '86
72050	Sentra all models '82 thru '94
72051	Sentra & 200SX all models '95 thru '99
72060	Stanza all models '82 thru '90

OLDSMOBILE
*73015	Cutlass '74 thru '88
	For other OLDSMOBILE titles, see BUICK, CHEVROLET or GM listings.

PLYMOUTH
	For PLYMOUTH titles, see DODGE.

PONTIAC
79008	Fiero all models '84 thru '88
79018	Firebird V8 models except Turbo '70 thru '81
79019	Firebird all models '82 thru '92
79040	Mid-size Rear-wheel Drive '70 thru '87
	For other PONTIAC titles, see BUICK, CHEVROLET or GM listings.

PORSCHE
80020	911 Coupe & Targa models '65 thru '89
80025	914 all 4 cyl models '69 thru '76
80030	924 all models incl. Turbo '76 thru '82
80035	944 all models incl. Turbo '83 thru '89

RENAULT
	Alliance, Encore - see AMC (14020)

SAAB
*84010	900 including Turbo '79 thru '88

SATURN
*87010	Saturn all models '91 thru '02

SUBARU
89002	1100, 1300, 1400 & 1600 '71 thru '79
89003	1600 & 1800 2WD & 4WD '80 thru '94

SUZUKI
90010	Samurai/Sidekick/Geo Tracker '86 thru '01

TOYOTA
92005	Camry all models '83 thru '91
92006	Camry all models '92 thru '96
*92007	Camry/Avalon/Solara/Lexus ES 300 '97 thru '01
92015	Celica Rear Wheel Drive '71 thru '85
92020	Celica Front Wheel Drive '86 thru '99
92025	Celica Supra all models '79 thru '92
92030	Corolla all models '75 thru '79
92032	Corolla rear wheel drive models '80 thru '87
92035	Corolla front wheel drive models '84 thru '92
92036	Corolla & Geo Prizm '93 thru '02
92040	Corolla Tercel all models '80 thru '82
92045	Corona all models '74 thru '82
92050	Cressida all models '78 thru '82
92055	Land Cruiser FJ40/43/45/55 '68 thru '82
92056	Land Cruiser FJ60/62/80/FZJ80 '80 thru '96
92065	MR2 all models '85 thru '87
92070	Pick-up all models '69 thru '78
92075	Pick-up all models '79 thru '95
*92076	Tacoma '95 thru '00, 4Runner '96 thru '00, T100 '93 thru '98
*92078	Tundra '00 thru '02, Sequoia '01 thru '02
92080	Previa all models '91 thru '95
*92082	RAV4 all models '96 thru '02
92085	Tercel all models '87 thru '94

TRIUMPH
94007	Spitfire all models '62 thru '81
94010	TR7 all models '75 thru '81

VW
96008	Beetle & Karmann Ghia '54 thru '79
*96009	New Beetle '98 thru '00
96016	Rabbit, Jetta, Scirocco, & Pick-up gas models '74 thru '91 & Convertible '80 thru '92
96017	Golf, GTI & Jetta '93 thru '98, Cabrio '95 thru '98
*96018	Golf, GTI, Jetta & Cabrio '98 thru '02
96020	Rabbit, Jetta, Pick-up diesel '77 thru '84
96023	Passat '98 thru '01, Audi A4 '96 thru '01
96030	Transporter 1600 all models '68 thru '79
96035	Transporter 1700, 1800, 2000 '72 thru '79
96040	Type 3 1500 & 1600 '63 thru '73
96045	Vanagon air-cooled models '80 thru '83

VOLVO
97010	120, 130 Series & 1800 Sports '61 thru '73
97015	140 Series all models '66 thru '74
97020	240 Series all models '76 thru '93
97025	260 Series all models '75 thru '82
97040	740 & 760 Series all models '82 thru '88

TECHBOOK MANUALS
10205	Automotive Computer Codes
10210	Automotive Emissions Control Manual
10215	Fuel Injection Manual, 1978 thru 1985
10220	Fuel Injection Manual, 1986 thru 1999
10225	Holley Carburetor Manual
10230	Rochester Carburetor Manual
10240	Weber/Zenith/Stromberg/SU Carburetor
10305	Chevrolet Engine Overhaul Manual
10310	Chrysler Engine Overhaul Manual
10320	Ford Engine Overhaul Manual
10330	GM and Ford Diesel Engine Repair
10340	Small Engine Repair Manual
10345	Suspension, Steering & Driveline
10355	Ford Automatic Transmission Overhaul
10360	GM Automatic Transmission Overhaul
10405	Automotive Body Repair & Painting
10410	Automotive Brake Manual
10415	Automotive Detailing Manual
10420	Automotive Eelectrical Manual
10425	Automotive Heating & Air Conditioning
10430	Automotive Reference Dictionary
10435	Automotive Tools Manual
10440	Used Car Buying Guide
10445	Welding Manual
10450	ATV Basics

SPANISH MANUALS
98903	Reparación de Carrocería & Pintura
98905	Códigos Automotrices de la Computadora
98910	Frenos Automotriz
98915	Inyección de Combustible 1986 al 1999
99040	Chevrolet & GMC Camionetas '67 al '87
99041	Chevrolet & GMC Camionetas '88 al '98
99042	Chevrolet Camionetas Cerradas '68 al '95
99055	Dodge Caravan/Ply. Voyager '84 al '95
99075	Ford Camionetas y Bronco '80 al '94
99077	Ford Camionetas Cerradas '69 al '91
99083	Ford Modelos de Tamaño Grande '75 al '87
99088	Ford Modelos de Tamaño Mediano '75 al '86
99091	Ford Taurus & Mercury Sable '86 al '95
99095	GM Modelos de Tamaño Grande '70 al '90
99100	GM Modelos de Tamaño Mediano '70 al '88
99110	Nissan Camionetas '80 al '96, Pathfinder '87 al '95
99118	Nissan Sentra '82 al '94
99125	Toyota Camionetas y 4-Runner '79 al '95

* Listings shown with an asterisk (*) indicate model coverage as of this printing. These titles will be periodically updated to include later model years - consult your Haynes dealer for more information.

Nearly 100 Haynes motorcycle manuals also available

8-03

Haynes North America, Inc., 861 Lawrence Drive, Newbury Park, CA 91320 • (805) 498-6703